THE PAPACY

ITS HISTORIC ORIGINS AND PRIMITIVE RELATIONS WITH THE EASTERN CHURCHES

THE PAPACY

Its Historic Origins and Primitive Relations

with the

Eastern Churches

Abbe Vladimir Guettée

Uncut Mountain Press

THE PAPACY
Its Historic Origins and
Primitive Relations with the Eastern Churches

© 2024
Uncut Mountain Press

uncutmountainpress.com

Originally published by
Sampson Low, Son, & Co., London, U.K., 1867.

All rights for this text are in the public domain.

Scriptural quotations are primarily taken from the King James Version.

Abbe Vladimir (Réné-Francois) Guettée, 1816–1892.

The Papacy: Its Historic Origins and Primitive Relations with the Eastern Churches.
Translated from the French, with an introduction by Arthur Cleveland Coxe (Bp. of Western NY), 1818–1896.
Edited by Kevin Kirwan and Joshua Reeves.

ISBN: 978-1-63941-035-4

I. Eastern Orthodox Church
II. Orthodox Christian History

THIS TEXT WAS FIRST PUBLISHED

IN GRATEFUL RECOGNITION OF THE HAND OF GOD

IN THE

EVENTS OF THE MEMORABLE YEAR,

A.D. MDCCCLXVII

LAUS DEO. AMEN.

Abbe Vladimir (Réné-Francois) Guettée

CONTENTS

Biographical Notice of the Author 9

Author's Introduction 21

I. The Papacy 29

II. The Papal Authority Condemned
    by the Word of God 33

III. Of the Authority of the Bishops of
    Rome in the First Three Centuries 51

IV. Teachings of Various Church Fathers 85

V. Of the Authority of the Bishops of
    Rome During the Sixth, Seventh,
    and Eighth Centuries 169

VI. That the Papacy, by Her Novel and
    Ambitious Pretentions, was the Cause
    of the Schism Between the Eastern
    and Western Churches 237

VII. The Papacy, Which Caused the
    Division, has Perpetuated and
    Strengthened It by Innovations
    and has Made It a Schism 285

Index 330

Cathedral at Blois, France. Birthplace of Abbe Guettée.

BIOGRAPHICAL NOTICE
OF THE AUTHOR
(BY THE EDITOR OF THE FIRST EDITION, AMENDED)

THE nature of the questions discussed in the following work would ordinarily lift them above all personal considerations and require that the argument be left to take care of itself in the honest vindication of catholic truth. There attaches to the present treatise, however, an interest quite separate from its merits as an argument, in its identification with the history of a man of whose remarkable career and labors, it is one of the most valuable fruits. It is believed, therefore, that it can scarcely fail to derive additional force from the account which it is proper here to give of the author.

Réné-Francois Guettée was born at Blois, on the banks of the Loire, in the Department of the *Loire et Cher*, on the first of December, 1816, of worthy parentage, but with no other inheritance than a good name and fair opportunities for education. Self-devoted from the beginning to Catholicism, his studies were pursued regularly and entirely in his native city. From a very early age his mind seems to have revolted against the wearisome routine that ruled the system of instruction, under which the seminarist becomes a mere receptacle in quantity and quality of the knowledge judged by Rome to be the needful preparation for the instruments of her despotic rule. Guettée, without comprehending then the evil results of such a system, felt its restraints and insufficiency. His mind, in its ardent desire for knowledge and its rapid acquisition, worked out of the prescribed limits with an instinctive appropriation of the whole domain of truth, and read and studied in secret. He consecrated to study the time devoted by others to amusement, and thus stored his mind with knowledge both varied and accurate. But such predilections, never viewed with favor by the Vatican, disquieted Guettée's professors and marked him as an *independent* young man, a character always regarded with jealousy and suspicion. All possible obstacles were accordingly thrown in his way and, had not his scrupulous regularity of conduct and unquestionable piety counterbalanced these unfavorable impressions, he might have found difficulty in obtaining orders.

At the age of twenty-one, M. Guettée was admitted to the sub-diaconate; at twenty- two he was made deacon, and at twenty-three years he was advanced to the priesthood, receiving his ordination on the twenty-first day of December 1839, at the hands of Mgr. de Sausin, Bishop of Blois. He began at once the faithful exercise of his ministry, first as vicar, then as curé. Mgr. de Sausin was succeeded in the see of Blois by Mgr. Fabre des Essarts, a man of liberal mind and of strong Gallican predilections. He soon perceived in the young curé qualities that inspired him with warm interest in his welfare. M. Guettée's studies, directed by a mind unshackled by prejudice, spurred by an ardent love of truth and insatiable thirst for knowledge, had led him, soon before his ordination to the priesthood, to conceive the idea of writing a *History of the Church of France*. To this work he gave himself with characteristic ardor immediately after his ordination. Having been appointed in 1841 to the curé of a small parish distant about twelve miles from Blois, where the duties left him the larger portion of his time for study, he frequently rose at daybreak and walked to the city for the purpose of studying in the public library, which is very rich in religious literature, and where can be found all the great historical collections and monuments of learning in France.

After devoting six hours to close study, he returned on foot to the solitude of his own chamber, where a large part of the night was consumed in work upon the materials he had gathered. Absorbed

Biographical Notice

thus between the cares of his ministry and his literary labors, he at length attracted the notice of his bishops who remarked that he never presented himself at the episcopal palace, although coming frequently to the episcopal city. He accordingly sent to him a request to know the subject of his laborious study at the library; and having learned the truth, asked to see the manuscript of the first volume, then nearly completed. This he caused to be carefully examined by his Vicar-General, the most learned the diocese, whose report was of the most flattering character. Mgr. des Essarts thereupon resolved to encourage the young writer and give him every facility for his work. M. Guettée was accordingly transferred to another parish very near the episcopal city, and where the charge of the ministry upon his time was equally light. The episcopal library was placed at his service and the emoluments of his post enabled him to go from time to time to Paris for such researches in the great libraries as became necessary.

Thus M. Guettée passed several years in the successful prosecution of his great work. In 1847 Mgr. Fabre des-Essarts proposed to his own publisher to begin the publication of the *History of the Church of France*. No sooner had the first volume appeared than the author received from a large number of the French bishops letters of the warmest commendation; while on the other hand there was formed against him in his own diocese a hostile party, composed of priests immediately surrounding the bishop, who were rendered jealous by the marks of episcopal favor lavished upon the new writer, and of the directors of the seminaries, who could not forgive one who had shown so little reverence for their narrow prescriptions, and who owed so little to them. The bitterness of this party could only acquire intensity in the steady progress of our author in the path of distinction. In 1849 M. Guettée, with the approbation of the Bishop, resigned his curé, and came to Blois to accept the editorial charge of a political journal which had been offered to him by the authorities of the department.

After the public excitement caused by the proclamation of the Republic in 1848 had somewhat subsided, the sincere democrats of the country, who did not sever the cause of order from that of liberty, felt the necessity of creating such organs of a true democracy as should enlighten the people upon their duties as well as upon the question of their rights. With this aim was founded *Le Republicain de Loire et Cher*, and some surprise was caused at seeing the editorship of the journal confided to a priest by democrats, who had until then passed for enemies of the clergy and of the Church. The confidence of his friends was fully justified in the influence which M. Guettée obtained for this journal by his earnest defense of the principles to which it was devoted, founding and strengthening them upon the authority of the Gospel and showing them to be in harmony with the principles of revealed religion.

By this service he attached more firmly to him the regard of the Bishop of Blois, who then conceived the design of drawing the Abbé into closer relations with himself by giving him a residence in the episcopal palace; but before this plan could be executed the Bishop was prostrated by the disease that was destined to remove him from life in the following year. M. l'Abbe Garapin, a vicar-general, an intelligent and learned man in the episcopal administration of Blois, who, like the Bishop, felt a strong regard for M. Guettée, informed him secretly of the Bishop's kind intentions but counselled him to decline them and thereby escape the machinations of his enemies in the administration, who would be certain, as soon as the Bishop's approaching death should put the power into their hands, to signalize it by driving him from the palace. M. Guettée followed this friendly advice and resigned the charge of the journal he had edited for eighteen months, because by this change of régime he could no longer edit it with independence. And seeing his friend the Bishop at the point of death, he resolved to quit the diocese of Blois and demand permission to establish himself at Paris, where he might enjoy more facilities for the completion of his *History of the Church of France*. Knowing that the first vicar-general would very joyfully seize the opportunity of ridding the diocese of one for whom he cherished so cordial a dislike, he asked and readily obtained a full letter of credit certifying to his learning and piety.

Thus furnished, M. Guettée arrived in Paris and made no other request of the archiepiscopal administration there than to be authorized to say mass within the diocese, attaching himself at the same time to an ecclesiastical college as professor. Mgr. Sibour, then Archbishop of Paris, having been apprised of the residence of M. Guettée in the capital, invited him to present himself at the episcopal palace and offered him a chaplaincy with such warmth of manner that he did not feel at liberty to refuse so evident a desire to serve him. By 1851, six volumes of the *History of the Church of France* had already been published, and the author had received for it the approbation of *more than forty* of the French bishops. This success caused great uneasiness to the ultramontane party. M. Guettée, it appeared, while so treating his great subject as to win the high suffrages just referred to, manifested so sincere a love of truth that his work became dangerous to a party with whom this was no recommendation. The design was immediately formed of gaining over the author, and accordingly Mgr. Gousset, Archbishop of Rheims, who was at the head of the ultramontane party, made overtures to him, intimating that honors and ecclesiastical preferment would not be tardy in rewarding his unreserved devotion to the ultramontane doctrines. But this dignitary quickly saw that he had to deal with one who could not be brought to traffic with his convictions, nor be intimidated by threats. From this moment began that war against him which issued in his present entire withdrawal from communion with Rome as schismatical in position and corrupted in doctrine. This alienation, however, was gradual, the fruit of his growing convictions and deeper insight into the principles of the complicated and powerful system with which now he had to grapple. The struggle called for all the resources of this thoroughly balanced and severely disciplined mind, as well as of his extensive learning. He saw at first, far less clearly than did the ultramontane party, the steady divergence of his views from the Papal doctrine. The Gallican tone that pervaded more and more his *History of the Church of France* proceeded not from a deliberate point of view from which he wrote, but was the scrupulous and truthful rendering of history by his honest mind, the impartial and logical use of the materials out of which his history was to be made. To such a mind, therefore, the forced revelation of this divergence from the doctrines of a party who for that reason solely demanded his retraction and unquestioning submission, could only increase the dissidence, and so it proved. The first seven volumes of the *History*, approved by more than forty bishops, and six of them published under the direction and with the sanction of the Bishop of Blois, were placed in the *Index* of books prohibited by the court of Rome. Mgr. Sibour gave his approbation to the resistance made at once by M. Guettée to this decree. The author was immediately attacked with great violence by the *Univers* and other Jesuit journals, and defended himself with great spirit and ability, all his replies being first submitted to Mgr. Sibour and approved by him. During this struggle, the eighth and ninth volumes of the *History* appeared. Mr. Sibour charged one of his vicars-general, M. l'Abbé Lequeux, with the mission of submitting them to the "Congregation of the Index," with the request that its objections might be made known to the author before they were censured.

The author had furnished M. Lequeux with letters bearing a similar petition. This ecclesiastic had himself suffered by the censure of the Congregation, passed upon his *Manual of Canon Law*, a classic of many years' standing in the seminaries. He had submitted and was on his way to Rome for the purpose of learning the objections of the Congregation and correcting his work. But he obtained no satisfaction either for himself or for M. Guettée, whose two new volumes were placed arbitrarily in the *Index* without a word of explanation as to the grounds of censure. Thus M. Guettée was baffled in his many respectful and patient endeavors to obtain the desired communication with the Congregation at Rome. He resolved, therefore, to pursue his work without concerning himself about censures so tyrannical and unreasonable. But matters were about to change their aspect at the archiepiscopal palace. In the course of the year 1854, the bishops were called to Rome to be present at the promulgation of the new dogma of the Immaculate Conception. Mgr. Sibour was not invited. He had addressed to Rome a paper in which he proved that this dogma, or belief, was not definable, because it was not taught either in Holy Scripture or by Catholic tradition. To punish him for this act he was not included among the bishops invited. Deeply mortified at this omission, he wrote to the Pope touching on it, and in a manner so submissive that he was at once rewarded with an invitation couched in the most gracious terms. The character of Mgr. Sibour was well understood at Rome as that of a weak and ambitious man, full of vanity and without fixed convictions, who could be won by flatteries and bought with promises. He was, therefore, received with studied politeness and lodged in the Vatican. His namesake and friend, M. Sibour, curé of the church of Thomas Aquinas in Paris, was made Bishop of Tripoli in *partibus*, and his friend, M. L'Abbé Darboy, the present Archbishop of Paris, was appointed *Prothonotaire Apostolique*. For himself he received the promise of a cardinal's hat. In return for these kindnesses he was constrained to sacrifice his Gallican friends among the clergy of Paris, and the promise made to that effect was well kept. M. L'Abbé Lequeux, his vicar-general, found himself dismissed to his old place among the Canons of Notre Dame; M. L'Abbé Laborde was persecuted and finally found no better refuge than the hospital, where he soon after died; M. L'Abbé Prompsault, who had been for nearly thirty years chaplain of the Hospice of les *Quinze Vingt*, was deprived of his position, left without resources, and subsequently died in the hospital not long after. Finally, regardless of all the encouragement he had given to M. L'Abbé Guettée in his resistance to the action of the Congregation of the Index, and of his repeated proofs of regard and confidence, he withdrew his support, deprived him of his place, and reduced him, like the others, to poverty. Here, however, he found a less submissive spirit roused by the injustice and tyranny of this act. M. Guettée printed a letter to Mgr. Sibour which proved a home thrust to this vacillating prelate. It recounted all the facts of his past relations with the Archbishop: his patient endeavors to be at peace with the court of Rome, his offers of every reasonable submission and earnest application directly to the Congregation of the Index, and afterward to Mgr. Sibour himself, to have his obnoxious work examined by a commission; how this was refused when proceeding from himself as an overture of conciliation, but was subsequently suggested by the Archbishop himself in the form of a menace, to induce the Abbé Guettée to withdraw from Paris voluntarily, and save himself from the threatened censure and disability; that he declined the latter course and opened himself and his work with every facility to the scrutiny of his judges. He set forth the action of the Council of Rochelle in 1853—the same which proposed to censure Bossuet—which attacked the eighth volume of the *History of the Church of France* and did not spare even the Abbé's personal character; that when he had prepared his defense and asked permission of the Archbishop to publish it, lest it should be seized as the pretext for depriving him of his functions, he was answered that before such permission could be accorded he must resign those functions in the diocese of Paris; that he refused to do this, and that by agreement certain copies of his defense were deposited with the Archbishop, and an agreement made that it should not be published that though this defense was not made the occasion of his premeditated removal, the pretext for a measure so determined upon was soon after made out of a petty difference of a personal kind between himself and a *confrére*, without any regard to the importance or the justice of the case; that Mgr. Sibour finally deprived him of the poor office of hospital chaplain, with the evident design of withdrawing from him such means of subsistence as alone prevented his quitting Paris.

This letter, addressed to Mgr. Sibour, protesting against his action and fully exposing the motives that could alone have operated to these persecutions, was printed and a copy sent to the Archbishop before it was published. Under the impression, however, that it had been published, the Archbishop immediately replied by depriving the Abbé of the permission to say mass in Paris, thus completing the disability cast upon him. But upon the Abbé's informing him that the letter had not been published, that it was designed as a defense of himself, not as an attack upon the administration of the diocese, and offering to deposit the edition of the letter at the archiepiscopal palace, to avoid the evils of publicity, Mgr. Sibour next day sent a very kind note to M. Guettée, expressing himself touched by the terms of his response, restoring to him the authority to celebrate mass, accepting the deposit of the copies of his printed letter, and desiring to see him to give him further proof of his satisfaction. At a personal interview the same evening, Mgr. Sibour promised him shortly new ecclesiastical functions.

It would seem, however, that the Archbishop's eyes were beginning to be opened toward Rome. His submission and absolute conversion had so satisfied that court that it was in no haste to confer the promised cardinal's hat; and Mgr. Sibour, feeling that he had been amused with words, repented of his acts of injustice and was meditating some reparation, of which his gentler disposition toward M. Guettée was a sign, when these better intentions were arrested by the tragic death he so suddenly met at the hand of the assassin Verger, in the church of *St. Etienne du Mont.*

His successor, Cardinal Morlot, was a man of political ideas and aspirations, astute and scheming, who never lost sight of the importance or neglected the means of maintaining the best relations with the powerful. He made every needful concession to the successive governments in France, and at the same time conciliated Rome, feeding its insatiable greed of riches by sending large sums of money for its necessities. Such a man could have no thoughts to bestow upon the trivial work of repairing the wrongs of his predecessor. On the contrary, he was not long in showing himself yet more severe against M. Guettée, and at the close of the year 1855 finally refused to renew his permission to say mass in Paris. From this moment began the war in earnest which ended in the separation of our author from Rome. After having in vain endeavored to procure from the Archbishop in writing the refusal to sanction the continuance of his ministry in the diocese of Paris—a refusal that was prudently communicated to him verbally by the proper official—he published his appeal to the Pope against the decision as a gross violation of canon law, and another to the government, as an abuse of authority and an invasion of his civil-ecclesiastical rights. These appeals, firm in their language and unanswerable in their facts and arguments, were not published with any hope of answer or justice, but for the purpose of exposing clearly the outrageous violation by his adversary of the ancient liberties of the Gallican church, and the arbitrary and despotic character of the whole proceeding. He did not imagine that the

Pope would ever be permitted to hear of his wrongs, or if he were, that he would listen to them at the expense of his own friends and of the principles upon which the power of the Papacy is built. Nor was it to be expected that the State would embroil itself with an individual conflict with Catholicism upon a question of canon law. Thus M. l'Abbé Guettée, innocent of the smallest offence against good morals, and with a character free from all taint, without any ecclesiastical censure resting upon him or any proceedings directed against him, was deprived of the exercise of his ministry with the evident purpose of driving him from Paris, where his enlightened views caused too much inconvenience to the ultramontane party.

It is unnecessary to say that the scheme failed, or to follow the controversy that ensued upon this open rupture. It had the natural result of disclosing more clearly than ever to M. Guettée the principles of the Papal institution and the despotic usurpation of the Papacy. The energy and industry with which he answered the attacks upon him developed his views, defined his objections, and thoroughly awakened the latent protest of his enlightened conscience against the pretensions of Rome. He became finally the watchful and open antagonist of the Papacy, and shortly after found himself the editor of the Review called l'*Observateur Catholique*, which had, and still has, for its object the resistance of Papal usurpations and corruptions in the Church by the principles of primitive truth and a pure catholicity. He has published successively a *History of the Jesuits*, in three volumes; the *Memoirs et Journal de l'Abbé Le Dieu sur la Vie et les Ouvrages de Bossuet*, in four volumes; also a refutation of Renan's *Vie de Jesus*. His latest and most important work is the *Papauté Schismatique*, now presented in English. Six years ago he founded, in conjunction with the Rev. Archpriest Wassilieff, titular head of the Orthodox Church in France, and especially attached to the Russian Church in Paris, *l'Union Chrétienne*, a weekly publication in quarto form, having for its specific object the diffusion of information upon the principles of the primitive Church as those of a true catholicity, calling for unity, and a resistless influence to oppose the invasions of the Papal principle and the corruptions it has introduced into the primitive faith. It is natural that such a consecration of his labor and such associations should have led M. Guettée into close and increasingly devoted relations with the Eastern Orthodox Church, and especially with the Orthodox Church of Russia. His views ceasing to be Roman and Papal only because more intensely Catholic, he sought a home in the East, where the Papal power could never seat itself, and especially in the Orthodox Russian Church, where its pretensions are held in abhorrence. All that is venerable, pure, and catholic in the faith and form of the Church of Christ, our author believes he has found in the Orthodox Church, and he has therefore attached himself warmly to it, making it the platform for his earnest and pure-minded labors for the restoration of visible unity. He is in turn held in high esteem by the authorities and learned men of the Russian Church, and has recently received from it the high and rare honor of a doctorate in theology. His labors for union are warmly appreciated and encouraged there as they are everywhere by all who understand them. M. Guettée is no enthusiast; he is fully aware of the difficulties and magnitude of the work to which his life is consecrated and looks for no marked progress or flattering results to show themselves in his lifetime, but is content to sow wide and deep the seeds of truth, leaving them to germinate and become fruitful in God's good time. He has a warm and intelligent appreciation of our American Christianity, and looks to its activity in the great endeavor as of the highest importance, believing that her catholic character and free and mobile structure peculiarly mark her as a powerful instrument to promote the interests of the Catholic faith. M. Guettée has in preparation a work of much interest and importance, designed to bring into a single view the harmonies and differences between Orthodox Christianity and heterodoxy. It forms a careful survey of the ground, and is likely to become a valuable help. This new production of M. Guettée will be translated without delay, and published simultaneously in French, Russian, and English.

The "Belgian Tiara"

AUTHOR'S INTRODUCTION

THE Pope is a king, and pretends to be sovereign pontiff of the Christian Church. We do not propose to occupy ourselves with his royalty. To what advantage? It will soon fall. Its ruin is decreed by Providence. Foreign bayonets will no more save it than the sophisms of its defenders. If, as is affirmed, these are necessary to uphold the sovereign pontificate, it is but another reason for desiring its fall—because this pontificate is an usurpation. This we proceed to demonstrate in the present work. To reach this end we shall have recourse neither to questionable arguments nor to declamation. Facts drawn from original sources are summoned as witnesses. We take the Roman episcopate at the origin of Christianity, follow it through centuries, and are able to prove incontestably that for eight centuries the spiritual Papacy, as we understand it in the present day, had no existence; that the bishop of Rome was for three centuries only a *bishop*, with the same rank as the others; that in the fourth century he received a primacy of honor without universal jurisdiction; that this honor has no other foundation than the decrees of the Church; that his *restricted* jurisdiction over certain neighboring churches is supported only upon a custom legalized by Councils.

As for the universal sovereignty, absolute, *of divine right*—in other words, the Papacy—facts and catholic testimony of the first eight centuries condemn instead of sustaining it.

History reveals to us the Papacy, after several fruitless attempts, taking its birth from circumstances and establishing itself in the ninth century, with its double political and ecclesiastical character. Its real founder was Adrian I; Nicholas I chiefly contributed to its development; Gregory VII raised it to its loftiest pitch.

Adrian I was in fact the first Pope. They who before this occupied the see of Rome were only bishops, successors not of St. Peter, as has been declared and repeated to satiety, but of Linus, who was already bishop of Rome when St. Peter arrived in that city, to seal there by his martyrdom the faith he had preached. At the outset, therefore, the defenders of the Papacy commit one of the grossest historical errors in tracing back the Papacy—that is, Papal sovereignty—to the origin of Christianity. This error has led them to a thousand others, impelled, as they have been, to seek proofs for the support of this false theory in the history of the Church and in the writings of the ancient fathers. They have thus wrested facts and distorted testimonies. They have even dared to attack Holy Scripture, and by delusive anti-Catholic interpretation, made it bear *false witness* in favor of their system. It is thus that the Church of Rome was the first to give example of those individual interpretations for which she so bitterly reproaches Protestantism. She was the first to abandon the *Catholic rule* of the interpretation of the sacred books; she has put aside the collective interpretation of which the fathers of the Church have been the faithful echoes, and upon her own authority she has presumed to discover in Scripture that which the Church Catholic has not found there. She has come thus to arrogate for her usurped sovereignty a *divine* foundation. She has drawn from this principle all its consequences: the Pope has become the vicar of Jesus Christ, the necessary center of the Church, the pivot of Christianity, the infallible organ of heaven. These Papal errors were so skillfully disseminated in the western countries that they were there gradually adopted. The protests which they drew forth were indeed continued, but partaking of the spirit of the age they were not sufficiently pointed; even protests that were raised against the abuses of the Papacy admitted as beyond question a divine basis for that institution.

Author's Introduction

At the present day, these errors have penetrated not only the clergy and religious men; the rationalists—anti-Christians themselves—admit the idea that the Pope is the sovereign chief of the Christian Church, and that his spiritual prerogatives are derived from Jesus Christ. Many Protestants themselves do not conceive of a *Catholic* Church without a Pope, and see this church only in the Roman Church.[1]

We ourselves have been misled by the common error, taught as we had been to regard it as a revealed and incontestable verity.

In embarking upon the extensive research we were obliged to make for the preparation of the *History of the Church of France*, it did not enter our thoughts to examine certain questions, which only in an indirect way entered into our subject and upon which we had blindly accepted certain opinions. Hence some expressions too favorable to the Papacy, and some errors of detail, appear in our book. We seize the occasion now offered to give warning of them, in order that our readers may be on their guard against these errors which, however, will find their correction in the present work.

Rome has censured the *History of the Church of France* because it was not sufficiently favorable to her pretensions. We ourselves censure it because *too many* concessions are there made to Roman prejudices which had been imparted to us as truth, and which we had not been at the pains thoroughly to examine. Should Providence ever put it into our power to reprint the *History of the Church of France*, we shall deem it an obligation of conscience to make the correction. This would have been done at the demand of Rome, had Rome condescended to convince us of our error. We shall do it, however, at the requirement of our own conscience, now more enlightened.

No man is infallible; hence, inasmuch as a man dishonors himself by changing his opinions without good reason or pretending such change from motives of interest, in the same degree does he honor

---

1   The author thus touches two of the greatest advantages which modern writers, unfortunately, concede to the Papists: (1) That of identifying historical Christianity with the medieval Roman system, and (2) that of calling the Trentine Church the Catholic Church.

himself when acknowledging and retracting errors he discovers himself to have committed.

We are therefore disposed to great tolerance toward Roman Catholics who believe in the divine origin of the Papal prerogatives; for we know that this prejudgment is communicated to all of them with the first elements of religious instruction, and that everything in the Roman Church tends to strengthen it in their souls. But the more deeply this delusion is rooted in the Roman Church, and generally in all the West, the more are we bound to combat it with vigor.

To this pursuit have we for several years perseveringly devoted ourselves, and, thanks to God, our labors have not been useless. We hope the new work we now send forth will also bear its fruits, and will come to the help of those religious men, daily increasing in number, who, in the presence of the abuses and excesses of every kind committed by the Papacy, can no longer be blinded into respecting it by old delusions.

Accustomed to see in it the divine center of the Church, they can no longer recognize such a center in this hotbed of innovations and of sacrilegious usurpations; they ask, therefore, where is the Church of Jesus Christ? We need only divest the Papacy of the glory it has usurped, that the Church Catholic[2] may at once appear in her majestic perpetuity, in her *universality*. The Papacy has narrowed it to the point of presuming to comprehend the whole Church in itself. Tear away these glittering pretensions and the Christian society will appear marching with unbroken progress through ages, preserving inviolate the deposit of revelation and protesting against every error, whether emanating from Rome or elsewhere; accepting as her rule only the *Catholic rule* founded upon the Word of God, of which the Councils and the Fathers are the organs.

In this holy society there are neither Greeks nor Barbarians, but *Christians* only, who can say with St. Pacian, "*Christian* is my name; *Catholic* my surname," because they believe *without exception* in all fullness (*Kath ólon*) the doctrine taught by the Master and preserved

---

2   The "Church Catholic" is in fact the Orthodox Church.

Author's Introduction

intact by the Church in all ages and in all places. This great truth is concisely expressed by the well-known words of Vincent of Lerins:
"Quod ubique, quod semper, quod ab omnibus."

The Pope would, in his own interest, limit the Church to such as acknowledge his sovereignty, that he might then absorb them and say, "*I am the Church.*" Let us break down the barriers he has raised, and we shall at once see the Church in all her beauty—expanding in freedom, unshackled by territorial boundaries, owning as its members all particular churches, bound together by the same faith, communing with one another through pastors alike apostolic, made one in Jesus Christ, the great Pontiff, the sole Head of the Church, and in the Holy Spirit its guide.

Who has broken this admirable unity of the first Christian ages? The Pope.

He has usurped the place of Jesus Christ, and has said to all churches, "It is in me and by me you shall be united; the ministry of your pastors shall proceed from me; from me are you to receive doctrine. I am supreme pastor. It is my right to govern all. I am supreme judge. I may judge all and be myself judged by no one whomsoever. I am the echo of heaven, the infallible voice of God."[3]

Shall the harmony of the Church Catholic be destroyed because the Papacy has availed itself of outward circumstances to extend its usurped domination over a certain number of individual churches? Assuredly not. Far from excluding from this concord churches which have resisted her usurpations, it is the Papacy itself that is to be thus excluded. Not only has she broken with churches truly Catholic, but she has violated the traditions of her own Church. She has divided them into two distinct parts, like the Roman episcopate itself. The Roman traditions of the first eight centuries are not the same as those of succeeding ages. The Papacy has, therefore, lost its true perpetuity in the very points wherein it has innovated. Thus a member of the Roman Church who returns to the primitive

---

3   To similar words, almost the same as those summed up by the author, the present pontiff, Pius IX, lately presumed to add the awful expression, "I am the way, the Truth, and the Life." – EDITOR.

doctrine of that Church, and who rejects the innovations of the Papacy, reenters at once into the Catholic concord, belongs to the true Church of Jesus Christ, to that Church which has maintained itself in its double character of perpetuity, of universality. Far from us be those deplorable accusations of schism hurled at venerable churches, which have preserved the revealed doctrine in its primitive purity, which have preserved the apostolic ministry! The Papacy calls them schismatical because they have refused to acknowledge its usurpations. It is high time such noisy misapprehensions should cease.

We proceed, then, to demonstrate that it is the Papacy itself which is guilty of schism; that after having provoked division, it has perpetuated and consolidated it by its innovations; in a word, that it has caused its divisions to pass into a state of *schism*.

This proved, we shall be at liberty to conclude that those who are considered by the Papacy as schismatics because of their opposition to her autocracy are in reality the true Catholics, and that it has, in seeking to separate others from it, become itself separated from the Church.

There are those in the West who would present the Papacy as the legitimate development of the Christian idea, as Christianity arrived at its completion. The truth is, that it is the negation of the evangelical idea, of the Christian idea. Can, then, the negation of an idea be considered as its development? There will be some astonishment perhaps in seeing us enter upon such a subject with this degree of candor. We answer that at the epoch in which we live, there is need to speak frankly without mental reserve. We do not understand circumlocution with respect to error. Indulgent, charitable toward men who are deceived, we believe that we obey a true instinct of charity in waging open war with the errors that deceive men. "To speak truth," as wrote the Patriarch Photius to Pope Nicholas, "is the greatest act of charity."

L'Abbe Guettée

Saint Photios the Great (+893)

*"For there must be also heresies among you,
that they which are approved may be made manifest among you."*
St. Paul, First Epistle to the Corinthians 11:19

THE PAPACY

I.

THE Christian Church is fundamentally divided. Were it desirable to expose the internal feuds which agitate all Christian societies, and the contradictory doctrines of the sects which have revolted against the Mother Church, they would form a sorrowful picture.

Yet conflicts and heresies have their purpose. Indeed, as to doctrines which do not belong to *the deposit* of revelation, and which have not been defined, controversy is permitted and the liberty of the human mind is to be respected. As for heresy, St. Paul tells us that it is *necessary*, in order that the faith of *believers* may be well-rounded and enlightened.

But above all divisions, there is one more serious, and which before all must attract attention because of its importance and of the facts which have provoked it; it is that which exists between the Oriental Catholic Church and the Roman Catholic Church.

Every Christian heart must be saddened in view of this separation, which has subsisted for so many centuries between churches which have alike an apostolic origin; which have, save one word, the same creed; which have the same sacraments, the same priesthood, the same ethics, the same worship. In spite of these elements of union, division has been since the ninth century an acknowledged fact between these churches. Upon whom recoils the responsibility for this great religious and social crime? This is one of the gravest questions upon which a theologian can enter; he cannot resolve it without bringing to judgment one of these churches, without accusing it of having despised the word of Jesus Christ, who made unity a condition essential to the existence of his Church. It is evidently only by the strangest perversion of Christian common-sense that the division could have been provoked and perpetuated. This is admitted in the two churches, Oriental and Roman. For this reason they return upon each other the accusation of schism, and are unwilling to accept before God and before the world the responsibility which they both regard as a stigma. One of the two must be guilty. For although reprehensible acts might be specified on either side, these minor faults would not account for the separation. Discussions upon secondary points, coldness, occasioned by vanity or ambition, can engender only transient controversies. To determine a fundamental and permanent division, there must be a more radical cause and one which touches the very essence of things.

It is not possible, then, to resolve the question we have put without seeking this powerful and deep-seated cause which has provoked the schism and kept it alive to the present day. In approaching this question, we have been struck at the outset by the difference that exists between the reproaches which the two churches, Oriental and Roman, urge against each other reciprocally. The latter alleges that the Oriental Church separated herself (from her) to satisfy a pitiful grudge, through interest, through ambition. Such motives could, philosophically, explain only temporary strifes. The Oriental Church, on the contrary, assigns for the schism a motive radical and logical: she affirms that the Roman Church has provoked it in seeking to impose in the name of God an unlawful yoke upon the Universal Church, that is, the Papal sovereignty, as contrary to the divine constitution of the Church as to the prescriptions of the ecumenical councils.

If the accusations of the Oriental Church are well founded, it follows that it is the Roman Church which is guilty. In order to enlighten ourselves upon this point, we have investigated the relations of the two churches before their separation. It is, indeed, necessary to establish clearly the nature of these relations in order to see from which side has come the rupture. If it be true that the Roman Church sought in the ninth century to impose upon the whole Church a rule unknown to the previous ages and therefore unlawful, we must conclude that she alone should bear the responsibility of the schism. We have pursued the study calmly and free from prejudice; it has brought us to these conclusions:

(1.) The bishop of Rome did not for eight centuries possess the authority of *divine* right which he has since sought to exercise.

(2.) The pretension of the bishop of Rome to the sovereignty of divine right over the whole Church was the real cause of the division.

We are about to produce the proofs in support of these conclusions. But before presenting them we think it profitable to interrogate the Holy Scriptures, and examine whether the pretensions of the bishop of Rome to universal sovereignty of the Church have, as is alleged, any ground in the Word of God.

"*The stone which the builders refused is become the head stone of the corner. This is the LORD'S doing; it is marvellous in our eyes.*"
Psalm 117:22-23 LXX

II.

THE PAPAL AUTHORITY CONDEMNED BY THE WORD OF GOD.

THE Church, according to St. Paul, is a temple, a religious edifice, of which the faithful are the stones. "You are," said he to the faithful of Ephesus (2: 20–22), "built upon the foundation of the apostles and prophets, Jesus Christ himself being the chief cornerstone; in whom all the building fitly framed together groweth unto a holy temple in the Lord: in whom ye also are builded together for an habitation of God through the Spirit."

Thus, according to St. Paul, the Church is the society of all the faithful of the Old as well as of the New Testament; the first, instructed by the prophets, and the second by the apostles, form together a spiritual habitation, having for its foundation Jesus Christ, waited for by the one as the Messiah, adored by the other as the Divine Word clothed in humanity.

The prophets and apostles form the first layers of this mystic edifice. The faithful are raised on these foundations and form the edifice itself; finally Jesus Christ is the principal stone, the cornerstone which gives solidity to the monument.

There is no other foundation or principal stone than Jesus Christ. St. Paul writes to the Corinthians (1 Cor. 3: 11), "For other foundation can no man lay than that is laid, which is Jesus Christ." Paul gave to the Corinthians this lesson, because among them many attached themselves to the preachers of the Gospel, as though they had been the corner-stone of the Church. "I have learned," said he to them, "that there are contentions among you...

"Every one of you saith, I am of Paul; and I of Apollos; and I of Cephas; and I of Christ. Is Christ divided? Was Paul crucified for you?" (1 Cor. 1: 12 –13).

Peter himself could not be, according to St. Paul, regarded as the corner-stone of the Church, as the first vicar of Jesus Christ, any more than himself or Apollos. Peter and all the other apostles were only in his eyes the ministers of Jesus Christ, the first layers of the mystic edifice.

St. Paul also compares the Church to a body, of which Jesus Christ is the head, and of which the members are the pastors and the faithful.

"Christ," said he, "gave some, apostles; and some, prophets; and some, evangelists; and some, pastors and teachers; for the perfecting of the saints, for the work of the ministry, for the edifying of the body of Christ: Till we all come in the unity of the, faith, and of the knowledge of the Son of God, unto a perfect man, unto the measure of the stature of the fullness of Christ: That we henceforth be no more children, tossed to and fro, and carried about with every wind of doctrine, by the sleight of men, and cunning craftiness, whereby they lie in wait to deceive... But speaking the truth in love, may grow up into him in all things, which is the head, even Christ: From whom the whole body fitly joined together and compacted by that which every joint supplieth, according to the effectual working in the measure of every part, maketh increase of the body, unto the edifying of itself in love" (Eph. 4: 11–16).

There is then but one Church, of which Jesus Christ is the head; which is composed of the faithful as well as the pastors, and in the bosom of which the pastors work in the various ministrations which are confided to them to develop the Christian life, of which charity is the sum.

Do we perceive, in these notions of the Church, a monarchy governed by a sovereign pontiff, absolute and infallible?

Now this Church which St. Paul regards as the depository of divine instruction—this Church as extended in its unity as in its

II. The Papal Authority Condemned by the Word of God

universality—it is this that he calls "the pillar and ground of the truth" (I Tim. 3: 15).

"The elders which are among you I exhort, who am also an elder, and a witness of the sufferings of Christ, and also a partaker of the glory that shall be revealed. Feed the flock of God which is among you, taking the oversight thereof, not by constraint, but willingly; not for filthy lucre, but of a ready mind; neither as being lords over God's heritage, but being examples to the flock. And when the chief Shepherd shall appear, ye shall receive a crown of glory that fadeth not away" (I Peter 5: 1–4).

St. Peter, then, whom the Roman theologians would make the absolute prince of the Church, knew but one chief Shepherd, Jesus Christ. As for himself, he was the colleague of the other apostles by his priesthood; he speaks neither of his primacy nor of his sovereignty. He does not raise himself above the other pastors of the Church, whom, on the contrary, he addresses as his equals and his brethren; justifying himself solely in giving them counsel, in that he was a witness of the sufferings of Jesus Christ and also of his future glory, which had been revealed to him upon Mount Tabor.

We have not met in Holy Scripture any text relating to the subject we are now considering, where Jesus Christ is not regarded as the sole held of the Church, nor in which the Church is not represented as a whole, one and identical, composed of the faithful as well as the pastors.

It cannot be disputed that these pastors have received from Jesus Christ the powers necessary to govern well the Church. Furthermore, it cannot be denied that these powers given to the apostles were also transmitted to their legitimate successors; for the Church and the body of pastors should, according to Christ's word, be perpetuated for all ages. Before leaving the earth, Christ said to his apostles: "Go teach all nations, baptizing them in the name of the Father, and of the Son and of the Holy Ghost; teaching them to observe all things whatsoever I have commanded you: and lo, I am with you always, even unto the end of the world." (Matt. 28: 19–20.)

Jesus Christ is then perpetually with the body of the pastors of the Church. It is to them He has said in the person of the apostles: "He that heareth you heareth me; and he that despiseth you despiseth me" (Luke 10: 16). It is still to them he says: "Receive ye the Holy Ghost; whosoever sins ye remit they are remitted unto them, and whosoever sins ye retain they are retained" (John 20: 22–23).

This power, given in a general manner to all the apostles, had been promised to St. Peter previously, and in the same terms. This is one of the proofs that the Popes bring to support their theory of a special and superior power that Peter had received from Jesus, and that has been transmitted to them; but they do not remark that the power was given to all, that it was not promised to Peter personally, but to all the apostles in his person. This is the observation of St. Cyprian, and of the greater number of the Fathers of the Church.

Other texts are also cited to support this theory. We will consider them. Here is the first:

"Thou art Peter, and upon this rock will I build my Church, and the gates of hell shall not prevail against it."[4]

If we believe with the Popes, this text proves that St. Peter and the bishops of Rome, his successors, have been established by Jesus Christ as the cornerstone of the Church, and that Error, figured by the gates of hell, shall never prevail against this stone or rock. Hence, they draw this result, that they are the sovereign heads of the Church.

If this reasoning be true, it follows that St. Peter, to the exclusion of the other apostles, was established as cornerstone of the Church, and that it was not merely a personal privilege to him but that it has passed to the bishops of Rome.

It is not thus.

First of all, Peter was not called the rock of the Church to the exclusion of the other apostles. He was not made the head of it. We

---

4   Matt. 16: 18, 19. It will here be remembered that both the text and its application lose nearly all their power when translated into English. In French, the word Stone and the Christian name Peter are both rendered "Pierre."

see a proof of this in the text of St. Paul, already cited, in which that apostle distinctly affirms that the foundation-stones of the Church are the prophets and apostles, joined together by the cornerstone, which is Jesus Christ.

The title of "rock of the Church" cannot be given to St. Peter without forcing the sense of Holy Scripture, without destroying the economy of the Church, nor without abandoning Catholic tradition. Jesus Christ has declared that he was himself that stone designated by the prophets, (Matt. 21: 42; Luke 20: 17, 18.) St. Paul says that Christ was that Rock, (1 Corinth. 10: 4.) St. Peter teaches the same truth, (1 Pet. 2: 7, 8.)

The greater number of the Fathers of the Church have not admitted the play upon words that our Ultramontanes attribute to Jesus Christ in applying to St. Peter these words, "And upon this rock I will build my Church."[5] In order to be convinced that their interpretation is most just, it is only necessary to recall the circumstances under which Jesus Christ addressed to St. Peter the words so much abused by the Roman theologians.

He had asked of his disciples, "Whom do men say, that I the Son of man am?" The disciples replied, "Some say John the Baptist, some Elias, and others Jeremias, or one of the prophets." "But whom," replied Jesus, "say ye that I am?" Simon Peter, answering him, said, "Thou art the Christ, the Son of the living God." Jesus answered him and said, "Blessed art thou, Simon Bar-jona; for flesh and blood hath not revealed it unto thee, but my Father which is in heaven. And I say unto thee, that thou art Peter, and upon this rock I will build my Church," etc. (Matt. 16: 13–17).

These words mean nothing but this: "I say unto thee, whom I have surnamed Peter because of the firmness of thy faith, I say to

---

5   Launoy, Doctor of the Sorbonne, known for a great number of works on theology and whose vast erudition no one will dispute, has shown the Catholic tradition upon that question. He has demonstrated, by clear and authentic texts, that but a small number of Fathers or Doctors of the Church have applied to St. Peter the title of rock upon which the Church should be built; while the most of them do not apply this to him at all, but understand these words of Christ in quite a different manner. His collection of Letters may be consulted, which are the treatises of a savant of the first order.

thee that this truth that thou hast professed is the foundation-stone of the Church, and that Error shall never prevail against it."

As St. Augustine remarks, it was not said to Simon, Thou art the rock, (la pierre,) but thou art Peter (Pierre.) The words of St. Augustine deserve to fix the attention: "It is not," said he, " upon thee as Peter, but upon that rock which thou hast confessed." "*Ce n'est pas, dit il sur toi qui es pierre, mais sur la pierre que tu as confessee ... tu es pierre, et sur cette pierre que tu as confessee, sur cette pierre cue tu as reconnue en disant, Thou art Christ, etc., sur cette pierre je batirai mon eglise,*" I will build thee upon myself, I will not be built upon thee. Those who wished to be built upon men said, "*I am of Paul, I am of Apollos, I am of Cephas, that is to say, of Peter*"; but those who did not wish to be built upon Peter, but upon the Rock, they said, "I am of Christ." In the French language, when the name given to a man is the same designation as that of a thing, there is an amphibology which is not found either in Greek or Latin. In these languages the name of the man has a masculine termination, while the name of the thing has a feminine, rendering it easier to perceive the distinction that Christ had in view; moreover, it is easy in these two languages to remark, by the aid of the pronoun and the feminine article that precedes the word la pierre, (the stone), that these words do not relate to the masculine substantive which designates the man, but to another object. Besides, the Greek word oti has not been sufficiently discussed, which in Latin is exactly rendered by the word quia, which means because (parce que.) In translating thus in French, the amphibology is avoided, upon which is founded all the reasoning of the popes and their partisans.

In Holy Scripture the Rock is frequently spoken of in a figurative sense. This word always signifies Christ, and never, directly or indirectly, St. Peter. The best interpreter of Scripture is Scripture itself. It is then with good reason that the immense majority of the Fathers and Doctors have given to the passage in question the interpretation that we claim for it—that the word rock, which the Saviour used—always refers either to Jesus Christ or to faith in his divinity. This interpretation has the threefold advantage of being more conformed to the text, of better accordance with other passages of Holy Scripture, and of not attributing to Christ a play upon words little worthy of his majesty.[6]

As for the few old writers who admitted this play upon words, it must be remembered that none of them interpreted the text in a manner favorable to Papal sovereignty, nor drew from it the exaggerated consequences of this system. These consequences are diametrically opposed to the whole of their doctrine.

It is true that Christ addressed himself directly to Peter; but it is only necessary to read the context to see that he did not, thereby, give him a title to the exclusion of the other apostles. In fact, after having pronounced the words we have quoted, Jesus Christ, still addressing himself to Peter, added:

"I will give unto thee the keys of the kingdom of heaven: and whatsoever thou shalt bind on earth shall be bound in heaven" (Matt. 16:18). In the two parts of this text, Christ simply made two promises to Peter: the first, that the Church should be so firmly

---

6   Among the Fathers who have given this interpretation to the famous passage, "Tu est Petrus," we will name St. Hilary of Poitiers, *The Trinity*, sixth book; St. Gregory of Nyssa, *Advent of Our Lord*; St. Ambrose, book 6, on chapter ix. of St. Luke and on second chapter of Epistle to the Ephesians; St. Jerome in the eighteenth verse of the sixteenth chapter of St. Matthew; St. John Chrysostom, homilies fifty-five and eighty-three on St. Matthew and the first chapter of the *Epistle to the Galatians*; St. Augustine, tracts seven and 123 on St. John, the thirteenth sermon on the words of the Lord, taken from St. Matthew, and the first book of *The Retractions*; Acacius, homily pronounced at the Council of Ephesus; St. Cyril of Alexandria, on the fourth book of Isaiah, the fourth book *of the Trinity*; St. Leo I, Sermons 2d and 3d, upon his *elevation to the episcopate*, Sermon *Upon the Transfiguration of our Lord*, Sermon 2d upon the nativity of the apostles Peter and Paul; St. Gregory the Great, third book, 33d epistle; and St. John Damascene, *On the Transfiguration*.

This interpretation of the Fathers was preserved in the West until the era when Ultramontanism was erected into a system by the Jesuits in the sixteenth century. It will suffice to prove this to cite Jonas of Orleans, third book on the worship of images; Hincmar of Rheims, thirty-third essay; Pope Nicholas I, sixth letter to Photius; Odo of Cluny, sermon on the see of St. Peter; Rupert, on the third book of St. Matthew and twelfth book of the Apocalypse; Thomas Aquinas, supplement Q. 25, art. 1; Anselm, on the sixteenth chapter of St. Matthew; Eckius, on the second book of *The primacy of St. Peter*; Cardinal de Cusa, Catholic Concordance, second book, chapters thirteen and eighteen.

established in the faith of his personal divinity that error should never prevail against that truth; the second, that he would give to Peter an important ministry in the Church.

It is not possible to sustain the doctrine that the power of the keys was granted exclusively to St. Peter, for Jesus Christ gave it to all of them at the same time, employing the same terms that he had used in promising, it to St. Peter, (Matt. 18: 18) moreover, he promised to all the apostles collectively, and not only to Peter, to be with them to the end of the world.

According to St. Matthew, (Matt. 28: 18, *et seq.*) Jesus approached his disciples and said to them: "All power is given unto me in heaven and in earth—, go ye teach all nations, … . and I am with you always, unto the end of the world."

We read in St. John, (John 20: 21, et seq.) "As my Father hath sent me, even so send I you." After having said these words, he breathed upon them, and said to them, "Receive ye the Holy Ghost; whosoever sins ye remit, they are remitted unto them; and whosoever sins ye retain, they are retained."

Evidently Christ gave to his apostles collectively the prerogatives he had promised to Peter. The promise made to Peter has been realized in respect to the whole body of pastors, which proves that Christ only spoke to Peter as representing his colleagues, as being a type of the apostolic body.[7]

But, it may be asked, should we not conclude that what was addressed to Peter alone under such solemn circumstances was the bestowal of prerogatives in a special and superior manner?

It must be remarked that nowhere in the Gospel is it seen that any such promise made to Peter alone has been realized. Peter received this power only with the other apostles. But, if in the designs of Christ there was to be in the Church a supreme and absolute head, this institution would have been of sufficient importance to cause a particular mention in the sacred volume, of some occasion when

---

7   It is thus this text is interpreted by Origen, upon St. Matthew; St. Cyprian, *Of the Unity of the Church*; St. Augustine, Tracts 50 and 118 on St. John, sermon 205 on the Nativity of the Apostles Peter and Paul; St. Ambrose on Psalm 38; St. Pacian, Third Letter to Sempronius.

II. The Papal Authority Condemned by the Word of God

Jesus Christ delegated superior powers to this supreme chief. On the contrary it is seen that special assistance for the preservation of revealed truth, as well as the power of the keys, was given to Peter only collectively with his fellow-workers in the apostleship.

St. Paul knew no more than the evangelists of superior powers having been conferred upon St. Peter. Beside the texts that we have already quoted, we read in the Epistle to the Galatians (2: 7, 8, 9) that Paul ascribes to himself, among the Gentiles, the same power that Peter had among the Jews, and that he did not regard Peter as superior to James and John, whom he calls, like Peter, the pillars of the Church. He even names James, Bishop of Jerusalem, before Peter when he gives them their title of pillars of the Church; he believed so little in any authority of Peter that he withstood him to the face, because he was to be blamed.

When the apostles assembled at Jerusalem, Peter spoke in council only as a simple member of the assembly, not even the first, but after many others. He felt himself obliged in presence of the other apostles—some old disciples and some faithful followers—to renounce publicly his opinion upon the necessity of circumcision and other Judaical ceremonies.

James, Bishop of Jerusalem, summed up the discussion, proposed the resolution which was adopted, and acted as the veritable president of the assembly (Acts 15: 7).

The apostles then did not consider St. Peter as the foundation-stone of the Church.

Consequently the papal interpretation of the famous text, *Tu es Petrus*, is as contrary to Holy Scripture as it is to Catholic tradition.

We cannot see any serious objection to the manner in which we understand it. Our interpretation necessarily results from the comparison of the various texts of Scripture relating to the same subject.

From a Catholic and traditional point of view, it presents every guarantee—in fine, the text considered in itself can receive no other legitimate rendering. From the simple reading of the passage, it appears that the Saviour's principal object was to concentrate upon himself and his divine mission the whole attention of his disciples.

His divinity is the idea to which evidently his questions and the answers of Peter had reference; the conclusion then should relate to that idea. It is not possible to apply it to Peter, as head of the Church, without pretending that Christ, after having spoken of His divinity, drew from it, as a consequence, the Pontifical power, which is an idea essentially different.

Let us now see if the other texts quoted by the Romish theologians in favor of the Papal authority prove that Jesus Christ has truly established this authority in his Church.

They support themselves upon this passage of the Gospel of St. Luke (22: 31, et seq.): "Simon, Simon, behold; Satan hath desired to have you that he may sift you as wheat. But I have prayed for thee, that thy faith fail not; and when thou art converted, strengthen thy brethren."

Jesus here addresses himself to the apostles in the person of Simon, surnamed Peter. He says that Satan has asked permission to sift them, that is, to put their faith to severe trial. It is necessary to discuss the word you, in Latin vos and in Greek imas. Satan did not obtain the opportunity that he desired. The apostles will not lose their faith in presence of the temptations which they will be made to endure in the ignominious death of their Master.

Peter only, in punishment for his presumption, shall yield and then deny his Master. But thanks to the special prayer of the Saviour, he shall return in repentance and will thus have a great duty to fulfill toward the brethren scandalized by his fall—the duty of strengthening them and repairing by his zeal and faith the fault he has committed.

Truly it is impossible to conceive how the Popes have been so bold as to set up this passage of St. Luke in order to establish their system. It must be remarked that these words quoted were addressed by Christ to St. Peter the very day that he was to betray him, and that they contain only a prediction of his fall. St. Peter understood this well, since he immediately replied, "Lord, I am ready to go with thee both into prison, and to death"; but Jesus added, "I tell thee, Peter, the cock shall not crow this day before that thou shalt thrice deny that thou knowest me."

II. The Papal Authority Condemned by the Word of God

The text of St. Luke's Gospel is a proof against the firmness of St. Peter's faith, rather than in favor of it-a fortiori, then, should no deductions in support of his superiority in the matter of doctrine or government be drawn from it. And the Fathers of the Church and the most learned interpreters of Holy Scripture have never dreamed of giving to it any such meaning. Aside from modern Popes and their partisans, who wish at any price to procure proofs, good or bad, no one has ever seen in the words above quoted more than a warning given to Peter to repair by his faith the scandal of his fall, and to strengthen the other apostles whom this fall must shake in their faith.[8] The obligation to confirm their faith proceeded from the scandal he would thus occasion; the words *confirma fratres* are only the consequence of the word *conversus*. Now if one would give to the first a general sense, why should it not be given to the second? It would result then, if the successors of St. Peter have inherited the prerogative of *confirming* their brethren in the faith, they have also inherited that of the need of conversion, after having denied Jesus Christ. We cannot see how the Pontifical authority would gain by that.

The Popes, who have found such a singular proof to support their pretensions in the thirty-first and thirty-second verses of the twenty-second chapter of St. Luke's Gospel, have been very guarded in their quotation of the preceding verses.

The evangelist relates that a discussion arose among the apostles as to who should be considered the greatest among them. The famous words, *Tu es Petrus*, were already pronounced—this should prove that the apostles did not receive them as understood by the Popes of modern times. The very eve before the death of Christ, they were ignorant that He had chosen Peter to be the first among them and the foundation-stone of the Church. Christ took part in the discussion. This would have been an excellent opportunity for Him to proclaim the power of Peter—moreover, it was time that it should be done, for on the morrow He was to be put to death. Did He do it? Not only did the Saviour not recognize the superiority He

---

8 It was not until the ninth century that any Father or ecclesiastical writer admitted the Ultramontane interpretation.

is said to have promised Peter, but He gave altogether a contrary lesson to His apostles, saying to them, "The kings of the Gentiles exercise lordship over them, and they that exercise authority upon them are called benefactors. But ye shall not be so; but he that is greatest among you, let him be as the younger, and he that is chief, as he that doth serve" (Luke 22: 25–26).

In comparing the recital of St. Luke with that of St. Mark, it will be seen that the discussion had been occasioned by the request that the mother of James and John had made of Christ in favor of her children. She had begged for them the first two places in his kingdom. Christ did not tell her He had given the first place to Peter, an answer which would have been very natural and even necessary if St. Peter had in fact been invested with a superior authority. The ten other apostles were indignant at the ambitious demand made by James and John through their mother; they agitated among themselves the question of superiority. Christ then gave them the lesson which we have related, and which immediately precedes the text upon which the Roman theologians pretend to support their system (Matt. 20: 20, *et seq.*)

The value of this pretended proof, after the context is considered, will be appreciated. They cite still in their favor a passage in the Gospel of St. John (21: 15, et seq.): "Jesus said to Simon Peter: 'Simon, son of Jonas, lovest thou me more than these?'

He saith unto him: 'Yea, Lord; thou knowest that I love thee.' He saith unto him: 'Feed my lambs.' He saith unto him again, the second time: 'Simon, son of Jonas, lovest thou me?' He saith unto him: 'Yea, Lord; thou knowest that I love thee.' He saith unto him: 'Feed my sheep.' He saith unto him the third time: 'Simon, son of Jonas, lovest thou me?' Peter was *grieved* because he saith unto him a third time, Lovest thou me? And he said unto him: 'Lord, thou knowest all things; thou knowest that I love thee.' Jesus said unto him: 'Feed my sheep.'"

The Roman theologians argue thus upon this text: "Jesus Christ has given to St. Peter in a general manner the care of the pasture of the sheep and lambs; now, the lambs are the faithful, and the sheep are the pastors; therefore, Peter, and in his person his successors,

II. The Papal Authority Condemned by the Word of God

have received a supreme power over the pastors (or shepherds) and over the faithful."

If this reasoning were just, it would necessarily prove: (1) that the function confided to St. Peter was not also given to the other pastors of the Church, and (2) that the lambs signify the faithful and the sheep the Pastors.

Now St. Peter himself teaches us that all the pastors of the Church have received the ministry of feeding the flock of the Lord. We have already quoted the passage of his first epistle, in which he said to all those who were the heads of different churches, "Feed the flock of God which is among you" (1 Pet. 5: 2).

Does the solemnity with which Christ gave that function to Peter imply that he possessed it in a superior manner? Nothing supports this idea. The Fathers of the Church and the most learned commentators have only seen the expiation of his threefold denial in this threefold attestation of love that Christ drew from Peter. Nor did Peter see anything else, since he *"was grieved."* Had he conceived that Christ therein conceded to him any superior powers, he would rather have rejoiced than have been saddened by the words that were addressed to him; but he was convinced that the Saviour demanded a triple public declaration of his fidelity, before reinstalling him among the shepherds of his flock, because he had given reason for legitimate suspicions by denying his Master again and again. Christ could only address himself to Peter, because he alone had been guilty of this crime.

Now, do the lambs signify the faithful and the sheep the pastors? This interpretation is altogether arbitrary, and there can be nothing found in Catholic tradition to confirm it; on the contrary, tradition formally contradicts it, and it would be impossible to quote one single Father of the Church in its support. Moreover, this interpretation is not conformable to Scripture. The words sheep and lambs are indifferently used in Holy Writ to describe the same object. Thus we read in St. Matthew: "I send you forth as sheep in the midst of wolves" (10: 16), and in St. Luke: "I send you forth as lambs among wolves (10: 3). The word *sheep* in Scripture signifies the faithful.

We read in Ezekiel (34: 6): "My sheep wandered through all the mountains." "Other sheep I have which are not of this fold."

"St. Peter, addressing himself to the faithful of Pontus, Galatia, Cappadocia, Asia, and Bithynia, said to them: 'Ye were as sheep going astray, but are now returned unto the Shepherd and Bishop of your souls'" (1 Pet. 2: 25).

It is not possible therefore to found or give different meanings to the words *sheep* and *lambs*, nor to interpret the word sheep in the sense of pastors or clergy.

If we feel obliged to give to the two expressions a different meaning, would it not be more natural to understand by *lambs* the young members who have need of the most tender care, and by *sheep* to understand those of more mature age, according to the faith?

Thus the Papal interpretation is so thoroughly divested of foundation that a commentator upon the Gospels—one who would not be suspected by Roman theologians, the Jesuit Maldonat—speaks of it in this language: "We should not reason acutely, in order to discover why Christ employs the word lambs rather than sheep. He who would do this, should carefully consider that he will only appear ridiculous to the learned, for it is incontestable that those whom Christ calls his lambs are the same as those he elsewhere designates as his sheep" (Comment. in cap. xxi. John, § 30.)

St. Peter then was instituted neither as the foundation-stone of the Church nor as its chief pastor.

It need not be denied, however, that a certain primacy was accorded to this apostle.

Although he was not the first, in order of time, chosen by our Lord as disciple, he is named the first by St. Matthew—this evangelist, wishing to name the twelve apostles, thus expresses himself: "The first Simon, who is called Peter, and Andrew his brother," (Matt.10: 2). St. Luke and St. Mark also name St. Peter the first, although otherwise they do not follow the same order in naming the others.

Upon many occasions Christ gave to Peter evidences of particular consideration. His surname of Peter, without having all the importance that the Roman theologians attach to it, was nevertheless given to him to signify the firmness of his faith, and

II. The Papal Authority Condemned by the Word of God

for the purpose of honoring him. Ordinarily Peter was always the first to question our Lord, and to answer him in the name of the other disciples. The evangelists use this expression, "Peter and those with him," to describe the apostolic body (Mark 1: 36; Luke 8: 45; 9: 32). From these facts can we conclude, with the Doctor de la Chambre, "That Christ had granted to St. Peter above all his colleagues in the apostolate, a primacy of jurisdiction and authority in the government of the Church?" (*Traite de l'Eglise*, 1st vol.) This consequence is not logical. In the first place it is possible to be first in a corporation without having necessarily jurisdiction and authority—to be, as it is said, *first among equals—primus inter pares.* Moreover, St. Peter is not always named first in the Holy Scriptures; thus St. John names Andrew before him (1: 44), St. Paul names him after James (Galat. 2: 9), even naming him after *the other apostles and the brethren of the Lord* (1st Corinth. 9: 5). "Peter then was only the first among the apostles as Stephen was the first among deacons": These words are St. Augustine's (Sermon 316).

Origen (on St. John) and St. Cyprian (seventy-first letter to Quint.) have the same idea. We can affirm that no Father of the Church has seen in the primacy of Peter any title to jurisdiction or absolute authority in the government of the Church. They would not have been able to draw these conclusions without contradicting Holy Scripture itself.

Christ forbade his apostles to take, in relation to each other, the titles of Master, Doctor, and even Father, or Pope, which signifies the same thing. His words are positive: "Be ye not called Rabbi: for one is your Master, even Christ; and all ye are brethren. And call no man your father upon earth, for one is your Father which is in heaven. Neither be ye called masters: for one is your Master, even Christ. But he that is greatest among you shall be your servant" (Matt. 23: 8).

Upon comparing these words of the Gospel with the pictures that the Roman theologians make of the prerogatives of the bishop of Rome, it will be easily seen that these theologians are not in the truth.

St. Matthew relates that, after Peter interrogated Jesus Christ upon the prerogatives of the apostles, our Lord answers him, saying: "Verily I say unto you, that ye which have followed me in the regeneration, when the Son of Man shall sit in the throne of his glory, ye shall also sit upon twelve thrones, judging the twelve tribes of Israel" (19:28).

If Christ had destined a superior seat to Peter—if he had granted to him a higher position than to the other apostles—would He have said to St. Peter himself that the twelve apostles should be seated upon twelve thrones without distinction?

The conclusion from all this is that there is in the church but one master, one lord, one chief shepherd.

Saith Christ: "I am the Good Shepherd" (John 10: 11); "Ye call me Master and Lord, and ye say well, for so I am" (John 13:13); and "One is your Master, even Christ" (Matt. 23: 10).

He is seated alone upon the throne of his majesty, in the heavenly city whose "wall has twelve foundations, and in them the names of the twelve apostles of the Lamb" (Rev. 21: 14). The first pastors are there upon their seats, judging the tribes of the new people of God. If any discussions arise that cannot be amicably settled, they must be carried to this tribunal—not to one alone, but before the whole Church, represented by those ordained to govern it.

There is nothing then in the writings of the New Testament which is even remotely favorable to that sovereign authority that the Romish theologians ascribe to St. Peter and to the bishops of Rome, whom they consider his successors.

It may be even said that Scripture formally contradicts this authority. We have already quoted some words of Christ sufficiently positive. The book of the Acts, and the Epistles, contain facts demonstrating that St. Peter did not enjoy any superiority in the apostolic college. In fact, it is said in the Acts (8 : 14): "Now when the apostles which were at Jerusalem heard that Samaria had received the word of God, they sent unto them Peter and John." Peter was subordinate, not only to the apostolic college, of which he was a member, but to a lesser number of apostles in convention at Jerusalem (since he received from them a mission). In the same book

II. The Papal Authority Condemned by the Word of God

(11: 2-3,) we read that the *faithful* of the *circumcision* reproached Peter for mingling with the uncircumcised, and Peter excused himself by relating that he had obeyed an express order of God. Is this the mode in which a chief is ordinarily treated, or that one supreme would act in relation to subordinates? At the Council of Jerusalem, (Acts 15: 7), Peter was not presiding; it was James who gave sentence (15:9). Peter spoke, but in his turn as a simple member. Yet the presidency would belong to him by right, if he had been vested with authority and jurisdiction over the whole apostolic body. St. Paul (Galatians 2: 7, etc.), too, refutes the primacy of Peter. He affirms that he is his equal and relates having reprimanded Peter for "walking not according to the truth of the Gospel" (Galatians 2:14). Again, St. Paul denies this (1 Corinth. 3: 4, 5, 22) when he affirms that Peter is but a simple minister like himself, and like Apollos, who must not attach the faithful to themselves but to Christ, their only Master. Finally, St. Peter himself denies the primacy with which he has since been invested by Romish theologians, when he addressed himself to the pastors of the churches which he had founded as their colleague (1 Pet. 1: 1).

Saint Clement of Rome (+101)

III.

OF THE AUTHORITY OF THE BISHOPS OF ROME IN THE FIRST THREE CENTURIES.

HISTORY shows us that the Fathers and Bishops, during the first eight centuries, have given to Holy Scripture the same interpretation that we have just set forth. If the Bishop of Rome had by divine right enjoyed universal authority in the Church; if, as the successor of St. Peter, he had been the vicar and representative of Christ, the necessary centre of the Church, there is no doubt that these prerogatives would have been recognized by Christian antiquity, the faithful guardian of the Faith and of Divine Institutions. Though the Church suffers, after the lapse of ages, some decline on her human side, that is to say, in the men that govern her, and form part of her, it will not be assumed that this decay appeared at the outset. It is natural and logical to go back to the beginnings of an institution to become acquainted with its true character; it is there we find the necessary starting-point from which to trace its development, its progress, or its lapses, age by age. If we prove that the primitive Church did not recognize in the Bishop of Rome the authority which he now assumes, that this authority is only an usurpation dating from the ninth century, it must necessarily be concluded that this authority is not of Divine origin, and that consequently it is the duty of every Church and all the faithful to protest against it and combat it.

Now we can affirm, after deep and conscientious study of the historical and doctrinal remains of the first eight centuries of the

Church, that the Bishop of Rome has no ground for claiming universal authority, that such authority has foundation neither in the Word of God nor the laws of the Church.

The first document by which the partisans of the Papal sovereignty justify themselves is the letter written by St. Clement in the name of the Church at Rome to the Church at Corinth. They assert that it was written by virtue of a superior authority attached to his title of Bishop of Rome.

Now, it is unquestionable, (1) that St. Clement was not Bishop of Rome when he wrote to the Corinthians, and (2) that in this matter he did not act of his own authority, but in the name of the Church at Rome, and from motives of charity.

The letter signed by St. Clement was written A.D. 69, immediately after the persecution by Nero, which took place between the years 64 and 68, as all learned men agree. Many scholars, accepting as an indisputable fact that the letter to the Corinthians was written while Clement was Bishop of Rome, assign its date to the reign of Domitian. But Clement only succeeded Anencletus in the See of Rome in the twelfth year of Domitian's reign, that is to say, A.D. 93, and held this See until A.D. 102. The testimony of Eusebius leaves no doubt upon this point.[9]

Now, it may be seen from the letter itself that it was written after a persecution; if it be pretended that this persecution was that of Domitian, then the letter must be dated in the last years of the first century, since it was chiefly in the years 95 and 96 that the persecution of Domitian took place. Now, it is easy to see from the letter itself that it was written before that time, for it speaks of the Jewish sacrifices as still existing in the temple of Jerusalem.

The temple was destroyed, with the city of Jerusalem, by Titus in A.D. 70. Hence, the letter must have been written before that year. Besides, the letter was written after some persecution, in which had suffered, at Rome, some very illustrious martyrs. There was nothing of the kind in the persecution of Domitian. The persecution of Nero lasted from the year 64 to the year 68. Hence it follows that the letter to the Corinthians could only have been written in the

---

9   Euseb., Eccl. Hist., Book III, chaps. xiii., xv., xxxiv.

III. Authority of the Bishops of Rome

year 69, that is to say, TWENTY-FOUR YEARS before Clement was Bishop of Rome.

In presence of this simple calculation, what becomes of the stress laid by the partisans of Papal sovereignty, upon the importance of this document as emanating *from* Pope St. Clement?

Even if it could be shown that the letter of St. Clement was written during his episcopate, this would prove nothing because this letter was not written by him by virtue of a superior and personal authority possessed by him, but from mere charity, and in *the name of the Church at Rome*. Let us hear Eusebius upon this subject:

"Of this Clement there is one epistle extant, acknowledged as genuine, ... which he wrote in the name of the Church at Rome to that of Corinth, at the time when there was a dissension in the latter. This we know to have been publicly read, for common benefit, in most of the churches, both in former times and in our own; and that at the time mentioned, a sedition did take place at Corinth, is abundantly attested by Hegesippus."[10]

Eusebius, further on, recurs to the letter of Clement, and again remarks that it was written in the *name of the Church at Rome*.[11] He could not say more explicitly that Clement did not in this matter *act of his own authority*, by virtue of any power he *individually* possessed. Nothing in the letter itself gives a suspicion of such authority. It thus commences: "The Church of God which is at Rome, to the Church of God which is at Corinth." The writer speaks of the Ecclesiastical Ministry, in relation to several Priests whom the Corinthians had rejected most unjustly; he looks upon this Ministry as wholly derived from the Apostolic Succession, attributing neither to himself nor to others any Primacy in it.

There is every reason to believe that St. Clement draughted this letter to the Corinthians. From the first centuries it has been considered as his work. It was not as Bishop of Rome, but as a disciple of the Apostles, that he wrote it. Without having been charged with the government of the Roman Church he had been made Bishop by St. Peter, and had been the companion of St. Paul

---

10 Euseb., Eccl. Hist., Book III, chap. xvi.

11 Ibid., chap. xxxviii.

in many of his Apostolic visitations. It may be that he had worked with St. Paul for the conversion of the Corinthians. It was natural, therefore, that he should be commissioned to draw up the letter of the Church of Rome to a Church of which he had been one of the founders. And so, Clement speaks to them in the name of the Apostles, and above all of St. Paul, who bad begotten them to the faith. Even had he written to them as *Bishop* of Rome, it would not be possible to infer anything from this in favor of his universal authority. St. Ignatius of Antioch, St. Irenæus of Lyons, and St. Dionysius of Alexandria have written letters to diverse churches, not excepting that of Rome, without thereby pretending to any other authority than that they possessed as bishops to do GOD'S work in all places.

Nothing can properly be inferred, either from the letter itself or from the circumstances under which it was written, that should make this proceeding appear in the light of an acknowledgment of any superior authority in the Bishop or the Church of Rome; or this answer in the light of an authoritative act. The Corinthians addressed themselves to a Church where dwelt the fellow-labourers of St. Paul, their father in the faith; and that Church, through Clement as her organ, recommended peace and concord to them, without the least pretension to any authority whatever.

Thus, in the intervention of Clement, no proof can be found to support the pretended authority of the Bishops of Rome. Clement was the deputy of the clergy of Rome in that affair, chosen because of his capacity, his former connection with the Corinthians, his relation with the Apostles, and the influence he had for these various reasons. But he did not act as Bishop of Rome, much less as having authority over the Church of Corinth.

In the second century the question concerning Easter was agitated with much warmth.

Many Oriental Churches wished to follow the Judaical traditions, preserved by several Apostles in the celebration of that feast, and to hold it upon the fourteenth day of the March moon; other Eastern Churches, in agreement with the Western Churches, according to

III. Authority of the Bishops of Rome

an equally Apostolic tradition, celebrated the festival of Easter the *Sunday* following the fourteenth day of the March moon.

The question in itself considered was of no great importance; and yet it was generally thought that all the Churches should celebrate at one and the same time the great Christian festival, and that some should not be rejoicing over the resurrection of the Saviour while others were contemplating the mysteries of his death.

How was the question settled? Did the Bishop of Rome interpose his authority and overrule the discussion, as would have been the case had he enjoyed a supreme authority?

Let us take the evidence of History. The question having been agitated, "there were synods and convocations of the Bishops on this question," says Eusebius,[12] "and all unanimously drew up an ecclesiastical *decree*, which they communicated to all the Churches in all places. There is an epistle extant even now of those who were assembled at the time; among whom presided Theophilus, Bishop of the Church in Cesarea and Narcissus, Bishop of Jerusalem. There is another epistle [of the Roman Synod] extant on the same question, bearing the name of Victor. An epistle also of the Bishops in Pontus, among whom Palmas, as the most ancient, presided; also of the Churches of Gaul, over whom Irenæus presided. Moreover, one from those in Osrhoene, and the cities there. And a particular epistle front Bacchyllus, Bishop of the Corinthians; and epistles of many others who, advancing one and the same doctrine, also passed the same vote."

It is evident that Eusebius speaks of the letter of the Roman synod in the same terms as of the others; he does not attribute it to Bishop Victor, but to the assembly of the Roman Clergy; and lastly, he only mentions it in the second place after that of the Bishops of Palestine.

Here is a point irrefragably established: it is that in the matter of Easter, the Church of Rome discussed and judged the question in the same capacity as the other churches, and that the Bishop of Rome only signed the letter in the name of the synod which represented that Church. The partisans of the Papal authority

---

12 Euseb., Eccl. Hist., Book V, chap. xxiii.

assert that it was Victor who commanded the councils to assemble. This assertion is altogether false.[13]

Several Oriental Bishops did not conform to the decision of the others. Polycrates of Ephesus, above all, protested against it.[14] Then a lively discussion arose between him and Victor, Bishop of Rome, who seemed to think that the Bishop of Ephesus would be alone in his opinion, and advised him, in consequence, to ask the opinion of the other Bishops of his province. Polycrates complied, and those Bishops declared themselves in favor of his opinion; he wrote thus to Victor, who threatened to separate them from his communion. This did not move Polycrates; he replied vigorously, saying to him particularly: "They who are greater than I have said 'we ought to obey God rather than men.' Upon this Victor, the Bishop of the Church of Rome forthwith *endeavored*[15] to cut off the Churches of all Asia, together with the neighboring Churches, as heterodox, from the common unity. And he published abroad by letters, and proclaimed that all the brethren there were wholly excommunicated." Thus Eusebius.

It is difficult to believe that the partisans of the Roman pretensions can find in these words of Eusebius and in the conduct of Victor any proof in favor of their system. Without much effort, they might find in them a proof to the contrary. The expression of Eusebius, that "Victor *endeavored*," etc., must first be noticed. It is clear that those who endeavor have not in themselves the power to do that which they have in view, otherwise the act would follow the will. Victor, however, did all he could in order that this excommunication should be recognized; he even pronounced it. But that act remained but an attempt, and it had to be ratified by the other Churches in order to be valid. Thus Victor did not have, as Bishop of Rome, the power to excommunicate other Churches, since the effect did not follow the

---

13 Among the Roman theologians who make this false assertion, we will particularly name Darruel in his work entitled *Du Pape et de ses Droits*. This book sums up all the errors and exaggerations of the Romish theologians.

14 Euseb., Eccl. Hist., Book V, chap. xxiv.

15 πειρᾶται; Euseb., loc. cit.

III. Authority of the Bishops of Rome

sentence which he believed himself entitled to give in the name of the Western Churches because of the importance of his See.

The Bishops, who would have submitted to his sentence, if they had recognized in him the Head of the Church, invested with universal authority, not only did not obey him, but strongly censured his conduct.

"But this," adds Eusebius, "was not the opinion of all the Bishops. They immediately exhorted him [Victor], on the contrary, to contemplate that course that was calculated to promote peace, unity, and love to one another."

Thus, instead of believing that unity consisted in union with Victor, the bishops exhorted him to observe better the true notions of unity. Many went even further. "There are also extant," continues Eusebius, "the expressions they used, who pressed upon Victor with much severity. Among these also was Irenæus, who, in the name of those brethren in Gaul, over whom he presided, wrote an epistle in which he maintains the duty of celebrating the mystery of the resurrection of our Lord only on the day of the Lord. He becomingly also admonishes Victor not to cut off whole churches of God who observed the tradition of an ancient custom." Irenæus endeavored to show to Victor that differences in practice, of which, he gives diverse examples, are not inconsistent with Unity of Faith." And when," adds Eusebius, " the blessed Polycarp went to Rome in the time of Anicetus, and they had a little deference among themselves likewise respecting other matters, they immediately were reconciled, not disputing much with one another on this head. For neither could Anicetus persuade Polycarp not to observe it, because he had always observed it" [a certain custom] "with John the disciple of our Lord, and the rest of the Apostles with whom he associated; and neither did Polyearp persuade Anicetus to observe, who said that he was bound to maintain the practice of the presbyters before him. Which thing being so, they communed with each other; and in the church Anicetus yielded to Polycarp the office of consecrating." And thus, though following different usages, all remained in the communion of the Church.

"And not only to Victor, but likewise to the most of the other rulers of the churches, he sent letters of exhortation on the agitated question."[16]

Thus Victor could not, *of his own authority*, cut off from the Church, in fact, those whom he had declared excommunicate; the other Bishops resisted him vigorously, and St. Irenæus, the great divine of the age, made war in his letters upon those which Victor had written to provoke the schism.

This discussion, invoked by the partisans of Papal pretensions in their favor, falls back upon them with all its weight, and with a force that cannot in good faith be contested.

Anicetus did not invoke his authority against Polycarp, nor did Victor against Irenæus and the other Bishops. Polycarp and Irenæus reasoned and wrote as equals of the Bishop of Rome in Episcopal authority, and recognized but one rule—*ancient tradition.*

How were the Churches reunited in a common practice? Eusebius thus relates that happy result, which certainly was not due to the Bishop of Rome:[17] The Bishops, indeed, of Palestine, Narcissus and Theophilus, and Cassius with them, the Bishop of the Church at Tyre, and Clarus of Ptolemais, and those that came together with them, having advanced many things respecting the tradition that had been handed down to them by succession from the Apostles, regarding the Passover, at the close of the epistle use the words: Endeavor to send copies of the epistle through all the Church, that we may not give occasion to those whose minds are easily led astray. But we inform you also, that they observe the same day at Alexandria which we also do; for letters have been sent by us to them and from them to us, so that we celebrate the holy season with one mind and at one time.

Nevertheless, many Churches preserved the tradition of the Churches of Smyrna and Ephesus, and were not on that account regarded as schismatics, although Victor had separated himself from their communion.

---

16   Euseb., Eccl. Hist., Book V, chap. xxiv.

17   Euseb., Eccl. Hist., Book V, chap. xxv.

III. Authority of the Bishops of Rome

The partisans of the Papal system attach much importance to the influence exercised by the Bishop of Rome in the question of Easter and some other matters: they transform that *influence* into *authority*. This is an untenable paralogism. It is not to be wondered at that the Bishop of Rome should have enjoyed from the first a high influence in religious questions; for he filled the first See of the West, and as Bishop of the Capital of the Empire, he was the natural link between East and West. It was then understood that the Catholic Church was not *exclusively* in any country; that the East possessed no more universal authority than the West. This is why certain heretics, born and condemned in the East, sought protection in the West, and above all at Rome, its representative. Thus it is that even some saints—as Polycarp of Smyrna—went themselves to Rome to confer with the Bishop of that city upon religious questions.

But it is not possible conscientiously to study these facts from reliable documents without eliciting this truth: that the influence of the Bishop of Rome did not arise in *an universal authority*—that it did not even have its source in an authority recognized by all the Western Churches, but was simply derived from the importance of his See.

Rome was the centre of all communications between different parts of the Empire. The faithful crowded thither from all quarters—for political business or private interests—and thus her testimony as an Apostolic Church was strengthened by the faithful who came thither from all parts of the world, bringing the witness of all the Churches to which they severally belonged.

Such is the sense of a passage of St. Irenæus, of which the Roman theologians have made the strangest misuse.[18] This great theologian, attacking the heretics who sought to corrupt the faithful at Rome, establishes against them the *Catholic rule* of faith, preserved everywhere and always. "But," he adds, "as it would be very tedious to enumerate in such a work the succession of all the Churches, we will trace that of the very great and very ancient Church and known of all, which was founded and established at Rome by the two very glorious Apostles, Peter and Paul; which possesses a tradition that

---

18 St. Irenaeus, In Hæres, Lib. III., cap. iii.

comes from the Apostles as much as the Faith declared to men, and which has transmitted it to us through the succession of her Bishops; by that, we confound all those who in any manner whatsoever, either through blindness or bad intention, do not gather where they should. For every Church, that is to say, the faithful who are from all places, are obliged to go *toward* that Church, because of the most powerful principality. In this Church, the tradition of the Apostles has been preserved by those who are of all countries.[19]

The Romish theologians choose a bad translation of this passage, in order to find in it an argument in favor of the papal sovereignty. Instead of saying that the faithful of the whole world were obliged to go to Rome, because it was the Capital of the Empire, the seat of government, and the centre of all business, civil and political, they translate *convenire* ad by the words *to agree with*—which is a misinterpretation; they make *potentiorem principalitatem* refer to the *Church of Rome*, and they see in this its primacy, whereas these words are only used in a general manner, and nothing indicates that they do not solely designate the capital and principal city of the Empire. Again, they translate *maximae antiquissimae* as *greatest and most ancient*, without reflecting that they thus attribute to St. Irenæus an assertion manifestly false; for, granting that the Church of Rome was the *greatest* of her day, she could not certainly be called the most ancient—everyone knew that a great number of churches had been founded in the East before that of Rome. Moreover, their translation does not make the author say in conclusion that the Apostolic tradition has been preserved at Rome, by those who were

---

19 We must quote the text of St. Irenaeus, that it may be compared with our translation: "*Quoniam valde longum est, in hoc, tali volumine omnium eccelsirum enumerate successiones; maximae et antiquissimae et omnibus cognitae, a gloriosissimis duobus apostolis Petro et Paullo, Romae fundatae et constitutae Ecclesiae, eam quam habet ab Apostolis Traditionem et annunciatam hominibus fidem, per suecessiones Episcoporum pervenientem usque ad nos, indicantes confundimus omnes eos, qui quoquomodo, vel per coecitatem et malam sententiam praeterquam oportet colligunt. Ad hane enim Ecclesiam, propter potentiorem principalitatem, necesse est omnem convenire ecclesiam, hoe est eos, qui sunt undique fideles; in qua semper ab his qui sunt undique, conservata eat ea, quae est ab Apostolis, Traditio.*"

III. Authority of the Bishops of Rome

of all countries (ab his qui sunt undique)—as the text requires—but like Pius IX, in his *Encyclical Letter to the Christians of the East*, "In all that the faithful believe," not reflecting that this is a misconstruction and that they are thus attributing nonsense to the good Father.

In the text as we render it all things hang together. St. Irenæus, after having established that only the *universal* Faith should be received, points out to the heretics of that city the Church of Rome as offering an Apostolic tradition that had been there preserved by the faithful of the whole world.

How then could St. Irenæus, whose purpose it is to give the *universal Faith* as the rule for private belief, and who enlarges precisely upon this point in the chapter from which the text is taken, logically say what is attributed to him by the Popes and their theologians? He would then have argued thus: *It is necessary* to adopt as the rule the belief of all the churches; but it *suffices* to appeal to that of the Church of Rome, to which there must be uniformity and submission, because of her primacy. St. Irenæus never expressed so unreasonable an opinion. He lays down as a principle the universal Faith as a rule, and he points out the Faith of the Church of Rome as true—thanks to the concourse of the faithful who assembled there from all parts, and who thus *preserved* there the Apostolic tradition.

How did they preserve it? Because they would have protested against any change in the traditions of their own churches, to which they were witnesses at Rome. St. Irenæus does not give the pretended Divine authority of the Bishop of Rome, as the principle of the preservation of tradition in the Church of that city—but *logically*, he attributes that preservation to the faithful of other Churches who controlled her traditions by those of their own Churches, and who thus formed an invincible obstacle to innovation.

It was natural that the Bishop of the Capital of the Empire, precisely because of the faithful who there gathered from all parts, should acquire a great influence in religious matters, and even occasionally take the lead. But all the monuments, as also the circumstances attending those transactions in which he took part, show that he enjoyed no authority superior to that of the other Bishops.

It is clear that all discussion relative to this text of St. Irenæus turns upon the sense to be given to the word *convenire*. If this word signifies to *agree with*, we must conclude that the venerable writer thought it all must necessarily agree with the Church of Rome, and without that it is impossible to be in unity. If the word means *to go*, all the Ultramontane scaffolding will fall of itself, for it cannot reasonably be affirmed that all the faithful must of *necessity* go to Rome, even though the Church established in that city should be the first and principal Church, the centre of Unity. It follows that the sense of this word should be determined in so evident a manner that there remains no doubt in respect to it.

We have already remarked that the preposition *ad* determined the sense of the word—we can add many others to this already conclusive proof

If we possessed the Greek text of the passage in question, there is no doubt there would not be the uncertainty resulting from the Latin word. But Eusebius and Nicephorus have preserved for us other fragments of the primitive text. Now it happens that in these fragments the good Father uses expressions which the Latin translator has rendered by the word *convenire*, and which have no meaning except just this one of *going*—whether *together* or separately.

In the second book, chapter xxii (Migne's edition, col. 785) St. Irenæus says: "All the priests who have gone to Asia, to John, disciple of the Lord, bear witness to it." The Greek Text reads: "καὶ πάντες οἱ πρεσβύτεροι μαρτυποῦσιν, οἱ κατὰ τὴν Ἀσίαν Ἰωάννῃ τῷ τοῦ κυρίου μαθητῇ συμβεβληκότες." while the Latin translation reads: "Omnes seniores testantur qui in Asia apud Joannem discipulum Domini convenerunt."

In the third book, 21st chapter, (Migne's edition, col. 947) speaking of the Septuagint interpreters of Scripture, St. Irenæus says of them, "Being assembled at Ptolemy's house," etc.

In Greek: "Συνελθόντων δὲ αὐτῶν ἐπὶ τὸ αὐτὸ παρὰ τῷ Πτολεμαίῳ," and in Latin translation: "*Convenientibus* autem ipsis in unum apud Ptolemaeum."

The Benedictine Massuet, editor of St. Irenæus's works, pretends that St. Irenæus must have used in the text in question,

III. Authority of the Bishops of Rome

the words συμβαίνειν πρὸς τὴν τῶν Ῥωμαίων Ἐκκλησίαν. And he pretends that συμβαίνειν πρός τινα is the same thing as συμβαίνειν τινί.

Even if this opinion were unimpeachable, such erudition would be worth nothing, for we must content ourselves with supposing that the good father has used the word συμβαίνειν. It would seem to us more natural and logical to look for the unknown word among the known words, which the translator renders convenire. Now from that study, it should appear that St. Irenæus did not use συμβαίνειν, but συμβεβληκότες, which has the sense of *a running together toward a place*, or of συνελθόντες, which has an analogous signification, since, in the Greek texts that have been preserved, he has used these words to express the idea for which the translator used *convenire*.

In general, the translator of St. Irenæus gives to the word *convenire* the sense of *to go*, and not *to agree with*. Why then give it this sense in the famous text in question, when in the text itself the preposition *ad* gives the idea of direction *toward a place*, and the adverb *undique* gives that of departure from all places other than Rome where the faithful were found?

Nothing is wanting to prove that it is impossible to give to the words of St. Irenæus the sense attributed to them by the Romish theologians. The good father then has simply said that *the concourse of Believers from all countries, drawn to Rome by the necessities of their business, because that city was the first and most powerful of the Empire, contributed to preserve there the Apostolic tradition, because those Believers carried there the Faith of the Churches to which they belonged.*

It is certain that Rome, in her position as an Apostolic Church, had a very great authority during the first centuries, and Tertullian is right in calling her as a witness against the heretic to whom he said, "Thou hast Rome, whose authority is close at hand. Happy Church to whom the Apostles gave all the doctrine with their blood!" (De Praescrip. c.xxxvi). But cannot an Apostolic Church *bear witness* to the Faith against heresy without enjoying universal and divine authority?

St. Cyprian was right in calling the Church of Rome *"the chair of Peter; the principal Church*, from whence sacerdotal unity emanated" (St. Cyp. 55th epis. to Cornelius). But for all that, did he pretend that the Bishop enjoyed authority by Divine right? He believed it so little, that in his *Treatise upon the Unity of the Church*, he understands by the *"chair of Peter,"* the entire *Episcopate*, he regards St. Peter as the equal of the other Apostles and denies his primacy, he makes St. Peter to be the simple *type* of the unity of the Apostolic College.[20] Therefore, it is in a limited sense that he calls the Church of Rome the *chair of Peter*; he makes her the principal Church—but that was a fact resulting from her exterior importance. She was the source of *Sacerdotal Unity* in this sense that Peter was the *sign* and *type* of the unity of the Apostolic College. To give any other sense to the text from the letter of St. Cyprian to Cornelius would be to contradict the *Treatise on the Unity of the Church*, to attribute to St. Cyprian two contradictory doctrines, and consequently to take from him all logic and all authority.

Those who have given such high importance to the text of St. Cyprian, taken from his letter to Cornelius, have forgotten another that so well explains it that it is difficult to understand how they have omitted it. It is that in which he declares that, "Rome should precede Carthage, *because of its great size—pro magnitudine sua.*"[21] This doctrine agrees with that of St. Irenæus and the other Fathers, who have never mentioned any *divine* prerogative with which the Church of Rome had been favored.

St. Optatus, St. Jerome, St. Augustine, and many other Western Fathers have praised the Church of Rome as an Apostolic Church, and have attached a high importance to her testimony in questions of faith. But *not one* of them ascribes to her any *such doctrinal authority that her testimony* would of itself be sufficient to determine questions under discussion. It must even be remarked that St. Augustine sets up the authority of the Oriental churches against the Donatists, and does not mention that of Rome, although she was the *Apostolic* Church of the West. St. Irenæus would be the only one to sustain that doctrine, if we should receive his text as translated by the Romish theologians.

---

20 Further on will be found the entire texts of St. Cyprian and Tertullian.

21 Cypr., Ep. 59 ad Cornel.

III. Authority of the Bishops of Rome

But we have seen that this interpretation is false, and that he has attributed to the testimony of the Church of Rome a great authority in this sense only: that it had received the Apostolic tradition, and, thanks to the Believers who congregated there from all parts, that tradition had been preserved pure *unto his times*. Therefore, it was not because the Church of Rome was *the principal, the first, the most Powerful* in Christendom that her testimony was chiefly valuable, but *because of* the Believers from other churches who strengthened it by their adherence.

When Constantinople had become the capital of the Roman Empire, St. Gregory Nazianzen said of that Church what St. Irenæus had said of that of Rome, and with still more formal expressions. "This city," said he, "is the eye of the world. The most distant nations press toward her from all parts, and they draw from her as from a spring the principles of the Faith" (42d dis., §10, col..470, Migne's edit.). The Latin translation of St. Gregory, like that of St. Irenæus, employs the word *convenire* to express the crowding of people toward Constantinople. Must we give to it the sense of *agreeing with*, because this Father calls Constantinople not only a powerful and principal Church but *the eye of the world, source of faith?*

The ninth canon of the Council of Antioch, held in 341, will of itself be sufficient to determine the sense of the text of St. Irenæus. The canon reads: "Let the bishops established in each province know that to the bishop of the metropolitan city is confided the care of the whole province, *because all those who have business* come to the metropolis from all parts. Therefore it has appeared advisable to grant a superior honor to him."

If the faithful were drawn to a mere metropolis to transact their business, how much more to the capital of the empire, which was for them a *necessary* centre, and in which they must meet from all parts of the empire. Such is the fact established by St. Irenæus, and from it he concludes that the witness of the Church of Rome should suffice to confound heretics.

Finally let us remark, that the chapter of the learned Father only relates to the heretics of Rome, for whom he destined the book; and that will convince us, that it is a strange abuse of the words to give them an absolute sense, making them relate to heretics in general, and to all ages; for he only affirmed that the Roman Church *had preserved* her apostolic tradition pure to his time, and not, that she would *always so preserve it.*

The discussion upon the baptism of heretics throws further light upon the question we are examining.

From all antiquity,[22] it was customary merely to impose hands upon those who had fallen into heresy, and wished to reenter the bosom of the Church. In the third century a grave discussion arose upon this subject. St. Cyprian, Bishop of Carthage, was the first in the West who maintained that baptism should be readministered to converted heretics.

Dionysius, Bishop of Alexandria, who at that time exerted a great influence throughout the Church by reason of his holiness, his zeal and learning, declared himself openly for the Bishop of Carthage, and wrote upon the subject to Stephen, Bishop of Rome. Stephen, persuaded that no change should be made in a tradition handed down from time immemorial, was very much grieved at an opinion which he looked upon as an innovation. St. Cyprian admitted the existence of the custom, but he contended that it was not lawful. He even took advantage of a contrary doctrine that he said his church had preserved, and according to which baptism administered by heretics was regarded as null.

St. Cyprian, having assembled several councils of bishops of the province of Africa, sent their transactions to Stephen with a letter,[23] in which he said, "I believe that I should write to you upon a subject that concerns the unity and dignity of the Church Catholic, and should confer upon it with a man *so grave* and *so wise as you.*"

It is not, as one may see, to a superior that he addresses himself, but to an equal whose gravity and wisdom he esteems. He even makes him understand that he is in error in supporting the custom of the Roman Church. He says: "I am persuaded that your faith and piety make that which conforms *to the truth* agreeable to you. However, we know there are some who will not abandon sentiments with which

---

22 Euseb., Eccl. Hist., Book VII, chaps. ii and iii.

23 Cyprian, Epp. 72, 73, ad. Steph.

III. Authority of the Bishops of Rome

they have been once imbued, and who maintain particular usages, without interrupting harmony among the Bishops. In such cases we do no violence and impose no law upon anyone."[24]

St. Cyprian does not wish here to impose his opinion upon Stephen; but he blames him for preserving that which he regards as a prejudice contrary to the truth.

Stephen rejected the doctrine of St. Cyprian; he further declared that he would not even communicate with him, nor with the Bishops of Cilicia, of Cappadocia and Galatia, who followed the same doctrine. Dionysius of Alexandria[25] wrote to him, to exhort him to peace; telling him that all the Oriental churches, although divided in their opinions on the doctrines of Novatus, were in most perfect union, and rejoicing in that happy result. He counseled him not to trouble again the Church in regard to the baptism of heretics.

At this stage of the matter Xystus succeeded Stephen. Dionysius of Alexandria hastened to write to him to dissuade him from following the way of Stephen. He says of this bishop:[26] "He had written before respecting Helenus and Firmilian, and all those from Cilicia and Cappadocia and Galatia and all the nations adjoining, that he would not have communion with them on this account, because they, said he, rebaptized the heretics; and behold, I pray you, the importance of the matter; for in reality, as I have ascertained, decrees have been passed in the greatest councils of the Bishops, that those who come from the heretics are first to be instructed, and then are to be washed and purified from the filth of their old and impure leaven. And respecting all these things I have sent letters entreating them."

St. Dionysius did not see an act of authority in the letter of Stephen, but an intervention that might throw a new germ of trouble in the Church; it was on this ground that he wished to check him. Instead of troubling the Church, Stephen would have pacified it if a universal authority had been recognized in him. This

---

24 Ibid.
25 Letter of St. Dionysius of Alex. In Eusebius, Eccl. Hist., Book VII, chap. v.
26 Letter of St. Dionysius of Alex. In Eusebius, Eccl. Hist., Book VII, chap. v.

consideration suffices to establish the entirely private and personal character of his letter.

What was the result? Was he obeyed, as he would have been had the Bishop of Rome had supreme authority? Was his separation regarded as breaking the unity of the Church? Assuredly not! St. Dionysius of Alexandria acted in this affair as St. Irenæus did in the question of Easter; he declared openly for those who differed with the Bishop of Rome, while to the latter he addressed earnest prayers for the peace of the Church. St. Cyprian assembled a new council of the bishops of Africa, who confirmed their first opinion; and he consulted with Firmilian, in order to oppose the entire Church against the Roman Church in this question.

Firmilian answered St. Cyprian in a letter that will show the belief of Oriental Christendom touching the authority of the Bishops of Rome:

"Firmilian to his brother in the Lord, Cyprian, greeting: 'We have received by our very dear deacon Rogatian, whom you have sent to us, the letter, beloved brother, that you have written us; and we have rendered thanks to God, that while being thus separated in body, we are united in spirit, as if we were dwelling, not only in the same country, but in the same house; which may well be said, since the spiritual house of God is one. In the last days, says the prophet, the mountain of the Lord, and the house of God, placed on the summit of the mountains, shall be manifested. Reunited in this house, we there enjoy the bliss of unity. It is what the psalmist asks of the Lord—to dwell in the house of the Lord all the days of his life. Whence, and from another passage, appears the happiness of the saints in being united: Oh! how good and pleasant a thing it is for brethren to live together in unity. In fact, union, peace, and concord confer a very great felicity, not only to faithful men who know the truth, but to the angels of heaven themselves, who according to the divine word experience joy when a sinner repents and returns to the bond of unity. This would not be said of the angels who inhabit heaven, if they also were not united to us, who rejoice over our union; as, on the other hand, they are grieved when they see hearts and minds in division, not only as though they did

III. Authority of the Bishops of Rome

not invoke the same and only God, but as if they would not speak to or hear each other. But in this we may be grateful to Stephen; for, by his violence, he has put your faith and wisdom to trial; yet if we have an advantage because of him, it is not to him that we owe it. Truly, Judas for his perfidy and treachery which he so criminally employed toward his Saviour, should not be regarded as the cause of the great blessings that the passion of the Lord procured for us, in delivering the world and all people. But for the present we will pass over what Stephen has done, fearing, lest in remembering his audacity and insolence, we experience too much grief at his bad actions.'"[27]

This preamble of Firmilian's letter demonstrates that he was very far from placing the centre of unity in the pope. In his eyes, Stephen was but a bishop, full of *audacity* and insolence, because he had dared to separate himself from the communion of those who had another belief from his own upon the question of the baptism of heretics; and he even goes so far as to compare him to Judas. Nor must it be forgotten that Firmilian was one of the holiest and wisest bishops of his time.

The principle of unity he placed in God; he says, "As it is but one and the same Lord that dwells in us, he joins and knits together his own among themselves, by the bond of unity, in whatever place they may be."

As for the Church of Rome, which it is sought to impose upon us now as the *centre of unity*, he thus speaks of her:

"Those who are at Rome do not observe all the things which were given at the beginning, and it is in vain that they pretend to support themselves upon the authority of the apostles: it is thus that, upon the day for the celebration of Easter, and upon a great number of other mysteries of religion, there are diversities among them and that they do not observe all that is observed at Jerusalem; likewise, in other provinces many varieties are encountered according to the diversity of places and tongues; yet they are not separated for all that from the peace and unity of the Church Universal."

---

[27] Firmilian to St. Cyprian among the letters of the latter. Seventy-fifth letter. Edit. Baluze—reviewed by the Benedictines.

The Church of Jerusalem was the *model church*, according to Firmilian; she was the mother of all the others, and the purest type after which all the others should form themselves. As for the Church of Rome, she could, like any other private church, be cut off from unity. This is why he declared so energetically against Stephen, who *had dared to break peace* with the bishops of Africa; who *slandered the Apostles Peter and Paul*, by pretending to follow their traditions. "I have reason," he said, "to be indignant at the manifest folly of Stephen, who, on the one hand, glories in his episcopal seat, and pretends to possess the succession of Peter, upon whom the foundations of the Church were placed, and who, on the other hand, introduces other stones (*Pierres*), and constructs new buildings for other churches, by asserting, upon his own authority, that they possess the true baptism...

"Stephen, who boasts of possessing the see of St. Peter by succession, shows no zeal against the heretics... You, Africans, you may say to Stephen, that having known the truth, you have rejected the custom of error; but for us, we possess at the same time, truth and usage; we oppose our custom against that of the Romans; our usage is that of truth, preserving, since the beginning, that which Christ and the Apostles have given to us... Yet Stephen does not blush to affirm, that those in sin can remit sins, as though the waters of life could be found in the house of the dead. What! dost thou not fear God's judgment, when thou showest thyself favorable to heretics against the Church! thou art worse than all the heretics; for when those among them, who have recognized their error, come to thee to receive the true light of the Church, thou then comest in aid of their errors, and extinguishing the light of the truth of the Church, thou gatherest around them the darkness of the night of heresy. Dost thou not understand that an account of these souls will be demanded of thee in the day of judgment, since thou hast refused the waters of the Church to those who were thirsty, and hast caused the death of those who wished to live? And yet thou art angered!

"Look at thy folly, who darest to attack those who fight against falsehood for truth's sake! Who is it, that is most righteously angry

III. Authority of the Bishops of Rome

with another? Is it he who agrees with the enemies of God, or rather, he, who for the truth of the Church, declares himself against those who agree with the enemies of God? . . What disputes, what discussions thou preparest for all the churches of the world! What grievous sin thou hast committed in separating thyself from so many flocks! Thou hast killed thyself; do not deceive thyself; for he is truly schismatic who renounces the communion of the unity of the Church! While thou thinkest that all others are separated from thee, it is thou who art separated from all others." Thus Firmilian speaks to the Bishop of Rome, and no one dreamed of taxing him with wrong, even among those who differed with him concerning the baptism of heretics.[28]

St. Dionysius of Alexandria, without openly taking part against the Bishop of Rome, endeavored to lead him to the idea of rebaptizing. It is to this end that he displays his doubts in regard to a man whom he had admitted to the communion without rebaptizing him, and who, nevertheless, scarcely dared to participate in the body of the Lord, because he had only received baptism among the heretics, and with guilty words and rites. "Brother,"[29] he wrote to Xystus, "I have need of your counsel, and I ask your opinion on an affair that has presented itself to me, and in which, indeed,

---

28 Some Ultramontanes have contested the authenticity of Firmilian's letter; but the most learned among them agree, with the learned of all the schools, to regard it as authentic. The strongest reason that Barruel alleges to contest its authority is that Firmillan could not have written such a letter, since, according to St. Dionysius of Alexandria, he was reconciled to the pope before the letter could have been written. If Barruel had been a little more learned, he would have known that in the letter of St. Dionysius of Alexandria to Stephen, the letter to which he alludes, he does not say that the whole church was in peace upon the subject of the baptism of heretics, since the discussion was just beginning; but that he only says that Stephen would be wrong to trouble the church by this discussion when she was in the enjoyment of peace after the troubles created by Novatus. The other pretended proofs of Barruel are still more feeble and do not deserve discussion. We only say that he has displayed an extraordinary audacity in confronting thus the most illustrious scholars of every school, who admit this letter as authentic without any dispute.

29 Euseb., Eccl. Hist., Book VII, chap. ix.

I am afraid I may be deceived." It is not to a superior he addresses himself, to ask a decision, but to an equal, to a brother, in order to know his views, that he may himself come to a determination. We ask every man in good faith, is it thus that the Bishop of Alexandria would have written to the Bishop of Rome, if the latter had enjoyed an authority universally acknowledged to terminate dogmatic or disciplinary discussions?

We find in the acts of the last council of St. Cyprian a very significant criticism upon the pretensions which the Bishop of Rome had begun to put forth. After having asked the advice of his colleagues, he speaks thus, "Let each one give his opinion without judging anyone and without separating from the Communion those who are not of his opinion; for none of us sets himself up for a bishop of bishops, nor compels his brethren to obey him by means of tyrannical terror, every bishop having full liberty and complete power; as he cannot be judged by another, neither can he judge another. Let us all wait the judgment of our Lord Jesus Christ, who alone has the power to appoint us to the government of his Church and to judge our conduct.[30]

It is evident that St. Cyprian had in view Stephen, Bishop of Rome, who had dared to declare those out of his communion who thought otherwise than he did upon the baptism of heretics. The Roman theologians choose to consider these excommunications by the Bishops of Rome as sentences which separated from the Church those upon whom they fell. But the manner in which the sentence of Victor in the Easter question and that of Stephen in the discussion upon the baptism were considered, proves that they were only regarded as personal acts of the Bishop of Rome, and had no other effect than to sever the relations between him and those who did not share his way of thinking. As for the Church, *that* remained intact, for the very simple reason that this unity did not consist in a union with the Bishop of Rome, and that those whom he separated from his communion communicated with the rest of the Church. Only those upon whom excommunication was declared by the

---

30 Concil. Carth., St. Cyprian, pp. 329, 330, Bened. edit.

III. Authority of the Bishops of Rome

Church itself in general council (or in particular councils to which the rest of the Church adhered) were considered out of the Church.

The criticism made by St. Cyprian upon the title of *bishop of bishops* leads one to think that the Bishop of Rome endeavored even then to assume it, and recalls a remark of Tertullian.[31]

This learned priest of Carthage said ironically of a Roman bishop whose teaching he censured: "I learn that an edict has been given, even a peremptory edict, the *Sovereign Pontif*, that is, the *Bishop of Bishops* has said: 'I remit the sins of impurity and of fornication to those who do penance.' O edict! Not less then can be done than to ticket it—*Good work*. But where shall such an edict be posted? Surely, I think upon the doors of the houses of prostitution." Tertullian equally ridicules the titles of Pope and *apostolic* which had been taken by the Bishops of Rome. Men like Zephyrinus and his successor Callistus[32] could well appropriate pompous titles that they did not deserve; but the Church, instead of recognizing their legitimacy, and regarding them as emanating from a divine right, censured them by her most learned doctors, and looked upon them as the evil fruit of pride and ambition. St. Cyprian would not have been consistent with himself if he had submitted and declared himself in favor of the pretensions of the Bishops of Rome. In fact, in his *Treatise upon Church Unity*, he positively denies the primacy of St. Peter himself; he makes that Apostle merely to be the type of unity, which resided in the apostolic college as a whole; and by succession in the whole episcopal body, which he calls the *see of Peter*. It is only by a series of the strangest of distortions that the Roman theologians understand by this last expression the *see of Rome*. They cannot give such a sense

---

31 Tertull., *De Pudicitia*, § 1.

32 See the work entitled *Filosofoúmena* upon the scandal of these two unworthy bishops, which with justice has been attributed to St. Hippolytus, Bishop of Ostia, or to the learned priest Calus. It is certain at any rate that this book is the work of a writer contemporary with the events recorded, and one who enjoyed great authority in the Roman Church. Tertullian reproaches a bishop of Rome with having adopted, owing to the seductions of Praxeas, the heresy of the Patripassians, (Lib. adv. Prax. § 1). The author of *Filosofoúmena* attributes this heresy to Zephyrinus and to Callistus, Bishops of Rome at that time. He did not believe, it is evident, in their infallibility.

to it without completely forgetting the rest of the text from which this is taken. We will give it as an example among a thousand of the want of good faith of the partisans of popery, when they cite from ancient traditions. After mentioning the powers promised to St. Peter, St. Cyprian remarks that Jesus Christ *promised* them to him alone, though they were to be given to all. "In order to show faith unity," he says, "the Lord has wished that unity might draw its origin from one only.[33] The OTHER APOSTLES certainly WERE JUST WHAT PETER WAS, having the SAME *honor* AND POWER AS HE.[34] All are shepherds, and the flock nourished by all the Apostles together is one, in order that the Church of Christ may appear in its unity."

The see of Peter, in St. Cyprian's idea, is the authority of the apostolic body, and, by succession, of the episcopal body; all the bishops had the *same honor* and the *same authority*, in all that relates to their order, as the Apostles had the SAME HONOR AND AUTHORITY AS PETER.

Since St. Cyprian admits this principle, how has it been possible to misconstrue some of his expressions as has been done? Even were it necessary to understand the see of Peter to mean the see of Rome, there would follow nothing favorable to the pretensions of the bishop of that see, since as bishop he would *possess no more honor,*

---

33 Here is the explanation of the passage, of which we have already spoken, where St. Cyprian calls the Church of Rome "Source of sacerdotal unity."

34 In some manuscripts, in this place it has been added, "But the primacy has been given to Peter, in order that there might be but one church and one see. *Sed primatus Petro datur ut una Ecclesia et cathedra una monstretur.*" These words could be explained in a sense not Ultramontanist, by that which precedes in St. Cyprian upon Peter—his type of unity; but it is useless to waste time in explaining an interpolated text. Thus it was regarded by the learned Baluze, who prepared the edition of the works of St. Cyprian, published subsequently by the Benedictine Don Maran. When that edition was published, one named Masbaret, professor at the Seminary of Angers, obtained authority from the government to reestablish the passage. It was at that time thought desirable not to oppose Rome, and the passage was inserted by means of a card. See *l'Histoire des Capitulaires*, in which notice the observations of Chiniac upon the Catalogue of the Works of Stephen Baluze.

III. Authority of the Bishops of Rome

no more authority, than the others; and, as St. Cyprian further proves, the *episcopate is one*, and the bishops possess it jointly and severally.

But the Bishop of Carthage calls the Church of Rome *root and womb of the Catholic Church*.[35] What follows if such expressions were generally employed in his time to designate all the apostolic churches? No one denies the Church of Rome was founded by the Apostles—it was thus *a root* of the Catholic Church, a mother church—but not exclusively THE ROOT—THE mother of the Church. In fact, Tertullian calls all the apostolic churches wombs and ORIGINATORS—which means, "mothers having given origin to others";[36] the same saint calls Jerusalem *mother* of *religion, matricem religionis*.[37] The first Council of Constantinople[38] gave to the Church of Jerusalem the title of *mother of all the churches*. In Africa the title of *matrix* or *mother* was given to all the great metropolitan churches.[39] A Gallican bishop of the fifth century, Avitus of Vienne, wrote to the Patriarch of Jerusalem: "Your apostolate exercises a primacy granted to it by God: and it is careful to show that it occupies a *principal place (principem locum)*, in the Church not only by its privileges, but by its merits."[40] Thus it is not surprising that St. Cyprian should give the title of *mother church/root of the church* to that of Rome, which had given birth to others, perhaps even in Africa, and whose origin was of apostolic date. Through the Apostles she was, like other apostolic churches, the mother and root of the Catholic Church. Since these qualifications are not given to her in an exclusive manner, they prove nothing in favor of the authority she claims. No one denies that Rome has been one of the most important centres of Christian radiation over the world; no one disputes that she was a powerful, venerable, and apostolic church. But all concurs to prove that her

---

35 St. Cyprian, Letter 45 to Cornelius.
36 Tertul., Præscript, c. xxi.
37 Tertul., Adv. Marcionem Book IV. c. xxxv.
38 Labbe, Collect. des Conciles.
39 See Conciles d'Afrique. Same collection.
40 Works of St. Avitus, edited by Father Sirmond, 2nd volume of the miscellaneous works of P. Sirmond.

importance did not confer universal authority upon her during the first centuries.

We see that as early as the third century the Bishops of Rome, because St. Peter had been one of the founders of that see, claimed to exercise a certain authority over the rest of the Church, giving themselves sometimes the title of bishop of bishops; but we also see that the whole Church protested against these ambitious pretensions, and held them of no account.

Since the Roman theologians attach so much importance to the testimony of St. Cyprian and Tertullian, we have been obliged to determine the sense of it in a clear and precise manner. To the texts of the great Carthaginian bishop we will add some of Tertullian, which are of high importance, because the Roman theologians have wished to interpret them in their favor.

In his book against Marcion,[41] he expresses himself thus: "If it be proved, to begin with: that is most true which is most primitive; that is most primitive which has been from the commencement; that which was from the commencement was established by the Apostles; it will then be equally unquestionable, that that has been given by the Apostles which has been held sacred by the apostolic churches. Let us see *what milk* the Corinthians have received of St. Paul; according to what law the Galatians have been corrected; what the Philippians, the Thessalonians, the Ephesians read; what the Romans our neighbors announce, they who have received direct from Peter and Paul the Gospel attested by their blood. We have also the churches nourished by John."

The Church of Rome is here assigned its proper place, which is after the apostolic churches, whose foundation was anterior to her own.

Tertullian does not esteem her witness superior to that of others; only he establishes *one fact*, namely, that the Church of Rome, the only apostolic Church of the West, was nearer than the others, and it was therefore easier for him and his opponents to ascertain her testimony touching the questions that divided them.

---

41 Tertull., Adv. Marcion, Book IV. § 5.

III. Authority of the Bishops of Rome 77

In his book *De Præscriptionibus* Tertullian develops the same doctrine of the *witness* of apostolic churches, and he appeals to that of the Church of Rome in the same manner as in his book against Marcion.

"That which the Apostles have preached," he said,[42] "that is to say, that which Christ has revealed to them, I claim *by prescription*, that it should only be proved by the churches that the Apostles have founded, teaching them, either *viva voce*, or by their epistles. If this be so, all doctrine that agrees with that of the apostolic churches, mothers *and sources of faith*,[43] is agreeable to the truth."

Further on, Tertullian applies this general principle.

"Let us glance,"[44] he says, "at the apostolic churches, where the sees of the apostles still remain, where their epistles are still read, where their voice still resounds, and their face, as it were, is still seen. Is it Achaia that is near thee? Thou hast Corinth; if thou art not far from Macedonia, thou hast the Philippians; if thou canst go to Asia, thou hast Ephesus; if thou dwellest near Italy, *thou hast-Rome, whose authority is near us. How happy is that church to whom the Apostles have given all its doctrine with their blood*—where Peter suffered death like his Lord, where Paul was crowned by the death of John the Baptist, whence the Apostle John, after being plunged into boiling oil without suffering any ill, was banished to an island. Let us see what that church says, what it teaches, what it testifies in common with the churches of Africa."

The Romish theologians ordinarily content themselves with quoting that part of the text we have put in italics. They are careful not to call attention to the fact that Tertullian speaks of the Church of Rome, only *after* the other apostolic churches, and in the same character; that he appeals specially to her evidence, only because it was the *apostolic church nearest to Africa*, whose testimony it was easiest to obtain. These observations, the importance and truth of which all will understand, destroy completely the interpretation that these

---

42   Tertul, De Præscript. § xxi.

43   Matricibus et originalibus fidei.

44   Tertul, De Præscript. § xxxvi.

theologians endeavor to give to the few lines they cite. This doubtless is why they ordinarily pass the others over in silence.

The Romish theologians have eagerly collected many causes brought for adjudication to the see of Rome during the first three centuries, and have instanced them as proofs of the superior authority of the bishops of this see over all the Church. Nevertheless, these appeals prove absolutely nothing in favor of that authority. The principal instances upon which they rely are those of Origen, of St. Dionysius of Alexandria, of Paul of Samosata, and of the Novatians. We will examine these cases in the light of authentic historical monuments.

First we will establish a general principle which determines their true character, as well as that of the appeals addressed subsequently to the Bishop of Rome; it is, that an appeal to a see or a bishop is not a proof in favor of its authority. During the first three centuries, frequent intercourse existed between the bishops; and if a discussion arose in one particular church, those who endeavored to prove to their adversaries that they were wrong, addressed themselves to other bishops, praying them to make known the belief of their churches, so as to condemn those who wished to give force to new opinions. Distant churches were most commonly appealed to, such as could not be suspected of partiality, apostolic churches, or bishops who enjoyed a high reputation for holiness or learning. Those who were condemned in the West appealed to the East, and those who were condemned in the East appealed to the West, and above all to Rome, which was the only apostolic church of that country.

It is very natural that the Church of Rome should not have been excluded from these appeals; but, before alleging these appeals in support of her supreme authority, it would be necessary to show her to have been the only one appealed to, and that her sentences were received as emanating from that authority. We shall see that such was not the case.

Origen never appealed to Rome, notwithstanding many Romish theologians affirming that he did. Condemned at first by the bishops of Egypt, subsequently by several others, and in particular by the Bishop of Rome, he saw fit to justify himself before those

III. Authority of the Bishops of Rome

who had condemned him. "But he also wrote," says Eusebius,[45] "to Fabianus, Bishop of Rome, and to many others of the bishops of churches, respecting his orthodoxy." Such is, in all its simplicity, the fact in which Roman theologians have found a proof of the primacy in authority and jurisdiction of the Bishops of Rome. They carefully avoid quoting the text of Eusebius, and have passed over in silence the opinion of St. Jerome touching the condemnations of which Origen had been the object. Jerome, after speaking of the innumerable labours of the learned priest of Alexandria, cries,[46] "What reward has he received for so much toil and sweat? He is condemned by Bishop Demetrius, and, excepting the bishops of Palestine, Arabia, Phœnicia and Achaia, he is unanimously condemned by all. Even Rome assembled her Senate (that is, her synod) against him; not that he taught new dogmas, not that he held heretical opinions, as those who bark after him like furious dogs would persuade us; but because they could not bear the brilliancy of his eloquence and learning, and because, when he spoke, all the others seemed dumb."

Thus, according to St. Jerome, the clergy of Rome associated themselves in low intrigues against Origen; and, according to Eusebius, this great man wrote to the Bishop of Rome as he wrote to many others to justify his faith.

We ask what this fact proves for the authority of the Bishops of Rome.

The case of St. Dionysius of Alexandria proves nothing more. Many of the faithful, not having understood the teaching of this great bishop against Sabellius and his partisans, went to Rome and attributed a heretical doctrine to him. A council was then holding in that city. The Roman bishop wrote, in the name of the council, a letter to Dionysius of Alexandria to ascertain if it were true that he taught the doctrine attributed to him. The Bishop of Alexandria sent to Rome a work he had composed and in which his sentiments were set forth with precision.

---

45 Euseb., Hist. Eccl., Book VI, chap. xxxvi.
46 Ap. Ruff, liv. ii.

Such is the substance of what St. Athanasius and Eusebius wrote on this point. Now, because one bishop asks in the name of a council for information from another bishop respecting his faith, must we conclude that the bishop who seeks this information possesses authority and jurisdiction over him to whom he writes? It is not only the *right* but the *duty* of every bishop to seek to enlighten a brother whom he believes in error, and to hold himself ready to give an account of his own faith. Thus, the bishops of Rome and Alexandria performed an imperative duty; neither of them exercised authority.

Again, because many went to Rome to accuse him, is there, therefore, no reason to say that they recognized a superior authority in this see?

Faustinus, Bishop of Lyons, wishing to have Marcianus of Arles condemned, accused him to St. Cyprian. Did he thereby acknowledge a superior authority in St. Cyprian? Two wicked bishops, who showed in their favor letters from the Bishop of Rome,[47] were condemned by St. Cyprian upon the accusation of the Spanish bishops. Shall we infer that the Spanish bishops acknowledged in Cyprian an authority not only over their church, but superior to that of the Bishop of Rome? The history of the Church affords numerous examples of bishops who appealed to each other, and that without recognizing any authority in those to whom the causes were submitted.

Dionysius of Alexandria[48] himself received complaints against the doctrine of Paul of Samosata, Bishop of Antioch, as the Bishop of Rome had received them against his. As that bishop had written to him, he wrote to the Bishop of Antioch to inform him of the accusations made against him. He addressed himself to Paul in the name of his clergy, as the Bishop of Rome had addressed him in the name of the Roman council. The Bishop of Antioch replied, in order to give explanations; and Dionysius, not finding them

---

47 Letters of St. Cyprian.

48 Euseb, *Eccl. Hist.*, Book VII, chap. xxviii. and xxx. Library of the Fathers, vol. xi.

III. Authority of the Bishops of Rome

sufficiently clear, wrote back to refute them. The bishops of Syria assembled at Antioch to judge Paul.

They wrote to Firmilian of Cæsarea in Cappadocia, and to Dionysius of Alexandria, praying them to come and judge with them. Had they thus written to the Bishop of Rome, the Romish theologians would have gloried in the fact, which, nevertheless, would prove nothing more in favor of the jurisdiction of that bishop than it proves in favor of that of Firmilian or of Dionysius.

The latter could not present himself at the council because of a serious malady that shortly after laid him in the tomb; but he wrote to the Council of Antioch a letter which was sent to the whole Church by a Second council that terminated the case of Paul of Samosata.

This heretical bishop wished to continue in the episcopal dwelling. The bishops, in order to have him expelled, wrote to the Emperor Aurelian at Rome, who, says Eusebius,[49] "decided most equitably, ordering the building to be given up to those to whom the *Christian bishops of Italy and Rome* should write."

The second Council of Antioch had written to the Bishop of Rome as well as to the successor of Dionysius in the see of Alexandria. The Church of Italy adhered to the sentence of the council against Paul of Samosata, who was driven from the Church.

It has been wished to find in the decision of Aurelian a proof in favor of the universal jurisdiction of the Bishop of Rome. It is more accurate to say that the Emperor, in the affair upon which he had been consulted, wished to hear the testimony of bishops, who could not be *reasonably challenged* by either party, because they were not interested to favor one more than another; of bishops whose sentence he himself could easily ascertain, since he lived among them. It must be remarked that the Emperor did not give as final the sentence of the Bishop of Rome; he named him with the other bishops of Italy, and *after them*; and if he mentioned him in a special manner, it was evidently because of the importance of his see, established in the capital of the empire, and not because he enjoyed any particular authority.

---

49 Eusebius, Eccl. Hist., Book VII, chap. xxx.

There must truly be great need of proofs in favor of the Roman supremacy when its supporters look for them in the conduct of a pagan emperor; while all the ecclesiastical details of the affair of Paul of Samosata prove that supremacy had not been recognized by the Church.

The case of the Novatians is not more favorable to their system. The schism of Novatus of Carthage is easily confounded with that of Novatian of Rome. The partisans of Novatian, like those of Novatus, affected an extreme rigor toward those whom persecution had overcome. Novatian having established his schism at Rome, as Novatus had done at Carthage, the schismatics of Rome endeavored to obtain the support of the Church of Africa, as the schismatics of Carthage that of the Church of Rome. From their relations and appeals one might as fairly infer the supremacy of Carthage over Rome. But the Romish theologians endeavor to fix the attention only upon that of Rome; wherefore is easily understood. Their efforts are useless, for facts confound them.

St. Cyprian in several councils severely condemned the opinions of Novatus and Novatian. The first, a most zealous partisan of sentiments which were not less than criminal seeing he was about to be brought to trial, fled to Rome. There he had an understanding with Novatian, who aspired to the Episcopate of that city, and caused him to be proclaimed bishop although Cornelius was already lawfully elected.

Cornelius and his competitor addressed themselves to the Bishop of Carthage.

Cyprian believed in the lawfulness of Cornelius's election; yet he did not admit him at once to his communion, because of the letters of his rival. He called a council of the bishops of Africa, who determined to send two of their number to Rome in order to learn what had happened there. The result being favorable to Cornelius, communion was established between him and the bishops of Africa.

Novatian still continued to call himself the Bishop of Rome, and renewed his appeals to the Church of Africa. He was foiled by the energy of Cyprian, but nevertheless gained some partisans. At Rome his party was considerable. Cyprian interfered to reestablish

III. Authority of the Bishops of Rome

the order of the Church and succeeded, and Cornelius informed him of the happy event.

Up to this time, it is rather the Bishop of Carthage who influences the affairs of the Church of Rome, than the Bishop of Rome who influences those of the Church of Carthage. But soon after, the schismatics of the latter city elected a bishop who sought communion with the Church of Rome. This party afterward divided in two portions, each one choosing a bishop; this division weakened them. Not having been able to gain any partisans in Africa, they presented themselves at Rome, to accuse Cyprian, as formerly they had accused

Cornelius before the Bishop of Carthage. The Bishop of Rome permitted himself to be shaken by their calumnies; but he arrived at other conclusions after having received the letters of Cyprian.

Novatian's party existed at Rome after the death of Cornelius. He had partisans in most of the churches. Marcianus, Bishop of Arles, was of the number.

Faustinus, Bishop of Lyons, believed it necessary under these circumstances to appeal for support to the principal bishops of the West in order to condemn Marcianus. He therefore addressed Stephen, Bishop of Rome, and Cyprian. The latter had written to the Bishop of Rome to tell him what he ought to do under the circumstances. He was himself too far from the seat of the trouble to give much attention to the case, and he entreated his brother of Rome to write to the clergy and people of Arles, advising them to depose Marcianus.

In all these facts, related exactly after authentic documents,[50] nothing can be seen but an equal intervention by the bishops of Rome and Carthage in the affairs of the Church, an equal desire to entertain friendly relations between them, and to be in perfect communion. If St. Cyprian *praises* Cornelius and the Church of Rome for condemning the schismatics of Africa, he had previously blamed them for having hesitated to pronounce between him and the illegitimate bishop who had presented himself at Rome. Happy that his adversaries had not found in that church the support they

---

50 See chiefly the Letters of St. Cyprian.

hoped for, he gave great praise to the Romans, and it was then he wrote that famous passage, which has been so much abused:

"They (his adversaries) dared to embark and carry their letters to the see of Peter, to the principal church from which sacerdotal unity has sprung, not thinking there were *the Romans* whose faith the Apostle has praised, and to whom perfidy can have no access."

We have explained according to St. Cyprian himself, the expressions from which the Romish theologians would draw such vast conclusions. It only remains for us, therefore, to notice that the circumstances and the context take from them all the importance it has been sought to attribute to them. It was right that St. Cyprian should thank the Church of Rome for declaring in his favor against his adversaries. In order to do this, he recalls the memory of its *two* founders—of St. Peter, who was the *type* of unity in the apostolic, and, by consequence, of the Episcopal body; of St. Paul, who had praised the faith of *the Romans*. It must be observed, it is not to the *Bishop* of Rome that he gives this praise, but to the clergy and faithful of that Church, who, at his prayer, had read his letters, and before whom he had pleaded his cause. In his eyes the bishop is nothing without his clergy and the faithful, and he grants him no personal prerogative. This text of St. Cyprian, therefore, is contrary, not favorable to the system of a Papal autocracy. Any one will be convinced of this who reads entire the letters of the bishops of Rome and Carthage. They both act only in concert with the clergy of their Church and the bishops of their province; neither assumes any personal authority.

IV.

TEACHINGS OF VARIOUS CHURCH FATHERS.

FACTS combine with doctrinal evidences to prove that the Papacy enjoyed no universal authority during the first three centuries of the Church; to prove that the bishops of Rome had in ecclesiastical affairs only such influence as was necessarily derived from the importance and dignity of their see; the *only one* in the West, which was generally recognized as apostolic.

Moreover, the Church of Rome was the mother of many other churches, over which she exercised a certain authority, as we learn from the sixth canon of the first œcumenical council held at Nicea in A.D. 325.

There has been a great deal of discussion upon this famous canon, in which the Roman theologians have endeavored to see an argument in favor of their opinions.

They have called in evidence all the manuscripts in order to find some that should favor their views; and they have, in fact, found some which serve them admirably, by reason of certain additions which would be very satisfactory if they were only authentic. For instance: "Since, then, the holy synod has confirmed the *primacy of the Apostolic See*, which is what is due to the merit of St. Peter, who is the prince of the whole episcopate (literally, of the episcopal crown) and to the dignity of the city of Rome."

This is certainly a beautiful preamble for the sixth canon of Nicea; but it is unfortunate that the forger should betray himself, even by his style,[51] which cannot be antecedent to the date of the manuscript itself, namely, the middle ages. In a Roman manuscript, at the head of the sixth canon, we read: "The Roman Church always had the primacy." These words, which we might otherwise adopt, are copied from the Acts of the Council of Chalcedon and in no wise belong to those of Nicea any more than this other formula interpolated in another manuscript, "Let the Roman Church have the primacy forever." All these additions were unknown in the ninth century, since the author of the *Fausses Décrétales*, who was then living, and who would not have failed to profit by them, has given the canons of the early councils, according to Dionysius Exiguus. This learned man, who made his collection of the canons at Rome itself, died in the first half of the sixth century. According to Cassiodorus, he had a perfect acquaintance with Greek; his version, consequently, deserves entire confidence, and in it we find none of the preceding additions; but it is thus we find the sixth canon of the Nicene Council:

"Let the ancient custom be preserved, that exists in Egypt, Lybia, and Pentapolis, that the Bishop of Alexandria have authority in all these countries, since that has also *passed into a custom* for the Bishop of Rome. Let the churches at Antioch and in the other provinces preserve also their privileges. Now, it is very evident, that if anyone be made bishop without the concurrence of the metropolitan, the great council declares that he may not be bishop," etc., etc.

The object of this canon was to defend the authority of the Bishop of Alexandria against the partisans of Meletius, Bishop of Lycopolis, who refused to recognize it in episcopal ordinations.

The object of the sixth canon, therefore, was merely to confirm the ancient customs respecting these ordinations, and, in general, the privileges consecrated by ancient usage. Now, *according to an ancient* custom, Rome enjoyed certain prerogatives that no one contested.

---

51 We give it as a specimen of its kind: *Cam igitur sedis apostolicæ primatum, sancti Petri meritum qui princeps est episcopalis coronæ et Romanæ dignitas civitatis, sacræ etiam synodi firmavit auctoritas.* It is only necessary to have read two pages of the Ecclesiastical Remains of the Fourth Century to discover at first sight the fraud and be persuaded that this ambitious and uncouth verbiage is of a much later age.

IV. Teachings of Various Church Fathers

The council makes use of this fact in order to confirm the similar prerogatives of Alexandria, Antioch, and other churches.

But what were the churches over which, according to custom, the Church of Rome exercised a right of supervision?

Ruffinus designates them Suburbicarian. This writer, who wrote his ecclesiastical history in the fourth century, who was born at Aquileia and dwelt at Rome, must have known the extent of the jurisdiction of the Roman Church in his times. Now, what does he understand by the *suburbicarian churches*? It is known that from and after Constantine's reign, the Church was divided in dioceses and provinces like the empire itself.[52] From this undeniable fact, we know the *suburbicarian* churches; they are those which existed in places of the same name in the fourth century—these places being those that were dependent upon the diocese or the prefecture of Rome—that is to say, the ten provinces called "Sicilia, Corsica, Sardinia, Campania, Tuscia, Picenum Suburbicarium, Apulia cum Calabria, Bruttium, Samnium, Valeria." Northern Italy formed another diocese, of which Milan was the prefecture, and was not dependent upon Rome. The diocese of Rome did not call itself Italy, but the Roman *Territory*. This is why St. Athanasius[53] calls Milan the *metropolis of Italy*, and Rome the *metropolis of the Roman Territory*. In the fourth century, therefore, the Jurisdiction of the Roman bishops extended only over southern Italy and the islands of Corsica, Sicily, and Sardinia.

When the Fathers of the Church speak of the see of Rome as the first of the West, they do not intend to speak of its universal jurisdiction, but of its greatness as the only apostolic episcopate of these countries.

The provinces which the Council of Nicea subjected to the jurisdiction of the Bishop of Alexandria formed *the diocese of Egypt*, just as those subject to the Bishop of Rome formed the diocese of Rome. It makes a comparison between them that perfectly agrees

---

52 A diocese was then a union of several provinces, and a province was a section of a diocese. The words have changed their sense, and at this time an ecclesiastical province is composed of several dioceses.

53 St. Athanas., Ep. ad Solit.

with the commentary of Ruffinus. The sixth and seventh canons of the Council of Nicea may be considered as the *legal* origin of the patriarchates; the title was not yet in use, but *the order* was established. According to the principle admitted by the first general council, the number of patriarchs was not limited to four; we are even given to understand that beside the four great apostolic churches of Rome, Alexandria, Antioch, and Jerusalem, there were others which enjoyed similar privileges. The bishops of these churches did not obtain the title of patriarch, but they enjoyed other titles that raised them above the simple metropolitans, such as *exarch* and *primate*.

In spite of the subterfuges of the Romish theologians, they cannot escape from two consequences of the sixth canon of the Council of Nicea:

1st. The council declared that the authority of the Bishop of Rome extended only over a limited *district*, like that of the Bishop of Alexandria.

2nd. That this authority was only based upon *usage*.

Hence, it follows that this authority in the eyes of the council was not *universal*; that it was not *of divine right*. The ultramontane system, being entirely based upon the *universal* and divine character of the Papal authority, is diametrically opposed to the sixth canon of the Nicene Council.

Nevertheless, it must be admitted that the council, by invoking the Roman custom in confirmation of that of Alexandria, recognized the legitimacy of the established *usage* and rendered homage to the dignity of the Roman see; but we must add that the prerogatives recognized in it were not those to which it has since laid claim.

The General Council of Constantinople, A.D. 381, which is the second œcumenical council, has well interpreted that of Nicea by its third canon, "Let the Bishop of Constantinople have the *primacy of honor (priores honoris partes)* after the Bishop of Rome, *because* Constantinople is the new Rome."

The Bishop of Rome was, therefore, regarded as the *first in honor*, because he was bishop of the capital of the empire. Byzantium having become the second capital, under the name of Constantinople, its bishop became entitled to be second in rank, according to the principle that had governed the Council of Nicea in the exterior constitution of the Church, and according to which the divisions of the empire were made the divisions of the Church.

The Œcumenical Council of Chalcedon, A.D. 451, which met a century after that of Constantinople, throws a new light upon this point and thus expresses itself in the twenty-eighth canon:

"In all things following the decrees of the holy Fathers, and recognizing the canon just read by the one hundred and fifty bishops well-beloved of God (third canon of the second council), we decree and establish the same thing touching the privileges of the most holy Church of Constantinople, *the new Rome*. Most justly *did the Fathers grant privileges* to the see of the ancient Rome, BECAUSE SHE WAS THE REIGNING (capital) CITY. Moved by the same motive, the one hundred and fifty bishops, well beloved of God, grant *equal privileges* to the most holy see of the new Rome, thinking, very properly, that the city that has the honor to be the seat of the empire and of the senate should enjoy in ecclesiastical things the same privileges as Rome, the ancient queen city, since the former, although of later origin, has been raised and honored as much as the latter." In consequence of this decree, the council subjected the dioceses of Pontus, of Asia,[54] and of Thrace to the jurisdiction of the Bishop of Constantinople.

The legates of Pope Leo I in the Council of Chalcedon opposed this canon. It was adopted, nevertheless; but the Fathers of the council addressed a respectful letter to Leo, in which, after alluding to the opposition of the legates, they add: "We therefore beg you to *honor our* JUDGMENT by your own decrees."

Romish theologians have claimed to see in this proceeding a proof that the Fathers of Chalcedon recognized in the Bishop of Rome a supreme authority over the decisions of the councils, which, they say, would be of no avail if not confirmed by him. But it is more just to see in this but an act of great propriety inspired by the love of peace and harmony. The council would of course desire

---

54 Asia Minor is understood, the ancient Metropolis of which was Ephesus. The part of Asia confided to the jurisdiction of the Bishop of Antioch is called the East.

that the West should be in concord with the East. The Bishop of Rome represented the West in the council, being the only bishop in the West possessing an *apostolic see*; again, his see was the *first in honor* in the universal Church, and evidently it was proper to entreat him to acquiesce in the decision of the council. He was not asked to *confirm* it, but by his own decrees to *honor* the judgment which had been rendered. If the confirmation of the Bishop of Rome had been necessary, would the decree of Chalcedon have been a judgment, *a promulgated* decision before that confirmation?

St. Leo did not understand the letter from the Council of Chalcedon as do our Romish theologians. He refused—not to *confirm it by his authority*—but simply to *admit* it. "This decree shall never obtain our consent," he said.[55] And why did he refuse his consent? Because the decree of Chalcedon took from the Bishop of Alexandria the second rank, and the third from the Bishop of Antioch, and was in so far forth contrary to the sixth canon of the Council of Nicea, and because the same decree prejudiced the rights of several primates or metropolitans.[56] In another letter addressed to the Emperor Marcianus,[57] St. Leo reasoned in the same manner: "The Bishop of Constantinople, in spite of the glory of his church, cannot make it *apostolic*; he has no right to aggrandize it at the expense of churches whose privileges, *established by canons of the holy Fathers* and settled by the decrees of the venerable Council of Nicea, cannot be unsettled by perversity nor violated by innovation."

The Church of Rome has too well forgotten this principle of one of her greatest bishops.

In his letter to the Empress Pulcheria,[58] St. Leo declares that he has "annulled the decree of Chalcedon by the authority of the blessed Apostle St. Peter." These words seem at first sight to mean that he claimed for himself a sovereign authority in the Church in the name of St. Peter; but upon a more careful and an unbiased examination of his letters and other writings, we are convinced that

---

55 St. Leo, epis. liii, vet. edit.; lxxxiv, edit. Quesn.

56 Ibid.

57 St. Leo, epis. iiv, vet. edit.; ixxxviii, edit. Quesn.

58 St. Leo, epis. iv, vet. edit.

IV. Teachings of Various Church Fathers

St. Leo only spoke as the bishop of an *apostolic* see, and that in this character he claimed the right, in the name of the apostles who had founded his church, and of the western countries which he represented, to resist any attempt on the part of the Eastern Church to decide, alone, matters of general interest to the whole Church.

The proof that he regarded matters in this light is that he does not claim for himself any *personal* authority of divine origin, descended to him from *St. Peter*, but that, on the contrary, he presents himself as defender of the canons and looks upon the rights and reciprocal duties of the churches as having been established by the Fathers and fixed by the Council of Nicea. He does not pretend that his church has any exceptional rights emanating from another source. But by ecclesiastical right, he is the first bishop of the Church; besides, he occupies the *apostolic* see of the West; in these characters he must interfere and prevent the ambition of one particular church from impairing rights that the canons have accorded to other bishops, too feeble to resist, and from disturbing the peace of the whole Church. After carefully reading all that St. Leo has written against the canon of the Council of Chalcedon, it cannot be doubted what he really meant. He does not claim for himself the autocracy which Romish theologians make the groundwork of papal authority. In his letter to the Fathers of the Council of Chalcedon, he only styles himself "*guardian* of the catholic faith and of the constitutions of the Fathers," and not chief and master of the Church *by divine right*.[59] He regarded the canon of the Council of Chalcedon as wrung from the members of that assembly by the influence of the Bishop of Constantinople, and he wrote to the Bishop of Antioch[60] that he ought to consider that canon as null, inasmuch as it was contrary to the decrees of Nicea. "Now," he adds, "universal peace can only subsist upon the condition that the canons be respected."

Modern Popes would not have written thus, but would have substituted their personal authority for the language of the canons.

Anatolius of Constantinople wrote to St. Leo that he was wrong in attributing the twenty-eighth canon of the Council of Chalcedon

---

59 St. Leo, epis. ixi, vet.edit.; lxxx, edit. Quesn.
60 St. Leo, epis. ixii, vet.edit; xcii, edit. Quesn.

to his influence; that the Fathers of the council had enjoyed full liberty; and that as far as he himself was concerned, he did not care for the privileges that had been conferred upon him. Nevertheless, these privileges remained in spite of the opposition of the Bishop of Rome, and were recognized even in the West. Let us give one proof among a thousand. It is a letter from an illustrious Gallican bishop—St. Avitus, metropolitan Bishop of Vienne—to John, Bishop of Constantinople.[61] At the same time we can perceive in the struggles between the bishops of Rome and Constantinople, respecting the canon of Chalcedon, the origin of the dissensions which afterward led to an entire rupture. In principle, Leo was right to defend the canons of Nicea; but he could not deny that one œcumenical council had the same rights as another that had preceded it; especially while it adhered to the spirit that had directed it. The Nicene Council, in consecrating the *usage* by which the Bishop of Rome was regarded as the *first in honor* in the Church, had in view not so much the *apostolic* origin of his see as the splendour which he acquired from the importance of the city of Rome; for many other churches had an equally *apostolic* origin, and Antioch, as a church founded by St. Peter, had priority over Rome. Why, then, should not the Bishop of Constantinople have been received as second in rank, Constantinople having become the second capital of the empire; since the Bishop of Rome was first in rank, only because of its position as the first capital? It was well understood that the Council of Chalcedon had not been unfaithful to the spirit that had inspired that of Nicea; and that if it had somewhat changed *the letter of* its decrees, it had done so in obedience to the same motives that had directed the first œcumenical assembly. It sustained itself, moreover, upon the second œcumenical council, which, without giving to the Bishop of Constantinople any patriarchal jurisdiction, had, nevertheless, conferred upon him the title of *second* bishop of the universal Church, and that too without any opposition on the part of the Bishop of Rome or any other Bishop in the West.

The twenty-eighth canon of Chalcedon was the consequence of the third canon of Constantinople. It was the more necessary

---

61 Works of St. Avitus, in the miscellaneous works of P. Sirmond.

IV. Teachings of Various Church Fathers

to give to a patriarch jurisdiction over the dioceses of Asia, Pontus, and Thrace, so that elections and consecrations occasioned in these dioceses not perpetuate struggles between the primates and the metropolitans. The Council of Nicea, having sanctioned the privileges founded upon usage, every primate and metropolitan pretended to have some such rights.

It was thus the Bishop of Antioch endeavored to stretch his jurisdiction over the isle of Cyprus; but from time immemorial this Church had governed herself by her bishops together with the metropolitan. The case was carried to the Œcumenical Council of Ephesus, which declared in favor of the Church of Cyprus. Its motive was "that it was necessary to beware, lest under pretext of the priesthood the liberty be lost which Jesus Christ, the liberator of all men, has given to us, at the cost of his blood."[62]

This is why the metropolitans of Cyprus styled themselves as *aftoképhali* (independent) and did not recognize the jurisdiction of any superior bishop. The Bishop of Jerusalem was likewise *acephalous*, or without chief, according to the seventh canon of the Nicene Council, and he retained the ancient honor *of his see*.

Thus Leo was right to pronounce in favor of respect for canons; but he was wrong in placing disciplinary canons in the same rank with dogmatic definitions. In fact, the first may be modified when grave reasons demand it, nay, *should be* modified, sometimes, in the *letter*, if it be desired to preserve them in *spirit*; while definitions of faith should never be modified as to the letter, much less as to the spirit.

The canons of the first œcumenical councils throw incontestably strong light upon the prerogatives of the Bishop of Rome. They are the complement to each other. The twenty-eighth canon of Chalcedon contains nothing less than the doctrine we defend, even though the opposition of the West, in the person of the Bishop of Rome, should strip it of its œcumenical character as certain theologians maintain; for it is well to notice that St. Leo did not protest against it as opposed to the *divine and universal authority* of the see of Rome, for which he only claimed an *ecclesiastical primacy*,

---

62 St. Leo, Epis. xcii. Labbe, Collec. of Councils. Cabassut. Not. Eccl., p. 209.

but simply because it infringed upon the sixth canon of Nicea in bringing down the Bishop of Alexandria to the third rank of the episcopate and the Bishop of Antioch to the fourth.

It is, therefore, incontestable that at that period the Bishop of Rome did not possess universal authority in the Church *by divine right*.

This is still more evident from the part that the bishops of Rome took in the councils. One fact is certain, that they did not convoke the first four œcumenical councils, that they did not preside over them, and that they did not confirm them

We will prove this for each of the Councils.

Here is what Eusebius relates of the convocation, presidence, and confirmation of the First Œcumenical council of Nicea:[63]

"Constantine declared that he must prosecute to the utmost this war against the secret adversary who was disturbing the peace of the Church."

"Resolved, therefore, to bring as it were a divine array against this enemy, *he convoked a general council*, and invited the speedy attendance of bishops from all quarters in letters expressive of the honorable estimation in which he held them. Nor was this merely the issuing of a *bare command*, but the Emperor's condescension contributed much to its being carried into effect: "For he allowed some the use of the public means of conveyance, while he afforded to others an ample supply of horses for their transport. The place, too, selected for the synod, the city of Nicea in Bithynia (which derived its name from *Victory*) was appropriate to the occasion. As soon, then, as the *imperial injunction* was generally made known, all with the utmost celerity hastened to obey it. The number of bishops exceeded two hundred and fifty, while that of the presbyters and deacons in their train, and the crowd of acolytes and other attendants was altogether beyond computation."

"Of these ministers of God some were very distinguished by wisdom and eloquence, others by the gravity of their lives and by patient fortitude of character, while others again united in themselves all these graces. There were among them men whose

---

63 Euseb., *Life of Constantine*, Book III, chap. v. et seq.

IV. Teachings of Various Church Fathers

years demanded the tribute of respect and veneration. Others were younger, and in the prime of bodily and mental vigor; and some had but recently entered on the course of their ministry. For the maintenance of all a sumptuous provision was daily furnished by the Emperor's command.

"Now when the appointed day arrived on which the council met for the final solution of the question in dispute each member attended to deliver his judgment in the central building of the palace. On each side of the interior of this were many seats disposed in order, which were occupied by those who had been invited to attend, according to their rank. As soon, then, as the whole assembly had seated themselves with becoming gravity, a general silence prevailed in expectation of the Emperor's arrival. And first of all, three of his immediate family entered in succession, and others also preceded his approach, not of the soldiers or guards who usually accompanied him, but only friends, who avowed the faith of Christ. And now all rising at the signal which indicated the Emperor's entrance, at last he himself proceeded through the midst of the assembly like some heavenly messenger of God...

As soon as he had advanced to the upper end of the seats, at first he remained standing, and when a low chair of wrought gold had been set for him, he waited until the bishops had beckoned to him, and then sat down, and after him the whole assembly did the same.

"The bishop who occupied the chief place in the right division of the assembly then rose, and, addressing the Emperor, delivered a concise speech."

This account shows that it was the Emperor who *convoked* the council, and gave formal orders to that effect, and that he occupied the place of president in the assembly. Doubtless he had no ecclesiastical *right to* convoke this council; yet while the direct intervention of the emperors in the convocation of councils in the first centuries does not prove that they had any ecclesiastical rights, it proves, at least, that the Church did not then possess any *central* power that could call all the bishops together. Otherwise the Christian emperors would have addressed that authority, and everything undertaken by them without that authority would have been null and void.

The bishop who occupied the highest place in the Nicene Council had only *the first place on the right of the Emperor*. Constantine was placed in *the middle*, at the end of the hall, and upon a separate seat. What bishop occupied the first place, Eusebius does not say; which leads one to think it was himself. The historian Socrates maintains, in fact, that it was really Eusebius, Bishop of Cæsarea in Palestine. This bishopric was one of the most important of the East, and the first in Palestine since the destruction of Jerusalem.

In the commencement of his *Life of Constantine*, Eusebius thus expresses himself: "I myself have recently addressed eulogies to the victorious prince, seated in the assembly of God's ministers." If these words are not a demonstrative proof, they nevertheless give great probability to the statement of Socrates.

But whether it be Eusebius of Cæsarea, or Eustathius of Antioch, as Theodoret affirms,[64] or Alexander of Alexandria, as Niectas[65] maintains, after Theodore of Mopsuestia, is of small account. This much is certain, that the envoys of the Roman Bishop did not preside. This is a fact admitted by all historians worthy of credence. We must come down to Gelasius of Cyzieus to learn that the Bishop of Rome presided at the Council of Nicea in the person of Hosius of Cordova, his deputy. In the first place, Hosius was not the delegate of the Bishop of Rome; he takes this title neither in the Acts of the Council nor elsewhere. The Bishop of Rome was only represented by the priests Vitus and Vincent, and not by Hosius. Thus, even if Hosius had presided over the Council, this fact would prove nothing in favor of the pretended authority. But it is certain that Hosius had not that honor, and that the ecclesiastical presidence of the assembly was in the Bishops of the great Sees of Alexandria, Antioch, and Cæsarea of Palestine, while the Emperor himself had the civil presidency.

After having heard the eulogies of the first bishop of the assembly, Constantine made an address in which he said that *he*

---

64 Theodoret, Eccl. Hist., Book I, ch. vii.

65 Nicet., Thesaur. fid orthodox, Book V, ch. vii.

IV. Teachings of Various Church Fathers

had convoked all the bishops to labor for peace, and he entreated them to secure it to the Christian world. When he had finished, he *invited the* PRESIDENTS OF THE COUNCIL to *speak*. There were, *therefore, several presidents*. With this declaration before us of Eusebius,[66] who was an eyewitness—a declaration that nothing contradicts—can it reasonably be contended that the Council was presided over by the Bishop of Rome, in the person of Hosius his proxy? What fact can authorize such an assertion, diametrically opposed to the authoritative and positive testimony of Eusebius?

This learned historian has accurately traced the functions of Constantine. From the time the bishops took the floor, animated discussions arose. "The Emperor," continues Eusebius,[67] "gave patient audience to all alike and received every proposition with steadfast attention, and by occasionally assisting the argument of each party in turn, he gradually disposed even the most vehement disputants to a reconciliation. At the same time, by the affability of his address to all, and his use of the Greek language (with which he was not altogether unacquainted), he appeared in a truly attractive and amiable light, persuading some, convincing others by his reasonings, praising those who spoke well, and urging all to unity of sentiment, until at last he succeeded in bringing them to one mind and judgment respecting every disputed question."

Constantine *convoked* the council and *presided over* it. These are *two facts* which no one in *good faith* can contest. A third fact, not less unquestionable, is that it was he who promulgated its decrees. To establish this, it is sufficient to translate the following passages of the letter that he addressed to all the bishops who had not attended the assembly, "in order," writes Eusebius,[68] "to assure them of what had been done." It is Eusebius himself who has preserved this letter for us:

---

66 Euseb., *Life of Constantine*, Book III, chap. xiii.
67 Ibid.
68 Euseb., *Life of Constantine*, Book III, chap. xvi and xvii.

CONSTANTINUS AUGUSTUS TO THE CHURCHES:

"Having had full proof in the general prosperity of the empire, how great the favor of God has been toward us, I have judged that it ought to be the first object of my endeavors, that unity of faith, sincerity of love, and community of feeling in regard to the worship of Almighty God, might be preserved among the highly favored multitude who compose the Catholic Church: and inasmuch as this object could not be effectually and certainly secured, unless all, or at least the greater number of the bishops were to meet together, and a discussion of all particulars relating to our most holy religion to take place; for this reason as numerous an assembly as possible has been convened, at which I myself was present, as one among yourselves (and far be it from me to deny that which is my greatest joy, that I am your fellow-servant), and every question received due and full examination, until that judgment which God, who sees all things, could approve, and which tended to unity and concord, was brought to light, so that no room was left for further discussion or controversy in relation to the faith."

After this preamble, which is of itself significant, Constantine publishes the decree of the Council upon the celebration of Easter. He explains the reasons for it and recommends its observance. Before dismissing the bishops, Constantine again addressed them, exhorting them to maintain peace among themselves. He particularly recommends "those in high places not to raise themselves above their inferiors in rank; for," he adds, "it belongs to God only to judge the virtue and superiority of each one."[69] He gave them some further advice, and then permitted them to return to their churches. They all withdrew joyfully, ascribing to the intervention of the Emperor the peace that had been established between those who had differed in opinion.

In respect to the most serious question that had been discussed in the Council—that of *Arianism*—Constantine wrote of it to Egypt, where the discussion had birth, *"confirming,"* writes Eusebius, "and *sanctioning* the decrees of the Council on this subject.[70]

Thus nothing is wanting in the intervention of Constantine at Nicea. It is he who *convokes* the Council, he who *presides*, and he who *confirms* the decrees. Eusebius, a contemporaneous historian,

---

69 Euseb., *Life of Constantine*, Book III, ch. xxi.
70 Euseb., *Life of Constantine*, Book III, ch. xxiii.

IV. Teachings of Various Church Fathers

an eyewitness of the events, who took part in the Council, positively asserts it; while subsequent historians, all worthy of confidence—Socrates, Sozomen, and Theodoret—bear witness to the fidelity of his recital.

Gelasius of Cyzicus, author of a romance founded upon the Council of Nicea, who lived in the fifth century, is the first, as we have said, to make mention of the Bishop of Rome in the convocation and presidency of the Council of Nicea. His mistake was propagated in the East, and the sixth general council in the seventh century did not protest against it when uttered in its presence. But it will be admitted that the erroneous assertion of a writer who entirely contradicts history and the clearest traditions cannot be received as truth because a council held at a much later period did not protest against it, when, even had it been competent, it was not called to pronounce upon that question. It is not possible, then, honestly to oppose such proofs to the multiplied evidences of contemporaneous writers, and to that of the Council itself, which, in its letters, never speaks of the intervention of the Bishop of Rome.

It is certain that Constantine did not claim any *ecclesiastical* rights for himself; that he only presided at the Council in order to assure liberty of discussion, and that he left the decisions to episcopal judgment. But it is nevertheless true that he convoked the Council, that he *presided*, that he *confirmed* its decrees; that under him there were *several bishop presidents*; that the delegates of the Bishop of Rome did not preside; that Hosius, who the first signed the acts of the Council, was not the delegate of the Bishop of Rome, whatever Gelasius of Cyzicus may say, whose testimony is worth nothing, even by the avowal of the most learned of the Roman theologians.[71]

---

71 See the judgement given by the Jesuit Feller upon this historian: "A Greek author of the fifth century, who wrote the *History of the Nicene Council*, held in 325. This history is *only a novel* in the opinion of the best critics—at least, in many respects, he is at variance with the documents and relations most worthy of belief." Like a good Ultramontane, Feller affirms that Gelasius had excellent motives, and *it is this which has made him embellish his history a little*. Thus, according to Feller, Gelasius has *lied*, but his falsehoods are excusable because of his *intentions*, and because his motives were good. Feller was faithful to the spirit of his Company.

What now was the intervention of the Bishop of Rome in the second œcumenical council? Nothing.

The Council was convoked by the Emperor Theodosius (A.D. 381), who did not even ask the opinion of the Bishop of Rome. That Bishop, Damasus, did not even send legates to it, nor did any other western bishop take part in it. The Council was composed of one hundred and fifty members, among whom we distinguish such men as St. Gregory Nazianzen, St. Gregory of Nyssa, St. Peter of Sebaste, St. Amphilochius of Iconium, and St. Cyril of Jerusalem. It was presided over by St. Meletius of Antioch.

For a long time there had been a schism at Antioch. That city had two bishops, Meletius and Paulinus. The Bishop of Rome was in communion with the latter, and consequently regarded Meletius as schismatic, which nevertheless did not prevent his being regarded as a *saint* by the Western churches as well as those in the East. The second œcumenical council was therefore under the presidency of a bishop who was not in communion with Rome. Meletius died during the sitting of the council. Those who were well known for eloquence among the Fathers pronounced his eulogy. There remains only the discourse of St. Gregory of Nyssa. The faithful vied with each other in lavishing marks of their veneration for the holy Bishop of Antioch; he was regarded by all as a Saint, and when his body was transported to Antioch the journey was an uninterrupted ovation.

After the death of St. Meletius, St. Gregory Nazianzen presided. The assembly did not recognize Paulinus as the legitimate Bishop of Antioch, although he was in communion with the Bishop of Rome, and they paid no heed to a compromise, by the terms of which the survivor Meletius or Paulinus was to be recognized as bishop by all the Catholics. They accordingly chose St. Flavianus to succeed Meletius, and, excepting the partisans of Paulinus, the Church of Antioch supported this choice.

St. Gregory Nazianzen, having obtained permission to resign his see of Constantinople, was succeeded as president of the council, successively by Timothy of Alexandria and Nectarius of Constantinople. These presidents had no relations with the Bishop of Rome.

IV. Teachings of Various Church Fathers

Nevertheless the council enacted important dogmatic decrees, and its decisions mingled with those of the Council of Nicea in the formula *of the creed*; moreover, it changed the order of the *ecclesiastical hierarchy* by giving to the Bishop of Constantinople the second place in the Church, and by placing after him the Bishops of Alexandria, Antioch, and Jerusalem. It enacted besides a great number of disciplinary canons which were adopted by the whole Church.[72]

The year following the Council of Constantinople, the Emperor Gratianus assembled another at Rome. Paulinus of Antioch was there. He was there sustained in his opposition to St. Flavianus, who was nevertheless recognized as the legitimate bishop by the majority of the provinces that depended upon the patriarchate. The West had raised an outcry against the East, for having decided on important matters without the concurrence of the West. But aside from the legitimacy of Flavianus, all the other acts of the Council were now concurred in, and the Council of Constantinople was universally considered as *œcumenical*, although neither convoked, nor presided over, nor yet confirmed by the Bishop of Rome.

In view of such facts, what becomes of the pretensions of the Bishop of Rome to an absolute autocracy in the Church? He claims, today, that all jurisdiction comes from him, and here is a council presided by a holy bishop with whom Rome is not in communion promulgating dogmatic and the most important disciplinarian decrees; and this council is one of those which St. Gregory the Great revered as one of the four gospels.[73]

The third œcumenical council held at Ephesus (431) was *convoked* by the Emperor Theodosius II and his colleague; both of them signed the letter of convocation addressed, as was customary, to the metropolitan of each province. "The troubles of the Church," they wrote,[74] "have made us think it indispensable to *convoke* the bishops

---

72 See the Acts of the Council in Father Labbe's Collection; Ecclesiastical Histories of Socrates, Sozomen, and Theodoret; the Works of St. Gregory of Nyssa and of St. Gregory Nazianzen, etc.

73 See Ecclesiastical Histories of Sozomen and of Theodoret; the Letters of St. Jerome and of St. Ambrose; the Collection of the Councils by Labbe.

74 See Works of St. Cyril of Alexandria; Collection of the Councils, by Labbe.;

of the whole world. In consequence, your Holiness will make arrangements to present yourself at Ephesus, at the Pentecost, and to bring with you such of the bishops as your Holiness may judge convenient," etc.

We read in the acts of the council that St. Cyril was the first, as occupying the place of Celestine, Bishop of Rome; but as Fleury remarks,[75] "He might as well have presided by right of the dignity of his see." This reflection is quite just. Nevertheless, since the second œcumenical council had given the second place in the episcopate to the Bishop of Constantinople, Nestorius might have disputed the presidency of the assembly with his antagonist, Cyril. Cyril had, therefore, a good reason to come to an understanding with Celestine, Bishop of Rome, in order that the heretic they had assembled to condemn should not preside over them.

We can thus understand why the Bishop of Alexandria thought fit to appear at the council with the prerogatives of the Bishop of Rome; but it would be wrong to conclude that he was the legate of that bishop, who was represented by two Western bishops and a Roman priest. In none of the acts of the council does Cyril mention his title of legate of the Bishop of Rome; and when the discussion was about him, he called to the chair not the delegates of the Roman Bishop, but the Bishop of Jerusalem, who was next to him in rank, since the Bishop of Antioch was not at the council.

After having read the Nicene Creed, a dogmatic letter was read from St. Cyril to Nestorius, and the bishops present adopted it as the expression of their faith. They next read a letter in which Nestorius set forth his doctrine: it was condemned. Juvenal of Jerusalem proposed to read the letter of the *very holy Archbishop of Rome* to Nestorius; then was read the third dogmatic letter of St. Cyril; this was the synodal letter with the twelve anathemas. *It was declared* that the doctrine of the Bishop of Rome and that of St. Cyril were agreeable to the Nicene Creed.

The testimony of the fathers in the East and West was then opposed to the errors of Nestorius. There was read a letter written

---

Eccl. Hist. of Socrates.

75 Fleury, Eccl. Hist., Book XXV, ch. xxxvii.

IV. Teachings of Various Church Fathers

by the Bishop of Carthage in the name of the African bishops, who could not be present at the council, and of whom St. Cyril was the delegate. That was approved. Finally the sentence was pronounced and signed by all the bishops. St. Cyril signed thus: "Cyril, Bishop of Alexandria, I have subscribed, judging with the Council." The other bishops adopted the same form. It must be observed that St. Cyril did not sign as representative of the Bishop of Rome. If he had consented to use the delegated powers of Celestine, it was simply to be prepared in case Nestorius should have wished to dispute his precedence. Consequently, that delegation had not the importance that Romish theologians delight in ascribing to it.

The Bishop of Antioch had not arrived when the condemnation of Nestorius was pronounced. They pretended that Cyril was judge in his own cause, against the Bishop of Constantinople. The Emperor declared in favor of the latter, and his party claimed that the discussion should be reopened. It was at this time that the Bishop of Rome sent three legates to represent him. They were bearers of a letter which commenced thus: "The assembly of the bishops manifests the presence of the Holy Spirit; for a council is holy and should be venerated, as representing a numerous assembly of Apostles. They were never abandoned by the Master whom they were ordained to preach. He taught by them, and told them what they should teach, and he declared that it was he who was heard through his apostles. This charge to teach has been transmitted to all the bishops alike, we all possess it by right of inheritance, we all who announce in *the place of the apostles*, the name of the Lord in diverse countries of the world, according to his word: '*Go teach all nations.*' You must observe, my brethren, *we have received a general order,* and that Jesus Christ willed we *should* all execute it in discharging this duty. We should all participate in the labors of those to whom we have all succeeded." A Pope writing thus to a council was very far removed from the theories of modern Papacy. Celestinus' letter was approved by the assembly, which in its enthusiasm cried out, "Celestinus the *new Paul!* Cyril the *new Paul!* Celestinus, *defender of the faith!* Celestinus, who *agrees with the council!* The whole council renders thanks to Celestinus! Celestinus and Cyril are one! The faith of the council is one! It is that of the whole earth!"

Celestine and Cyril were put in the same category as defenders of the Catholic faith.

Neither had any authority except through the conformity of their doctrine with that of the council. Instead of considering Celestine as having inherited a universal authority from *St. Peter*, they compare him to *St. Paul*, the Doctor-Apostle.

The legates examined the Acts of the Council, and declared that they regarded them as *canonical*, "since," they said, "the Bishops of the East and West have taken part in the council, in person or by proxy." It was not, then, because the Bishop of Rome had *directed* or *confirmed* it.

The council, in its synodical letter addressed to the Emperor, relies upon the *adhesion of the Bishops of the West, of whom Pope Celestine was the interpreter*, to prove that its sentence against Nestorius was canonical.

In view of these facts and this doctrine, it will be admitted that St. Cyril might have presided at the council without any mandate from the Pope; that if he rejoiced that he represented Celestine, it was only because he thereby took precedence of Nestorius, in spite of the canon of the Council of Constantinople, which gave to Nestorius the first rank after the Bishop of Rome; and that the three deputies of the Pope did not go to Ephesus to direct the assembly or confirm it, but to convey the adhesion of the Western bishops assembled in council by Celestine.

It is false, therefore, to say that the Pope presided at the council by St. Cyril, who in such case would have been his legate. It is one thing to yield for a particular reason the honors attached by the Church to the title of *first bishop*, and quite another to delegate the *right* to preside at an œcumenical council. The position of legate of the Bishop of Rome did not carry with it the *right to preside*, as we see in councils where the deputies of that bishop were present, but did not preside. The prerogatives of first bishop delegated to St. Cyril gave him precedence over Nestorius—in case that heretic had chosen to insist on presiding over the Council of Ephesus, by

IV. Teachings of Various Church Fathers

virtue of the third canon of the Council of Constantinople. The Romish theologians have, therefore, grossly misunderstood the facts which they would make a weapon against the Catholic doctrine. They have not observed that even after the arrival of the legates of the Bishop of Rome at Ephesus, when St. Cyril did not preside at the council, it was Juvenal, Bishop of Jerusalem, who had that honor. After the Bishop of Antioch, who took sides with Nestorius and did not attend the assemblies, the right to preside fell upon the Bishop of Jerusalem; since, according to the hierarchy established by the Councils of Nicea and Constantinople, he was fifth in order. This fact alone is strong proof against the opinion that attributes to the Bishop of Rome the right to preside at councils either in person or by proxy. Had he been present, and if the council had had no reason for putting him on his trial, or excluding him, he would without doubt have presided, in virtue of his *ecclesiastical title of first Bishop*; but when he caused himself to be represented there, his deputies had no right to preside, and in fact never did preside. The Bishops of Rome themselves knew so well that they had not this right that they oftenest delegated simple priests or deacons who could not properly preside in a council of bishops.

The Acts of the Fourth Œcumenical Council, held at Chalcedon in 451, are not favorable to the Papal system, whatever may be said by Romish theologians.

The council was *convoked* by the Emperor Marcianus,[76] who gave notice of it to the Bishop of Rome, St. Leo. The Empress Pulcheria also wrote to him, and said that it had pleased the very pious Emperor, her husband, to assemble the *Eastern bishops* in council in order to consider the necessities of the Catholic faith. She entreats him (the Bishop of Rome) to give his consent, in order that its decisions may be according to rule. It was, in, fact, just and necessary to demand the adhesion of the West, so that the council might be œcumenical. St. Leo replied that the *doubts which had been raised concerning the orthodox faith* made a council necessary; consequently,

---

[76] All the documents to which we refer in this account may be found in Labbe's Collection of the Councils. See also, the works of St. Leo.

the Emperor Marcianus and Valentinian, his colleague, addressed letters of convocation to all the bishops.

It must be remarked that St. Leo only consented to the convocation of the council. He, therefore, believed neither in his right to convoke it, nor to terminate the discussions himself, by virtue of his authority. His letters to Marcianus, to Pulcheria, and to the Fathers of the council leave no doubt of this.

This preliminary fact is of great importance.

Leo had requested that the council should take place in Italy; but the Emperor refused this, and convoked it at Nicea and afterward Chalcedon. In nearly all its sessions the council recognizes *having been convoked by the most pious Emperors*, and never mentions the Bishop of Rome in this connection. A Roman council under Pope Gelasius asserts that the Council of Chalcedon was assembled by the intervention of the Emperor Marcianus, and of Anatolius, Bishop of Constantinople. The original conception was in fact theirs; yet, as St. Leo consented to it, his prerogatives as *first bishop* were allowed him, as they should have been. Consequently, he sent to Chalcedon his legates, who were Boniface, one *of his fellow priests of the city of Rome*—as he says in several of his letters to Marcianus—Paschasinus, Bishop of Sicily, Bishop Julian, and Lucentius.

"Let the brethren," said he, in his letter to the Fathers of the council, "believe that by them I preside in the council. I am present amongst you in the persons of my vicars. You know from ancient tradition what we believe; you cannot therefore doubt what we wish."

As this shows, St. Leo appeals to the old traditions, and leaves the council to judge all questions without interposing his pretended doctrinal authority.

But does he use the word *preside* in its strictest sense?

If we attentively examine the Transactions of the Council, we see that the delegates of the Emperor occupied the first place; that the assembly had several presidents; that the legates of the Bishop of Rome and Anatolius of Constantinople acted simultaneously as *ecclesiastical presidents*. Such was the case in the twelfth session particularly; and accordingly a council of Sardinia says, in a letter

IV. Teachings of Various Church Fathers

addressed to the Emperor Leo:[77] "The Council of Chalcedon was presided over by Leo, the very holy Archbishop of Rome, in the persons of his legates, and by the very holy and venerable Archbishop Anatolius."

Photius, in the seventh book of *The Synods*, designates as presidents of the Council Anatolius, the legates of the Bishops of Rome, the Bishop of Antioch and the Bishop of Jerusalem. Cedrenus, Zonarius, and Nilus of Rhodes relate the same thing.[78]

On the other hand, in the report addressed to St. Leo by the Fathers of the Council, we read that the assembly was presided over by the delegated officers of the Emperor. We must, therefore, admit that the Council of Chalcedon was held under the same conditions as that of Nicea; that the civil authority held the *first place* there; and that the bishops of sees since called patriarchal presided together. We have no difficulty after this in admitting that the Bishop of Rome occupied the first place among the bishops in the persons of his legates; but it is one thing to occupy the first place and another thing to *preside*, especially in the sense that Romish theologians give to this word.

It is an undeniable fact that the *dogmatic* letter addressed by St. Leo to the Fathers of the Council was there examined and approved for this reason: that it agreed with the doctrine of Celestine and Cyril, confirmed by the Council of Ephesus. When the two letters of St. Cyril were read, in the second session, the *"most glorious judges"* and all the assembly said: "Let there now be read the letter of Leo, most worthy in God, Archbishop of Royal and Ancient Rome." At the close of the reading the bishops exclaimed: "Such is the faith of the Fathers; this is the faith of the Apostles! We all believe thus! Anathema to those who do not thus believe! Peter has spoken by Leo. Thus taught the Apostles. Leo teaches according to piety and truth; and thus has Cyril taught." Some of the bishops, having raised doubts as to the doctrine contained in St. Leo's letter, determined that after five days *they should meet at the house of Anatolius, Bishop of Constantinople,* in order to confer with him and receive further

---

77 Int. act. Counc. Chalced.
78 Ced. Compend. Hist.; Zonar., Annal.; Nil., Rhod. de Synod.

explanations. If such a commission had been given to the legates of the Bishop of Rome, there is no doubt that the Romish theologians would draw numerous conclusions from it in favor of their system. But the legates were only called upon by Anatolius to explain certain Latin words that seemed obscure to those who doubted and who, after the explanation of the legates, gave their adherence with the others to Leo's letter. All that was done in this council in the matter of this letter proves, in the most evident manner, that it was not approved *as coming from a bishop having authority*, but rather because it agreed with traditional teachings. It suffices to glance through the *Transactions* to find abundant evidence of this. Some Romish theologians can see nothing but these words, "Peter has spoken by Leo," as if that expression could have an Ultramontane sense, placed as it is in the midst of other exclamations, and taken with a host of other declarations, which give it only the meaning we have indicated.

As those honorary titles which are found in the Transactions of the Council, addressed to the Bishop of Rome, have been much abused, we must point out their true meaning.

St. Gregory the Great in his letters against the title of Ecumenical *bishop* assumed by John the Faster, the Patriarch of Constantinople, teaches us that the Council of Chalcedon had offered this title to the Bishop of Rome. In fact we see, in the Transactions of the Council, that this title was given to him by his legates. The first of them subscribed to the profession of faith in the sixth session in these terms:

"Paschasinus, bishop, vicar of his Lordship Leo, Bishop of the universal church, of the city of Rome, president of the Synod. I have ordered consented, and signed." The other legates signed in about the same terms.

Again in the third session, the legates in speaking of St. Leo said: "The holy and blessed Pope Leo, *head of the universal Church*, endowed with the dignity of the Apostle Peter, who is the foundation of the Church and the rock of faith," etc., etc.

In the fourth session, the legate Paschasinus gave also to Leo the title of *Pope of the universal Church*.

IV. Teachings of Various Church Fathers

The Fathers of the council saw in these expressions nothing more than an *honorary* title, which the Bishop of Rome, no doubt, desired the better to determine his superiority over the Bishop of Constantinople, whom the second œcumenical council had raised to the second rank, and who as bishop of the new capital of the empire must naturally gain a preponderant influence in the affairs of the Church because of his frequent relations with the emperors.

There is then every reason to believe that the council, in order to humor the jealousy of the Bishop of Rome, accorded to him the title of *œcumenical bishop*. It was one way of causing Rome to adopt the twenty-eighth canon, of which we have already spoken, and in which was developed that of the second œcumenical council, concerning the elevation of the Bishop of Constantinople to the second rank in the episcopate. But the Bishops of Rome, if we are to believe St. Gregory, their successor, regarded this title as *illegal*.

In view of such a decision by the popes themselves, can much importance be attached to the words of the legates, and is it fair to use them as proofs of an autho*rity* of which the *expression* alone was condemned at Rome? Let us observe, moreover, that the council, in offering a title to the Bishops of Rome, indirectly decided that they had no right to it in virtue of their dignity, and that they should never claim for this title anything more than a purely *ecclesiastical* value.

As for the confirmation of the Acts of the Council, we must observe two things: that it was the council that confirmed the dogmatic letter of St. Leo, and that the Fathers only addressed him in order to ask his *adherence* and that of the Western Church. Leo refused to admit the twenty-eighth canon, as we have said; yet that did not prevent its being universally admitted in the West no less than in the East.

Thus the Bishop of Rome did not convoke the Council of Chalcedon; he did not preside alone by his deputies, who only had the first place because he was the *first bishop* in virtue of the canons; he did not confirm the council; and the *honorary* titles conferred upon him prove nothing in favor of the universal and sovereign authority that is sought to be ascribed to the Papacy.

The accounts we have given can leave no doubt as to the view which was universally taken of the authority of the Bishops of Rome in the fourth and fifth centuries.

Yet, in order not to leave unanswered any of the assertions of the Romish theologians, we will proceed to examine the *facts and texts* in which they have sought proofs to support their system.

The principal events of the fourth and fifth centuries upon which they rely, are those relating to St. Athanasius, to the Donatists, and to St. John Chrysostom. Let us consult the positive and admitted data of history in relation to this subject.

One of the results of the sixth canon of Nicea bad been to give the first rank in the Church to the Bishop of Rome. Moreover, by reason of the circumstances in which the West was placed, he must be considered as its interpreter. Consequently, the following *ecclesiastical rule*[79] became a usage: that he should always be invited to the oriental councils when they should assemble, and that they should *decide nothing without having his* opinion. This was a just rule; for the East, in itself, no more forms the universal Church than the West; and the Bishop of Rome represented the entire West at a period when these countries were overrun by barbarians, when the bishops could not leave their sees to go to the East, to testify in discussions in which their particular churches were not interested. This is the reason given by Sozomen:[80] "Neither the Bishop of the city of Rome," he says, "nor any other bishop of Italy, or of the more distant provinces, assembled at this council (Antioch), for the Franks were then ravaging Gaul."

Paul of Constantinople and Athanasius of Alexandria, faithful to the faith of Nicea, being persecuted and condemned by some of the oriental bishops sustained by the imperial power, naturally addressed themselves to the Western Church, appealing to the Bishop of Rome who represented it. "The Bishop of the city of Rome," says Sozomen,[81] "and all the bishops of the West, regarded the deposition of the orthodox bishops as an insult to themselves;

---

79 Socrates, Hist. Eccl., Lib. II. c. xvii.

80 Sozom., Hist. Eccl., Lib. III. c. vi.

81 Sozom., Hist. Eccl., Lib. III. c. vii.

IV. Teachings of Various Church Fathers

for, from the beginning, they had approved of the Nicene faith, and still continued of the same opinion. Hence, they graciously received Athanasius, who went to them, and they claimed the right to judge his cause. Eusebius (of Nicomedia) was much grieved at this, and wrote of it to Julius."

Eusebius of Nicomedia represented the Eastern Arians, and it was the Bishop of Rome who represented the Western bishops. That bishop was Julius. He assumed the defence of the persecuted bishops, sustained them against the Eastern bishops, and, using thus the *prerogatives of his see*,[82] recognized as legitimate bishops those whom the Arians had unjustly deposed. The latter assembled at Antioch and addressed a letter to Julius, in which they sharply told him that it was no more his business to meddle with those whom they had expelled than it had been theirs to concern themselves with the affair of Novatus, whom he had driven from the Church. Sozomen[83] gives further particulars of this letter. We learn from him that the oriental bishops said, "That the Church of Rome was glorious, because it had been the abode of the Apostles, and that from the beginning she had been the metropolis of piety, although the teachers of the faith had come to her from the East. Yet it did not appear just to them, that they (the Eastern churches) should be regarded as inferior, because they were surpassed in number and in magnificence by a church to whom they were superior in virtue and courage."

Julius did not reply to them that he was chief of the Church by *divine right*, but he reminds them of the *ecclesiastical* rule already quoted, in virtue of which he had the right to *be summoned* and consulted. Sozomen adds[84] that "*this prerogative, due to the dignity of his see, gave him the right to take care of all those* who had appealed to him, seeking refuge from the persecutions of the Arian faction of the East, and that he should restore to each one his church."

The pretensions of the Bishop of Rome did not extend beyond an *ecclesiastical prerogative*. The Eastern bishops would not believe that

---

82   Socrates, Hist. Eccl., Lib. II. c. xv.

83   Sozom., Hist. Eccl., Lib. III. c. viii.

84   Sozom., Lib. III. c. viii.

Julius was the interpreter of the Western Church, as he claimed in the answer which he addressed to them.[85]

For this reason the bishops of that part of the Catholic Church were convoked, that they might decide between the Eastern bishops and the Bishop of Rome in the case of the persecuted bishops—especially St. Athanasius. That was the object of the Council of Sardica (A.D. 347).[86]

This fact alone is sufficient to prove that the universal authority of the Bishop of Rome was not then recognized, and that his *ecclesiastical prerogative* was subordinate to the judgment of the council.

Julius wrote to the Council of Sardica, *excusing* himself from personally responding to the letter of convocation that had been addressed to him. He sent two priests and a deacon to represent him, and the assembly was presided over by Hosius, Bishop of Cordova.

The cause of Athanasius and that of the other bishops deposed in the East by the Arian faction, with the support of the imperial power, was examined. Their innocence and orthodoxy were established, and they were confirmed as legitimate bishops of their respective sees. A council assembled at Rome by Julius had already pronounced a similar sentence, but that had been found insufficient. Another council of the West, held at Milan, requested the Emperor Constans to make arrangement with his brother, who resided at Constantinople, to assemble the bishops of the two empires. It was then that the two emperors convoked the Council of Sardica, where the Eastern clergy were to meet the Western, and terminate the discussion. The Arian bishops, finding themselves in the minority, pleaded some technical objection for not attending the council, which held its sessions nevertheless under the presidency of Hosius, Bishop of Cordova.

The Council of Sardica was neither convoked nor presided over by the Bishop of Rome. Nor was Hosius there as his legate, as some

---

85 Letter of Julius to the Eastern Bishops, in the Apology of St. Athanasius, § 26.

86 Socrates, Eccl. Hist., Lib. I. c. xx.

IV. Teachings of Various Church Fathers

say, without being able to prove it; nor were his delegates treated with any particular honor.

In his letter, written to the Eastern bishops in the name of the Roman council,[87] Julius had blamed them for having judged Athanasius and the other bishops who adhered to the Nicene Creed without regard to *the custom* which had obtained of deciding nothing in the East without referring to the Apostolic See of the West. "Are you ignorant," he said, "that it is the custom to write first to us?"[88]

The Council of Sardica strengthened that *custom by* its third canon, which was proposed in these terms by Hosius: "If two bishops of the same province have a discussion, neither of them shall choose as umpire a bishop of another province. If a bishop who has been condemned is so certain of his being right that he is willing to be judged again *in council*—LET US HONOR, IF YOU FIND IT WELL TO DO SO, the memory of the Apostle St. Peter: let those who have examined the cause WRITE TO JULIUS, BISHOP OF ROME: if he think well that the case have a rehearing, let him designate the judges; if he think there be no necessity for reviewing, his decision shall be final."

This proposition was approved by the council, and the Bishop Gaudentius added (canon 4) that, during the appeal, no bishop should be appointed to the place of the one deposed until the Bishop of Rome should judge the case.

The council (Can. 5, Greek; 7 Latin) prescribed the practice of these appeals to Rome.

The Romish theologians exult in these canons. Yet it is only necessary to read them carefully to perceive that they are altogether contrary to that system. In fact the council, far from recognizing in the Bishop of Rome an universal and divine authority, did not even sanction, in any general manner, the *usage* which had grown up of appealing to the Bishop of Rome as the representative of the West. It merely so decided for *certain particular cases.*

Beside the bishops of the great sees, whom the Arians persecuted, and whose cause it was the province of the councils to judge, there

---

87 Athanas., Apolog. § 36.

88 Athanas., Apolog. § 35.

were many less important bishops and priests in the East whose causes the entire Church could not consider.†

It is these bishops that the council refers, in the last resort, to *Julius, Bishop of Rome*. It does not refer them to the Bishop of Rome generally, but to Julius. Nor does it make this rule *obligatory*; the appeal is purely optional; and lastly, the council proposes to *honor the memory of St. Peter by granting to a Bishop of Rome* a prerogative which it considers new and exceptional. Is not such a decision tantamount to a formal declaration that the Pope had no legal rights, even in the decision of questions of discipline and the general government of the Church? If the council had believed that the Pope had any *right* whatever, would it have thought *to do him so great* an honor in *granting him* a temporary prerogative?

The council published its declarations in several synodical letters,[89] in which are examined in detail the cases of St. Athanasius and the other orthodox bishops persecuted by the Arians and unjustly deprived by them of their sees.

The Romish theologians quote, with an especial pride, the synodal letter to the Bishop of Rome, in which the following language occurs:

"And thou, beloved brother, though absent in body, thou hast been with us in spirit, because of thy desire and the accord that is between us. The excuse thou hast given for not taking part in the council is a good one, and based on necessity; for the schismatic wolves might, during thine absence, have committed thefts and laid traps; the heretical dogs might have yelped, and, in their senseless rage, have effected mischief; finally, the infernal serpent might have diffused the venom of his blasphemies. It would have been well and very proper to convoke the bishops of all the provinces at the capital, that is to say, at the see of St. Peter; but you will learn from our letters all that has been done; and our brethren in the priesthood, Archidamus and Philoxenus, and our son Leo the deacon, will make all things known to you by word of mouth."

---

89 Athan., Apolog. Adv. Arianos; Hillary of Poitiers, Fragments; Theodoret, Eccl. Hist.

IV. Teachings of Various Church Fathers

We have translated the word *caput* by *capital*, and we believe that such was the meaning of the council; for it places it in contrast to the word *province* in the same phrase. It would have been well, according to the council, to hold the assembly as Julius desired, at Rome, for the double reason that Rome was the capital of the empire, and also the see of St. Peter.

The Romish theologians translate the word *caput* by that of *chief*; but they do not thereby help their cause; for this word signifies both head *and first in hierarchical order*.

That the Bishop of Rome is the *head* of the Church, as being first bishop and holding the highest see, we do not deny; that he is the first in the hierarchical order established by the Church, everyone allows; what then is the use of translating illogically a text of the Council of Sardica for the sake of propping up a system which it really can in no wise be made to favor?

While endeavoring to draw such great advantage from one word employed by the Council of Sardica, these theologians have kept out of sight the facts which clearly appear from the transactions of that holy assembly, namely, that it was convoked by the Emperors Constans and Constantius—as the council itself and all the historians affirm; that it was convoked in order to pass upon a decision rendered by the Pope, in a council at Rome; that Hosius presided, and not the legates;[90] and finally, that, instead of being itself confirmed by the Pope, it was the council that confirmed the sentence of the Pope, and that granted him certain ecclesiastical privileges.[91]

These incontrovertible facts are more significant than a *mistranslated word* can be in the question of Papal authority, and give to the appeal of St. Athanasius its true character.

Let us now examine the case of the Donatists.

---

90 To establish this fact, it is only necessary to quote the first line of the signatures of the council: "Hosius of Spain, Julius of Rome, by the Priests Archidamus and Philoxenus," etc. St. Athan., Apolog. adv. Arian. § 50.

91 St. Athanasius, Apol. adv. Arian., and History of the Arians for the monks. Eccl. Hists. of Socrates, Sozomen, and Theodoret. Acts of the Council in Father Labbe's Collection.

It is not our purpose to explain in detail the causes of this schism which so long afflicted the Church of Africa. From the numerous facts connected with it, we only intend to draw this conclusion, that both the schismatics and the Catholics recognized in the episcopate the only authority competent to decide the questions that divided the Church. Hence the numerous councils that were called on both sides, and which mutually condemned each other. Constantine, immediately upon his elevation to the throne, wrote to Cæcilianus, Bishop of Carthage, to offer him money and the protection of his lieutenants to enable him to bring the schismatics to order. The latter endeavored to justify themselves before the prince, claiming that the bishops who had condemned them were judges in their own cause, and praying the Emperor to allow them to be tried by bishops from Gaul, where he then was. He consented, and named as judges three of the most learned and distinguished bishops of the age—Matenus of Cologne, Rheticius of Autun, and Marinus of Arles. He sent them to Rome to join with Miltiades, bishop of that city, and Mark,[92] in hearing the conflicting depositions of Cæcilianus and his opponents. Eusebius has preserved the letter which Constantine wrote upon this occasion to the Bishop of Rome and to Mark. We will translate that letter, together with an extract from the petition of the Donatists to Constantine. These documents will determine the character of the appeal of the Donatists, and will prove that the Romish theologians are wrong in citing it in support of their opinions.

Here is, first, the extract preserved by St. Optatus.[93]

"We beseech thee, O Constantine! most excellent emperor, thou that comest from a righteous family (for thy father was not a persecutor like his colleagues; and Gaul is free from this crime).[94] Since between us bishops in Africa there are dissensions, we beseech thee let thy piety give us judges who are of Gaul!"

---

92 It is very generally admitted by the learned that Mark was an influential priest, who was Bishop of Rome after Sylvester.

93 St. Optat., Book I against Parmenianus.

94 The Donatists here refer to the crime of having given up the Holy Scriptures during the persecutions.

IV. Teachings of Various Church Fathers

In consequence of this petition, Constantine chose the three bishops we have mentioned, adding to their number the Bishop of Rome and Mark, to examine and give judgment in the case. Constantine writes thus to the two Roman judges:[95]

"Constantine Augustus, to Miltiades, Bishop of Rome and to Marcus.[96] As many communications of this kind have been sent to me from Anulinus, the most illustrious proconsul of Africa, in which it is contained that Cæcilianus, the Bishop of Carthage, was accused in many respects by his colleagues in Africa, and in this appears to be grievous, that in those provinces which divine Providence has freely entrusted to my fidelity, and in which there is a vast population, the multitude are found inclining to deteriorate, and in a manner divided into two parties, and among others, that the bishops were at variance; I have resolved that the same Cæcilianus, together with ten bishops, who appear to accuse him, and ten others, whom he himself may consider necessary for his cause, shall sail to Rome. That you (*imón*) being present there, as also Reticius, Maternus, and Marinus, your colleagues, whom I have commanded to hasten to Rome for this purpose, he may be heard, as you may understand most consistent with the most sacred

---

95 Euseb., Eccl. Hist., Book X, ch. v.
96 This Mark has been very troublesome to the Romish theologians. If he had not been named with the Bishop of Rome, it would have been far easier to have made of the latter a *sovereign* judge to whom the three Gallican bishops were added merely from motives of expediency, and to remove every pretext on which the Donatists could oppose the sentence. But the bare name of this Mark is sufficient to forbid that conclusion. Baronius was so thoroughly convinced of this, that he has tried to prove that there was in this place an error of the copyist. He therefore proposes to replace the words *Ke Márko* by *ierárhi*. There are many inconveniences attendant upon this, besides that of distorting Eusebius's text. The first is the word hierarch signifies bishop, and Miltiades is already called by Constantine *Bishop of Rome*. Why should he have given him twice the same qualification in the superscription of his letter? The second is, that the word *ierárhi*, to mean bishop, was not yet in use, in the fourth century. All the learned oppose these reasons to Baronius, and call attention to the further fact that all the manuscripts clearly bear the words *Ke Márko*. Must a text be distorted and a bad word introduced in order to please the Romish theologians? The end will not justify the means.

law. And, indeed, that you may have the most perfect knowledge of these matters, I have subjoined to my own epistle copies of the writings sent to me by Anulinus, and sent them to your aforesaid colleagues. In which your gravity will read and consider in what way the aforesaid cause may be most accurately investigated and justly decided, since it does not escape your diligence that I show such regard for the Holy Catholic Church, that I wish you, upon the whole, to leave no room for schism or division. May the power of the great God preserve you many years, most esteemed."

From the foregoing documents we must conclude that the Donatists did not appeal to Rome, but to the Emperor; that they did not ask the arbitration of the Bishop of Rome, but of the Gallican bishops; that it was the Emperor who added of his own motion the Bishop of Rome *and* Mark to the three Gallican bishops whom he had chosen. Is there in all this the shadow of an argument in favor of the sovereign authority of the Bishop of Rome? Could the choice of the place seem important? Evidently not, for there is nothing peculiar in Constantine's choosing the city whither one could most easily go from both Africa and Gaul; and this choice explains why he added Miltiades and Mark to the judges asked for by the Donatists. It would have been very improper to send bishops to Rome to judge an ecclesiastical cause without asking the intervention of those who were at the head of the Roman Church. It is thus easy to see why Constantine named Miltiades and Mark judges in the case of the Donatists, although their intervention had not been asked.

Fifteen other Italian bishops went to Rome for this affair. The council pronounced in favor of Cæcilianus. The Bishop of Rome, having been of the council, the sentence would necessarily have been regarded as final if his sovereign authority had been recognized. Such was not the case.

The Donatists complained that the Gallican bishops whom they had asked for were too few in number at Rome, and demanded a more numerous council in which their cause should be examined with more care.

Constantine convoked this council at Arles. He invited there a large number of bishops from different provinces of his empire—that

IV. Teachings of Various Church Fathers

is to say, of the West, for at this time he only possessed that part of the Roman empire. Eusebius has preserved Constantine's letter to the Bishop of Syracuse, inviting him to come to Arles.[97] This letter is important as showing that the judgment at Rome was not considered final, and that it was the Emperor who convoked the Council of Arles. But the Fathers of the council themselves say so in their letter to Sylvester, Bishop of Rome, who had succeeded Miltiades. The Bishop of Rome sent thither as his legates, the priests Claudianus and Vitus, and the deacons Eugenius and Cyriacus. The council took place in 315, ten years before the great Council of Nicea.

Marinus of Arles presided. After confirming the sentence of the Council of Rome, the bishops saw fit to make several ordinances, which they sent to Sylvester with this letter:

"*Marinus, etc., etc., to the well-beloved Pope Sylvester, eternal life in the Lord.*

United by the bonds of mutual charity and in the unity of the Catholic Church, our mother, from the city of Arles, where our most pious emperor has caused us to meet, We salute you, most glorious father, with all the respect which is due to you.

We have had to do with men both licentious and most dangerous to our law and tradition; but thanks to the power of God who is present in our midst, and to tradition and the rule of truth, they have been confounded, silenced, and rendered unable to carry out and prove their accusations; wherefore by the judgment of God and the Church, who knows her own, they have been condemned.

Would to God, beloved brother, you had condescended to be present at this spectacle! We think that the sentence given against them would have been still more overwhelming, and, if you had given judgement with us, we would have experienced a still greater joy; but you could not leave those places where the apostles still preside, and where their blood renders a continual witness to the glory of God.

Well-beloved brother, we have not thought it necessary to confine ourselves solely to the business for which we assembled, but have also considered the necessities of our respective provinces; and we send you our ordinances, that

---

97 Euseb., loc. cit. Saint Opatus, Book I. Letters of St. Augustine, passim. Father Labee's Collect. of Gallican Councils in Sirmond.

through you, who have the greatest authority, they may become universally known."

It is generally claimed in the West that by these last words the Council of Arles recognized the universal authority of the Bishop of Rome. But it is not sufficiently remembered that this council was held without any cooperation on the part of that bishop; that he did not preside; that in the letter of the Fathers no mention is made of his authority among the motives that caused to condemn the Donatists; that they do not wait for his approbation or confirmation in order to issue their disciplinarian ordinances; that they merely apprise him of them, in order that, since in his position of bishop of an apostolic see he had the greatest authority, he might make them known to all.

This only proves that the Bishop of Rome was recognized as the first in the West, because of the *apostolic* authority and of dignity of his see; that he was thus the natural medium between the West and the apostolic sees of the East. To find more than this in the words of the Council of Arles would be to distort them. It suffices to notice that this council, convoked without the Bishop of Rome, acted independently, and that it confirmed a sentence of a council of Rome, at which the Pope presided, to be convinced that the papal authority as received at this day in the West was then unknown.

It thus appears that the Romish theologians are without a show of reason when they cite the appeal of the Donatists as favorable to papal pretensions.

Let us now examine the case of St. John Chrysostom:

This great Bishop of Constantinople drew upon himself the hatred of the Empress Eudoxia, and of many bishops and other ecclesiastics, by his firmness in maintaining the rules of the purest discipline.[98] His enemies were supported by Theophilus, Bishop of Alexandria. This bishop had condemned some poor monks as

---

98 The facts we are about to analyze all rest upon the authority of Palladius the historian, a disciple of St. John Chrysostom; the Ecclesiastical Histories of Socrates, Sozomen, and Theodoret; the works of St. John Chrysostom; and upon the official documents inserted either in the work of Baronius or in the Collection of Councils by Father Labbe.

IV. Teachings of Various Church Fathers

Origenists. They had come to Constantinople to seek for redress. The famous question of *Origenism* was thus revived.

Chrysostom did not think it profitable to examine it. But Eudoxia, who busied herself with theological questions more than was becoming in a woman, took the part of the monks against Theophilus, who was accordingly commanded to appear at Constantinople. But before Theophilus arrived there, Chrysostom incurred the hatred of the Empress, and she determined upon using Theophilus to avenge her of that great man, who had not known how to yield a servile submission to her caprices.

It was not long before Theophilus, who had been summoned to Constantinople under accusation of guilt, bore himself as the judge of that innocent archbishop, who out of respect for the canons had refused to judge him. He conspired with certain bishops who were courtiers; and he corrupted sundry ecclesiastics by money and promises. Sustained by the court, he, with thirty-five other bishops assembled in a place called *The Oak*, near Chalcedon (A.D. 403). These bishops were at once prosecutors, witnesses, and judges. They had not dared to assemble at Constantinople, where the broad light of day would have fallen upon their calumnies, and where they had cause to fear the faithful people who venerated their pastor. Of the thirty-five bishops, twenty-nine were of Egypt. While the enemies of Chrysostom assembled at *The Oak*, the faithful bishops, forty in number, had gathered around Chrysostom, at the call of the Emperor, to judge Theophilus. Chrysostom was conferring with these bishops when two messengers from the pseudo-council of The Oak came to summon him to appear there. The holy bishop refused to recognize his enemies as judges. They nevertheless proceeded to depose him, and wrote to the Emperor Arcadius that it was his duty to banish him and even to punish him for the crime of high treason for having in his sermons insulted the Empress Eudoxia. This amounted to a demand for his death. The whole people rose against the conventicle of *The Oak* in favor of Chrysostom, who would not leave the city without being forced to do so. The Emperor then commanded one of his counts to expel him, using violence even, if necessary. The saint took advantage of a moment when his faithful children had somewhat relaxed their vigilance to leave his house and give himself up to the soldiers commissioned to arrest him. He was put in ward until evening, and was conveyed by night to the port. But in spite of these precautions, the people found out that their pastor was taken from them. A great crowd followed him weeping.

Chrysostom was put on board of a ship, and hurried off before daylight, and he was landed on the coast of Bithynia.

Such gross injustice gave universal umbrage. Several of the enemies of the saint repented of their calumnies; the people besieged the churches and filled them with their clamour. A dreadful earthquake at this time filled Eudoxia, the first cause of the crime, with terror. She attributed it to her injustice and hastened to recall Chrysostom. The people received him in triumph, and his enemies hid themselves or fled. He asked a council before which to justify himself. Theophilus, afraid to face incorruptible judges, fled to Egypt. But Eudoxia, having recovered from her first fright, renewed her persecutions against Chrysostom, who, with apostolic freedom, preached against her numerous acts of injustice.

Theophilus was summoned to return, that the intrigues of the pseudo-council of The Oak might be carried out. But the Bishop of Alexandria contented himself by sending perfidious counsels from a distance. A new council was assembled; forty-two bishops pronounced in favor of the saint. The others, influenced by the court, accepted as legitimate his deposition by the pseudo-council of *The Oak*, and decided that Chrysostom, having been deposed by a council and having reassumed his see without having been reinstated by another council, was guilty and deserved to be deposed.

Chrysostom, indeed, had asked for a council immediately after his return to Constantinople; the Emperor had granted it; but Eudoxia had given contrary orders, for she did not desire a regular council but an assembly composed of the enemies of the saintly Archbishop. She carried her point, and caused Chrysostom to be condemned for not having been reinstated by a council, when she herself had rendered that council impossible.

IV. Teachings of Various Church Fathers

Renewed persecutions followed this unjust sentence. It was then that Chrysostom addressed himself to the West, represented by the bishops of the most important sees, to set before them the violence and injustice of which he had been the victim. The object of his letter was to warn the Western bishops against the calumnies that his enemies might perhaps already have published against him, and to entreat them not to take from him their charity and their communion. He addressed his letter to the Bishop of Rome, who was then (A.D. 404) Innocent Venerius of Milan, and to Chromatius of Aquileia. This fact, which is not denied, suffices to prove that he did not appeal to the Pope as a chief having authority over all the Church. He added in his letter that he was disposed to defend himself, provided his adversaries would give him a fair trial; which is a further proof that he did not carry his case to Rome as to a superior tribunal. It was natural that the Bishop of Constantinople, persecuted in the East by unworthy bishops and by the imperial power, should look to the Western Church for assistance. The bishops who had declared for Chrysostom, as well as the people of Constantinople, wrote also to the Western Church; their letters were carried to Rome by four bishops and two deacons. They believed that Theophilus of Alexandria would endeavor to seduce the bishops of the West, and they were not mistaken. In fact, a messenger from Theophilus had arrived in Rome some days before the deputies from Constantinople, and he had handed to Innocent a letter in which, without entering into any details, the Bishop of Alexandria said that he had deposed Chrysostom. Sometime after, he sent to Rome the acts of the pseudo-council at *The Oak*. Innocent declared that he would remain in communion with Chrysostom and Theophilus until such time as a council composed of Eastern and Western bishops should pronounce canonically upon the case. He accordingly requested the Emperor of the West to come to an understanding with his brother Areadius, Emperor of the East, in order that this council might be assembled. Honorius did, in fact, write to this effect; but the court at Constantinople wished to be revenged upon Chrysostom, and not to have him regularly tried. The holy Archbishop, after suffering most unjust treatment, was accordingly again exiled. Arsacius was placed in his see, without the observance of the canonical forms. He died the following year, and was quite as uncanonically succeeded by Atticus.

These renewed persecutions did not cool the zeal of St. Chrysostom's friends. Several of them took refuge in Rome and brought to Innocent a letter from those of the clergy and people of Constantinople who remained faithful to their bishop. Innocent answered, consoling them and endeavoring to inspire them with the hope that God would soon deliver them *by means of the æcumenical council* which he was labouring to have assembled.

It was to a lawful council that Chrysostom and his friends had appealed; and Innocent, far from assuming the right to determine the affair by his own authority, placed all his hopes as well in the council.

These facts speak loudly, and need no comment.

Other bishops of the West were of the same opinion. The Bishop of Aquileia, in particular, joined his efforts to those of Innocent in order to obtain from Honorius the convocation of a council in the West that should consult upon the means of terminating the affair that so justly engaged their thoughts. The Italian bishops assembled by order of Honorius and gave as their opinion that an æcumenical council should be assembled at Thessalonica, whither the bishops of the East and West could go with equal facility; and that such a council was necessary in order to close the discussion by a final award.

They prayed him to write to this effect to Arcadius. Honorius wrote to ask Innocent to send him five bishops, two priests and one deacon, to carry the letter which he should write to his brother. It was the third that he wrote him on the same subject.

In view of the difficulties raised by Arcadius against the convocation of a council, this was certainly a proper occasion for the Pope of Rome to settle the question himself, in virtue of his sovereign authority, if he had possessed any. But neither Chrysostom nor his friends of the East, nor the bishops of the West, nor the Pope himself, dreamed of this mode, which was to them unknown.

IV. Teachings of Various Church Fathers

They all were satisfied to ask of the emperors a council, which alone had the authority to give a final decision.

The deputies who bore the letter of Honorius were likewise entrusted with several other letters, from Innocent of Rome, from Chomatius of Aquileia, from Venerius of Milan, and other bishops of Italy. Moreover, they were bearers of a note from the council of Italy, to the effect that Chrysostom should in the first place be reinstated in his see and in communion with the Eastern bishops, before appearing at the œcumenical council where his cause was to be decided.

Areadius did not even allow the deputies to land at Constantinople, but sent them to Thrace where they were treated as prisoners. The letters they carried were taken from them by force, and they were cast upon a rotten vessel to be returned to the West. Four Eastern bishops who had accompanied them were roughly handled and exiled to the most distant parts of the empire. Many Eastern bishops then became the victims of the cruelest treatment, and Areadius entered upon an organized persecution against all those who had remained faithful to Chrysostom.

Palladius relates that the Roman Church and the Western council resolved thereupon to communicate no longer with the partisans of Atticus and Theophilus, until it should please God to provide the means of assembling the œcumenical council. Theodoret also relates that the bishops *of Europe* acted thus. Some Eastern churches followed the same rule; but other churches, and those of Africa in particular, did not separate themselves from the communion of Chrysostom's adversaries, although they took the part of this holy patriarch and hoped that justice would be done to him.

This was the state of things when St. John Chrysostom died. From his remote place of exile, a short time before he quitted this life, he had written to Innocent, thanking him for the zeal he had displayed in his cause. He wrote similar letters to the Bishop of Milan and other bishops who had openly declared for him.

The entire East rendered justice to the great Archbishop after his death, recognizing him as a saint, which recognition restored the communion between all the Eastern and Western churches.

Such is the exact analysis of facts relating to the affair of St. Chrysostom. It appears from it that the saint did not appeal to Rome; that he sought in the Western Church a support against his enemies of the East; that the Western bishops only acted collectively to cause his case to be determined; that they only ascribed to a general council authority to pronounce final sentence; that they only claimed for themselves the right to separate themselves from the communion of such as they deemed accomplices of injustice; and lastly, that Innocent of Rome acted with no more authority in all these discussions than the Bishop of Milan or of Aquileia.

From these facts, is it not clear that the care of St. John Chrysostom, far from furnishing evidence in favor of the sovereign authority of the Papacy, proves precisely the contrary?

Some Romish theologians, having asserted, in the face of all historical documents, that Chrysostom had appealed to Rome for the purpose of suspending the proceedings against him by the interposition of the papal authority, we will remark that, according to St. Chrysostom himself, he addressed his protest not only to the Bishop of Rome, but to other bishops. "I have also addressed this same letter," he says, "to Venerius, Bishop of Milan, and to Chromatius, Bishop of Aquileia."

Here is what he asks of his colleagues in the West: "I pray you, therefore, to write letters declaring null and void all that has been done against me, granting me inter-communion with you as in the past, since I am condemned without a bearing, *and since I am ready to justify myself before any impartial tribunal.*"

What was the tribunal to which he appealed? The Bishop of Rome affirms that there was no other except a council; he expresses himself substantially to this effect in his letter to the clergy and people of Constantinople: "From the friendly letter that Germanus the priest and Cassianus the deacon have handed to me from you, I have gathered with an anxious mind the scene of woe you describe, and the afflictions and the trial that the faith has endured among you. *This is an evil for which there is no other remedy than patience...* I derive from the beginning of your affectionate epistle the consolation which I needed... Innocent bishops are driven from their sees. John, our brother and *colleague*, and your bishop, has been the first to suffer from this violence, without having been heard, and without our knowing of what he is accused... As regards the canons, we declare that only those made at the Council of Nicea should be recognized... Nevertheless, what remedy can be applied to so great an evil? *There is no other than to convoke a council... Until we are able to obtain the convocation of a council*, we cannot do better than to await from the will of God and our Saviour Jesus Christ the remedy of these evils... We are continually devising means to assemble a general council, where all dissensions may be set at rest at the command of God. Let us then wait, entrenched within the bulwark of patience."

We could multiply such texts; but to what purpose, when all the facts demonstrate the error of these Romish writers?

We will now endeavor to learn, with the aid of doctrinal texts, what has been the teaching of the Fathers of the fourth and fifth centuries respecting the authority of the Bishops of Rome.

After studying profoundly and critically, and without bias or prejudice the historical and dogmatic remains of the first centuries of the Church, we cannot read without pain the works of Romish theologians in favor of the papal authority.

We have had the patience to read most of those regarded as authorities, such as Bellarmine, Rocaberti, André Duval, Zaccaria, and many of the most renowned of the modern theologians who have taken these as their guides—such as Gerdil, Perrone, Passaglia. We have read the principal works of the modern Gallicans—those, namely, of the seventeenth and eighteenth centuries—and particularly the works of Bossuet, Nicole, Tournely, and La Chambre. We are convinced that the latter have borrowed from the Ultramontanes those of their texts which appear to have the greatest weight, limiting the sense to a primacy of divine right and a restricted authority of the Pope, while the others extend it to an absolute authority and infallibility. Among them all we have remarked, first, a crowd of broken and corrupted texts distorted from their true sense and isolated from the context expressly to give them a false interpretation. We have remarked, secondly, that the texts of each particular Father are isolated from other texts of the same Father touching the same point of doctrine, although the last may modify or absolutely destroy the sense attributed to the first. We have remarked, thirdly, that these writers deduce from these texts conclusions clearly false, and which do not logically follow from them. Of this we shall give two examples, among the many we could point out.

Launoy, as we have already mentioned, has analyzed the Catholic tradition upon the interpretation of the text, "*Thou art Peter,*" etc. He has found but seventeen Fathers or Doctors of the Church who have applied to St. Peter the word the stone (*la pierre*). He has pointed out more than forty of them who have understood this expression as applied to the confession of faith made by St. Peter, that is to say, to the divinity of Jesus Christ. The Ultramontanes cannot dispute this, but they pretend that by giving *the faith of Peter* as the foundation of the Church, the Lord necessarily granted to that Apostle not only an indefectible faith, but also infallibility, and that these gifts have passed to his successors.

Now, all the Fathers of the Church, quoted for the latter interpretation, have meant by the confession of St. Peter *only the belief he had confessed his objective* faith, or the object of that faith, and not the *subjective* faith or the personal adherence that he had given to it.

The belief confessed by St. Peter being the divinity of Jesus Christ, the Fathers quoted have interpreted the text, "Thou art Peter," etc., in this sense, that the divinity of Jesus Christ is the rock upon which the Church rests. All speak *in the clearest terms* to this effect. Not one of them speaks of any privilege whatever granted to St. Peter personally—and *á fortiori*, not of any privilege descended to the Bishops of Rome as his successors. Thus, even had St. Peter received any prerogative from Jesus Christ, it would be necessary to prove that this prerogative was not personal; but the Ultramontanes dispose of that difficulty with extreme facility. *They simply affirm* that the privileges granted to St. Peter belong to his successors; they rest these privileges upon texts which say nothing at all about them; they affirm, on the strength of these falsified texts, that the Bishops of

IV. Teachings of Various Church Fathers

Rome are the only successors of St. Peter, because that Apostle died Bishop of Rome.

What they say upon this last point is the second example that we shall give of their false reasoning. They rely chiefly upon St. Irenæus, Tertullian, and Eusebius to prove this.

Now, Eusebius expresses himself thus: "After the martyrdom of Paul and Peter, Linus was the first that received the episcopate at Rome."[99] "Clement also, who was appointed the third Bishop of this Church (Rome)."[100] "After Anencletus (or Cletus) had been Bishop of Rome twelve years he was succeeded by Clement."[101] "After Evaristus had completed the eighth year as Bishop of Rome, he was succeeded in the episcopal office by Alexander, the fifth in succession from Peter and Paul."[102] Thus it makes no difference to Eusebius whether he places Paul before Peter, or Peter before Paul, when he speaks of the foundation of the Church of Rome. The bishops are the successors of the one as well as of the other, and neither of them is counted among the Bishops of Rome. St. Irenæus has nowhere said that Peter had been Bishop of Rome; he even asserts the contrary in a most incontestable manner. He expresses himself in substance as follows: "The blessed Apostles (Peter and Paul), when they founded and organized the Church of Rome, gave to Linus the episcopate and the care of governing that Church... Anencletus succeeded Linus; after Anencletus, Clement was the third since the Apostles, who had charge of this episcopate."[103]

St. Peter and St. Paul *founded* and *organized* the Church of Rome, but it was Linus who was made the first Bishop, even during the life of the Apostles. Observe that Peter and Paul are here coordinated by the holy doctor. Thus if we prove the episcopate of St. Peter at Rome by the text quoted, we also prove that of St. Paul by the same

---

99 Eccl. Hist., Book III, ch. 2.

100 Book III, ch. 4.

101 Book III, ch. 15.

102 Book IV, ch. 1.

103 St. Irenæus, *Agt. the Heret.*, Book III, ch. 8.

text. Rome would then have had two *Apostle-Bishops* at one and the same time.

Tertullian mentions the Bishops of Rome in the same order as St. Irenæus, and designates Linus as the first, and Anencletus as the second.[104] He only claims for Rome the succession of St. Peter *by ordination*, from St. Clement, third bishop of that city. "Let those," he said, "who boast of dating back to apostolic times, show by the succession of their bishops that they derive their origin from an Apostle or an apostolic man, as the Church of Smyrna proves that Polycarp was ordained by John, or as the Church of Rome shows that Clement was ordained by Peter."[105] We might infer from this that Linus and Anencletus were ordained by St. Paul, who in that case had *organized* the Roman Church before Peter.

When Tertullian says that St. Peter sat on the *chair of Rome*, he does not mean that he was *Bishop*, but that he *taught* there; for the word chair signifies nothing more than teaching in the writings of the Fathers. If he had meant otherwise, he would have made Linus the *second* bishop, not the first.

Thus the evidence brought by Romish theologians to prove the episcopate of St. Peter at Rome tells against them, and only establishes the fact that St. Peter and St. Paul founded the Roman Church, and consequently that this Church is *Apostolic* in its origin, which no one denies. Besides these *historical* evidences which confound them, the Romish theologians have invoked the letter of Firmilianus, already quoted, and those few texts from St. Cyprian, the true meaning of which we have already explained. As regards the letter of Firmilianus, it is only necessary to read it, in order to understand its true sense, and to wonder that they should have ventured to appeal to its evidence. As to St. Cyprian, we will now in a general way sum up his doctrine, in order to make apparent the abuse that has been made of it.

St. Cyprian[106] proves: First, that the Church of Rome was built upon St. Peter as the type and representative of the unity of the

---

104 Tertullian, *Agt. Marcion*, Book IV.

105 Tertullian, *De Prescription*, chap. xxxii.

106 St. Cyprian, *De Unitat.*, Eccl. Letters 27, 55, 59, 75.

IV. Teachings of Various Church Fathers

Church; secondly, that the Church of Rome is the chair of Peter; thirdly, that the Church of Rome is the principal church from which sacerdotal unity proceeded; fourthly, that treachery and error cannot gain access to the Roman Church.

From this, the Romish theologians argue that the Popes, as successors of St. Peter, are the centre of unity, and that beyond them and their Church, all is schism.

Such are not the legitimate conclusions from the doctrine of St. Cyprian; for the holy Doctor lays down other principles besides, which clearly determine the sense of the former ones: First, that St. Peter, in confessing the divinity of Jesus Christ, answered for all the Apostles and spoke in the name of them all, and not in his own name personally; secondly, that the other Apostles were equal to St. Peter in power and dignity; thirdly, that all the Bishops who are successors of the Apostles are successors of St. Peter, in the same way as those of Rome.

If St. Peter answered Jesus Christ in the name of his colleagues, it was because the question was addressed to them as well as to him. St. Cyprian positively asserts this: "Peter, upon whom the Lord had built the Church, speaking *alone, for* all, and answering *by the voice of the Church.*" If the personality of that Apostle *was not concerned* in Christ's question and in Peter's answer, can it be said that *his person* is the foundation of the Church? It is evident that *all the Apostles* have been so many foundations of that mystical edifice; as Holy Scripture affirms very plainly, and as we have already endeavored to show. Peter in replying alone, was, therefore, but the *symbol* of the unity which was to govern the Apostolic body, and afterward the episcopate. But in being the symbol or sign, was he necessarily the source *and principle* of it, so that without him it could not subsist? What if he were? Would the Bishop of Rome inherit this privilege? St. Cyprian was so far from this opinion that he united with Firmilianus in rebuking Stephen, Bishop of Rome, for breaking this unity and putting himself outside of this unity when he separated himself from the communion of those who differed with him in belief concerning rebaptism. The question is not whether Stephen was right or wrong, but what Cyprian thought of his opposition.

Now so far from believing that unity with Stephen was necessary to unity with the Church, he affirmed that Stephen had separated himself from that unity. Can it be said, after this, that Cyprian placed in the Bishop of Rome the *source and principle* of the unity of the Church? He did not even attribute that prerogative to the person of St. Peter. He saw in him only the *symbol* of that unity, which resided in the entire *apostolate* as it was subsequently to reside in the *episcopate*, which is one; which episcopate, in its unity, is the *see of Peter*. He fully develops that reflection in one of his letters.[107] "Jesus Christ," he says, "in order to determine the honor due to *a bishop*, and all that concerns the government of the Church, speaks in the Gospel and says to Peter, '*I say to thee, thou, art Peter,*' etc. Thus Christ does not confer upon Peter, by these words, a personal prerogative; he confers upon all the Apostles a power common to them all, and not only upon the Apostles, but upon all the Bishops their successors, who *jointly and severally* possess the episcopate, which is one, and which is thus the foundation of Church unity.

Is it consistent with this doctrine of St. Cyprian to affirm, as do the Romish theologians, that Christ gave to Peter a *personal* privilege, and that this exclusive privilege has passed to the Bishops of Rome?

The great principle that runs through the remarks of the Bishop of Carthage is that in the Church there is but *one apostolic see*; that is to say, as he himself explains it, *but one legitimate episcopate* transmitted from the Apostles; lest this episcopate be attacked at Rome or elsewhere, it is an attack upon the unity and upon *the apostolic see*, which must remain one, as Christ has taught us by answering to one for all. It is this episcopate which is the *chair of St. Peter*. Therefore, when Novatus would establish at Rome, side by side with the legitimate episcopate another episcopate which does not come from the Apostles, this last episcopate is out of the unity of the apostolic see—the universal see, the unity of which is typified in Peter; he is therefore *schismatic*, as well as all others who would establish in any place whatsoever an episcopate separate from the one which constitutes the apostolic inheritance.

---

107 St. Cyprian, 27th Letter.

Instead of thus comparing the several points of the doctrine of St. Cyprian upon the Church, the Romish theologians have only consented to notice some few words standing alone, such as *see of Peter, source of unity*, for the sake of applying them without reason to the *particular church* of Rome, while they might so easily have convinced themselves that the holy Father understood by these words nothing more than the apostolic Church or the legitimate episcopacy in general. It is thus that he speaks of the *lawful episcopate of Carthage* as the *see of Peter*, as well as of that of Rome;[108] that he speaks of the early bishops of Rome as the pre*decessors of himself,* the Bishop *of Carthage*, which obviously means that he possessed the same legitimate episcopate that they had;[109] and accordingly, in the famous letter to Pope Cornelius, which has been so much abused by the Romans, because in it the holy Doctor calls the Church of Rome *the principal church, from which sacerdotal unity proceeded.*[110] In this letter, St. Cyprian exclaims with indignation against a handful of unprincipled men who sought an appeal to Rome, *as if the bishops of Africa were not possessed of the same authority.*

If, contrary to all evidence, we should accept the construction given by some Romish theologians to a few isolated words of St. Cyprian, we must conclude that the good Father was wanting in common-sense. For on the one hand he would make Peter the foundation and chief of the Church, while on the other he would teach that all the Apostles had the same honor and power as Peter; he would make the Bishop of Rome sole inheritor of St. Peter's prerogatives, while maintaining that all lawful bishops are his heirs in the like manner; he would teach that the episcopate is but *one*, possessed jointly and severally by all legitimate bishops, and at the same time he would make the Roman episcopate a separate and superior authority; he would regard the Pope as the source of unity, and in the same breath reprove the Pope for seceding from unity; he would recognize a superior jurisdiction in the see of Rome, while

---

108 St. Cyprian, 40th Letter.

109 St. Cyprian, 67th Letter.

110 St. Cyprian, 55th Letter. We have already explained these words.

he would call those men unprincipled who did not see in Africa the same episcopal authority as in Rome.

We have already seen that St. Cyprian blamed Pope Stephen for pretending to be *bishop of bishops*, which, according to his real teaching, was in fact monstrous; but had he taught the doctrine that Rome ascribes to him, he could not have blamed him, for it would have been legitimate.

Is it just, then, for the sake of favoring the papal system, to make of St. Cyprian a writer wanting in good sense and logic, and to isolate out of his writings a few words that may be interpreted in favor of this system without noticing the rest?

We think it more proper to compare the several parts of the doctrine of one to whose genius and holiness all Christian ages have rendered homage. In this manner we find in his works a broad, logical, and *catholic* doctrine, but one opposed to the papal system. Whence it follows that the champions of the modern Papacy cannot rest upon his evidence, without falsifying his works, without insulting his memory, without denying by implication both his genius and his sincerity, which alone can give any authority to his words.

It follows from all this that Rome cannot establish her pretended rights upon the testimony of St. Irenæus, Tertullian, St. Cyprian, Firmilianus, or Eusebius of Cæsarea without resorting to such subterfuges as are unworthy of an honest cause.

Such is also their practice with respect to numerous testimonies that prove the falsity of their interpretation of the famous text, "*Thou art Peter.*" The Fathers, who understand it to refer to the person of St. Peter, are the most ancient, say these theologians; they were nearer to the apostolic times, and understood the text better than those of later centuries. Upon that point they emphatically quote Tertullian, who, in fact, says:[111] "Could any thing have been hidden from Peter, who was called the rock of the church which was to be built?"

At first sight, one might indeed think that Tertullian had applied the word rock (*la pierre*) to the person of Peter, but he explains

---

111 Tertullian, *De Prescription*, cap. xxii.

IV. Teachings of Various Church Fathers

himself in another of his works, where he says:[112] "If Christ changes the name of Simon to that of Peter, it is not only to signify the strength and firmness of his faith, for then he would have given him the name of such solid substances as are strengthened and made more durable by admixture and cohesion; but he gives him the name of Peter [*the stone*] because, in Scripture, *the stone* typifies and represents Christ, who is *the stone* of which we read that it is laid to be a stumbling-stone and rock of offence.[113] Since, then, he thus changes his name, it is to express the change he is going to make in the world, by transforming idolatrous nations into stones similar to him, and fit for the building of his Church."

With this explanation of Tertullian himself before us, where are the deductions that it is sought to draw from his first text?

And further, when we see Tertullian, in the work from which we have quoted, maintaining that in addressing Peter Christ addressed all the Apostles; teaching, moreover, that the twelve Apostles were equal among themselves, like the twelve wells of Elim, the twelve precious stones of Aaron's breast-plate, and Joshua's twelve stones from Jordan; can it be said in good faith that he acknowledged in St. Peter any exceptional or superior prerogative? Above all, can he be said to have acknowledged these prerogatives in the Bishops of Rome?

One thing is certain, that the Fathers who seem to have understood the words "upon this rock" to apply to the person of St. Peter really meant to apply it only to the object of his Faith, namely, Jesus Christ, the Man-God. We will give as an example St. Hilary of Poitiers.

This Father, in his commentary upon St. Matthew and upon the Psalms, applies to St. Peter the word rock of the Church and regards him as its foundation.[114]

But in his work upon the Trinity he acknowledges that it is upon the *rock of his confession*—that is to say, upon the divinity of Jesus

---

112 Tertul., adv. Marc., Lib. IV.

113 Rom. 9:33.

114 St. Hil. of Poit., Commentary upon the 16th chap. of St. Matt., and upon the 181st psalm. § 4.

Christ—that the Church is built.¹¹⁵ "There is," he adds, "but one unchangeable foundation,¹¹⁶ *this is the one blessed rock of faith* confessed by the mouth of St. Peter, '*Thou art the Son of the living God.*' Upon that are based as many arguments for the truth as perversity can suggest doubts, or infidelity calumnies."

It is evident that in this place the holy Father means only the *object* of St. Peter's confession of faith—that is, the divinity of Jesus Christ. If it should be claimed that he meant his subjective faith—that is to say, his adherence—and that the Bishops of Rome have inherited that unfailing faith, it suffices to recall the anathema of the same Father against Pope Liberius, who had grown weak in the confession of the divinity of Christ: "I say to thee anathema, O Liberius, to thee and to thine accomplices. I repeat, anathema. And again I say it to thee a third time; to thee, Liberius, then prevaricator."¹¹⁷

According to St. Hilary of Poitiers, therefore, if St. Peter may be considered as the rock of the Church, it is only because of the confession of faith that he made in the name of the whole Apostolic College, and through the very object of that faith, which is the divinity of Christ. His doctrine thus agrees with that of Tertullian and the other Fathers who have only in this sense applied to Peter himself the title of *rock* of the Church. If we add that this Father and the others nowhere imply that this title belongs to the Bishops of Rome, and further, that their teaching is even altogether opposed to that opinion, it will be admitted that it is only by a strange abuse of some of their words, taken alone and misconstrued, that the Romish theologians have sought to prop the papal authority upon their testimony.

St. Epiphanius taught the same doctrine as St. Hilary of Poitiers.¹¹⁸ "Peter, prince of Apostles," he says, "has been for us as a solid stone, upon which the faith of the Lord rests as upon a foundation; upon which the Church has been in every way edified.

---

115 St. Hil. of Poit., *On the Trinity*, Book VI, chap. 36.

116 St. Hil. of Poit., *On the Trinity*, Book II, chap. 23.

117 St. Hil. de Poit., Fragm.

118 Epiph., Hæres. 59.

It was chiefly because he confessed the Christ, Son of the living God, that it was said to him, 'Upon this rock of solid faith I will build my Church.'"

The Apostle Peter is not separated from the dogma he confessed; and it is this dogma itself which is the foundation of the Church.

We do not deny that St. Epiphanius called Peter prince of Apostles; but in what sense?

The Romans cite the following text in their favor:[119] "Andrew first met the Lord, because Peter was the younger. But subsequently when they had renounced everything else, it was Peter who was first; he then takes precedence over his brother. Add to this that God knows the bent of all hearts, and knows who is worthy of the first place. It is for this reason that Peter was chosen to be prince of his disciples, as is very clearly declared."

Did St. Epiphanius mean by this, that Peter was the foundation and chief of the Church, or that the Church was founded upon the *objective* faith of that Apostle that is to say, the divinity of Christ, to which he had rendered homage? He answers for himself, as we have already seen.

"Upon Peter," he says, "the Church is built, because he confessed Christ as Son of the living God, and because it was said to him, *Upon this rock of solid faith I will build my Church.*"

In the same place St. Epiphanius teaches that the words "feed my sheep" were not said by the Lord to commit to Peter the government of the Church, but to reinstate him in his apostolic dignity, which he had forfeited by denying Christ. "The Lord," he says, "CALLED PETER AGAIN after his denial; and to EFFACE the three denials, he calls upon him thrice to confess him."

Elsewhere[120] he makes St. Paul the equal of St. Peter at Rome, saying of them, "Peter and Paul, the first of all the Apostles, were equally Bishops of Rome." And he thus speaks of St. James of Jerusalem:

---

119 Epiph., Hæres. 51.
120 Epiph., Hæres. 27.

"He [James] first received the see [of Jerusalem]; it is *to him first that* THE LORD ENTRUSTED HIS THRONE UPON EARTH."[121]

It is clear that he did not believe that it was Peter who had inherited *the throne of the Lord* in this world. He believed then that the primacy granted to St. Peter was a mere *priority*, as Pope Leo[122] explains it in the following passage: "The disposition of the truth remains: and the blessed Peter has persevered in that strength of the rock which he had received, and has never abandoned the reins of the Church which had been confided to him; *he received ordination before the others, in order that when he is called rock (pierre) and foundation,* ... we might know, by the mystery of these titles, what union exists between him and Christ."

This text proves that St. Leo saw in St. Peter nothing more than a *priority of ordination*. He believed that it was by his ordination uniting him to Christ that he was the rock (*Pierre*) and the foundation of the Church.

He understands the power of binding and loosing committed to Peter in an equally orthodox sense. "This power is confided to him," he says,[123] "in a special manner, *because the type (forma) of Peter is proposed to all the pastors of the church.* Therefore the PRIVILEGE OF PETER DWELLS WHEREVER JUDGMENT IS GIVEN WITH HIS EQUITY." Hence he concludes that only that will be remitted or retained which might be so by a just sentence and one worthy of Peter.

It is difficult to understand how the Romish theologians have dared to quote the two preceding texts in support of the papal autocracy, so evident is it that St. Leo ascribes to St. Peter only a *primacy*, or rather *a priority of ordination*, and that instead of ascribing to the Bishop of Rome only the power of Peter he regards that Apostle only as the *form or figure* of the apostolic power, which is exercised in reality wherever it is exercised with equity.

And this also explains these other words of St. Leo:[124]

---

121 Epiph., Hæres. 78.

122 St. Leo, Sermon II (III in Migne), upon the anniversary of his elevation to the Pontificate.

123 St. Leo, Sermon III (IV Migne.)

124 Ibid.

IV. Teachings of Various Church Fathers

"From the whole world is Peter chosen to lead the vocation of all peoples, all the Apostles, and all the Fathers of the Church; so that, though there are many priests and many pastors, nevertheless, Peter governs all those whom also Christ governs in chief.

"The divine condescension gave to this man a great and wondrous participation in His power; whenever He willed there should be something in common between him and the other princes, he never gave save through him what he did not deny to the others."

Such phrases that smack of panegyric should have their doctrinal interpretation according to the positive instruction which we find in the other texts of the same father.

St. Leo does not pretend that St. Peter's power, whatever it was, passed to the Bishops of Rome. His letter to the Council of Chalcedon proves this, as we have seen, sufficiently; and this power of the first Apostle did not make him master of the others; it has passed to all bishops who exercise it lawfully; Peter was only distinguished by *the priority of his ordination*.

Romish theologians have misused the eulogiums that St. Leo and other Fathers have addressed to St. Peter, in an oratorical way, without choosing to see that even literally understood they do not constitute privileges transmissible to the Bishops of Rome, since none of these Fathers have recognized any in them; but no one who is familiar with the Fathers could take these eulogies literally. We will prove this by the works of St. John Chrysostom, whose writings have been most abused by the Ultramontanes, and whom they most prefer to quote in support of their system. They have accumulated texts to prove that the great Bishop of Constantinople gave to St. Peter the titles *of first*, of *great apostle*, of *Coryphæus*, of *prince*, of *chief*, and of *mouth of the Apostles*.

But if he has given the same titles to the other Apostles, what can we conclude in favor of St. Peter?

Now, in several places in his writings he says of all the Apostles that they were the *foundations*, the *columns*, the *chiefs*, the *doctors*, the *pilots*, and the *pastors* of the Church.

He calls Peter and John in the same sense, *princes of the Apostles*.[125] He says of Peter, James, and John *collectively* that they were "first in dignity among the Apostles, the foundations of the Church, the first called, and princes of the disciples."[126]

If he says of St. Peter, "Peter so blotted out his denial, that he became the first of the Apostles, and that the entire universe was confided to him,"[127] he likewise says elsewhere of Peter *and John*, that *the universe was confided to them*;[128] he says of St Paul: "Angels often receive the mission of guarding the nations, but none of them ever governed the people confided to him as Paul *governed the whole universe*... The Hebrew people were confided to Michael the Archangel, and to Paul were committed the earth, the sea, the inhabitants of all the universe—even the desert."[129] "In the kingdom of heaven," he says, "it is clear that no one will be before Paul."[130] He further calls him *the pilot of the Church*,[131] vessel of election, the celestial trumpet, the leader of the spouse of Christ; that is, the Church.[132] In the following passage, he evidently places him above St. Peter: "In the place where the cherubim are covered with glory, and where the seraphim soar, there shall we see Paul with Peter, (Paul) who is the prince and president (*prostátis*) of the choir of saints."[133]

It is most important to observe that St. Chrysostom attributes an equal dignity to these two Apostles when he mentions both of them together. We will give some few examples.

In his second sermon on prayer, he tells us that prayer has such power that it "delivered from great perils both Peter and Paul, the

---

125 Upon St. Matthew, Homily 32.

126 Upon the First Chapter of Galatians.

127 Against the Jews. Eighth Discourse.

128 Upon St. John, Eighty-eighth Homily.

129 Panegyric upon St. Paul, Second Homily.

130 Upon St. Mathew, Sixty-fifth Homily.

131 Sermon on the Twelve Apostles.

132 Homily upon the words, "May it please God that ye be patient awhile."

133 Thirty-second Homily upon Epistle to Romans.

IV. Teachings of Various Church Fathers

columns of the Church and princes of the Apostles, the most glorious in heaven, the walls of the universe, and guardians of earth and sea."[134]

Speaking of the rebuke which Paul gave to Peter at Antioch, he says: "Is anyone troubled to hear that Paul resisted Peter, that the *columns of the Church* came into collision and fell upon each other? For they are *the columns* that bear and sustain the roof of faith; and not only *the columns,* but also the *shields* and e*yes of the body of the Church,* the source and *treasury* of all *good* things; and if one should say of them all that could be imagined, he could not sufficiently describe their dignity."[135] Later he compares these Apostles to two coursers drawing together the chariot of the Church, adding, in allusion to his fall, that one of them, Peter, appears to halt.[136] He finally adds, "How, O Paul! didst thou, who wast so gentle and good with thy disciples, show thyself cruel, inhuman toward thy fellow-apostle" (*Sinapóstolos*).[137] Is it possible to say more distinctly that Paul was equal with Peter in dignity?

We find the same truth in the following passage, which deserves very particular attention:

"Christ confided the Jews to Peter, and set Paul at the head of the Gentiles. *I do not say this of myself,* but we have Paul himself who says: 'For he that wrought effectually in Peter to the apostleship of the circumcision, the same was mighty in me toward the Gentiles (Galat. 2: 8). For as a wise king (*vasiléfs*) who, after having carefully estimated the capacities of each, gives to one the command of the cavalry, and to another that of the infantry, Christ also did certainly divide his army in two parts, and confided the Jews to Peter, and the Gentiles to Paul. The two divisions of the army are indeed several, BUT THE GENERAL IS ONE."[138]

Here, then, is the true doctrine of St. John Chrysostom: The Apostles were equal in dignity; Peter and Paul were alike first among

---

134 Upon Prayer, Second Discourse.

135 Homily on the words, "I withstood him to the face."

136 Ibid.

137 Ibid.

138 Homily on the words, "I withstood him to the face."

them, the one for the Jews, the other for the Gentiles; Peter never received any exclusive supremacy over all Christendom; the only chief of the Church was, is, and ever shall be, Jesus Christ himself. Let us carefully observe these words of St. Chrysostom *"I do not say this of myself,"* which signifies: this is not a mere personal opinion; it is a truth which the Holy Ghost has taught us by the Apostle Paul.

St. John Chrysostom has not recognized in the Church any dignity superior to the *apostolate* in general.

Of all spiritual magistratures," says he, "the *greatest is the apostolate*. How do we know this? Because the apostle precedes all others. As the consul is the first of civil magistrates, so is the apostle *the first of* spiritual magistrates. St. Paul himself, when he enumerates these dignities, places at their *head the prerogatives of the apostolate*. What does he say? 'And God has set some in the church; first, apostles; secondarily, prophets; thirdly, teachers.' Do you observe the summit of these dignities? Do you mark that *the apostle is at the apex of the hierarchy—no one before, none above him*. For he says: '*First, apostles*.' And not only is the apostolate *the first* of all dignities, but also the root and foundation thereof."[139]

St. Chrysostom recognized no supremacy in the apostolate. Had he believed that Christ had set one of the Apostles above the rest to be his representative on earth and the visible chief of his Church, he certainly would have said so, for manifestly then or never was the time to speak of it.

We can now appreciate the audacity which the Romish theologians display in asserting that according to St. Chrysostom, the authority of Peter was the most fundamental and essential thing, *in the organization of the hierarchy*, which the Church has received from Christ. The great and holy Patriarch is his own defense against those who have falsified his doctrine, when he tells them that the apostolate belongs equally to all the Apostles. "THAT IT IS THE FIRST OF ALL DIGNITIES, THAT THE APOSTLE IS AT THE SUMMIT OF THE HIERARCHY, THAT NONE IS BEFORE AND NONE ABOVE HIM." The Romish theologians make the most capital of this passage on the election of St. Matthias: "Peter always speaks first, because he is full of zeal;

---

139 Homily upon the Utility of Reading Holy Scripture.

because it is to him that Christ has committed the care of the flock; and because he is the first among the Apostles." A little further on, asking whether Peter would not, himself, have designated someone to take the place of Judas, he adds, "Without doubt he could have done this, but be refrained in order not to seem to do a favor to the one he would name."

In the first place, these expressions that "Peter always speaks first, *because* he is full of zeal and *because* he is first among the Apostles," are the best evidence that Chrysostom never meant to say *because* he was the chief of the Church. And thus the third *because*, inserted between the other two, "*because* it is to him that Christ has committed the care of his flock," is no longer susceptible of the meaning attached to it by the Romanists; unless one would make the good Father contradict himself, not only in this passage, but in all his writings. This is abundantly confirmed by the explanation that the great Patriarch gives of the words "*feed my lambs, feed my sheep*," upon which our adversaries most rely when they claim that it was to Peter alone that these words were addressed, and that to him alone was confided the care of the flock. "This," writes St. Chrysostom, "was not said *to the Apostles and bishops* only, but also *to each one of us, however* humble, to whom has been committed the care of the flock."[140] Thus, according to St. Chrysostom, these words were not said to Peter alone and only for him; they did not confer upon him the dignity of supreme pastor of the Apostles and the Church; but were addressed to all the Apostles in common, and to all bishops and pastors who are equally the successors of the Apostles. Moreover, St. Chrysostom perceived neither honor nor authority in these words, but an exhortation to zeal and carefulness. "Three times," he says, "the Lord questioned Peter, and three times he gave him this command, in order to show him how much care must be taken for the salvation of the sheep."[141]

St. Chrysostom himself has refuted the conclusions that the Romanists would draw from the remainder of the text.

---

140 Upon St. Matthew, 77th homily.
141 Upon St. John, 88th homily.

"Behold," he says, "how Peter does all things by common consent, and decides nothing by his own authority and power..."[142]

"It was not Peter who presented them [Matthias and Joseph], but all [the Apostles]. Thus Peter did nothing but give them counsel, showing moreover that it did not come from him but had been announced of old in the prophecies, and *thus he was the interpreter, but not the master.* "And again: "Remark the modesty of James, although he had received the Bishopric of Jerusalem, he says nothing on this occasion; consider also the great modesty of the other disciples, who, after unanimously *giving the throne to James,* no longer disputed among themselves. For that Church was, as it were, in heaven, having nothing of earth- shining not by its walls or its marbles, but by the unanimous and pious fervour of its members."

The Romish theologians quote the first part of this text, but carefully abstain from quoting the last; such, indeed, being their habit.

According to this Father, therefore, the Apostles acted by common consent; they chose together the candidates for the election; Peter did not speak as master, but as interpreter of the prophecies; James, *who was the first in dignity*, and the other Apostles, allowed him to speak alone because of their modesty, not because they did not possess the same power as he. If St. Chrysostom recognized a superior dignity in any of the Apostles, we should say it was in St. James of Jerusalem. In fact, beside the text already quoted, we find the following amongst his writings:

"Behold, after Peter it is Paul who speaks, and no man objects; James looks on and remains quiet, for the *primacy had been committed to him.* John and the other Apostles do not speak, but remain silent without the least vexation, because their soul was free from all vainglory. After they [Barnabas and Paul] ceased speaking, James answered and said,

'Simeon hath declared how God, at the first, did visit the Gentiles.' Peter's language had been more vehement; that of James is more moderate. It is thus *those should always act who possess great*

---

142 Upon the Acts of the Apostles, 8th hom.

IV. Teachings of Various Church Fathers 145

power. He leaves severity for others, and reserves moderation for himself."

Again, where he analyzes the words of St. James, he reasons thus:

"What means, *I judge?* It means, *I affirm*, with authority, that the thing is thus... *James, therefore, decided the whole question.*"[143]

This passage may not seem to the Romanists to prove the primacy of James, but it assuredly disproves that of Peter—if by primacy we mean authority.

Romish theologians also quote St. Chrysostom upon the fall of St. Peter as follows:

"God permitted him to yield, because He meant to establish him prince of the entire universe; so that, remembering his own faults, he should pardon those who might fall."

We have already seen that St. Chrysostom does not use this title of *prince of the universe*, in the sense that Rome struggles to give it; and without that interpretation, the passage quoted presents nothing further in favor of the papal theory. As to St. Chrysostom's opinion of Peter's fall, he himself explains it:[144]

"Wishing to *correct Peter* of this fault of contradiction, Christ permitted that this Apostle should deny Him... Hear what He says to him: '*I have prayed for thee, that thy faith fail not.*' He holds this language to him in order to touch him the more forcibly, and to show him that his fall would be heavier than that of the others, and that *it would need a greater aid*. For his was a double crime—that of contradiction, and that *of exalting himself above the others*. There was yet a third, still more serious—that of relying entirely upon his own strength. *In order to cure* Peter, the Saviour allows him to fall; and, passing by the other disciples, He says to him, 'Simon, Simon, behold, Satan hath desired to have you, that he may sift you as wheat'—that is, to trouble, to tempt you—'but I have prayed for *thee*, that thy faith fail not.' Why, if Satan hath desired to sift all the Apostles, does not the Lord here say, 'I have prayed for you'? Is it not, evidently, for the reasons I have stated? Is it not in order to

---

143 Upon the Acts of the Apostles, 33d hom.
144 Upon Chapter 1st of Galatians.

touch Peter, and to show him that his fall would be heavier than that of the others, that He speaks to him only? How, then, could Peter deny Christ? Because Christ did not say to him, 'that thou shouldst not deny me,' but 'that thy faith fail not, *that it do not entirely perish.*'"[145]

How is it possible to discover in such language the faintest allusion to a supremacy of authority given to St. Peter upon the occasion of his fall? What singular boldness to maintain that our Lord meant to establish a distinction in favor of Peter, and to notify him of his elevation over the other Apostles, precisely at the moment when He foretold him his fall and denial!

The following words most evidently determine the meaning which Chrysostom gives to Peter's primacy. He says, in the first place, that this Apostle was "first in the church." Now "the first in a society" does not mean "the chief of that society." Again he adds: "When I say Peter (Pierre), I say the solid rock (*la pierre*), the unshaken base, the great Apostle, the first of the Apostles, the first called, the first obedient."[146] Evidently he praises Peter for the solidity of the faith he had confessed; he calls him "first of the Apostles" because he was the first called to the apostolate. He does not say *"first in authority,"* but "the *first obedient."* St. Peter had, therefore, the glory of being called first to the apostolate, and of being also the first servant of Jesus Christ.

As regards the alleged succession from St. Peter that is claimed for the Roman bishops, the Romish theologians sum up the doctrine of St. Chrysostom as follows:

"The Church of Antioch had the honor of possessing St. Peter for a time. She acknowledges him as her founder, but she did not keep him. It was to Rome that he removed his see; it was at Rome that he received the palm of martyrdom; and Rome has his tomb—Rome, preeminently the royal city."

What says the Father?

"One of the prerogatives of our city (Antioch) is to have had for her teacher Peter, the leader of the Apostles. It was just that the city which first of all the world was adorned with the name of

---

145 Upon St. Matthew, 82d homily.

146 Upon Almsgiving, 3d homily.

IV. Teachings of Various Church Fathers

Christian, should have for her Bishop the first of the Apostles. But having received him as teacher, we did not keep him always; we yielded him to the imperial city of Rome; or rather, *we have always kept him*; for if we have not the body of Peter, we have kept the faith of Peter as our Peter, *since holding Peter's faith is as though we held Peter himself.*"[147]

Peter is therefore nothing except for the sake of the truth to which he testified. St. Chrysostom says this expressly in the same discourse, and adds: "When I mentioned Peter, another Peter was brought to mind [Flavian, Bishop of Antioch, at the time the discourse was written], a father and doctor common to us all, who has inherited St. Peter's virtue *and has received his see in heritage*." Again, in his eulogy of St. Ignatius, Bishop of Antioch, we read: "St. Ignatius was the successor of Peter in his principality."[148] The Latin translation thus renders it: "St. Ignatius succeeded (St. Peter) in the dignity of the episcopate." This is incorrect. The principality in the style of the Fathers is the *apostolate*, which is indeed the source of the episcopate, but surpasses it in dignity and power. But whether translated *principality or episcopate*, St. Chrysostom's testimony is equally opposed to the Romish doctrine that the Bishop of Rome is the sole successor of St. Peter. According to St. Chrysostom, St. Peter cannot in fact have occupied the see of any one city, being equally and in a *general sense* the apostle-bishop of all the churches where he preached the Gospel, and where his teachings are preserved.

In this same discourse, St. Chrysostom calls St. Ignatius of Antioch, "teacher of Rome in the faith," and gives the following as the reason why Peter, Paul, and Ignatius died at Rome: "You [inhabitants of Antioch] have, through God's blessing, no further need of instruction, for you have struck root in religion; but the people of Rome, because of the great wickedness that prevailed there, needed more powerful aid; *therefore, were Peter and Paul, and Ignatius with them, put to death there.*"[149] In developing this subject, he

---

147 2nd Homily upon the Title of the Acts of the Apostles.
148 Eulogy of St. Ignatius.
149 Ibid.

adds: "The death of these Apostles and Ignatius was a visible proof and a preaching in action of the resurrection of Jesus Christ."

In another discourse, St. Chrysostom shows just as plainly that he ascribes no right of superiority to the city of Rome, although Peter and Paul died there. He says: "I love Rome for her magnificence, her antiquity, her beauty, for the multitude of her inhabitants, her power, her wealth, her military glory; but, above all, I call that city blessed because Paul wrote to the Romans during his life, because he loved them, because he spoke with them, during his sojourn among them, and ended his life in their midst."[150] He thus merely expresses a personal sentiment of affection for the city of Rome. The praises he gives her are earthly and temporal. He merely says, "I love Rome," but he does not say that he recognizes the Church of that city as the Queen of Churches—the *mother and mistress* of all others. He ascribes no privilege to her on account of St. Peter. We see, therefore, that in seeking to give the sanction of so great a name to their doctrine of papal prerogative, the Romish theologians have distorted the works of this great divine. And no less the doctrine of St. Gregory Nazianzen, which, in respect to St. Peter, may be entirely summed up in this text: "Thou seest," he says, "how among Christ's disciples, all equally great, high, and worthy of election, this one is called the Rock, in order that on *his faith* he may receive the foundations of the Church."[151] He does not say that it was upon the person of St. Peter that the Church was to be built, but upon his faith; nor yet upon his *subjective* faith, which was to fail so sadly at the moment of his threefold denial; but upon his *objective* faith—that faith which he had confessed in the divinity of Christ.

Romanists invoke the testimony of St. Gregory of Nyssa,[152] who says:

"We celebrate the memory of St. Peter, who is the chief of the Apostles; and in him we honor the other members of the Church, for it is on him that the Church of God rests, since, in virtue of the

---

150 Homily 22, on the Epistle to Romans.
151 S. Greg. Nazian., 26th Discourse.
152 Greg. of Nyssa, Panegyric of St. Stephen.

prerogative he holds from the Lord, he is the firm and solid rock on which the Saviour has built his Church."

Such is the translation of Roman theologians. Here is the literal translation from the Greek:

"We celebrate the memory of St. Peter, who is the chief of the Apostles; and *together with him* are glorified the other members of the Church; and the Church of God is *strengthened*, since, in virtue of the GIFT that the Lord has given him, he is the firm and most solid rock upon which the Saviour has constructed the Church."[153]

By their translation, the Romish theologians endeavor to convey the idea that Peter received an exceptional gift that made him the sole foundation of the Church. St. Gregory positively denies the errors they would attribute to him in the following passages, taken from the same discourse they misquote:

"We chiefly commemorate today those who have shone with a great and dazzling splendour of piety. I mean Peter, James, and John, who are the *princes of the apostolic order*... The Apostles of the Lord were stars that brightened all under heaven. *Their princes* and *chiefs*—Peter, James, and John—whose martyrdom we celebrate today, suffered in various ways.... .

"It is just to celebrate on the same day the memory of these men, not only because they were unanimous in their preaching, but because of the EQUALITY OF THEIR DIGNITY, *protosthátis*. The one [Peter] who held *the first place, ton omótimon*, and who is *the chief of the Apostolic college*, received the favor of a glory suitable to his dignity, being honored with a passion similar to that of the Saviour. But James was beheaded, aspiring to the possession of Christ, who is TRULY *óntos* HIS HEAD, *for the head of man is the Christ, who is at the same time* HEAD OF ALL THE CHURCH.

"They [the Apostles] are the foundations *of the Church*, the columns and pillars of truth. They are never-failing springs of salvation, from which flow abundant torrents of divine doctrine."

---

153 "*Mnimoné Pétros kefalí ton Apostólon Ke sindoxázete men aftó ta lipá méri tis Ekklisías, Epistrízete de I Ekklisia Tov Theoú. Oútos gar estí Katá tin dóthisan aftó pará tov Kiríov doreán I arrayís Ke Schirotáti pétra ef in Tin Ekklisian O Sotíe okodómise*" (Greg. of Nyssa).

After again giving the same titles to Peter, James, and, John, St. Gregory adds: "Nevertheless, we have not said this *to debase the other Apostles,* but to bear witness to the virtue of those of whom we speak; or, better still, in order to *speak the common praise of all the Apostles.*

All these titles, all this praise, given by St. Gregory to Peter, James, and John, refer not to the dignity of their apostolate—that dignity was the same in all—but merely to their personal virtue. He is at particular pains to leave no doubt as to the true value of these encomiums, and upon the doctrine of the real equality of the Apostles, for he adds:

"As regards the truth of the dogmas, they [the Apostles], like members, represent one and the same body; and whether one *member be honored,* as the Apostle says, (1 Cor. 12: 26), all the members rejoice with it. As their labours for religion *were in common,* so also the honors deserved for their preaching of the faith are in common. Why," he continues, "should we be so bold as to endeavor to express what is above our power, and to strive worthily to celebrate the virtues of the Apostles? Our encomiums are not for Simon (Peter), known as having been a fisherman, but for his firm faith, that supports the church. Neither do we exalt the sons of Zebedee [James and John], but the Boanerges, which means the *sons of the thunder.*"

It is, therefore, not the person of Peter that is the rock of the Church, but the faith he confessed; that is, *Jesus Christ, the Son of God,* or the divinity of Christ, to which he bore witness.

Among the Greek Fathers there is not one who has taught a different doctrine from that of Chrysostom and Gregory of Nyssa. St. Cyril of Alexandria says expressly, "The word *rock* has only a denominative value—it signifies nothing but the steadfast and firm faith of the Apostle."[154] This forbids us to ascribe to Cyril the opinion that founds so great privileges upon that word, and yet this text has been quoted in favor of the modern Papacy by its champions. They quote yet another passage: "He (Christ) teaches his disciple (Peter) that it was He that knew all things before they were created; He announces to him that his name shall be no more Simon, but Peter;

---

154 St. Cyril of Alexandria, *Of the Trinity*, Fourth Book.

giving, him to understand by this word that He would build his Church upon him as upon a stone and a very solid rock."[155]

Has he taught that Peter should be *exclusively the foundation* of the Church? No; for he teaches elsewhere[156] that *"Peter and John were equal in dignity and honor."* In another place[157] he teaches that *"Christ is the foundation* of all—the unshaken base upon which we all are built as a spiritual edifice." Has he in this taught that the privileges of Peter would pass to the Bishops of Rome?

He nowhere makes the least mention of such a thing. Why, then, do Romish theologians call him to witness? For we have seen that the application of the word *rock* to Peter does not prove that this Apostle enjoyed any exceptional prerogatives; much less does it prove that the Bishops of Rome have inherited any from that Apostle.

St. Cyril had, touching the prerogatives of St. Peter, no other teaching than that of the learned school of Alexandria. Clement, one of the great luminaries of that school, taught distinctly that no primacy—in the sense of authority—ever existed among the Apostles.

"The disciples," he says,[158] "disputing for *primacy*, Christ made a law of equality, saying, 'Ye must become as little children.'"

Origen taught no other doctrine. Romish theologians quote some texts in which he seems to apply to the *person* of St. Peter the title of the *rock*, but they omit this passage in which he clearly explains himself: "If you believe," he says,[159] "that God has raised the whole building of his Church on Peter alone, what will you say of John, the son of the Thunder? What will you say of each of the Apostles? Will you venture to say that the gates of hell shall not prevail against Peter in particular, but shall prevail against the others? Are not the words, *the gates of hell shall not prevail against it,*

---

155 St. Cyril of Alexandria upon St. John, Book II, ch. xii.
156 St. Cyril of Alexandria, Letter to Nestorius.
157 St. Cyril of Alexandria, Second Discourse of Isaiah.
158 St. Clement of Alexandria, Stromat. Fifth Book, fifth section.
159 Origen, Commentary on St. Matt.

addressed to them all? Have not these words had their fulfillment in each one of the Apostles?" And such also is the teaching of Cyril of Alexandria, ever faithful to the traditions of his fathers.

The same is true of that of St. Basil of Cæsarea. Romanists have in vain sought to use him as an authority. It is sufficient to read him to be assured that he has nowhere made the Apostle Peter the rock of the Church, as they pretend. "The house of the Lord," he says,[160] "built in the top of the mountains," is the Church—according to the Apostle who says that *one should know how to conduct one's self in the House of God, which is the Church of the living God*. Its foundations are in the holy mountains, for it is built upon the foundations of the Apostles and Prophets. *One of these mountains* was Peter, *upon which rock* the Lord promised to build his Church. It is just that sublime souls, lifted above terrestrial things, should be called mountains. Now, the soul of the blessed Peter was called a *sublime rock, because he was firmly grounded in faith*, and that it bore constantly and courageously the blows that were laid upon it in the day of trial. St. Basil concludes that by imitating that faith and courage we shall also become mountains upon which the house of God may be raised.

Some Western fathers of the fourth and fifth centuries *seem*, more than those of the East, to favor the papal authority. But it is not so in fact. We have already given the doctrine of Tertullian, of St. Cyprian, of St. Hilary of Poitiers, and of St. Leo. That of Ambrose, Augustine, Optatus, and Jerome is the same.

According to St. Augustine, St. Ambrose had made the word rock in his hymns relate to the person of St. Peter, and this had at first led him to adopt this construction. St. Ambrose, however, explains himself in other writings, as in the following:[161] "Faith is the foundation of the Church, for it was not of *the person* but of *the faith* of St. Peter that it was said that the gates of hell should not prevail against it; it is the confession of faith that has vanquished hell." The truth confessed by St. Peter is, therefore, the foundation of the

---

160 St. Basil on second chapter of Isaiah.
161 St. Ambrose, *On the Incarnation*.

IV. Teachings of Various Church Fathers

Church, and no promise was made to his person, nor, consequently, to his *subjective faith*.

Among the texts of St. Ambrose, Rome relies chiefly upon this:[162] "The Lord, who questioned, did not doubt; he questioned, not to learn, but in order to teach which one he would leave, as the vicar of his love, before ascending to heaven... Because, alone of them all, he confessed Him, he is preferred to all... The Lord does not ask the third time, *likest* thou me,[163] but lovest thou me; and then He does not commit to him, as the first time, the *lambs* that must be nourished with milk, nor, as at the second time, the young sheep; but he commands him to pasture all, that, being more perfect, he may govern the most perfect."

Now, say with much gravity the Romish theologians, after quoting this text, who are these *most perfect* sheep if not the other Apostles? Then they go one step further, and suppose that the Pope takes Peter's place, and the Bishops that of the other Apostles; and thus they arrive at the conclusion that the Bishops are the sheep as regards their relation to the Pope.

St. Ambrose never said a word that would sustain such inferences. He gives no dogmatic character to what he says of St. Peter. He proposes a mystic and devout interpretation—he has no intention to confound the Apostles, who are *the shepherds*, with the sheep. Much less does he dream of any privileges of the Bishops of Rome, whom he does not even mention. A tottering foundation, indeed, for so lofty an edifice! St. Ambrose, like Hilary of Poitiers, ascribes sometimes to the person of Peter, sometimes to his faith, or rather to the *object* of his faith, the title of the *rock*. To his person he only attributes the title in a figurative manner, and by extension. "Jesus Christ," he says, "is the rock. He did not deny the grace of this name to his disciple when he called him Peter, because he borrowed from the rock the constancy and solidity of his faith.

---

162 St. Ambrose on St. Luke, and passim.

163 Thus only can we do justice to the text. In fact *agapás* and *filís* are both properly translated "lovest," as in our common English version; but in the Greek the two words indicate different degrees or loving—*agapán* being stronger than *filín*).—ED.

Endeavor, then, thyself to be a rock—thy rock is thy faith, and faith is the foundation of the Church. If thou art a rock, thou shalt be in the Church, for the Church is built *upon the rock.*"

This explanation leaves no shadow of doubt upon the sense in which St. Ambrose took this famous saying, upon which Romanists rear the prodigious monument of papal prerogatives. Why was this name given to Peter? "Because," adds St. Ambrose, "the Church was built on Peter's faith." But what faith? His *personal* belief, or the truth he believed? St. Ambrose replies in the same place, "Peter was thus named because he was *the first* who laid the foundation *of faith* among the nations." What did he preach? Certainly not his personal assent. What he taught is, then, the *truth* that he believed; and *that truth* is the foundation of the Church.

The works of St. Ambrose are full of proofs against papal pretensions. But why multiply texts? One only needs to glance over his works to be convinced that he is no authority in favor of the Ultramontane system. We shall therefore be content to quote only the following texts, in which he sets forth his belief concerning Peter's primacy.

In explaining these words in the epistle to the Galatians, "*I went up to Jerusalem to see Peter,*" he says: "It was proper that Paul should go to see Peter. Why? Was Peter superiour to him and to the other Apostles? No; but because, of all the Apostles, he was the first to be entrusted by the Lord with the care of the churches. Had he need to be taught, or to receive a commission from Peter? No; but that Peter might know that Paul had received "*the power which had also been given to himself.*"

St. Ambrose also explains these other words: "*When they saw that the Gospel of the uncircumcision was committed to me...* He [Paul] names only Peter, and only compares himself with him, because as Peter had received the primacy to found the Church of the Jews, he, Paul, had been chosen in like manner to have the primacy in founding the Church of the Gentiles." Then he enlarges upon this idea, which completely demolishes the papal pretensions. In fact, according to St. Ambrose, Rome, which confessedly did not belong to the Jews, should not glory in the primacy of St. Peter, but in that

IV. Teachings of Various Church Fathers

of St. Paul. Besides, she would then come closer to historic truth: for it is demonstrated that Paul evangelized Rome before Peter; that her first two bishops were ordained by Paul; and that her succession through Peter only dates from Clement, her third Bishop.

Finally, what does St. Ambrose mean by the word *primacy*? He attached no idea of honor or authority to it, for he says positively: "As soon as Peter heard these words, '*Whom say ye that I am?*' remembering his place, he exercised this primacy, a *primacy* of confession, not of *honor*; a primacy of faith, not of rank."[164] Is not this to reject all idea of primacy as taught by the Romanists? It is clear, then, that they wrong St. Ambrose in making him their authority.

No less St. Augustine. This Father indeed said,[165] "Peter, who a short time before had confessed that Christ was the Son of God, and who in return for that confession had been called *the rock* upon which the Church should be built." But he explains his meaning in several other works. Let us give a few specimens:[166] "Peter received this name from the Lord to Signify the Church; for it is Christ who is THE ROCK, and Peter is the CHRISTIAN PEOPLE. THE ROCK is the principal word; this is why Peter is derived from *the Rock*, and not *the rock* from Peter; precisely as the word *Christ* is not from Christian, but *Christian* from *Christ*. 'Thou art therefore Peter, and upon *this rock* I will build my Church. I will build thee on myself—I will not be built on thee.'"

"The Church," he says again, "is built on the rock after which Peter was named. That rock was Christ, and it is on this foundation that Peter himself was to be raised."[167]

In his book of the Retractations, the same Father says:[168] In that book, I said in one place, in speaking of St. Peter, that the Church had been built on him as on *the rock*. This thought is sung by many in the verses of the blessed Ambrose, who says of the cock, that

---

164 St. Ambrose on the Incarnation.
165 St. Augustine on 69th Psalm.
166 St. Augustine, 18th Sermon.
167 St. Augustine, 124th Tract.
168 St. Augustine, Retractions, Book I, ch. 21.

"when *it crew the Rock of the Church deplored his fault.*' But I know that subsequently I very frequently adopted this sense, that when the Lord said, 'Thou art Peter, and *upon this rock I will build my Church,*' he meant by this rock, the one which Peter had confessed in saying, '*Thou art the Christ, the son, of the living God*'; so that Peter, called by the name of *this rock*, represented the *person of the Church* which is built upon that rock, and which has received the keys of the kingdom of heaven. In fact, it was not said to him, Thou art the rock; but thou art Peter. The rock was Christ. Peter having confessed him as all the Church confesses him, he was called Peter. Between these two sentiments, let the reader choose the most probable."

Thus St. Augustine condemns neither of the interpretations given to the text, *Thou art Peter*, etc. But he evidently regards as the better the one which he most frequently used. Yet this does not prevent the Romish theologians from quoting this Father in favor of the first interpretation, which he admitted but once, and renounced, though without formally condemning it.

St. Augustine teaches, like St. Cyprian, that Peter *represented the Church*—that he was the *type* of the Church. He does not infer from this that the whole Church was summed up in him; but, on the contrary, that he received nothing *personally*, and all that was granted to him was granted to the Church.[169] Such is the true commentary upon the belief of the Fathers—that Peter *typified* the church whenever he addressed Christ, or the Lord spoke to him. St. Augustine, it is true, admits that Peter enjoyed *the primacy*, but he explains what he means by that word. "He had not," he says, "the primacy *over the disciples (in discipulos) but among the disciples (in discipulos)*. His primacy among the disciples *was the same as that of Stephen among the deacons.*" He calls Peter *the first (primus)* as he calls Paul *the last (novissimus)*, which conveys only an idea of time. And that this was indeed St. Augustine's idea, which appears from the fact that, in this same text,[170] which is so much abused by Romanists, when Augustine grants Peter the primacy he distinctly asserts that Peter and Paul, the first and the last, were

---

169 Sermons 118 and 316, Sermon 10 on Peter and Paul, Tract 124 on John *et alibi*.

170 Sermon 10 on Peter and Paul.

equal in the honor of the apostleship. Therefore, according to St. Augustine, Peter received only the high favor of being *called first to the Apostleship*. This distinction with which the Lord honored him is his glory, but it gave him no authority.

According to Romish theologians, St. Augustine recognized the supreme authority of the Roman Church when he said that the principality of the Apostolic chair has always been in vigour there;[171] but what did he mean by these words? It is certain that the Church of Africa, under the inspiration of St. Augustine himself, who was her oracle, wrote vigorously to the Bishop of Rome, warning him not to receive to his communion thereafter those whom she had excommunicated, as he had done in the case of a certain Appiarius,[172] because he could not do so without violating the canons of the Council of Nicea. Far from recognizing the supreme authority of Rome, the Church of Africa, in accord with St. Augustine, refused to that Bishop the title of *summus sacerdos*. St. Augustine did not, therefore, recognize the superior jurisdiction of the Roman Church. What, then, does he mean by *principality of the Apostleship*? He leaves no doubt upon the subject. After having ascribed this *principality of the Apostleship* to St. Paul as well as to St. Peter, he observes that it is something higher than the episcopate. "Who does not know," says he, "that the *principality of the Apostleship* is to be preferred to *every episcopate*?"[173] The Bishops were considered, indeed, as successors of the Apostles; but while they inherited from them the apostolic ministry, they had no share in certain superiour prerogatives, which only belonged to the first Apostles of Christ. These prerogatives constitute the principality of the Apostleship, which thus belongs equally to all the first Apostles. And in fact, the title of Apostle-prince is given to them all indifferently by the Fathers of the Church. Every Apostolic Church, therefore—that is, every Church that has preserved the legitimate Apostolic succession—has *preserved this principality of the see*, that is, of *Apostolic teaching*. St. Augustine merely says that, in his time, the Church of

---

171 St. Aug. Ep. to the Donatist Bishops.
172 Epist. Episcop. Afric. ad Celestin. et Conc Carth. III.
173 St. Augustine's 10th Sermon on Peter and Paul.

Rome had preserved this succession of Apostolic teaching. Does that prove that he recognizes in her a superiour authority, and one universal in the government of the Church? Assuredly not. So far was he from recognizing any such authority that, by preference, he sends the Donatists to the Apostolic churches of the East to be convinced of their error; not because he did not believe Rome to have inherited the Apostolic teaching—for we have seen to the contrary—but because Rome, mixed up as she was already with their discussions, did not offer equal guarantees of impartiality as the Apostolic churches of the East.

St. Augustine, who did not even recognize the right of Rome to interfere with the discussion of mere matters of discipline in the African Church, was still further removed from recognizing her doctrinal authority. In many of his writings he sets forth the *rule of faith*, and never in that connection does be mention the doctrinal authority of the Church of Rome. In his eyes, the rule of faith is the constant and unanimous consent of all the Apostolic churches. His doctrine is the same as that of Tertullian, and it has been copied, so to speak, by *Vincent Lirinensis*, whose admirable *Commonitorium* sums up perfectly the doctrine of the first five centuries upon this fundamental question. In view of this great doctrine so clearly stated by the Fathers, and in which not the faintest foreshadowing of Roman authority is to be found—a doctrine, on the contrary, diametrically opposed to this pretended authority—it is difficult to understand how the partisans of the Papacy have ventured to invent their system; for they must have known that they were thus putting themselves in direct opposition to all Catholic tradition.

Romish theologians quote with much pomp and circumstance two other passages from St. Augustine. In the first, this Father, speaking to the Pelagians,[174] says: "As regards your cause two councils have been sent to the Apostolic See. Rescripts have returned, *the case is finished*—may it please God that also the error be so!" The advocates of the Papacy thus translate this passage: "*Rome has spoken—the case is finished; Roma locuta est—causa finita est.*" This

---

174 St. Aug., Serm. 131. *De Verb. Evang.*

IV. Teachings of Various Church Fathers

expression, *Rome has spoken—Roma locuta est*, is a mere invention. It does not occur in St. Augustine. The other—*the case is finished*—is there. We shall presently see what it means.

The second passage, similar to the first, is thus conceived: "Your cause is finished," he said to the Pelagians,[175] "by a competent judgment of the bishops in general; there is nothing for you to do except to submit to the sentence that has been given; or to repress your restless turbulence if you cannot submit!"

The first text dates back to the year 419, when the Pelagians had been condemned by two African councils and by Pope Innocent I. The second is of the year 421, when eighteen Pelagian bishops had appealed from this sentence to a general council. According to this text, say the Romish theologians, the condemnation of the Pope, confirming that of the African councils, had a doctrinal authority from which there was no appeal to a general council, and therefore Rome enjoyed a superiour and final authority in dogmatic questions.

These inferences are not just. In the first place, St. Augustine did not regard a sentence of Rome as final. Thus, speaking of the question of rebaptism, he asserts that St. Cyprian had a right to oppose his belief to that of Pope Stephen; and be says that he himself would not give so positive an opinion on that point if a general council had not settled it.[176] At the same time be admits that Stephen had with him the *majority*. He says to the Donatists that, after having been condemned by the council of Rome, they had one resource left—an appeal to the plenary or œcumenical council.[177] It thus appears that he did not regard the sentence of the Pope, even given in council, as final and without appeal.

It must be remarked, moreover, that in the case of the Pelagians, St. Augustine only once mentioned a sentence from Rome—in the first text quoted. In the second text, and everywhere else, he only speaks of a judgment given by all the bishops; particularly those of the East.[178] This, then, is St. Augustine's argument: "You have

---

175 St. Aug., Adv. Julian, Lib. III.
176 St. Aug., De Baptismate ad. Donat. De Baptismate ad. Petil.
177 St. Aug., Epist. 4.
178 St. Aug., Lib. I. adv. Julian.

been condemned everywhere—in the East and in the West—why then appeal to the Church in council, when all the churches unanimously condemn you?" The Pelagians relied on a sentence in their favor given by Pope Zosimus, Innocent's successor. How does Augustine answer them? "If I should concede (what is not true) that the Roman Church passed this judgment upon Celestius and Pelagius, and that she approved their doctrines, it would only follow that the Roman clergy were prevaricators."[179] This answer of St. Augustine overthrows the whole theory that the Ultramontanes would build upon this *enlarged* and *distorted* text. He did not exclude Rome in the judgment given against the Pelagians, because that church is Apostolic and a part of the Church Catholic; yet his argument is wholly summed up in the following words: "Where will you go?" he says to the Pelagians. "Do you not see, wherever you turn, the army of Jesus Christ arrayed against you the world over; at Constantinople quite as much as in Africa and in the most remote lands?"[180]

Beside all this, another proof that even at Rome—as well as elsewhere in the church—the sentence of Innocent I was not regarded as *terminating* the case is found in the fact that, after his sentence, the case was reexamined at Rome itself by Zosimus, the successor of Innocent, by the several churches in a great number of synods; and finally[181] by the Œcumenical Council of Ephesus, which judged the case and confirmed the sentence given at Rome and in all other places where it had been examined.

When we are told how Pope Innocent I happened to be called upon to give an opinion in the case of Pelagius, we see very clearly that the Romish theologians have misapplied the text.

The African bishops had condemned the errors of Pelagius in two councils, without a thought of Rome or its doctrine. The Pelagians then set up, to oppose them, the alleged faith of Rome, which they said harmonized with their own. Then the African

---

179 Ibid. Lib. II.

180 Ibid.

181 Epist. Conc. Ephes. ad Cælest. v. et St. Prosp. Opera, Phot. Biblioth. Cardinal Noris. Hist. Pelag. Lib. II. cap. ix. Rom. ed.

IV. Teachings of Various Church Fathers

bishops wrote to Innocent to ask him whether this assertion of the Pelagians was true. They were the rather moved to this that the Pelagians had great influence at Rome.[182] They did not write to the Pope to ask of him a sentence that should guide them, but that they might silence those who claimed that *heresy* was maintained at Rome. Innocent condemned it, and therefore Augustine says: "You pretended that Rome was for you; Rome condemns you; you have also been condemned by all the other churches; hence the case is finished." Instead of asking a decision from Rome, the African bishops pointed out to the Pope the course he should pursue in this affair.[183]

Here then again have the Romish theologians not only abused the text of St. Augustine, *but also invented a part of it* to suit the necessities of their cause.

Another text which at first sight seems very favorable to Romish pretensions, is that of St. Optatus of Melevia, which is quoted on all occasions by those theologians. Reasonably interpreted, this text is no more in their favor than those of the other Fathers. The holy bishop of Melevia was opposing the Donatists who had established a bishopric at Rome. He wished to prove to them that this bishopric was not legitimate. To do this it was necessary to prove that the only legitimate bishopric was that which had descended in direct line from the Apostles—for there was but one only *Apostolate* of which Peter typified the unity, and nothing outside of that Apostolic see—that is, this apostolate—could claim to be legitimate.

St. Optatus, therefore, thus addresses his adversary:[184]

"Thou canst not deny it—thou knowest that the bishop's chair was first given to Peter in the city of Rome; upon that chair sat Peter, the chief of all the Apostles; thou knowest why he was called Peter; that thus in that *one* see, unity should be preserved by all; lest each of the other Apostles should claim a separate see for himself;

---

182 Epist. Snyod Carthag. ad Innocent int. St. Aug. Op. Aug., Ep. 191 and 194, Possid., int. Op. Aug. St. Prosp. Charon. Ad ann. 418.

183 Epist. Quinque Episcop. int. Aug. Op.

184 S. Optat., Lib. II. cont. Parm.

and that he should be schismatic and sinful who should establish another bishopric beside that only see."

"For the sake of unity," he elsewhere says,[185] the blessed "Peter (for whom it had been enough had he only obtained pardon after denying his Master) deserved to be preferred to all the Apostles, and *alone* received the keys of the kingdom of heaven to impart them to others."

St. Optatus was arguing against a man who denied the unity of the ministry and its Apostolic origin. In order to convince him he holds up before him Rome—the only *Apostolic* church of the West whose origin was incontestable. He shows him that Peter, who was *the type of sacerdotal unity*, founded the see of Rome; that, consequently, he must be with this see, if he would be in the unity and would give an Apostolic character to his ministry; but from this to an authority over the whole Church is a long step.

The whole argument of St. Optatus proves this to have been his idea in the preceding texts.

"Our angel,"[186] he says, "dates back to St. Peter—yours only to Victor.[187] Address yourself, if you like, to the seven angels which are in Asia; to our colleagues—those churches to whom St. John wrote, and with which you are evidently not in communion. Now all outside of these seven churches is foreign. If you have any one of the angels of the seven churches with whom you are one, you commune through him with the other angels; through them with the churches, and through the churches with us. Such not being the case, you have not the characteristics of a *Catholic* church—you are no true *Catholics*."

Such is a faithful analysis of the argument of St. Optatus. He does not seek in his work to prove that the legitimate Bishop of Rome had universal authority—he only proves that he was descended in direct line from the Apostles, and that his Donatist rival was illegitimate. He proves that all the Apostolic churches of the East

---

185 Ib. Lib. I. cont. Parm.

186 He alludes to the angels of the churches, which in the Apocalypse mean the bishops.

187 This was the bishop the Donatists had established at Rome.

IV. Teachings of Various Church Fathers

were in communion with the Apostolic Bishop of Rome, and that, consequently, the Donatists were not in Catholic or universal unity. We really cannot see how such teaching can be quoted to support the pretensions of the modern Papacy. Nay, more. We may certainly justly quote it against them.

We have now reviewed the strongest texts upon which the Ultramontanes and modern Gallicans have rested their theories about the papacy. The former see in them the papal autocracy, the latter a limited monarchy of which the Pope is the head—not absolute or infallible, but subject to the laws and decrees of the councils. Both have misinterpreted the texts and have drawn false conclusions from them; it would be sufficient to set them the one against the other in order to confound them. The only facts proved by the texts are the following:

First: St. Peter was the first among the Apostles; but this title gave him no authority.

Second: Peter cooperated with St. Paul in founding the Church of Rome.

Third: This Church is consequently an Apostolic see.

The advocates of papal authority would conclude from these facts that the Bishops of Rome, as successors of St. Peter, have inherited that Apostle's prerogatives. But the texts prove neither the prerogatives of Peter nor their descent to the Bishops of Rome. That Bishop is no more the heir of St. Peter than of St. Paul. He merely holds his bishopric in the same church where those Apostles exercised their apostleship. Peter and Paul died at Rome, but if by their death they glorified the Church, *non constat* that they have bequeathed their apostolate any more than the other apostles have bequeathed theirs to the churches in which they died. Those prerogatives, which were intended to be perpetuated in the Church, have been transmitted not by the death of the Apostles, but by *ordination*. It is to this end that they *ordained* and established bishops in all the churches they founded; at Rome as much as anywhere else. Accordingly, as appears from the records of the first centuries, the *first Bishop* of Rome was Linus, and not St. Peter. The Roman episcopate, therefore, only dates back to Linus, and that episcopate draws its origin from the Apostolate; from Paul first, who ordained the first two bishops, then from Peter, who ordained Clement, who was chosen to fill the see of Rome after the death of Anencletus, and long after Peter's death. The Bishops of Antioch are traced in precisely the same manner to the apostolate of Peter and Paul; those of Alexandria also go back to Peter by St. Mark, who was the delegate and disciple of that Apostle. The other Apostolic Sees, Jerusalem, Smyrna, Byzantium, etc., can be traced like that of Rome to some one of the Apostles. Their *episcopate* is thus *Apostolic*, but it is not the Apostolate.

Before concluding our examination of the Fathers of the fourth and fifth centuries, we must mention, in the way of objection, some texts of St. Jerome that seem favorable to such papal extravagances. We must premise:

First: That even should the words of this Father be taken literally, they could prove nothing, since he would be alone against all; and the opinion of a single Father proves absolutely nothing as to Catholic doctrine.

Second: That these texts of St. Jerome cannot be taken literally without making him contradict himself.

Writing to Pope Damasus, his friend and protector, Jerome thus expresses himself:[188] "Although your greatness awes me, your goodness reassures. I ask of the priest the saving sacrifice—of the shepherd the help he owes to the sheep. I speak to the successor of the fisherman, to the disciple of the cross. Following NO CHIEF save *Christ*, I am united in communion with your Holiness; that is to say, with the see of Peter. I know the Church is built upon this rock. Who eats not of the lamb in this house is defiled. Whoever dwells not in Noah's ark will perish at the time of the deluge. I do not know Vitalis; I repel Meletius; I ignore Paulinus.[189] Whoever does not reap with you, scatters his harvest; that is, he who is not of Christ is of Antichrist." Then he asks Damasus if he shall speak of the divine hypostases, or be silent.

---

188 St. Hieron., Epis. 57 ad Damas.

189 This alludes to the dissensions in the church of Antioch.

IV. Teachings of Various Church Fathers

And addressing Damasus or the Roman ladies, particularly Eustochia, Jerome speaks in very nearly the same terms of the Roman see.

Should his words be taken literally, or should we not rather see in them only a bit of flattery addressed to the Pope—the rather that Damasus had given to Jerome pledges not only of protection but of friendship? At all events, it is certain that we cannot take them literally without making St. Jerome contradict himself. We notice, in the first place, that he recognized but ONE FIRST in the Church—Jesus Christ; that he calls the Apostle Peter *the rock* on which the Church is built, asserting at the same time that Christ alone is that rock, and that the title of *secondary stones* belongs *equally* to all the Apostles and to the Prophets. "*The stones,*"[190] he says, "must be understood to mean the Prophets and the Apostles. The Church is the rock founded upon the most solid stone." He teaches that the Church is represented by the Apostles and Prophets, meaning that it is *established* upon both—"*super prophetas et apostolos constituta.*" Yet, in his letter to Damasus, he seems to say that Peter is the foundation of the Church, to the exclusion of the others.

But did he not, perhaps, mean to imply that Peter had some superiority as a foundation of the Church? Not so; for he clearly says the contrary: "The solidity of the Church," he says, "is supported upon them [the Apostles and Prophets] equally.[191] He calls Peter *prince* of the Apostles; but he also says: "He [Christ] shows us Peter and Andrew—princes of the Apostles—established as teachers of the Gospel."

Was this principality of Peter an *authority*, as might be inferred from the letter to Damasus? Jerome answers that question in the following passage:[192] "What can be claimed for Aristotle that we do not find in Paul? For Plato that does not belong to Peter? As Plato was *the prince of philosophers*, so Peter was the prince of Apostles, upon whom the Church of the Lord was built as upon a solid rock."

---

190 St. Hieron., adv. Jovinian.

191 St. Hieron., adv. Jovin.

192 St. Hieron., adv. Pelag. Lib. I. ch. 4.

Elsewhere,[193] he represents St. Paul saying: "I am in *nothing* inferior to Peter; for we were *ordained* by the same God for the same ministry." Clearly, if inferior *in nothing (in nullo)*, then equal in *everything*.

The Romish theologians cannot deny that the Fathers have generally taught the *equality* of the Apostles among themselves; on this point, tradition is unanimous. No Father of the Church has taught any other doctrine. But these theologians affect to give no weight to so important a fact. They try to evade the overwhelming testimony of the Fathers by this distinction: the Apostles, they say, were *equal in respect of the apostolate, but not in respect of the primacy*.[194] But clearly, such a primacy, as it is understood at Rome, cannot coexist with any equality whatsoever. The Fathers cannot teach the equality of the Apostles without denying the superiority of any one of them. They teach that equality absolutely. To resort, then, to a distinction that takes away this absolute character, is to falsify their testimony.

After all, has St. Jerome conceded to the see of Rome any exceptional prerogatives, as we might be led to think from his letters to Damasus and Eustochia? Let us see what he says in another letter:[195]

"We must not believe that the city of Rome is a different church from that of the whole world. Gaul, Britain, Africa, Persia, the East, India, all the barbarous nations, adore Jesus Christ, and observe *one and the same rule of truth. If one is looking for authority, the world is greater than one city.* Wherever there is a Bishop, be he at Rome or at Eugubium, at Constantinople or at Rhegium, at Alexandria or at Tanis, he has *the same authority*, the same merit, because he has the same priesthood. The power that riches give, and the low estate to which poverty reduces, render a Bishop neither greater nor less."

---

193 St. Hieron., comment. in Epist. ad Galat.

194 Lest we be accused of falsely attributing this distinction to the Romish party, let us here say that it may be found in the works of a theologian of great authority in that party, Father Perrone. Tract de Loc. Theol. part 1, sect. 2, chap. 1. Difficult respons. ad 6.

195 St. Hieron., Epist. 146 ad Ev.

IV. Teachings of Various Church Fathers

It cannot be more distinctly stated that the rule of truth dwells only in the entire episcopal body, and not at Rome; that the Bishop of Rome is no more, as bishop, than the humblest bishop of the Church; that the power he possessed because of his riches did not make him superiour to the rest. One might almost think that St. Jerome exerted himself, in all his works, to refute his own letters to Damasus.

But, say the Roman theologians, the papal prerogatives were so well recognized that even the heretic Jovinian mentions them. And, in fact, in order to prove to St. Jerome that the estate of marriage was superior to that of virginity, he says: "St. John was a virgin, and St. Peter was married; why, then, did Christ prefer St. Peter to St. John to *build his Church on him?*" The Romanists stop here, but do not give us St. Jerome's answer to Jovinian—a proceeding not creditable to their good faith, as we shall see. Here is St. Jerome's answer:[196] "If he chose Peter rather than John for this honorable distinction, it was that it was more expedient not to confer it upon a young man, nay a child, as John was, in order to excite no jealousy. But if Peter be an Apostle, so is John also. The one is married, the other is virgin; but Peter is *only an* Apostle, and John is an Apostle, an Evangelist, and a Prophet."

St. Jerome could not have reasoned thus if he had had the same idea of St. Peter's primacy as is held at Rome concerning that of the Pope. His reasoning against Jovinian would have been worthless if that heretic had considered Peter's primacy otherwise than as a priority, in virtue of which he was the representative of the Apostolic college and the *type of unity*; for he (St. Jerome) grounds his argument upon this *conceded* point: that St. Peter was but an Apostle like the others. If Jovinian had believed that Peter was anything more than this, St. Jerome's argument would have been ridiculous. And if St. Peter had been the *chief—the prince* of the Apostles in the sense that Rome now gives to these expressions—would St. Jerome have laid down as the first principle of his argument that St. John was superiour to St. Peter because of his characters of Evangelist and *Prophet?*

---

196 St. Hieron., Lib. I., adv. Jovin.

After the review we have given of the constant and universal tradition of the Church, during the first five centuries, we may well be amazed to hear Cardinal Orsi[197] assert that nothing could be opposed to papal pretensions except a few isolated texts, which do not contain the true sense of Catholic tradition; to hear all the advocates of the Papacy declare that Catholic tradition is in favor of their system, especially in the first centuries!

---

197 Orsi, de Infallib. Rom. Pontif.

V.

OF THE AUTHORITY OF THE BISHOPS OF ROME DURING THE SIXTH, SEVENTH, AND EIGHTH CENTURIES.

WE have already seen that the œcumenical councils of Constantinople and Chalcedon had given to the Bishop of Constantinople the second place in the Catholic episcopacy, and that St. Leo, Bishop of Rome, had opposed this law as changing the hierarchal order established at the first Œcumenical Council of Nicea.

We may believe that St. Leo was indeed only moved to this opposition by his respect for the canons. But his successors, probably, had another motive. They feared lest the Bishop of Constantinople should soon supplant them in the primacy. Such fears were the more reasonable because the Council of Chalcedon had only given as the reason of the primacy the dignity of the city of Rome, the capital of the empire. Now Rome was daily growing less influential. The Roman empire in the West had fallen under the blows of the barbarians; Rome was passing successively through the hands of various tribes, who destroyed everything—even to the signs of her former greatness. Constantinople had become the only centre of the empire, and increased in splendour in proportion as Rome was humbled. On the other hand, the emperor added daily to the prerogatives of the Bishops of Constantinople, thus increasing their influence, while they quite forgot the Bishops of Rome. It was therefore natural that the Roman Bishops should be jealous of the prerogatives and honors of their brethren of Constantinople, and that jealousy betrayed itself in the relations necessary to be preserved between them. It was no less natural that the Bishops of Constantinople should show some degree of arrogance toward those of Rome, who had merely the semblance of a primacy and the memories of a glory that each day left dimmer.

Such was the beginning of the struggles between the sees of Rome and Constantinople during the sixth, seventh, and eighth centuries, and the motive that impelled the Roman Bishops to aid in the establishment of a new Western empire, in which, thanks to the new emperors, they might so enlarge their prerogatives that they should eclipse those of the see of Constantinople.

We must not lose sight of these general considerations if we would comprehend the history of the Papacy and those struggles which led to the rupture between the Eastern and Western churches.

No one denies that the emperors of Constantinople strove to increase the influence of the bishops of that city. They issued numberless decrees for this purpose; and the Emperor Zeno even made the twenty-eighth canon of the Council of Chalcedon a law of the state. The heads of the new empire of the East thought that they were adding to their own glory when they surrounded the see of their capital with splendour and power. In consequence of his position, the Bishop of Constantinople was the sole medium of intercourse not only between them and the other Oriental, but also the Western bishops. He became so powerful that there grew up a custom to choose him from the members of the imperial or the most illustrious families.

The Bishop of Constantinople had, at first, only enjoyed an honorary title in virtue of the third canon of the second œcumenical council (381). Sometime after, the Emperor Theodosius the younger made two laws for the purpose of giving him a real authority over the provinces of Asia and Illyria. The Council of Chalcedon (451) gave its ecclesiastical sanction to these laws and extended the authority of the Bishop of Constantinople over Pontus and Thrace, in consequence of the ecclesiastical troubles that afflicted these

V. Roman Bishop Authority of the 6th, 7th, and 8th Centuries 171

countries. The Bishop of Constantinople thought himself entitled to extend his jurisdiction over the other Patriarchal sees of the East.

To trace the beginning of these undertakings we must go back to the fifth century. In 476 Acacius was Bishop of Constantinople, and Simplicius Bishop of Rome.

Basiliscus, having driven Zeno from the imperial throne, declared himself in favor of the heretics condemned by the Council of Chalcedon and recalled from exile Timothy Ælurus, the heretic Bishop of Alexandria, and Peter the Fuller, heretic Bishop of Antioch, both canonically deposed. These churches were filled with confusion and a new council was talked of to revoke the decrees of Chalcedon. Simplicius wrote to Basiliscus against the heretics, and at the same time applied to Acacius to obtain from the Emperor the expulsion of Timothy and to dissuade that prince from convoking a new council.[198] But Basiliscus was overthrown, and Zeno reascended the imperial throne. Simplicius at once wrote to him, praying him to expel the heretics, especially Timothy of Alexandria.

Acacius sent a deacon to the Bishop of Rome, that he might consult with him upon the best means to remedy the evils of the churches. Simplicius replied that, under God, the Emperor only could remedy them; and advised that he should issue a decree exiling Timothy and John of Antioch, who had supplanted Peter the heretic and was no better than he had been; in a word, all the heretical bishops opposed to the Council of Chalcedon.

It is noteworthy that if the universal and absolute authority of the Bishop of Rome, now ascribed to him, had been recognized at that time, he would not have needed imperial intervention to reestablish order and respect for the laws in the churches. The usurpers of bishoprics and the deposed bishops could not have had so numerous partisans.

Simplicius invoked the good offices of Acacius with Zeno in order to obtain the decree he desired, and to cause those to be excommunicated who were to be exiled. The Emperor issued the decree that Simplicius and Acacius asked for, and convoked a council of Eastern bishops who excommunicated the heretical bishops, and

---

198 See Simplic., Epist. in Labbe's Collection. Evag. Hist.

particularly Peter and John, the usurpers of the see of Antioch, and Timothy of Alexandria. The council wrote to Simplicius, praying him not to receive into his communion any of those who had been condemned. Then Simplicius, on his part, excommunicated them and gave Acacius notice of his sentence, entreating him at the same time to solicit from the Emperor the execution of the decree of proscription.

Timothy Ælurus, already feeble through age and infirmity, was permitted to die at Alexandria. After his death, his supporters elected Peter, surnamed Mongus, or "the Hoarse"; but the Emperor Zeno had him driven away and reestablished in the chair of Alexandria Timothy Salofaciolus, who had been unjustly expelled.[199] The three Bishops of Rome, Constantinople, and Alexandria were thus in perfect communion, and mutually pledged themselves thereof.

But the Bishop of Antioch, who had taken the place of the two usurpers, Peter and John, was then killed in a riot. For that church was sadly divided, and the religious parties carried on a war to the knife there. To obtain pardon of the Emperor, they now agreed to give up their right of election and asked that Zeno should himself choose a bishop for them. He chose Stephen, who was consecrated at Constantinople by Acacius. This choice was not canonical; they knew *that* at Constantinople as well as at Rome; but they alleged the peculiar circumstances of the case as their excuse, and notified the Pope of what had occurred in order that he should not refuse to enter into communion with the new bishop. Simplicius agreed to what had been done by the Emperor and Acacius, insisting, however, that such a choice, contrary to the canons of Nicea, should not establish a precedent. This was agreed to at Constantinople; but it is certain that the troubles of the churches of Antioch and Alexandria served to extend the influence of the Bishop of Constantinople over the whole Eastern Church; for the Emperor necessarily interfered in these troubles and availed himself, in ecclesiastical matters, of the cooperation of the bishop nearest at hand whose advice he could

---

199 The Roman court is now so little acquainted with these facts that in a work published by it against the Eastern Church, over the name of Mr. Pitzipios, it makes Peter the Hoarse a Patriarch of Antioch. See Part I, ch. 2.

most easily obtain. Simplicius was not blind to the progress of the rival see, and that is why he so carefully appealed to the canons to prevent the interference of Acacius from becoming a matter of custom.

Nevertheless, upon Stephen's death, the Emperor chose Calandion to succeed him; and Acacius conferred the ordination.

Calandion, according to custom, wrote a letter of notification to the Bishop of Rome, who entered into communion with him.[200]

The see of Alexandria, after the death of Timothy Salofaciolus, gave greater trouble.

John Talaïa was regularly elected and ordained; but Acacius declared against him and persuaded the Emperor that John was unfit to be a bishop, urging him to restore the see to Peter the Hoarse. This seemed to him to promise a restoration of peace; for Peter promised to abandon, with his followers, his opposition to the Council of Chalcedon; and the faithful would have no further objection to him if he were canonically consecrated. The Bishop of Rome did not agree with Acacius and declared that, though he would not grant intercommunion to John Talaïa, he never could recognize Peter the Hoarse as the legitimate bishop. Zeno overruled his opinion and established Peter; and Acacius, deceived by the orthodox declarations of this wicked bishop, granted him communion.

John Talaïa, flying from Alexandria, went to Antioch and thence to Rome. In these two cities he made the most overwhelming charges against Mongus, and was received into communion by Calandion and Simplicius. He wrote to Acacius to ask for his removal; but Acacius replied that he did not recognize him as legitimate Bishop of Alexandria. Simplicius at once wrote to Acacius, blaming him for having granted communion to Mongus. He died before receiving the answer of the Bishop of Constantinople (483). He was succeeded by Felix, before whom John Talaïa at once pleaded his cause. John wrote a petition against Acacius; and Felix assembled a council at

---

200 In the work before mentioned *letters of communion* are confounded with *requests for confirmation*, proving that the Roman court is no better acquainted with canon law than with historical facts. See Part I, ch. 3.

Rome, which decided that Acacius must reply to the petition of John and pronounce an anathema against Peter the Hoarse. These decisions were sent to the Emperor.[201] In the letters that Felix wrote to Zeno and to Acacius, he bitterly complains that there had not even been an answer to the letters of his predecessor concerning the troubles of the Church of Alexandria. Zeno, by mingled terror and flattery, induced the envoys of Felix to communicate with Acacius and Peter Mongus; but the adversaries of these two bishops denounced these legates at Rome, and they were deposed. They had brought back letters in which Acacius and Zeno explained their conduct respecting Peter Mongus, and denied the accusations against that bishop.

This conduct wounded the Pope, who at once assembled a council of Italian bishops to excommunicate Acacius and depose him. He served on him a notice of the sentence, which was signed, "Felix, Bishop of the holy *Catholic Church of Rome.*"

This sentence pronounced against Acacius was null and anticanonical, since it was rendered outside of the district where the accused resided, and without the participation of the Eastern bishops, who were *necessary* judges in this case. The sentence has, moreover, a very passionate character; and in it Felix affects to give to his *see of Rome* the title of *Catholic—that is*, universal—in order that his authority should seem to extend over the whole Church.

From this we perceive that if the Bishops of Rome did not, as Gregory the Great tells us, accept for their persons the title of œcumenical or *universal* which the Council of Chalcedon is said to have offered them, they endeavored, shortly after, to claim for this see not merely an *honorary* title, but an *œcumenical* authority, as contrary to the intentions of the council as to the traditions of the entire Church. The Bishop of Rome showed himself disposed to exaggerate his prerogatives, in proportion as Acacius became more influential in the direction of the affairs of the Eastern Church; he became more angry as the Bishop of Constantinople treated him with more arrogance. Acacius despised the sentence of the Bishop of Rome, and even refused to receive it. Some bishops

---

201 Felic., Epist. Labbe's Collection, vol. iv. Evag. Eccl. Hist.

V. Roman Bishop Authority of the 6th, 7th, and 8th Centuries 175

having declared against him, he caused them to be deposed; and Rome, on her part, excommunicated his adherents. After the death of Acacius, in 489, the dissension respecting him continued. If one could doubt the share that the jealousy of Rome had in her opposition to Acacius, such doubt would not survive the perusal of what Pope Gelasius wrote on this subject in 495. Having received a letter from the bishops of Dardania in which he was informed that the partisans of Acacius relied principally upon the irregularity of the sentence passed against him by the Italian Council, Gelasius replied to them, justifying himself by the Council of Chalcedon, which, he claimed, "condemned in advance those who should oppose it."[202] But this was precisely the question—whether Acacius had failed in the respect due to the Council of Chalcedon, by endeavoring to quiet the troubles raised in the East respecting that assembly. One evident fact is that Acacius, in his efforts to settle these troubles, and in showing himself tolerant toward men, had sacrificed nothing of the Catholic doctrine defined at Chalcedon. No less clear is it that the men condemned first at Constantinople, and afterward at Rome, had never been heard face to face with their accusers; that they had numerous supporters; that they had been condemned, banished, and persecuted through the imperial power from which the Roman bishops were incessantly demanding severity, as their letters show. It is not, therefore, to be wondered at that Acacius, even after his death, should have been regarded in the East as a great and holy bishop, and that the sentence of the Italian Council should have been considered as null and void. Gelasius is not happy in his answer to the objection of the bishops of Dardania to the illegality of this sentence. In return, he shows a great deal of temper when he tries to confute the argument drawn in favor of Acacius from the importance of the Byzantine see. "We laughed," he says,[203] "at the prerogative that they [the Eastern bishops] claim

---

202 It was therefore under the false pretext of his opposition to the council of Chalcedon that Rome had deposed Acacius, which bellies the assertion contained in the work already cited, that no dogmatic question was pending between Rome and Constantinople under Acacius. Part I. ch. 3.

203 Gelas., Ep. ad Episcop. Dard.

for Acacius because he was bishop of the imperial city. Did not the Emperor reside for a long time at Ravenna, Milan, Sirmium, and Tréves? Have the bishops of these cities exceeded, on this account, the limits that antiquity has prescribed to them? If the question be upon the dignity of cities, the bishops of a second- or third-rate see have more dignity than the bishops of *a city which is not even a metropolis*. The power of the secular empire is one thing, and the distribution of ecclesiastical dignities quite another. However small a city may be, it does not diminish the greatness of the prince who dwells there; but it is quite as true that the presence of the emperor does not change the order of religion; and such a city should rather profit by such an advantage to preserve the freedom of religion by keeping peaceably within its proper limits."

But what, then, was the foundation of the dignity of the Roman Church? Gelasius could indicate none other but the Council of Nicea. Now has not one œcumenical council the same rights as another? If at Nicea the Church had so ruled the hierarchal rank that Rome and Alexandria should be superior to Antioch and Jerusalem, because their sees were more important, why should not the Council of Chalcedon have had the right to put Constantinople before Alexandria, and even before Rome? If, in the spirit of the Council of Nicea, Rome and Alexandria must precede Antioch and Jerusalem, it was evidently only because of their political importance, as was very properly expressed by the Council of Chalcedon. Why, then, should not Constantinople—already more important than Alexandria, and now the capital of the empire—why should she not be raised to a superiour hierarchal rank?

Gelasius was far from the point when he spoke of the imperial *residences* of Trèves, Milan, Ravenna, and Sirmium; for these cities were never *reigning cities or capitals*, like Rome and Constantinople. He went so far in his anger as to refuse Constantinople the bare title of metropolis, because the ancient Byzantium was not one. It is thus that, while accusing and condemning Acacius for his alleged opposition to the Council of Chalcedon, Rome affected to trample on the decrees of that very same Council. Of what consequence is it that Pope Leo protested against these decrees under cover of

V. Roman Bishop Authority of the 6th, 7th, and 8th Centuries 177

those of Nicea? It is none the less true that those of Chalcedon are of equal value, since that assembly was equally œcumenical.

It is not our business, however, to notice all the historical blunders and erroneous assertions of the letter of Gelasius. We have only sought to show that the more Constantinople increased in influence the more Rome sought to humble her. The motive of this is easily understood. Rome was in the hands of the barbarians, losing each day more her *prestige*, while Constantinople, on the contrary, was at the height of her splendour.

In one of his treatises against Acacius,[204] Gelasius reviews the decree of the Council of Chalcedon, which granted the second rank in the Church to the Bishop of Constantinople.

He pretends that this decree is of no force because it was rejected by the Roman see. Why, then, does this see take for the foundation of its argument the Council of Nicea as having of itself a superiour authority to which Rome herself should submit? Was it not because the Council of Nicea was œcumenical? But was not the Council of Chalcedon equally so, and hence was not its authority the same as that of the Nicene Council?

Evidently Rome, by reason of her antipathy against Constantinople, put herself in a false position. To escape from it there was but one course open to her, namely, to proclaim that she held her authority from God, and was superiour to that of the councils. This course she took. She so affirmed timidly at first, openly when she saw a favorable opportunity.

These papal tendencies first appeared in the letters and instructions from the Popes in matters connected with those troubles which had arisen from the pretended deposition of Acacius. Nearly the entire East regarded this sentence as null. The Popes sustained it and confounded that affair with that of the Council of Chalcedon, in order to give it more importance; nevertheless, the prevailing doctrine, even in these documents, is that the council could alone determine the basis of reconciliations, thus excluding the idea of a central and sovereign authority at Rome or elsewhere. That thought chiefly pervades the writings of Gelasius and Hormisda, who took

---

204 Gelas. de. Anath.

the chief part in the troubles of the East.[205] Peace was restored in a council held at Constantinople (A.D. 519), and upon conditions discussed with equal authority by either side. When in 525 Pope John I went to Constantinople by order of Theodoric, King of Italy, to plead for the Arians, he was invited to celebrate mass on Easter day. He accepted on condition *that he might be permitted to occupy the first seat*. None denied him this privilege; still the demand betrays in the Papacy a serious anxiety on the subject of the Roman primacy. The Bishop of Constantinople was then rich and influential; the Bishop of Rome, on the contrary, subject to the whims of heretical kings, was in such povert that in 536, when Agapitus was made to go to Constantinople by order of Theodotus, king of the Goths, he was forced to sell some of the consecrated vessels in order to raise money sufficient for the journey. Agapitus was received by the Emperor Justinian with honors. The Emperor had called to the see of Constantinople Anthymus, Bishop of Trebizond, known for his attachment to the errors of Eutyches. The bishops who were at Constantinople availed themselves of the presence of the Pope, to hold with him a council against Anthymus, who preferred to return to his see of Trebizond, rather than to make a Catholic confession of faith. Mennas, chosen in his place by the clergy and people, and confirmed by the Emperor, was consecrated by the Pope. In a letter from the Eastern bishops, it is remarked that they give to Agapitus the titles of *Father of fathers and Patriarch*, and that in a letter from the monks he was *called Archbishop of the ancient Rome and œcumenical Patriarch*.[206] These titles were merely honorary and in the style of the age, especially in the East. They gave the title of *Father of fathers* to every bishop whom they particularly wished to honor. This proves nothing in favor of an authority which the Popes themselves did not yet claim.

The discussions relating to the "*Three Chapters*" furnish an incontestable proof of our assertion.

Ever since the Council of Chalcedon, the East had been filled with the most animated discussions; the most subtle reasoning

---

205 See their letters in Labbe's Collection of Councils, vol. iv.

206 Labbe, vol. v.

was resorted to. Some openly tampered with the doctrine of the council, in order that they might attack it to better advantage; others denied its orthodoxy, as contrary to the Council of Ephesus and to St. Cyril. The latter charge arose from this, that the Fathers of Chalcedon had given cause to believe that they approved of the doctrine of Theodorus, Bishop of Mopsuestia; a letter of Ibas; and the writings of Theoderet against the anathemas of St. Cyril. The Emperor Justinian took great part in theological discussions, partly from inclination, and also because the various factions, each seeking to enlist him on their side, referred their causes to him. He thought that he had found the means of reuniting men's minds on the subject of the Council of Chalcedon by clearing up the misunderstandings which the three writings above mentioned had occasioned, and condemning them, which he did, in fact. These are called the *Three Chapters*. They certainly had a Nestorian tendency; the authors were no longer at hand to explain them; and all that was requisite was to condemn the Nestorianism in their writings.

Justinian sent the condemnation of the Three Chapters to all the bishops, with orders to sign it. Some obeyed this; others resisted, regarding that condemnation only as an attack on the Council of Chalcedon. Pope Vigilius was ordered to Constantinople by Justinian.

After refusing to concur in the condemnation, he consented *without prejudice to the Council of Chalcedon*. This reservation left unsatisfied the enemies of the council, while it did not excuse the condemnation in the eyes of the other party. The bishops of Africa, Illyria, and Dalmatia, and many other bishops individually, separated from the communion of Vigilius. Those of Africa solemnly excommunicated him in a council in 551.[207]

Without passing on the question at issue, these facts show clearly that in the sixth century the Bishop of Rome was regarded neither as infallible nor as the *centre* of Catholic unity; that this centre was believed to rest only in the pure and orthodox faith, and in the councils that represented the whole Church.

---

207 See Facundi, op. edit. of Father Sirmond; and for the documents, Labbe's Collection of Councils. See also the Eccl. Hists. of Evag. and Theoph.

Vigilius, alarmed by the condemnations that were showered upon him, asked the Emperor for an œcumennical council to close the discussion. Justinian consented and convoked the bishops. Vigilius withdrew his signature, and it was agreed that all should let the matter rest until the decision of the council. This proves that at Rome, as elsewhere, no infallible doctrinal authority was recognized, except that of the episcopate—the only interpreter of the universal faith.

Vigilius refused to attend the meetings of the council under pretext that the West was not as numerously represented as the East. He was told that the number of Western bishops then at Constantinople was greater than it had been at the other œcumenical councils. This objection raised by Vigilius proves that he did not think he could, *by his presence or by delegation*, give an œcumenical character to a council, as is now assumed at Rome.

Nevertheless, Vigilius sent to the council his opinion upon the *Three Chapters*, opposing their condemnation. The council paid no heed to his opposition, examined carefully the three writings, and condemned the doctrine in them as opposed to anteriour councils, particularly to that of Chalcedon, which was solemnly recognized as œcumenical and thus on the same ground with those of Nicea, Constantinople, and Ephesus.

Before giving sentence, the council rehearsed its proceedings in respect to Vigilius. "When The Most Pious Vigilius," it said,[208] "was in this city; he took part in all the discussions concerning the Three Chapters, and condemned them several times both in writing and by word of mouth. After this he agreed, in writing, to come to the council and examine them with us, in order to come to a common decision. The Emperor having, in pursuance of our agreement, exhorted us to assemble, we were obliged to entreat Vigilius to fulfill his promise, recalling to him the example of the Apostles, who, filled with the Holy Ghost individually, and needing no deliberation, would not, nevertheless, determine the question 'whether the Gentiles must be circumcised,' until they had met in council and had strengthened their opinions by passages from

---

208 Labbe's Collection of Councils. Counc. of Const. session 8.

Scripture. The Fathers who in times past have held the four councils have followed the ancient examples, and have decided together all questions concerning heretics; *for there is no other way of knowing the truth in questions of faith.*

"According to Scripture, each one has need of his brother's aid, and when two or three are gathered together in the name of Jesus Christ, he is in the midst of them. We have therefore repeatedly invited Vigilius, and the Emperor has sent officers to him for the same object; but he has only promised to give his judgment *in private* touching the Three Chapters. Having heard his reply, we have all considered what the Apostle says, *'That everyone shall give account of himself to God'*; and on the other hand, we have feared the judgment with which those are threatened who scandalize the brethren."

Then the council relates all that was done in examining the Three Chapters; it condemns them, while it declares its respect for the Council of Chalcedon. By this wise decision, the fifth œcumenical council disproved the accusations that passionate men had spread among the Westerns touching the evil dispositions of most of its members. At the same time, it exposed the pretexts held out by the adversaries of the Council of Chalcedon for rejecting the decisions of that holy assembly. It thus powerfully contributed to quiet the dissensions.

Vigilius saw he had been wrong in undertaking the defence of a bad doctrine, under pretence of his respect for the Council of Chalcedon. Six months after the closing of the council, he wrote to Eutychius, the Patriarch of Constantinople, acknowledging *that he had sinned against charity in separating himself from his brethren.* He adds that no one should be ashamed to retract, when he discovers the truth. "Having," he says, "examined the matter of the Three Chapters, I again find them condemnable." Then he declares against those who sustain them, and condemns his own writings in their defence. He publishes finally a long memorial to prove that the Three Chapters contained unsound doctrine.[209] He returned to communion with those whom he had previously anathematized, and peace was restored.

---

209 Labbe's Collection, vol. v.

The fifth œcumenical council was neither convoked nor presided over by the Bishop of Rome, although he was present in the city where the council was held. The meetings were held not only without him, but against him. Nevertheless, the decision of this council was considered canonical, and the Pope himself, after some objections arising out of his ignorance of certain facts, submitted to it. The West concurred with the council thus assembled without the Pope and against the Pope, and thus the assembly acquired its œcumenical character.

All the circumstances of this great fact of ecclesiastical history prove, beyond dispute, that nothing was known in the sixth century, even at Rome, of these pretended prerogatives that are now ascribed to the Papacy.

The discussions that took place at the close of that century, between John the Faster, successor of Eutychius, at Constantinople, and Pope Gregory the Great, clearly establish the same truth.

We have already mentioned that the title of *œcumenical* had been given to the Bishop of Rome as a mere honor in the Council of Chalcedon; that Pope Felix had affected to give to his see the title of *catholic* in the same sense; and that some Oriental monks had called Pope Agapitus ecumenical Patriarch. These precedents were copied at Constantinople. The emperors were bent upon raising the Patriarch of that capital, which they called *the new Rome*, to the same degree of honor as belonged to the one of ancient Rome, still keeping him in the second rank but only in respect of seniority. The Emperor Maurice thus gave to John the Faster the title of œcumenical *Patriarch*.

Pope Pelagius II and his successor Gregory the Great protested against this title.

Gregory then wrote those famous letters which so absolutely condemn the modern Papacy. We will give some extracts from them.

At the beginning of his episcopate, Gregory addressed a letter of communion to the Patriarchs John of Constantinople, Eulogius of Alexandria, Gregory of Antioch, John of Jerusalem, and to Anastasius, formerly Patriarch of Antioch, his friend. If he had considered himself the chief and sovereign of the Church; if he had

V. Roman Bishop Authority of the 6th, 7th, and 8th Centuries

believed he was so by *divine right*, he would certainly have addressed the Patriarchs as subordinates; we should find in that encyclical letter some traces of his superiority. The fact is quite the reverse of this. It speaks at great length of the *duties* of the episcopate, and not even dreams of mentioning the *rights* which such a dignity would have conferred on him.

He particularly insists upon the duty of a bishop not to permit himself to be engrossed by the cares of external things, and concludes his encyclical letter with his confession of faith, in order to prove himself in communion with the other Patriarchs, and through them with all the Church.[210]

Such silence on St. Gregory's part concerning the pretended *rights* of the Papacy is of itself significant enough, and Romish theologians would find it difficult to explain.

What, then, shall they oppose to the letters from which we are about to give a few extracts, and in which St. Gregory most unreservedly condemns the very idea which is the foundation of their Papacy as they understand it—that is, the universal character of its authority?

Gregory to John, Bishop of Constantinople:
"You remember, my brother, the peace and concord which the Church enjoyed when you were raised to the sacerdotal dignity. I do not, therefore, understand how you have dared to follow the inspiration of pride, and have attempted to assume a title which may give offence to all the brethren. I am the more astonished at it that I remember your having taken flight to avoid the episcopate; and yet you would exercise it today, as if you had run toward it, impelled by ambitious desires. You who used to say so loud that you were unworthy of the episcopate, you are no sooner raised to it than, despising your brethren, you aspire to have alone the title of bishop. My predecessor, Pelagius, of saintly memory, wrote very seriously to your Holiness upon this subject. He rejected, in consequence of the proud and magnificent title that you assumed in them, the acts of the synod which you assembled in the cause

---

210 St. Greg. Pap. Epist. 25, lib. 1.

of Gregory, our brother and fellow-bishop; and to the archdeacon, whom, according to usage, he had sent to the Emperor's court, he forbade communion with you. After the death of Pelagius, having been raised, notwithstanding my unworthiness, to the government of the Church,[211] it has been my care to urge you, my brother, not by writing, but by word of mouth, first by my envoy,[212] and afterward through our common son, Deacon Sabinian, to give up such assumption. I have forbidden him also to communicate with you if you should refuse to yield to my request, in order that your Holiness may be inspired with shame for your ambition, before resorting canonical proceedings, in case shame should not cure you of pride so profane and so reprehensible. As before resorting to amputation, the wound should be tenderly probed, I pray you—I entreat you—I ask with the greatest possible gentleness, that you, my brother, will resist all the flatterers who give you an erroneous title, and that you will not consent to ascribe to yourself a title as senseless as vainglorious. Verily I have tears for this; and from the bottom of my heart I ascribe it to my own sins that my brother has not been willing to return to lowliness—he who was raised to the episcopal dignity only to teach other souls to be lowly; that he who teaches others the truth would neither teach it to himself, nor consent, for all my prayers, that I should teach it him.

"I pray you, therefore, reflect that by your bold presumption the peace of the whole Church is troubled, and that you are at enmity *with that grace, which was given to all in common.* The more you grow in that grace, the more humble you will be in your own eyes; you will be the greater in proportion as you are further removed from usurping this extravagant and vainglorious title. You will be the richer as you seek less to despoil your brethren to your profit. Therefore, dearly beloved brother, love humility with all your heart. It is that which ensures peace among the brethren, and *which preserves unity in the Holy Catholic Church.*

---

211 According to St. Gregory, every bishop has a part in the government of the Church, the authority residing in the episcopate.

212 The Bishop of Rome had kept representatives at the court of Constantinople ever since that city had become the imperial residence.

"When the Apostle Paul heard certain of the faithful say, '*I am of Paul of Apollos, and I of Cephas,*' he could not see them, without horror, thus rending the body of the Lord to attach his members to various heads; and he exclaimed, 'Was Paul crucified for you?—or were ye baptized in the name of Paul?' If he could not bear that the members of the body of the Lord *should be attached piecemeal to other heads than that of Christ, though those heads were Apostles*, what will you say to Christ, who is the head of the universal Church—what will you say to him at the last judgment—you who, by your title of universal, would bring all his members into subjection to yourself? Whom, I pray you tell me, whom do you imitate by this perverse title if not him who, despising the legions of angels, his companions endeavored to mount to the highest that he might be subject to none and be alone above all others; who said, '*I will ascend into heaven; I will exalt my throne above the stars of God; I will sit also upon the mount of the congregation, in the sides of the North; I will ascend above the heights of the clouds; I will be like the Most High*' ? What are your brethren, the bishops of the universal Church, but the stars of God? Their lives and teaching shine, in truth, through the sins and errors of men, as do the stars through the darkness of the night. When, by your ambitious title, you would exalt yourself above them and debase their title in comparison with your own, what do you say, if not these very words, *I will ascend into heaven; I will exalt my throne above the stars of God?* Are not all the bishops the clouds that pour forth the rain of instruction, and who are furrowed by the lightnings of their own good works? In despising them, my brother, and endeavoring to put them under your feet, what else do you say than that word of the ancient enemy, *I will ascend above the heights of the clouds?* For my part, when, through my tears, I see all this, I fear the secret judgments of God; my tears flow more abundantly; my heart overflows with lamentations to think that my Lord John—a man so holy, of such great abstinence and humility, but now seduced by the flattery of his familiars—should have been raised to such a degree of pride that, through the lust of a wrongful title, he should endeavor to resemble him who, vaingloriously wishing to be like God, lost, because he was ambitious of a false glory, the grace of the divine resemblance that had been granted to him, and the true beatitude. Peter, the first of the Apostles, and a *member* of the holy and universal Church; Paul, Andrew, John—were they not the chiefs of certain nations? And yet all are members under *one only head*. In a word, the saints *before the law*, the saints *under the law*, the saints *under grace*—do they not all constitute the body of the Lord? Are they not members of the Church? Yet there is none among them who desired to be called universal. Let your Holiness consider, therefore, how much you are puffed up when you claim a title that none of them had the presumption to assume. Not even Peter.

"You know it, my brother; hath not the venerable Council of Chalcedon conferred the honorary title of universal upon the bishops of this Apostolic See, whereof I am, by GOD'S will, the servant? And yet none of us hath permitted this title to be given to him; none hath assumed this bold title, lest by assuming a special distinction in the dignity of the episcopate we should seem to refuse it to all the brethren.

....'The Lord, wishing to recall to a proper humility the yet feeble hearts of his disciples, said to them, 'If any man desire to be first, the same shall be last of all'; whereby we are clearly taught that he who is truly high is he who is most humble in mind. Let us, therefore, beware of being of the number of those 'who love the chief seats in the synagogues, and greetings in the markets, and to be called of men, Rabbi, Rabbi.' In fact, the Lord said to his disciples, *'Be ye not called Rabbi, for one is your Master... and all ye are brethren. Neither be ye called Fathers, for ye have but one Father.'*

"What then could you answer, beloved brother, in the terrible judgment to come, who desire not only to be called Father, but universal Father of the world? Beware then of evil suggestions; fly from the counsel of offence. *'It is impossible,'* indeed, *'but that offences will come*; but, for all that, WOE unto *him through whom they come!'* In consequence of your wicked and vainglorious title, the Church is divided and the hearts of the brethren are offended.

... "I have sought again and again, by my messengers and by humble words, to correct the sin which has been committed *against the whole Church. Now* I myself write. I have omitted nothing that humility made it my duty to do. If I reap from my rebuke nothing better than contempt, there will nothing be left for me but to appeal to *the Church*."

By this first letter of St. Gregory we see, first, that ecclesiastical authority *resides in the episcopate*, and not in any one bishop, however high in the ecclesiastical hierarchy; second, that it was not *his private cause* that Gregory defended against John of Constantinople, *but that of the whole Church*; third, that he had not himself the right to judge the cause, and was compelled to refer it *to the Church*; fourth, that the title of *universal* bishop is contrary to God's word, and vainglorious and wicked; fifth, that no bishop, however high in the ecclesiastical hierarchy, can assume universal authority, without invading the rights of the entire episcopate; and last, that no bishop in the Church can claim to be Father of all Christians without assuming a title which is contrary to the Gospel, vainglorious, and wicked.

When John of Constantinople received his title of *universal* from the Emperor, Gregory wrote the following letter to that prince:[213]

"Our very pious lord does wisely to endeavor to accomplish the peace of the Church that he may restore peace to his empire, and to condescend to invite the priesthood to concord and unity. I myself desire it ardently; and as much as in me lies, I obey his worshipful commands. But since not my cause alone, but the cause of God is concerned; since it is not I alone who am disturbed, but the whole Church that is agitated; since the canons, the venerable councils, and the commandments of our Lord Jesus Christ himself are attacked, by the invention of a certain pompous and vainglorious word; let our most pious lord cut out this evil; and if the patient would resist him, let him bind him with the bonds of his imperial authority. In binding such things you will give liberty to the commonwealth, and by excisions of this sort you will diminish the malady of your empire.

"All those who have read the Gospel know that the care of the whole Church was confided by our Lord himself to St. Peter, first of all the Apostles. Indeed, he said to him, *'Peter, lovest thou me? Feed my sheep.'* Again it was said to him, *'Satan has desired to sift thee as wheat:*

---

[213] Letters of St. Gregory, Book V, Letter 20, Benedictine edition.

but I have prayed for thee, that thy faith fail not: and when thou art converted, strengthen thy brethren.' It was also said to him, '*Thou art Peter, and upon this rock I will build my Church: and the gates of hell shall not prevail against it: and l will give thee the keys of the kingdom of heaven: and whatsoever thou shalt bind on earth shall be* bound in *heaven*; *and whatsoever thou shalt loose on earth shall be loosed in* heaven.' He thus received the keys of the celestial kingdom; the power to bind and loose was given to him; the care of all the Church and the primacy were committed to him; and yet he did not call himself *universal Apostle*. But that most holy man, John, my brother in the priesthood, would fain assume the title of *universal bishop. I* can but exclaim, *O tempora! O mores!*"

We cannot pass over these words of St. Gregory without pointing out their great importance. This learned doctor interprets, as we have seen, the texts of the Gospel which refer to St. Peter in the sense most favorable to that Apostle. He exalts Peter as having had the primacy in the Apostolic college; as having been entrusted by the Lord himself with the care of the whole Church. What does he infer from all this? Ever since the Popes have abused the texts that he quotes, in order to attribute to themselves an *absolute* and *universal* authority in the Church, we know how they reason. They give to the language of the Gospel, in the first place, the very broadest and most absolute sense, and then apply it to themselves as the successors of St. Peter. St. Gregory acts quite otherwise: he places Peter's prerogatives side by side with his humility, which kept him from claiming universal authority; he is so far from holding himself out as Peter's heir that he only quotes the example of that Apostle to confound John of Constantinople, and all those who would claim universal authority in the Church. Thus he attacks, by St. Peter's example, the same authority that the popes have since claimed in the name of St. Peter and as his successors.

St. Gregory continues:

"Is it my cause, most pious lord, that I now defend? Is it a private injury that I wish to avenge? No; this is the cause of Almighty God, the cause of the universal Church.

"Who is he who, against the precepts of the Gospel and the decrees of the canons, has the presumption to usurp a new title?

V. Roman Bishop Authority of the 6th, 7th, and 8th Centuries

Would to Heaven there were but one who, without wishing to lessen the others, desired to be himself *universal*...

"The Church of Constantinople has produced bishops who have fallen in the abyss of heresy, and who have even become heresiarchs. Thence issued Nestorius, who, thinking there must be two persons in Jesus Christ, mediator between God and man, because be did not believe that God could become man, descended thus to the very perfidy of the Jews.

Thence came Macedonius, also, who denied that the Holy Spirit was God consubstantial with the Father and the Son. But if any one usurp in the Church a title which embraces all the faithful, the *universal* Church—O blasphemy!—will then fall with him, since he makes himself to be called the *universal*. May all Christians reject this blasphemous title—this title which takes the sacerdotal honor from every priest the moment it is insanely usurped by one!

"It is certain that this title was offered to the Roman Pontiff by the venerable Council of Chalcedon, to honor the blessed Peter, prince of the Apostles. But none of us has consented to use this particular title, lest, by conferring a special matter upon one alone, all priests should be deprived of the honor which is their due.

How, then, while we are not ambitious of the glory of a title that has been offered to us, does another, to whom no one has offered it, have the presumption to take it?"

This passage of Gregory is very remarkable. He first asserts that it was a council that offered the Bishops of Rome the honor of being called *universal*. Would this council have done this with a view to honor these bishops if it had believed that they already had universal authority by *divine right?* Moreover, St. Gregory asserts that the council wished to honor the bishops as an honor to St. Peter. He, therefore, did not believe that *universal authority* came to them by *succession from that Apostle*. The Church of Rome has cause to glory in St. Peter, for he made her illustrious by his martyrdom. It was, therefore, in remembrance of this martyrdom, and to *honor* this first of the Apostles, that the General Council of Chalcedon *offered* the Bishops of Rome this *honorary* title. How shall we reconcile these statements of St. Gregory with the pretensions of the modern

Bishops of Rome, who believe that of *divine right* they are invested not only with the title of *universal Bishop* and common *Father of the Faithful*, but also with a *universal sovereignty*?

These letters of St. Gregory are unquestionable records attesting that the universal Church was startled from the moment there appeared in her bosom the first glimmerings of a universal power residing in a single bishop. The whole Church understood that such authority could not be established without depriving the entire episcopate of its rights; in fact, according to divine institution, the government of the Church is *synodical*. Authority can, therefore, only reside in the entire body of legitimate pastors and not in any individual pastor.

We cannot declare in favor of the universal authority of one without destroying the divine principle of the organization of the Church.

This truth stands out prominently from the writings of Pope Gregory the Great.

He writes upon the same subject to Eulogius, Bishop of Alexandria, and Anastasius, Bishop of Antioch. He says to them: "Eight years ago, in the life of our predecessor, Pelagius, of saintly memory, our brother and fellow-bishop, John, taking occasion from some other matter, assembled a synod in the city of Constantinople and sought to assume the title of universal, which our predecessor no sooner learned than he sent letters by which, in virtue of the authority of the Apostle St. Peter, he nullified the acts of the synod."

Romish theologians have strangely misused this passage in favor of their system.

Had they compared it with the other texts from St. Gregory on the same subject, and with the whole body of his doctrine, they might have convinced themselves of two things: First, that in this passage Gregory only refers to the primacy granted by the councils to the Bishop of Rome because of the dignity of his see, made glorious by the martyrdom of St. Peter, first of the Apostles. Secondly, that the only question before the synod of Constantinople was one of mere discipline, in which the accused priest had appealed to Rome. Pelagius, then Bishop of Rome, was therefore judge in the last

V. Roman Bishop Authority of the 6th, 7th, and 8th Centuries 191

resort in this matter, in virtue of the primacy granted to his see. This primacy had been granted to his see for the sake of St. Peter. The Council of Chalcedon, in order *to honor St. Peter*, had also offered the title of *universal* to the Bishops or Rome, as we learn from St. Gregory.

But between this and a *sovereignty of divine right* coming to the popes by *succession from* St. Peter, there is a great gulf; yet Romanists have found it all in the text from St. Gregory above quoted; carefully avoiding, to quote, however, the other texts that limit its meaning, and teach us the true doctrine of this Pope. They often act thus in respect of their quotations from the councils and the Fathers of the Church, as we have already repeatedly shown.

St. Gregory continues:

"As your Holiness, whom I particularly venerate, well knows, this title of universal was offered by the holy Council of Chalcedon to the Bishop of the Apostolic see, which, by God's grace, I serve. But none of my predecessors would use this *impious word*, because, in reality, *if a Patriarch be called universal, this takes from all the others the title of Patriarch*. Far, very far, from every Christian soul be the wish to usurp anything that might diminish, however little, the honor of his brethren! When we deny ourselves an honor that has been offered to us, consider how humiliating it is to see it violently usurped by another."

Roman theologians have carefully avoided calling attention to this passage, where St. Gregory considers himself *a Patriarch* equal to the other Patriarchs; where he clearly says, if one of the Patriarchs may claim to be universal, the others are, *ipso facto*, no more Patriarchs. This doctrine perfectly agrees with that of the *primacy* granted to the Patriarch of Rome, for St. Peter's sake, and in remembrance of the *martyrdom* suffered by this *first of the Apostles* at Rome; but does it agree with a UNIVERSAL *sovereignty*, coming by *divine right* to the Bishops of Rome, through Peter, their assumed predecessor? Assuredly not.

St. Gregory continues to unfold a teaching contrary to the modern Papal system: "Therefore," he says, "let your Holiness not give to anyone in your letters the title of *universal*, lest you deprive yourself of your own due by offering to another an honor *that you do not owe to him*. For my part, though separated from you by great distance of land and sea, I am, nevertheless, closely bound to you in heart. I am confident that such are also the sentiments of your Holiness toward me; if you love me as I love you, no distance can separate us. Thanks be, then, to that grain of mustard-seed which was, indeed, in appearance, small and contemptible, but which, spreading afar its branches, sprung all from one root, has formed a shelter for all the birds of the air! Thanks be, also, to that leaven which, hidden in three measures of meal, has joined in one unity the whole of mankind.

Thanks, again, for that little stone, broken without effort from the mountain that has covered the whole surface of the earth, which has so extended itself as to make out of the human race, now united, the body of the universal Church, which has even made distinctions of the parts serve to rivet the bonds of unity.

"Hence it follows that we are not far from you, since we are *one* in Him who is everywhere. Let us give Him thanks for having so destroyed all enmities that, in his humanity, there is in the world but one fold and one flock, under one shepherd, which is Christ himself. Let us always remember these warnings of the Preacher of truth: '*Endeavoring to keep the unity of the Spirit in the bond of peace*' (Ephes. 4: 3). '*Follow peace with all men, and holiness, without which no man shall see the Lord*' (Heb. 12: 14). The same said to HIS DISCIPLES, '*If it be possible, as much as lieth in you, live peaceably with all men*' (Romans 12: 18). He knew that the good could have no peace with the wicked; therefore, he says at once, as you know, '*If it be possible.*'"

Let us pause a moment over this part of Gregory's letter. Is it not remarkable that, in speaking of the Church as *one* flock under the guidance of a *single pastor*, which is Jesus Christ, he expressly says that Jesus Christ is the only *visible* pastor of the Church, or, which is the same thing, that he is the pastor *in his humanity, in his flesh*, according to the whole strength of the expression, "*in carne suâ?*"

Does not this exclude all idea of a universal pastor, taking the place of and representing Christ? Therefore, does it not, in one

V. Roman Bishop Authority of the 6th, 7th, and 8th Centuries   193

word, destroy all the assumptions of the modern Papacy, and reduce the true Papacy to a primacy established by the Church?

Further, St. Gregory, in quoting the epistle *to the Romans*, calls these *Romans "disciples" of St. Paul*. St. Paul only wrote his epistle to the Christians at Rome, A.D. 58. There were then at Rome very few Christians—not established as a Church, properly so called, and assembling at, the house of Aquila, one of their number. They had come to Rome from various countries that had been evangelized by St. Paul, and are thus called by St. Gregory his disciples. They wrote to him, beseeching him to visit and instruct them. Paul replied to them by his letter, in which he promises to evangelize Rome. He went there *two years* later. There he found some Jews, who only knew the Christians by name, and who, therefore, cannot have already been converted by St. Peter, their special Apostle. Paul formed a church at Rome and gave it for a bishop one Linus, his disciple, whom Tertullian, St. Irenæus, and Eusebius mention, as we have already seen, as the first Bishop of Rome.

Where, now, is the alleged episcopate of St. Peter at Rome, upon which the Ultramontanes base all their systems? St. Peter evidently came to Rome but a short time before he suffered martyrdom there. It was *because of the martyrdom of the first* of the Apostles, and not because of his episcopate at Rome, that the councils, like that of Chalcedon and that of Sardica, for example, granted certain special privileges to the Bishops of Rome.

Nor does St. Gregory, in his letters to the Patriarchs, endeavor to ascribe to himself, by right of Apostolic succession from St. Peter, an authority which was not his; he even very justly traces his Church back to St. Paul, and not to St. Peter. Thus, when in another place he calls the authority of his predecessor the *authority of St. Peter*, he means by that only the rights which the Bishops of Rome had received from the councils for the *honor of St. Peter*, who had made that Church illustrious by his glorious death!

Could anyone find in St. Gregory's "Letter To the Patriarchs" the language of a superiour toward his subordinates? St. Gregory, *as first bishop* of the Church, *as first of the Patriarchs*, takes the lead, calls the attention of the other Patriarchs, *his brethren*, to the encroachments of one of their number. He entreats them to join him in resisting what he regards as a misfortune for the whole episcopate; nay, for the *universal* Church. He does not make the slightest allusion to any superiour authority in himself; he appeals only to the divine precept and to the canons, against a usurpation which he calls diabolical. Is this the language of a chief, of a universal monarch? Clearly not. We cannot read this beautiful letter of St. Gregory to the Patriarchs of Antioch and Alexandria without being convinced that such a Papacy, as is now assumed to be of divine *right*, was unknown to him; that he cried out against tendencies that may be looked upon as the first attempts at *universal jurisdiction*; that he looked upon those first attempts as an enterprise which might upset the Church and which threatened the rights of the entire priesthood. Perhaps he attached too much importance to a purely *honorary* title which only emanated from the imperial authority; but he saw, under this title, an anti-canonical undertaking and the first attempts at a universal Papacy. What would he say of this Papacy itself, with all its modern pretensions? He would justly show himself its greatest enemy, and would see in it the source of all the evils with which the Church has been for centuries overwhelmed.

The Patriarch of Alexandria, not replying to him, Gregory wrote asking for his opinion.[214]

Thereupon John of Constantinople died. Gregory wrote at once to his successor, Cyriacus, who had sent him a letter of communion. He congratulates him upon his faith, but adds, concerning the title of *universal*, which he had followed the example of his predecessor in taking:

"We shall truly be at peace[215] if you renounce the pride of an impious title, according to the word of the Apostle of the Gentiles, '*Timothy, keep that which is committed to thy trust, avoiding profane and vain babblings*' (1 Tim. 6:20). It is indeed too unjust that those who have become the preachers of humility should glory in a vain title of pride. The Preacher of truth says, '*God forbid that I should glory save in the cross of our Lord Jesus Christ*' (Gal. 6: 14). Hence he is truly glorious

---

214 Letters of St. Gregory, Book VI, Ep. 60, Benedictine Ed.

215 Ibid., Book VII, Ep. 4.

V. Roman Bishop Authority of the 6th, 7th, and 8th Centuries

who glories not *in temporal power, but in what he suffers for the name of Christ*. In this we heartily embrace you; in this we recognize you as priest, if, repelling the vanity of titles, you occupy a holy see with holy humility.

"For we have been offended in respect to a sinful title; we have had a grudge concerning it, and we have declared loudly on the subject. Now you know, my brother, that the Truth hath said, '*If thou bring thy gift to the altar, and there rememberest that thy brother hath something against thee, leave there thy gift before the altar, and go thy way; first be reconciled to thy brother, and then come and offer thy gift*' (St. Matt. 5:23–24). Thus, although every fault is wiped away by the sacrifice, the evil of giving offence to the brethren *is* so great that the Lord will not accept from him who is guilty of it the sacrifice that usually atones for sin. Hasten, therefore, to purify your heart of this offence, that the Lord may look with favor upon the offering of your gift."

Gregory, having occasion to write again to Cyriacus, alludes again to the subject, so much importance did he attach to it:

"I could not express to you in this letter," says he,[216] "how my soul is bound to you; but I pray Almighty God, by the gift of his grace, to strengthen still more this union between us, and destroy all occasion of offence, in order that the holy Church, united by a confession of the true faith, of which the bonds are riveted by the reciprocal sentiments of the faithful, may suffer no damage from any discussions that the priests may have among themselves. As for me, in spite of all I say, and through all the opposition that I make to certain acts of pride, I preserve charity in the depth of my heart, God be thanked, and while I sustain externally the claims of justice, I do not inwardly repel those of love and affection.

"On your part, reciprocate my sentiments and respect the rights of peace and affection, that, remaining in unity of spirit, there may be left no subject of division between us. We shall the more easily obtain the grace of the Lord if we come before him with united hearts."

---

216 Ibid., Book VI, letter v.

Cyriacus was not touched by Gregory's tender exhortations, who, sometime after, wrote to the Patriarch of Antioch, blaming him, in a friendly way, for not attaching enough importance to the usurpation of their brother of Constantinople. We see by that letter that the Patriarch of Antioch feared to draw upon himself the displeasure of the Emperor if he declared against the Patriarch of Constantinople. He wrote his friend, St. Gregory, a very flattering letter. "But," replied the great Pope, "your Holiness, I perceive, would have your letter like the bee that carries both honey and a sting, that you might both satisfy me with honey and sting me. But I have found in this an occasion to reflect upon these words of Solomon, 'Faithful are the wounds of a friend; but the kisses of an enemy are deceitful.' (Prov. 27:6).

"As regards what You say to me concerning the title whereat I am offended, that I should yield, because the thing is of no importance, the Emperor has written me to the same effect. That which he says, by virtue of his power, I know you say out of friendship. I am not surprised to find the same expressions in your letter as in that of the Emperor, for love and power have many things in common; both are in the first rank, and they always speak with authority.

"When I received the synodical letter from our brother and fellow-bishop, Cyriacus, I did not see fit to put off replying to him, in spite of the impious title he assumed in it, lest I should thereby trouble the unity of the holy Church; but I took care to tell him my opinion touching this grand and superstitious title; I told him that he could not have peace with us if he did not refrain from taking this title of pride, which was but an *invention of the first apostate*. You must not consider this same affair as unimportant; for, if we tolerate it, *we corrupt the faith of the whole Church*. You know how many, not heretics only but heresiarchs, have arisen in the church of Constantinople. Not to speak of the injury done to your dignity, it cannot be denied that if any one bishop be called *universal*, all the Church *crumbles* if that *universal one* fall. But far be it from me to lend an ear to such folly, to such *levity*! I confide in the all-powerful Lord, who will fulfill the promise he has made, '*Whosoever exalteth himself shall be abased*'" (Luke 14:11).

No one could more wisely estimate than does St. Gregory the serious inconveniences that the Church might suffer from a central authority assuming to *represent* and sum up the Church. Man, whatever he may be, and frequently from the superiour dignity itself with which he is invested, is subject to error: *if the Church be summed up in him*, the Church falls with him. Such is St. Gregory's reasoning. He foresaw but too well; and the Roman Church has fallen into endless errors, with a Pope who claims to sum her up in his own person and to be her infallible personification.

Happily, the Church of Jesus Christ is neither that of *one time* nor that of *one place*, and she may always be distinguished by the *Catholic criterion* so clearly set forth by the Fathers of the Church. Otherwise, we must cease to believe the promises of Christ, and must say in an absolute sense what St. Gregory said hypothetically, *The universal one has fallen, the whole Church has fallen*!

They said at the court of Constantinople that Gregory only made such fierce war against the title of *universal* from jealousy of the Bishop of the New Rome, and to debase him. The Emperor and Cyriacus wrote thus to him with all the respect that was his due; but Gregory made Cyriacus clearly understand that he had misjudged him. He sent to him and to the Emperor a deacon, Anatolius by name, to undeceive them, giving him letters for the Emperor and the Patriarch. To the latter, after thanking him for his flattering words, he says:[217]

"It must be not only by words, but by deeds, that you show to me and to all your brethren the splendour of your charity, by hastening to renounce a title of pride, which has been a cause of offence to all the churches. Fulfill these words, *'Endeavor to keep the unity of the Spirit in the bond of peace'* (Eph. 4:3), and this other, *'Give none occasion to the adversary to speak reproachfully'* (1 Tim. 5:14). Your charity will shine forth if there be no division between us in respect to a vainglorious title. I call Jesus to witness, from the depth of my soul, that I do not wish to give offence to any person, from the least to the greatest. I desire all to be great and honored, provided such honor detracts nothing from that which is due to Almighty God. Indeed, who*ever*

---

217 Letters of St. Gregory, Book VII, Ep. 31.

would be honored against God is not honorable in my eyes... In this matter I would injure no one; I would only defend that humility which is pleasing to God and the peace of the holy Church. Let the things newly introduced be therefore abrogated in the same manner as they have been established, and we shall preserve amongst us the purest peace of the Lord. What kindly relations can exist between us if our sentiments are but words, and we wound one another with our deeds?"

In his letter to the Emperor, Gregory devotes himself to refuting the argument that was drawn from the insignificance of this honorary title, to which they pretended, at Constantinople, not to attach any great importance. "I pray your Imperial Piety," he says,[218] "to observe that there are some frivolous things that are inoffensive, but also some others that are very hurtful. When Antichrist shall come and call *himself* God, it will be in itself a perfectly frivolous thing, but a very pernicious one. If we only choose to consider the number of syllables in this word, we find but two (De-us); but if we conceive the weight of iniquity of this title, we shall find it enormous. I say it without the least hesitation, *whoever calls himself the universal bishop, or desires this title, is, by his pride,* THE PRECURSOR OF ANTICHRIST, because he thus attempts to raise himself above the others. The error into which he falls springs from pride equal to that of Antichrist; for as that Wicked One wished to be regarded as exalted above other men, like a god, so likewise whoever would be called *sole bishop* exalteth himself above others."

Nowadays they teach, in the name of the Church and in favor of the Bishop of Rome, the same doctrine that St. Gregory stigmatized with so much energy. The partisans of the Papacy teach continually that the Pope has a universal authority—that he is *the universal bishop*—that, properly speaking, he is the *only bishop*, the *source* whence flows all ecclesiastical dignity, including the *episcopate*, which is but *indirectly* and *mediately* of divine right.

Such is the instruction that they would now foist upon us as *Catholic doctrine*. Do our modern innovators apprehend that Pope Gregory the Great regarded such a doctrine as *diabolical*, and has, in

---

218 Letters of St. Gregory, Book VII, Ep. 33.

V. Roman Bishop Authority of the 6th, 7th, and 8th Centuries

anticipation, called this Pope, so invested with an assumed universal episcopate, Antichrist?

St. Gregory was in the habit of taking no important decision without giving information of it to the other Patriarchs. He therefore wrote to those of Alexandria and Antioch to inform them what course he had adopted with regard to the new Patriarch of Constantinople. Eulogius, Patriarch of Alexandria, was persuaded, and announced to Gregory that he would no longer give the title *universal* to the Bishop of Constantinople; but, thinking to flatter Gregory, whom he loved and who had done him service on many occasions, he gave the same title to him, and wrote that if he did not give it to the Bishop of Constantinople, it was in submission to the COMMANDS of Gregory. Gregory answered at once, and the following passage from his answer shows what idea he had of his own authority as bishop of Rome:

"Your Holiness has been at pains to tell us that in addressing certain persons you no longer give them certain titles that have no better origin than pride, using this phrase regarding me, *I as you have commanded.*' I pray you let me never again hear this word command; for I know who I am and who you are. BY YOUR POSITION YOU ARE MY BRETHREN; by your virtues you are my fathers. *I have, therefore, not commanded; I have only been careful to point out things which seemed to me useful.* Still I do not find that your Holiness has perfectly remembered what I particularly wished to impress on your memory; for I said *that you should no more give that title to me than to others*; and lo! in the superscription of your letter, you give to me, who have proscribed them, the vainglorious titles of *universal* and of *Pope*. May your sweet Holiness do so no more in future, I beseech you; *for you take from yourself what you give in excess to another. I do not ask to increase in dignities, but in virtues. I do not esteem that an honor which causes my brethren to lose their own dignity.* My honor is that of the whole Church. My honor is the unshaken firmness of my brethren. I consider myself truly honored when no one is denied the Honor due to him. If your Holiness calls me *universal Pope, you deny that you are yourself what I should then be altogether.* God forbid! Far from us be the words that puff up vanity and wound charity."

Thus did Pope Gregory condemn, even in the person of the Bishop of Rome, the title of *Pope* and that of *universal*. He acknowledges that the Patriarch of Alexandria is his equal, that he is not entitled to lay any commands upon him, and consequently that he has no authority over him.

How is this orthodox doctrine of St. Gregory's to be reconciled with the modern teaching that ascribes to the Pope a *universal authority of divine right*? Let the defenders of the Papacy answer.

St. Gregory, consistent with himself, sees the unity of the Church only in the true faith, and never makes the least allusion to the necessity of being in communion with the Church of Rome.

And no wonder; for he did not regard the see of Rome as the only see of St. Peter. He expressly acknowledged that the sees of Alexandria and Antioch were, quite as much as that of Rome, the see of the first of the Apostles, and that these three sees were but one. Let us quote his words. He writes thus to Eulogius, Patriarch of Alexandria:[219]

"Your Holiness has spoken to me at large, in your letters, of the see of St. Peter, prince of the Apostles, saying that he still resides here by his successors. Now, I acknowledge myself unworthy not only of the honor of the chiefs, but even to be counted in the number of the faithful. Yet I have willingly accepted all that you have said, because your words regarding the see of Peter *came from him who occupies that see of Peter*. A special honor has no charms for me; but I greatly rejoice that you, who are very holy, only ascribe to me what you also give to yourself. Indeed, who is ignorant that the holy Church has been made fast upon the solidity of the prince of the Apostles, whose name is the type of the firmness of his soul, and who borrowed from the rock his name of Peter?—that it was said to him by the Truth, 'I will give unto thee the keys of the kingdom of heaven ... . *When thou art converted, strengthen thy brethren... . Simon, Son of Jonas, lovest thou me? Feed my sheep.*" Therefore, though there were many Apostles, the single see of the prince of the Apostles prevailed by his princedom; which see now exists in three places; for it is he

---

219 Letters of St. Gregory, Book VII, Ep. 39.

V. Roman Bishop Authority of the 6th, 7th, and 8th Centuries 201

that made glorious that see where he condescended to rest (*quiescere*) and close his present life.

It is he who adorned the see, whither he sent the Evangelist, his disciple. It is he who strengthened the see which he occupied for seven years, although finally compelled to leave it. Since then there is but one see of the same Apostle, and three bishops now hold it by divine authority.

"All the good I bear of you I also impute to myself."

Observe that St. Gregory, in speaking of Rome, only says that St. Peter *rested* there and died there. To Alexandria he only sent his disciple; but at Antioch he *held the see* for seven years. If, then, in the strict acceptation of the words, any bishop has inherited *the see of* St. Peter, it must be, according to St. Gregory, the Bishop of Antioch. The great Pope was well aware that Peter only went to Rome to die there; that the Roman Church was already founded and governed by a bishop; he accordingly limits himself to saying that he made *glorious* the see of Rome by the martyrdom he suffered there, while he designates Antioch as the true episcopal see of Peter. We believe that St. Peter was, strictly speaking, no more *Bishop* of Antioch than of Rome; but we only wish to show what was the opinion of St. Gregory; and that opinion, whatever it was, is no less a withering argument against the pretensions of the court of Rome.

Writing to Anastasius, Patriarch of Antioch, to offer consolation in his sufferings, Gregory says:[220] "Behold now, your Holiness is weighed down with many tribulations in your old age; but remember what was *said of him whose seat you fill. Is it not of him that the Truth himself said, 'When thou shalt be old... another shall gird thee, and carry thee whither thou wouldest not?'*" (John 21: 18).

We know that these words were addressed by our Lord to St. Peter. In another letter to the same Anastasius, St. Gregory thus expresses himself after having quoted what he believed to be the words of St. Ignatius of Antioch:

"I have introduced in my letter these words drawn from your writings, that your Holiness may know that your own holy Ignatius is also ours. For as *we have* in common the master, the prince of the

---

220 Letters of St. Gregory, Book VIII, Ep. 2.

Apostles, we must neither of us exclusively claim the disciple of this prince of the Apostles."[221]

St. Gregory wrote to Eulogius, Patriarch of Alexandria, "We have received, with the same tenderness as it was given us the benediction of St. Mark the Evangelist, or rather, more properly speaking, of the Apostle St. Peter."[222]

He wrote again to the same, after having congratulated him upon his refutation of the errors of the *Monophysites*:

"Praise and glory be in the heavens to my saintly brother, thanks to whom the voice of Mark is heard from the *chair of Peter*, whose teaching resounds through the Church as the cymbal in the tabernacle when he fathoms the mysteries—that is to say, when, as priest of the Most High, he enters the Holy of Holies."[223]

Was anything more flattering ever said to the Bishops of Rome than Gregory here says to Eulogius of Alexandria? Does not the saintly Pope seem to copy the very words of the Council of Chalcedon, "Peter has spoken by the mouth of Leo"? Why draw such vast consequences from the words of the Fathers of Chalcedon, spoken in praise of the Bishop of Rome, and yet draw none whatever from those of the great Pope addressed to the Patriarch of Alexandria? He wrote again to the same:[224] "The bearers of these presents, having come to Sicily, were converted from the errors of the Monophysites and have joined the holy Church universal. *Desiring to go to the Church of the blessed Peter, prince of the Apostles*, they have besought me to give them commendatory letters to your Holiness in order that you might assist them against the attacks of their heretical neighbours."

In another letter, in which he discourses of simony, he writes to Eulogius: "Root out this simoniacal heresy from your *most holy see*, which is ours also." He calls the Church of Alexandria a *most*

---

221 Ibid., Book V, Ep. 39.

222 Ibid., Book VIII, Ep. 39.

223 Ibid., Book X, Ep. 35.

224 Ibid., Book XII, Ep. 50.

V. Roman Bishop Authority of the 6th, 7th, and 8th Centuries 203

holy church.[225] With such evidence before us, how can we draw any conclusion in favor of the Roman see from expressions like these of *apostolic see*, or *holy see*? Such epithets were common, during the first eight centuries, to all the churches founded by the Apostles, and were never exclusively employed to describe the Church of Rome.

From what we have shown of the doctrine of St. Gregory respecting the see of St. Peter, it is easy to see that no absolute sense can be honestly attached to such expressions as these: "My son, the lord Venantius has *come toward the blessed Apostle Peter* to beg me to commend his cause to you," etc.[226] "The care of the whole Church was confided to Peter, prince of the Apostles."[227] "He received the keys of the heavenly kingdom; the power to bind and to loose was given to him, the care of the whole Church and the princedom were intrusted to him."[228] "Who does not know that the holy Church has been strengthened by the firmness of the prince of the Apostles?"[229]

These expressions certainly belong to St. Gregory; but is it fair to quote them separately and give them an absolute sense? Yet this is the course of the Romish theologians, not only with the works of Gregory, but with all those of the other Fathers of the Church. In this manner they have succeeded in deceiving a great number of the faithful, and even many sincere theologians; the latter could not suspect such a strange dishonesty in writers who at every turn are boasting of their devotion to the cause of the Church and truth, and they have thought it safe to quote from them at second hand.

We can now understand what St. Gregory meant by the *see of St. Peter*, and by the titles of *first and prince of the Apostles*. But that we may throw still stronger light upon his thoughts, we will quote a few more texts, both decisive and clear, which shall determine the exact meaning of these phrases that have been so culpably misused by the advocates of Popery.

---

225 Letters of St. Gregory, Book XIII, Ep. 41.
226 Ibid., Book II, Ep. 53.
227 Ibid., Book V, Ep. 20.
228 Ibid.
229 Ibid., Book VII, Ep. 40.

St. Gregory, in his book upon the *Pastoral Rule*, lays down this principle: that the pastors of the Church should not use their authority toward blameless believers, but only toward sinners whom gentleness could not correct. In support of this principle he quotes the examples of the Apostles Peter and Paul. "Peter," he says, "*the first pastor holding the princedom of the holy Church, by the will of God, (auctore Deo)*, showed himself humble toward the faithful, *but showed how much power he had beyond others when he punished Ananias and Sapphira*; when it became necessary to punish sins, he remembered *that he was the highest in the Church (summus)* and, in taking vengeance of the crime, he exercised *the right of his power*."[230]

In the same passage he proves by the example of St. Paul, as well as by that of St. Peter, that the pastor should be humble toward the faithful and only exercise his power when he is compelled to take in hand the cause of justice. Thus St. Paul declared himself the servant of the faithful, the least among them; "but," adds St. Gregory, "when he finds a fault to correct, he remembers he is master, and says, 'What *will ye? I will come to you with a rod of iron.*' "Hence," concludes St. Gregory, "the highest places are best filled when he who presides rules rather his own vices than the brethren. But when *those who preside* correct those who are subject unto them, they should observe this duty," etc.[231]

It appears from this that St. Gregory regarded St. Paul as well as St. Peter and their successors as *filling the highest place* in the Church, as *presiding* in the Church. If he says that Peter held the *princedom*, he also says that Paul was *master*; he uses the same word (summus) to signify the authority of St. Peter and that of St. Paul, and of all those who have the right to exercise authority in the Church. Would he have expressed himself in a manner so general if by this word princedom he had meant to signify a superiour authority ascribed exclusively to St. Peter? Just as by the *see of St. Peter* he means the first degree of the episcopate represented by the Patriarchs; so likewise by the words "*superiour authority*" he only means that of the episcopate which the pastors of the Church have inherited.

---

230 St. Greg., Pastoral Rule, Part II, Chap. vi.

231 St. Greg. loc. cit.

V. Roman Bishop Authority of the 6th, 7th, and 8th Centuries

The more intimate we grow with the works of the Fathers of the Church, the more we are convinced of their unanimity in considering the authority in the church as one and possessed jointly and severally by the first pastors or the bishops. At first blush we might believe that the word "princedom," or that of *"prince"* of the Apostles, given by them to St. Peter, clashed with this principle. St. Gregory has shielded us from this false interpretation. For while ascribing to Peter the prince*dom* of the Church, he has not exalted him more than St. Paul. He shall tell us so most clearly in his own words. We read in his *Dialogues*:

"Peter. How can you prove to me that there be those who do no miracles, and yet are not inferior to those who do them?

"Gregory. Dost thou not know that the Apostle Paul is the *brother* of Peter, first of the Apostles in the *princedom*?

"Peter. I know this perfectly," etc., etc.[232]

Thus Paul was the equal or *brother* of Peter in the *Apostolic princedom*. Is it possible to say with greater clearness that by such titles no particular personal and exclusive dignity was intended?

In another place St. Gregory regards St. Paul as having a right, as well as St. Peter, to the title of *first* Apostle. In relating in his Dialogues the death of one Martin, a priest, he says that this holy man saw Peter and Paul calling him to heaven: "I see, I see," said Martin. "I thank you. I thank you!"

As he often repeated these words, his friends about him asked him to whom he spoke. He wondered at their question, and said, "Do you not see here the holy Apostles? Do you not perceive Peter and Paul the *first of the Apostles?*"[233]

And lastly, Gregory leads us to think that St. Peter was never Bishop of Rome. We have already quoted some positive texts on this point. Here is another to confirm them:

"It is certain," he says, "that at the time when the holy Apostles Peter and Paul suffered martyrdom, the faithful came from the East to beg the bodies of these *Apostles, who were their fellow-countrymen.* They carried these bodies as far as the second mile stone and deposited

---

232 St. Greg., Dialogues, Book I, Chap. 12.

233 Ibid., Book IV, Chap. 11.

them in the place called *the Catacombs*. But when they would have taken them up, to continue their journey, the thunder and lightning threw those who attempted it into such a panic that no one has ever again dared to attempt their removal."[234]

It is not our business to discuss the truth of this story; but one truth may be clearly inferred from this recital, namely, that the Eastern people could claim the body of St. Peter *because he was of their country*, and that the Romans never dreamed of answering that his body belonged by a better title to them because he had been their bishop.

Thus the doctrine of Gregory the Great upon the Church destroys, piece by piece, the whole Papal system. We defy the Romanists to find in the writings of this great Pope a single word which gives any idea of that universal monarchy whose centre is in the Church of Rome, and whose sovereign is the bishop of that city. This doctrine runs utterly counter to that of St. Gregory. According to him, the unity of the Church results from the reciprocal relations of its chiefs. "May your piety," he wrote to Anastasius, Archbishop of Corinth, "reply to our letters in which we have notified him of our ordination, and by *replying* (litteris reciprocis) *give us the pleasure of knowing that the Church is united.*"

He defines the "unity of the Catholic Church" as "the totality (*compago*) of the body of Christ."[235] He does not swerve from this: the individual churches are the members of the church; each church is governed by its pastors; the authority is the same, of divine right, in all the pastors of the Church; the whole edifice is supported upon the see of St. Peter; that is, upon the patriarchates of Alexandria, Antioch, and Rome, which exercise, *of ecclesiastical right*, a supervision over the whole Church.

Can anything be conceived more diametrically opposed to the Papal system than this doctrine of St. Gregory?

When Maurice was killed by Phocas, Pope Boniface III hastened to apply to the murderer that he might obtain official recognition of

---

234 Letters of St. Gregory, Book IV, Ep. 30.

235 Ibid., Book II, Ep. 47.

the primacy of the Roman Church. He saw it imperiled by the title of *œmmenical* that Maurice had granted to John the Faster.

That pious emperor had been the chief support of the title taken by the Bishop of Constantinople. The Patriarch did not long enjoy the good graces of Phocas, whose violence he condemned. Rome made advances to the tyrant; Gregory the Great himself covered him with adulation; and Boniface III, who was raised to the see of Rome after the short episcopate of Sabinian, wrote to the murderer of Maurice to ask for the same title of *œcumenical* that Gregory the Great had so energetically condemned.[236] It was generally understood that the Bishop of Constantinople assumed by this title to be *the first* in the Church. Accordingly, the historian of the Popes, Anastasius the Librarian, thus mentions this proceeding of Boniface III:

"He [Boniface][237] *obtained* from the Emperor Phocas that the Apostolic see of the blessed Apostle Peter, that is to say, the Roman Church, *should be the chief (caput*, the head) of all the churches, *because* the Church of Constantinople wrote that she was *the first* of all the churches."

Paul the Deacon thus records the same fact§: "*At* the *request* of Pope Boniface, Phocas *decreed* that the see of the Roman and Apostolic Church should be the chief (*caput*) of all the churches, because the Church of Constantinople wrote that she was the *first* of all the churches."

Such is for the Church of Rome the official origin of the title of *chief* of the universal Church, which she claims for her bishop. It had been given to him occasionally before, but only in flattery, and without attaching to it any other meaning than that of *head* of the episcopate, or *of first bishop*; it was occasionally given to the Roman Church itself, and then the word *caput* only meant *chief* in the sense of *head*. She had been called *head* of the Church, that is, *first of the churches*. This title, becoming official, thanks to Phocas, soon changed its signification. "Chief" no longer meant *head*, but sovereign prince; today it means absolute *monarch, infallible autocrat*.

---

236 Noël Alexandre, Eccl. Hist.

237 Anast., De Vit. Rom. Pontif. §67. Bonif. III.

Such is the progress of this title of *caput*, given to the Roman Church by Phocas, one of the vilest men that ever occupied a throne.

Some years later (633) arose the quarrel of the Monothelites, which gives us further proofs against the Papal system and demonstrates that in the seventh century the self-styled universal authority of the Bishops of Rome was not recognized.[238]

An Arabian bishop named Theodore, starting from this Catholic truth, defined at Chalcedon, that there is but one person in Christ, inferred that there was in Christ but one will and *one operation*. He thus neglected the distinction of the two natures, divine and human, which are hypostatically *united* in Jesus Christ, but not mingled, and which retain their respective essence, each consequently with its own *will* and its own *proper action* or *operation*, since will and action are as necessary attributes of the human being as of God. Theodore thus confounded being with personality. Sergius, Bishop of Constantinople, consulted by Theodore, fell into the same error with him. He believed that his system was calculated to bring back to the Church those who were still opposed to the Council of Chalcedon. Accordingly, he sent them a paper upon this subject and opened communications with them. Cyrus, Bishop of Alexandria, who shared his views, did the same, and many of the opponents of the Council of Chalcedon accepted its decrees with this pretended explanation.

This result encouraged the Monothelite bishops, who were also sustained by the Emperor Heraclius. Sophronius, a monk of Alexandria, had declared against his bishop, and had gone to Constantinople to confer upon the question with Sergius, whom he found in perfect agreement with Cyrus. Sophronius, in despair for this new error, was returning when he was elected Bishop of Jerusalem. Sergius, believing that in his high position Sophronius would declare against him, and would seek the support of the West, wrote to Honorius, Bishop of Rome, setting forth his doctrine and its good results in the East, particularly at Alexandria. Honorius replied with his famous letter in which he also only recognizes

---

238 See Theoph., Eccl. Hist., and Labbe's Collection of the Councils, vol. vi, for the documents. See also *Histoire du Monothélisme*, by Combefis.

one will and one operation in Jesus Christ; he censured those who were in favor of admitting two, and promised to remain in perfect harmony with Sergius, telling him, however, at the same time, that the Church should not be troubled by this new question, whether there were one or two wills or operations, and that such a war of words should be left to grammarians.

Sophronius, ordained Bishop of Jerusalem, at once assembled his synod and read before it the letter of communion, which, according to custom, he was to address to the other Patriarchs of the Church. He sent it to Sergius and also to Honorius. This letter was very explicit in regard to the two wills and two operations. Honorius, having read it, told the messengers of Sophronius that, for the good of the Church, it was best not to agitate that question. The messengers agreed to this, and Honorius wrote to the Patriarchs of Constantinople and Alexandria, making the same request.

Sophronius, who saw that the faith was in peril, wrote a paper, in which he proved from the Fathers that, according to the constant traditions of the Church, two wills and two operations should be recognized in Jesus Christ. He proved this to be the necessary consequence of the two natures. In despair of convincing Sergius and Cyrus, who had openly declared in favor of the contrary doctrine, he sent one of his suffragan bishops to Rome, hoping to overcome her hesitancy rather than to convert Constantinople or Alexandria. We are ignorant of the result of this embassy. Honorius died in 638 and was succeeded by Severinus, who in turn was succeeded soon after by John IV. It was during the brief pontificate of Severinus that the Emperor Heraclius published his *Êkthesis*, or *Exposition*, to give an official character to the *Monothelite* doctrine. This *Êkthesis* was addressed to all the bishops, and was solemnly accepted by those of Alexandria and Constantinople. It is not known whether Severinus approved it or not. But after the death of Heraclius, John IV condemned it in a Roman council. We perhaps owe that condemnation to the explanations of the envoy of Sophronius. Sergius had died before this decision of the Roman council. Pyrrhus, his successor, set up in opposition to the decision of John IV the letter of Honorius, John's predecessor. John attempted an apology; but the letters of Sergius and Honorius still exist; they prove that John's defence was untenable; that Honorius had perfectly understood Sergius; that he had answered him, agreeing with the letter he had received from him; that both rejected in a general way the *two distinct wills* and operations. It was with justice, then, that Honorius was condemned as a heretic by the sixth œcumenical council, as we shall shortly see.

After the publication of the *Êkthesis* of Heraclius, the discussions upon the two operations and two wills assumed greater proportions. The whole East was filled with them. Many bishops declared against the new doctrine and appealed to the West, in the person of the Bishop of Rome, to sustain the Catholic faith. Pyrrhus, having abandoned his see, was succeeded by Paul, who wrote letters of communion to Theodore, then Bishop of Rome.

Theodore replied, praising the orthodoxy of Paul's faith but expressing surprise that he had not condemned the *Êkthesis* of Heraclius. Yet he himself did not dare to censure that document openly; he ought, therefore, to have understood why Paul, who was then at Constantinople, had not solemnly condemned it. In his answer, Theodore urged that Pyrrhus, Paul's predecessor, must be canonically deposed or be sent to Rome to be judged. This opinion was not followed. But Pyrrhus himself, having been proved to be in error by the monk Maximus of Constantinople, asked to go to Rome, where he was received with all honors due to his title of ex-Patriarch, by Theodore, to whom he entrusted a perfectly orthodox confession of faith.

Rome took advantage of the occasions offered by Monothelism to enlarge her authority. The two Patriarchs of Constantinople and Alexandria, having declared in favor of the new doctrine all those who were orthodox in the East, had occasion to turn to the Patriarch of Rome and write to him as the bulwark of the faith which was threatened throughout the East. At such a time the title of successor of St. Peter was not withheld from him, and some bishops went so far as to trace back to that Apostle the authority of the Roman see. This flattered the tendencies which were destined to be daily more and more developed at Rome.

V. Roman Bishop Authority of the 6th, 7th, and 8th Centuries 211

Some Popes, particularly St. Leo, had made altogether too much of the prerogatives of the Apostle Peter, and possibly with a purpose. St. Gregory the Great, indeed, came in to determine the orthodox sense of the expressions of his predecessors; but it is certain that, beginning with St. Leo, the Bishops of Rome *were tending* to exaggerate the prerogatives of the first of the Apostles in order to appropriate them *by right of succession.* As the small patriarchate of Jerusalem was under the authority of St. Sophronius, the most illustrious defender of orthodoxy in the East, the Pope thought he might properly have himself represented there. He chose for his legate Stephen of Dora, who had been *sent* to Rome by Sophronius himself to enlighten Honorius. This was a step unheard of before in the East, and therefore it should not pass unnoticed; it sustains our allegation that the Popes intended to profit by every circumstance in order to increase their authority, the more as it was threatened by the Bishops of Constantinople. The two highest Patriarchs of the East had fallen into heresy, and now or never should Rome speak out. The Popes did not let the opportunity go by. Nevertheless, the authentic documents concerning the question of Monothelism agree in proving that all the Patriarchs discussed the dogmatic questions among themselves on a footing of equality. Many bishops, having declared against Paul of Constantinople, gave explanations that might be interpreted either way, and which satisfied no one. But as he was continually found fault with for his silence respecting the *Êkthesis,* he prevailed upon the Emperor Constans to publish a new edict, which received the name of *Type*. By this edict the *Êkthesis* was withdrawn, and both parties were silenced.

This was precisely what Honorius had formerly asked in the letter in which he declared in favor of Monothelism. But Theodore was no longer satisfied with this. He assembled a council of Italian bishops, and there deposed Paul of Constantinople and Pyrrhus, who had relapsed into Monothelism after he left Rome. He dared to sign this anti- canonical sentence with a pen dipped in the consecrated wine. Such impiety might satisfy the rancour of Rome, but it could only have calamitous results. Paul continued to consider himself legitimate Bishop of Constantinople, and replied to the violence of the Bishop of Rome with corresponding violence. He caused to be overthrown the Roman altar of the palace of Placidia, where the two envoys of the Roman Bishop resided, and forbade them to celebrate the holy mysteries. This was to declare them and their bishop excommunicate.

They returned to Rome, and one of them, Martin, was elected to succeed Theodore, who died soon after throwing this new element of discord into the Church by his sentence (649). Martin was no sooner consecrated than he assembled at Rome a numerous council of bishops from the environs of Rome, from the Exarchate of Ravenna, from Sicily, and from Sardinia. Some African bishops, Stephen of Dora, and some Greek monks, refugees in Rome, were present. The question of the two wills and two operations was examined; the *Êkthesis*, the Type, and their defenders were condemned. Martin signed the acts of the council as follows: "Martin, by the grace of God, Bishop of the holy *catholic* and apostolic Church of the city of Rome. I have signed as judge this sentence in confirmation of the orthodox faith, and also the condemnation of Theodore, formerly Bishop of Pharan, of Cyrus of Alexandria, of Sergius of Constantinople, of Pyrrhus and Paul his successors, and of their heretical writings, of the impious *Êkthesis*, and the impious *Type*, published by them."

All the bishops, one hundred and five in number, employed the same formula in signing. They concurred in the condemnation, as *judges*, as well as the Bishop of Rome, who merely had the first place in the council.

Martin sent the transactions of the Council of Rome to the East, and named John, Bishop of Philadelphia, his vicar for the entire East, condemning as heretics the Patriarchs of Antioch and Alexandria as well as the Patriarch of Constantinople. Martin declared in the commission given to John of Philadelphia that he gave it to him "by virtue of the power that he had received from St. Peter," and because of the unhappy condition of the East now ravaged by Muslims.

It was thus that the Bishop of Rome availed himself of the misfortunes of the East to seize upon universal power in the Church

V. Roman Bishop Authority of the 6th, 7th, and 8th Centuries 213

by virtue of an alleged succession from St. Peter. These formulas became more and more the fashion at Rome after the middle of the seventh century, and Martin particularly contributed to carrying them out. He claimed authority such as his predecessors never enjoyed. Thus, being dissatisfied with the letter of communion he had received from Paul, the new Bishop of Thessalonica, he dictated the formula he should accept. When Paul refused to comply, Martin announced to him without the form of a trial that he was deposed from his see. He was the more inclined to make this bishop feel his power, because his province had been submitted to the jurisdiction of Constantinople in spite of Rome.

The patriarchal churches of Alexandria, Antioch, and Jerusalem had enough to do to defend themselves against the ferocious conquerors of the East; they, therefore, took no notice of the encroachments of Rome, nor the acts of her vicar. They only protested by their silence and by ceasing to keep up any relations with the Roman see. For them, Constantinople became the first see of the Church, and they remained in communion with it. The only contest was now between the Bishops of Rome and Constantinople.

By the Council of Rome, Martin had obviously desired to pay back the last Council of Constantinople in which his predecessor, Vigilius, had been, as he himself confessed, convicted of error. But be had not imitated the prudence of this council, which, while it condemned the errors of Vigilius, had not sought to depose him and thus violate the rights of the bishops of the Roman province. Moreover, Martin attacked the Emperor himself in condemning *The Type*, which had been promulgated as a law of the state. He had, indeed, endeavored to ascribe that document to the Bishop of Constantinople, and had written to the Emperor to persuade him that he was not personally concerned in the decision. But these precautions only irritated Constans, who had Martin ousted from Rome. He accused him not only of heresy, but of rebellion and high treason. One Eugene was substituted for Martin in the episcopate of Rome. Martin, speaking of his deposition, says in one of his letters:[239] "It has never been practiced in this manner; for, in

---

239 Mart., Epist. ad Theod.

the absence of the bishop, he is replaced by the archdeacon, the archpriest, and the dean."

He never dreamed of appealing to any exclusive privilege in favor of the Bishops of Rome, and acknowledged that they were subject to the common law.

The anti-canonical deposition of Martin answered to that which he had himself pronounced as uncanonically against Paul of Constantinople. It may be safely said that if Martin had had, like Paul, the imperial power at his disposal, he would have treated his antagonist as he himself was treated.

The letters of the Roman bishops to the emperors will satisfy anyone that it was a matter of tradition among them to ask for violent measures against all whom they considered heretics; and we know how faithful they were to these traditions when they had in their own hands both the spiritual and the temporal power.

From a purely ecclesiastical point of view, it was natural that the first encroachments of the Papacy should excite a powerful reaction. Martin, coming to Constantinople (654), was treated as a prisoner of state; insults were heaped upon him, and he was shamefully maltreated. The Bishop of Constantinople, who was ill, disapproved of such violence and besought the Emperor not to treat a bishop thus. He died soon after expressing these kindly sentiments. Martin was banished to Cherson. Thence he wrote several letters. He complains that the Roman Church sent him no aid; and in one of his letters he thus expresses himself in regard to the Roman clergy and of the successor who had been appointed to his place:[240] "I am amazed at those who belong to the Church of St. Peter, because of the little care they have of one who is of them. If that Church have no money, she lacks, thank God, neither grain, nor wine, nor other provisions that she could send to my aid... Have I been such an enemy to the Church, and particularly to them? I pray God nevertheless, by the intercession of St. Peter, to preserve them unshaken in the orthodox faith, and chiefly the pastor who now governs them." Thus Martin regarded Eugene, who had been put in his place, and whose promotion had been approved

---

240 Mart., Epist. xviii. Labbe's Collection.

V. Roman Bishop Authority of the 6th, 7th, and 8th Centuries 215

by the Roman clergy, as the legitimate Bishop of Rome. It must be acknowledged that his letter is not very favorable to the pretensions of the modern Papacy, and is a more than sufficient answer to what he himself said of his universal power inherited from St. Peter. He died about a year after writing this letter.

Pyrrhus, the former Bishop of Constantinople, was the same year reinstalled in that see; but he only survived his restoration a few months, and was succeeded by Peter. Eugene, Bishop of Rome, was succeeded by Vitalianus in 658. Constans, going to Rome under his episcopate, was received by him with great honors and communicated with him, although this Emperor had never revoked his *Type* and had persecuted Pope Martin and the monk Maximus, who was regarded in the East as the great defender of orthodoxy. During the episcopate of Vitalianus—fourteen years—no differences existed between the sees of Rome and Constantinople. In 664 Constans died, and Constantine Pogonatus ascended the imperial throne. In 674 Vitalianus was replaced by Adeodatus, who was succeeded by Donus. He died in 679, and Agatho was elected to the see of Rome. Peter of Constantinople had been succeeded by Constantine, who gave place, in 678, to Theodore. This Patriarch, full of pacific intentions, had sent to Donus a letter exhorting him to peace. But the Bishop of Rome did not reply, imitating his predecessors, who had given no answer to the synodical letters of the later bishops of Constantinople. This schism grieved the Emperor, who determined to reestablish friendly relations between the Eastern and Western churches. He therefore inquired of Theodore and of Macarius of Antioch as to the cause of the division.[241] They replied: "There have been introduced new modes of speaking of the mysteries, either through ignorance or from excessive curiosity; and never, since these questions have been under discussion, have the two sees assembled to search out the truth." The Emperor concluded that the remedy for these divisions was a council, and consequently wrote thus to Donus: "Circumstances do not allow the assembling of a complete council; but you may send discreet and learned men, who, with the Patriarchs Theodore and Macarius, shall solve these

---

241 V. Theoph. Eccl. Hist. and vol. vi of Labbe's Collection.

questions. They shall enjoy complete security here, and even for their return, in case they do not come to an understanding. After this we shall be justified in the sight of God; for while we can exhort to union, we are unwilling to compel anyone. Send us from your holy Church three men at most, if you will, and from your council [i.e., of his ecclesiastical province] about twelve bishops, including the metropolitan." Beside this, the Emperor offered every assistance and safeguard to the deputies for their journey. Donus was dead when the imperial missive reached Rome (679). It was given to Agatho, who convoked at Rome a large council, to choose the delegates that should be sent to Constantinople. All the provinces of Italy took part in that assembly, in which were also several bishops from France. Agatho did not, then, it should seem, claim for himself the right to send delegates by his own authority to Constantinople. The council sent the Emperor a letter, signed by the Pope and all the members of the assembly. Agatho addressed him another in his own name. The delegates were well received at Constantinople by the Emperor. Theodore was no longer Patriarch; George had succeeded him. He and Macarius of Antioch assembled the metropolitans and the bishops depending from their sees. The churches of Alexandria and Jerusalem were represented there. All united with the Western delegates to form what is known as the *sixth* œcumenical council.

The first session took place on the seventh of November, A.D. 680. The Emperor occupied the first place, in the middle; on his *left* were the delegates from Rome and Jerusalem; on his right, the Patriarchs of Constantinople and of Antioch, and the delegate from Alexandria; next, on each side, quite a great number of metropolitans and bishops. During several sessions the Emperor caused the acts of the Councils of Ephesus and Chalcedon to be read, together with all the texts cited for or against the two wills and two operations in Christ. The question being discussed, all agreed, except the Patriarch of Antioch and his disciple Stephen, in condemning Monothelism and all those who had supported it, including Honorius, Pope of Rome. This important decree, which

V. Roman Bishop Authority of the 6th, 7th, and 8th Centuries 217

so loudly refutes the pretensions of the modern Papacy, deserves to be quoted verbally.[242]

"Having examined the pretended dogmatical letters of Sergius of Constantinople to Cyrus, and the replies of Honorius to Sergius, and finding them opposed to the doctrine of the Apostles, to the decrees of the councils, and to the sense of all the Fathers, but agreeable, on the contrary, to the false doctrines of the heretics, we entirely reject them, and detest them as calculated to corrupt souls. And while we reject *their impious dogmas*, we also think that their names should be banished from the Church—namely, of Sergius, formerly Bishop of this city of Constantinople, who first wrote upon this error; of Cyrus of Alexandria; of Pyrrhus Paul, and Peter, Bishops of Constantinople; of Theodore, Bishop of Pharan; all of whom Pope Agatho mentions in his letter to the Emperor, and hath rejected. We pronounce anathema against them all. With them we think we should expel from the Church, and pronounce anathema against Honorius, formerly Bishop of Old Rome. We find in his letter to Sergius that he follows, in every respect, and authorizes his impious doctrine."

In the sixteenth session, after the profession of faith of the Patriarch George of Constantinople, the council rung with declamations, and among others, with the following: "Anathema to Theodore of Pharan, to Sergius, to Cyrus! ANATHEMA TO HONORIUS THE HERETIC!" In the profession of faith of the council, read in the last session, Honorius is condemned with the other heretics; anathema is again pronounced against him as well as against the other Monothelites.

The council enacted many canons. The thirty-sixth renewed those of Constantinople and Chalcedon touching the rank of the Patriarchs in the Church. It is thus worded: "Renewing the decrees of the hundred and fifty holy Fathers assembled in this royal city, blessed of God, and of the six hundred and thirty assembled at Chalcedon, we decree that the see of Constantinople shall enjoy the same prerogatives as that of Old Rome that it shall be as great in ecclesiastical matters, being the second after it. After these shall

---

[242] Conc. Constant, see xiii in Labbe's Collection.

be the sees of Alexandria, Antioch, and then that of the city of Jerusalem. "Thus did the council answer the pretensions of Rome. The legates of Agatho and one hundred and sixty bishops subscribed to the acts of the council. Five copies were made of them, which were signed by the Emperor's hand—one for each of the five Patriarchal churches. Fifty-five bishops, and the delegates of the Oriental churches, addressed a letter to Agatho, requesting him to concur in what had been done.

Those who had been condemned by the council—six in number—hoping, without doubt, to prevail on the West not to concur in these acts, asked to be sent to the Pope. The Emperor granted this, and banished them to Rome.

Meanwhile (682), Agatho having died, Leo II was elected Bishop of Rome. It was he that received the legates and the transactions of the council. The Emperor wrote two letters—one to the Pope, the other to the members of the Western councils—in reply to those he had received. Leo II solemnly concurred in the acts of the council by his letter to the Emperor of May 7, 683. Among other passages, we read: "*We anathematize* the inventors of the new error, to wit, Theodore of Pharan, Cyrus of Alexandria, Sergius, Pyrrhus Paul and Peter of Constantinople, and *also Honorius*, who, instead of purifying this Apostolic Church by the doctrine of the Apostles, *has come near to overthrowing the faith by an impious treason.*"

Nothing is wanting, as we see, to the condemnation of Pope Honorius as a heretic; yet this has not prevented Romish theologians from saying he was not so condemned. They have written long disquisitions upon this subject in which they have distorted all the facts. The acts which we have quoted are clear enough of themselves to prove, to any honest man, that the sixth œcumenical council did not believe in the doctrinal authority of the Bishops of Rome; that those bishops themselves did not believe themselves possessed of any such authority.

Is it not incredible that the Romish theologians should have dared to cite this council in favor of their system? Among their acclamations the Fathers said, "Peter has spoken by Agatho"; "therefore," say the Romanists, "they recognized the same doctrinal

V. Roman Bishop Authority of the 6th, 7th, and 8th Centuries 219

authority in Agatho as in Peter." They will not reflect that this acclamation was made *after the examination* of Agatho's letter, when it appeared to be in conformity with Apostolic doctrine. The council *approved* of Agatho's letter as it *condemned* that of Honorius, his predecessor. It was therefore the council that possessed *doctrinal authority*; and no more of it was recognized in the see of Rome than in other Apostolic sees.

The doctrine of one Pope was esteemed to be that of Peter, because it was seen to be Apostolic; that of another Pope was condemned as contrary to Peter's teaching, because it differed from Apostolic tradition. This fact stands out so prominently in the Acts of the Sixth Council, that it is difficult to understand how men who claim to be in earnest have ever contested it.

Under the reign of Justinian II there assembled at Constantinople two hundred and eleven bishops, of whom the four Patriarchs of Constantinople, Alexandria, Antioch, and Jerusalem were the chiefs.[243] This assembly is known under the title of the Council in *Trullo*, because it was assembled under the *Trullus* or dome of the imperial palace. Its object was to add to the acts of the fifth and sixth œcumenical councils, which had not made any disciplinary rules. Church discipline was alone discussed. Customs widely different already prevailed in the Eastern and Western churches, particularly in regard to the marriage of priests. The Roman Church even then was drifting toward ecclesiastical celibacy as a general law. The Eastern Church, on the contrary, solemnly proclaimed the ancient law respecting marriage of priests, deacons, and sub-deacons. Rome, therefore, refused to receive the laws of the Council in *Trullo*. This embittered the antagonism already existing between Rome and Constantinople. In thus disavowing ancient discipline, and refusing to subscribe to the canons which were its exact expression, she was laying, the groundwork of that wall of separation which was so soon to be raised between the two churches. It was Pope Sergius (692) who refused to admit the canons of the Council in *Trullo*. He particularly relied upon this, that the council prescribed to the Roman Church to change her practice regarding the Saturday

---

243 See the transactions of this council in Labbe's Collection, vol. vi.

fast, a practice that she had followed from time immemorial. Some zealous Romans, like the priest Blastus, had tried as early as the fifth century to impose the Roman custom upon the whole Church; at the close of the seventh century the East undertook to impose hers upon Rome. It must be granted that a council of two hundred and eleven bishops had more authority than Blastus and his followers; but it was a matter of mere discipline, and the Eastern usage should not have been imposed upon the Western Church but submitted to the judgment of the bishops of that Church. We may believe that the Eastern Church assembled in *Trullo* meant, by several of her canons, to remind the Roman Church how far she had removed from the primitive discipline, and that the Roman Church would not accept that lesson, chiefly because it came from Constantinople.

Official relations were not interrupted between the two churches; but for a long time they had been far from fraternal. The opposition of Rome to the Council in *Trullo* did not prevent her intercommunion with Constantinople; but these relations were feebly kept up until the discussion regarding images arose in 726.

The Emperor Leo the Isaurian[244] declared himself the enemy of that "cultus" which was addressed to images, alleging that it was idolatrous. This idea does not speak very well for his judgment; but he had the power, and many bishops took sides with him.[245]

Constantinople at that time possessed a great and holy Patriarch, Germanus, who energetically opposed the Emperor's errors. He wrote concerning them to several bishops, and particularly to Gregory II, then Bishop of Rome, who assured him that he was of his opinion.

The Emperor resorted to every expedient to corrupt Germanus. Failing in this, he persecuted him. Germanus preferred to resign his office rather than concur in the Emperor's decree against images. He retired to his father's house, where he lived like a monk and died like a saint. Anastasius, his assistant, was put in his place by the Emperor. He was an ambitious man, who had sold his faith to the

---

[244] Leo III.

[245] See Eccl. Hist. of Theoph. and Niceph., and Labbe's Collection of the Councils.

Emperor for the Patriarchal See. Leo also endeavored to corrupt Gregory II; but his promises and threats had no other effect than to raise against him in rebellion all those who still recognized the imperial authority in the West.

Anastasius sent a letter of communion to the Pope, who refused to recognize him and even threatened his deposition if he should continue to maintain heresy. Meanwhile Gregory II died (731) and was succeeded by Gregory III. This Pope wrote to the Emperor several letters full of excellent doctrine and the most valuable information.[246] Thus, in the first, he says to the Emperor: "The decisions of the Church belong not to emperors but *to the bishops*; accordingly, as these do not meddle in civil affairs, so likewise should the emperors not busy themselves with ecclesiastical matters. If the emperors and the bishops agree, then they form in common a single power to treat of affairs in the spirit of peace and charity."

Leo proposing a council, Gregory told him that such an assembly was not needed, since it was only necessary for himself to return to order that peace might be universal respecting the question at issue. "You think to frighten us," he said, "by saying, 'I will send to Rome and break the image of St. Peter, and will carry off Pope Gregory loaded with chains. I will treat him as Constans treated Martin.' Know, then, that the Popes are mediators and arbiters of peace between the East and the West. We do not, therefore, fear your threats; at one league from Rome we shall be in safety."

These words depict exactly the position which the Bishops of Rome had taken in the midst of all the nations who had dismembered the Roman empire in the West—a position that became one of the elements of their power. As to any pretensions to any sort of political authority, or the supreme authority in the Church, no trace of either can be found in the letters of Gregory III. He saw this authority only *in the bishops*; that is, he only saw a *collective* authority in the Church. The Emperor replying that he possessed both imperial and sacerdotal power, Gregory wrote him an admirable letter upon the distinction of the two powers, still placing the ecclesiastical authority in the *episcopate*. Agreeably to his

---

246 Letters of Greg. III in Labbe's Collection.

principles, Gregory III called a council at Rome to give a collective decision concerning images. He sent that decision to the Emperor and to Anastasius of Constantinople, with private letters to lead them back to the right way. His efforts only served to redouble the persecutions against the Catholics of the East. The bishops of those countries could neither come together in convention nor obtain a hearing. In their stead John Damascene took up the defence of the Church. The Mohammedan yoke gave the great theologian liberty boldly to attack the Emperor and those who served as his instruments to give sanction to his errors or execute his cruelties.

The doctrinal whims of Leo the Isaurian had a political result which he was far from foreseeing. The West renounced him, and Rome, threatened by the Lombards, turned to Karl Martel, Duke of the Franks, to offer him the *Roman Consulate*. Gregory III made this proposition to Karl. This terrible warrior died then, and Gregory III also. But the idea remained. Pepin, the son of Karl, and Pope Zachary renewed the negotiations. Zachary approved for Pepin's benefit the deposition of the first race of Frankish kings. In return, the new king delivered Rome from the attacks of the Lombards, became its lord paramount, and gave it in appanage to the Pope. Thus the relations ceased between the Popes and the Eastern emperors, whom they no longer recognized as sovereigns. The separation became complete when the son of Pepin, Karl the Great, better known as Charlemagne, was proclaimed at Rome Emperor of the West.

This political rupture made way for the religious schism between the East and the West. Rome was rising again from her ruins at the same moment that Constantinople was falling into decay. The Popes, more rich and powerful than ever, crowned with the diadem of temporal power, could not but meditate revenge for the humiliations to which in their pride they imagined they had been subjected.

While the West was quite escaping him forever, Constantine Copronymus, the son of Leo, assembled councils and caused the condemnation of images in an assembly of bishops, bereft of conscience, who endeavored to dishonor the memory of the

V. Roman Bishop Authority of the 6th, 7th, and 8th Centuries 223

Patriarch St. Germanus and the learned John Damascene. Pope Stephen II (756) prevailed upon Pepin, King of France, to take the cause of the Church in hand. Constantine Copronymus had sent to this prince an embassy which troubled the Pope. Stephen feared lest politics should binder his plans and the Emperor of the East should resume some influence in the affairs of the West. He therefore wrote thus to Pepin:[247] "We earnestly entreat you to act toward the Greeks in such manner that the Catholic faith may be forever preserved, *that the Church may be delivered from their malice* and may recover all her patrimony." The Church of Rome had had considerable property in the East, which had been confiscated since the rupture between Rome and the empire. "Inform us," adds the Pope, "how you have talked to the envoy, and send us copies of the letters you have given him, that we may act in concert."

Paul, who succeeded Stephen II, continued in the same relations with Pepin. His letters[248] show that he had to struggle against the influences of certain politicians, who were endeavoring to effect an agreement between the King of France and the Emperor of Constantinople. The latter particularly depended upon the Lombards against Rome. The Popes were alarmed at what might be the results of such an alliance. They accordingly strove to excite the Frankish kings against the Greeks and Lombards.

We have now come to the last years of the eighth century. The Eastern empire, delivered from Copronymus and his son Leo IV, breathed again under the reign of Constantine and Irene.

Charlemagne reigned in France, Adrian I was Bishop of Rome; Tarasius, a great and saintly Patriarch, ruled at Constantinople. Before consenting to his election, Tarasius addressed to the court and people of Constantinople a discourse from which we quote the following passage: "This is what I principally fear [in accepting the episcopate)]: I see the church divided in the East; we have different languages among, us, and many agree with the West, which *anathematizes us daily*. Separation (anathema) is a terrible thing; it drives from the kingdom of heaven and leads to outer darkness.

---

247 Steph., II Epist. in Cod. Carol.
248 Paul et Steph., III Epist. in Cod. Carol.

Nothing is more pleasant to God than *union*, which makes us one Catholic Church, as we confess in the creed. I therefore ask you, brethren, that which I believe is also your will, since you have the fear of God: I ask that the Emperor and Empress *assemble* an œcumenical council, in order that we may make but one body *under a single chief, who is Jesus Christ*. If the Emperor and Empress grant me this request, I submit to their orders and your votes; if not, I cannot consent. Give me, brethren, what answer you will."[249]

All but a few fanatics applauded the project of a council, and then Tarasius consented to be ordained and instituted bishop. He at once addressed his letters of communion to the churches of Rome, Alexandria, Antioch, and Jerusalem.[250] In these he made as usual his profession of faith, and invited those churches to the Council which the Emperor was about to assemble. The Empress-regent and her son wrote to Pope Adrian that they had resolved to assemble an œcumenical council; they begged him to come to it, promising to receive him with honors; or to send representatives if he could not personally accept their invitation.

Adrian's answer to the Emperor and Empress is a very important document, in regard to the question we are examining. We find in it a style which the Bishops of Rome had not hitherto allowed themselves to adopt toward the emperors.

Rome, jealous of Constantinople, was soon to crown Charlemagne Emperor of the West, and thus to break all political ties with the East. The Pope enjoyed great temporal authority in that city under the protection of the Frankish kings; he was rich, and he was ambitious to surround his see with still greater magnificence and splendour. Adrian therefore replied arrogantly to the respectful letter he had received from the court of Constantinople.

He insisted upon certain conditions, as one power dealing with another, and particularly upon this point: *that the patrimony of St. Peter in the East*, confiscated by the iconoclastic emperors, *must be restored in toto*. We will quote from his letter what he says respecting

---

249 Theoph., Annal. Labbe's Collection of Councils, vol. vii., Vit. Taras. ap. Bolland. 14 February.

250 See all the documents in Labbe's Collection of the Councils, 7th vol.

the Patriarch of Constantinople: "We are very much surprised to see that in your letter you give to Tarasius the title of *œcumenical* Patriarch. The Patriarch of Constantinople would not have even the second rank WITHOUT THE CONSENT OF OUR SEE; if he be œcumenical, must he not therefore have also the primacy over our church? All Christians know that this is a ridiculous assumption."

Adrian sets before the Emperor the example of Charles, King of the Franks. "Following our advice," he says, "and fulfilling our wishes, he has subjected all the barbarous nations of the West; he has given to the Roman Church in perpetuity provinces, cities, castles, and patrimonies which were withheld by the Lombards, and which by right belong to St. Peter; he does not cease daily to offer gold and silver for this light and sustenance of the poor."

Here is language quite new on the part of Roman bishops, but henceforth destined to become habitual with them. It dates from 785; that is, from the same year when Adrian delivered to Ingelramn, Bishop of Metz, the collection of the False Decretals.[251]

---

251 Here are some details regarding the *False Decretals*:

It appears from the acts of the Council of Chalcedon, in 451, that the Church had already a *Codex Canonum*, or collection of the laws of the Church. Several of these laws are held to have emanated from the Apostles themselves. What they had commenced the councils continued, and, as soon as the Church began to enjoy some little tranquillity, these venerable laws were collected and formed the basis of ecclesiastical discipline; and, as they were mostly in Greek, they were translated into Latin for the use of the Western churches.

At the beginning of the sixth century Dionysius, surnamed Exiguus, a monk at Rome, finding this translation incorrect, made another at the request of Julian, curate of St. Anastasia at Rome, and a disciple of Pope Gelasius. Dionysius collected, besides, whatever letters of the Popes he could discover in the archives, and published in his collection those of Siricius, Innocent, Zosimus, Boniface, Celestine, Leo, Gelasius, and Anastasius, under which last he lived. The archives of Rome at that time possessed nothing prior to Siricius—that is, to the end of the fourth century.

At the beginning of the seventh century, Isidore of Seville undertook to complete the collection of Dionysius. He added the canons of some national or provincial councils of Africa, Spain, and France, and some letters of a few of the Popes, going back no further than to Damasus, who died in 384 and was the predecessor of Siricius. This collection of Isidore of Seville begins

There is something highly significant in this coincidence. Was it

with the cannons of the Council of Nicea. He used the old translation, and not that of Dionysius for the Greek canons.

His collection was but little known, and in history we do not meet it until 785, and then disfigured and interpolated by an unknown forger who gave his name as Isidore Mercator. This collection contained, beside the pieces contained in the collection of Isidore of Seville, certain Decretals which he ascribed to the Popes of the first three centuries. Several scholars make Isidore Mercator and Isidore of Seville separate writers, while others think that the latter had added, through humility, the word *Peccator* to his name, which was corrupted to *Mercator*. However this may be, the best Ultramontane critics, as well as the Gallicans, agree that the *Decretals* ascribed to the Popes of the first centuries in the collection of Isidore Mercator are spurious. Marchetti himself admits their spuriousness. "Learned men of great piety," he adds, "have declared against this false collection, which Cardinal Bona frankly calls a *pious fraud*... Baronius does not as frankly regard them as a *fraud*; nevertheless, he would not use them in his Ecclesiastical Annals, less it should be believed that the Roman Church needed suspicious documents to establish her rights."

The Ultramontanes cannot openly sustain these Decretals as true, for it has been abundantly proved that they were manufactured *partly* from ancient canons, with extracts from the letters of the Popes of the fourth and fifth centuries. Entire passages, particularly from St. Leo and Gregory the Great, are found in them. The whole is strung together in bad Latin, which for even the least critical scholar has all the characteristics of the style of the eighth and ninth centuries.

The collection of Isidore Mercator was disseminated chiefly by Riculf, Archibishop of Mayence, who took that see in 787. Several critics have concluded from this that this collection first appeared at Mayence, and even that Riculf was its author.

Were these *False Decretals* fabricated in Spain, Germany, or Rome? We have no certainty on the subject. The oldest copies tell us that it was Ingelramn who brought this collection to Rome from Metz, when he had a lawsuit there in 785; but other copies tell us that it was Pope Adrian who, upon that occasion, delivered it to Ingleramn on September 19, 785. Certain it is, that *at Rome* we find the first mention of it. Yet Adrian knew that these Decretals were false, since, ten years before, he had given Charlemagne a copy of the canons, which was no other than that of Dionysius Exiguus.

The *False Decretals* were so extensively circulated in the West that they were everywhere received, and particularly at Rome, as authentic.

The Ultramontanes, while they do not dare to maintain the authority of the writings ascribed to the Popes of the first three centuries, nevertheless indirectly sustain them. Several works have been written with this object

Adrian himself who authorized this work of forgery?

against Fleury, who justly asserted and abundantly proved that they changed the ancient discipline. We will quote among these Ultramontane works those of Marchetti, of Father de Housta, and Father Honoré de Sainte-Marie:

"We may conjecture," says Marchetti, "that Isidore gathered the Decretals of ancient Popes which the persecutions of the first centuries had not permitted to be collected, and that *animated* by a desire to transmit the collection to posterity, he made such haste that he overlooked some faults and chronological errors which were afterward corrected by more exact criticism."

Thus, then, the *Decretals* of the first three centuries are false; neverthless they are substantially true. Such is the Ultramontane system. It only remains to say, to make the business complete, that the texts of St. Leo and St. Gregory the Great, which are found in these Decretals, do not belong to those fathers, who, in that case, must have copied them from the Decretals of their predecessors. It would be quite as reasonable to maintain this opinion, as to say that we only find in the False Decretals a few faults and chronological errors.

To this first system of defence, the Ultramontanes add a second. They make a great display of eloquence to prove that an unknown person without any authority could never have introduced a new code in the Church. We think so too. But there is one great fact of the very highest importance which our Ultramontanes have left out of sight, that, at the time when the *False Decretals* appeared, the see of Rome had for about two centuries taken advantage of every occurrence to increase her influence and to put into *practice* what the *false Decretals* lay down as the law. Everyone knows that after the fall of the Roman empire, most of the Western nations were essentially modified by the invasion of new races; that the Church seriously felt this change; that the pursuit of learning was abandoned, and that after the seventh century the most deplorable ignorance reigned in the Western churches. From that time the Bishops of Rome began to take part directly in the government of individual churches, which frequently lay in the hands of only half-Christianized conquerors. They sent missionaries to labour for the conversion of the invading tribes; and these missionaries, like St. Boniface of Mayence, retained for the Popes who sent them the feelings of disciples for their masters. The churches newly founded by them remained faithful to these sentiments. It would not, therefore, be surprising if the fabricator of the *False Decretals* lived in or near Mayence. He composed that work of fragments from the councils and the Fathers, and added regulations which were in perfect harmony with the usages of the see of Rome at the end of the eighth century, and which Rome, doubtless, inspired.

This coincidence, joined to the ignorance which then prevailed, explains sufficiently how the *False Decretals* could be accepted without protest—the see

We do not know; but it is an incontestable fact that it was in of Rome using all its influence to spread them. As most of the churches had been accustomed for two centuries to feel the authority of the Bishops of Rome, they accepted without examination documents which seemed to be no more than the sanction of this authority. The *False Decretals* did not therefore create a new code for the Western churches; they only came in aid of a *régime* which, owing to political disturbances, the Popes themselves had created.

Thus the Romanists have their labour for their pains, when they seek to defend *the Decretals* by saying that an unknown author without authority could not have established a new code.

Here are the objections that Fleury makes to the *False Decretals*: "The subject matter of these letters [Eccl. Hist., liv. xliv.] reveals their spuriousness. They speak of archbishops, primates, patriarchs, as if these titles had existed from the birth of the Church. They forbid the holding of any council, even a provincial one, without permission from the Pope, and represent appeals to Rome as habitual. Frequent complaint is therein made of usurpations of the temporalities of the Church. We find there this maxim, that bishops falling into sin may, after having done penance, exercise their functions as before. Finally, the principal subject of these *Decretals* is that of complaints against bishops; there is scarcely one that does not speak of them and give rules to make them difficult. And Isidore makes it very apparent in his preface that he had this matter deeply at heart."

The object of the forger in this last matter was to diminish the authority of the metropolitans, who, from time immemorial, had enjoyed the right to convoke the council of their province to hear complaints against a bishop of that province, in particular, and judge him. The forger, whose object it was to concentrate all authority at Rome, would naturally first endeavor to check the authority of the metropolitan, and to make the appeals to Rome seem to offer greater guarantees and to be more consonant with episcopal dignity.

One must be utterly ignorant of the history of the first three centuries not to know that at that period the Church had no fixed organization; that it was not divided into provinces and dioceses until the reign of Constantine and by the Council of Nicea; that it was this council that recognized in the sees of Rome, Alexandria, and Antioch a superiority common to them all over a certain number of churches to which they had given birth, and over which, *according to customs*, they exercised a special supervision. But the forger does not hesitate for all this to bring into play archbishops, primates, and patriarchs during the first three centuries, and ascribes to the first Bishops of Rome, as *rights*, prerogatives which the councils had never recognized, and which these bishops had usurped in the West since the invasions of the barbarians had overthrown the ancient Roman polity.

After our deep study of the history of the Church, we feel at liberty to

Rome itself under the *pontificate of Adrian*, and in the year in which he wrote so haughtily to the Emperor of the East, that this new code of the Papacy is first mentioned in history. Adrian is the true creator of the modern Papacy. Not finding in the traditions of the Church the documents necessary to support his ambitious views, he rested them upon apocryphal documents written to suit the occasion, and to legalize all future usurpations of the Roman see. Adrian knew that the *Decretals* contained in the code of Ingelramn were false. For he had already given, ten years before, to Charles, King of the Franks, a code of the ancient canons identical with the generally received collection of Dionysius Exiguus. It was, therefore, between the years 775 and 785 that the *False Decretals* were composed.

The time was favorable to such inventions. In the foreign invasions which had deluged the entire West with blood and covered it with ruins, the libraries of the churches and monasteries had been destroyed; the clergy were plunged in the deepest ignorance; the East, invaded by the Mussulman, had now scarcely any relations with the West. The Papacy profited by these misfortunes and built up a power half political and half religious upon these ruins, finding no lack of flatterers who did not blush to invent and secretly propagate their forgeries in order to give a divine character to an institution that has ambition for its only source.

---

assert that it is impossible to accumulate more errors than the Ultramontanes have done to defend the alleged legal force of the False Decretals; that the *False Decretals* established in the ninth century a new code completely opposed to that of the first eight Christian centuries; and that the forger had no other object than to sanction the encroachments of the court of Rome during the two centuries preceding the composition of his work. We have carefully studied what has been said pro and contra upon this subject. The writings of the Romanists have convinced us that this forger of the ninth century has never been defended but by arguments worthy of him; that is to say, by the most shameful misrepresentations. The works of the Gallicans are more honest and show deeper research. Yet even in them we perceive a certain reticence which injures their cause, and even now and then a forced and unnatural attitude concerning Papal prerogatives, which they do not dare to deny. (See the works of Hincmar of Rheims, and the Annals of Father Lecointe.)

The *False Decretals* make as it were the dividing point between the Papacy of the first eight and that of the succeeding centuries. At this date, the pretensions of the Popes begin to develop and take each day a more distinct character. The answer of Adrian to Constantine and Irene is the starting-point.

The legates of the Pope and those of the Patriarchal churches of Alexandria, Antioch, and Jerusalem, having gone to Constantinople, Nicea was appointed as the place of assembling the council. The first session took place September 24, 787. This second Council of Nicea is reckoned the *seventh œcumenical*, both by the Eastern and Western churches.[252] Adrian was represented by the Archpriest Peter, and by another Peter, Abbot of the monastery of St. Sabas at Rome. The Bishops of Sicily were the first to speak, and said, "We deem it advisable that the most holy Archbishop of Constantinople should open the council." All the members agreed to this proposition, and Tarasius made them an allocution upon the duty of following the ancient traditions of the Church in the decisions they were about to make. Then those who opposed these traditions were introduced, that the council might hear a statement of their doctrine. Then were read the letters brought by the legates of the Bishops of Rome, Alexandria, Antioch, and Jerusalem, for the purpose of ascertaining what the faith of the East and the West might be. The Bishop of Ancyra had shared the error of the iconoclasts. He now appeared before the council to make his confession of faith, and commenced with the following words, well worthy of being quoted: "It is the law of the Church, that those who are converted from a heresy should abjure it in writing and confess the Catholic faith. Therefore do I, Basil, Bishop of Ancyra, wishing to unite myself with the Church, with Pope Adrian, with the Patriarch Tarasius, with the Apostolic sees of Alexandria, Antioch, and Jerusalem, and with all Catholic bishops and priests, make this confession in writing and present it to you, who have power by apostolic authority."

This most orthodox language clearly proves that at that time the Pope of Rome was not regarded as the *sole centre* of unity; the *source*

---

[252] See its transactions in Labbe's Collection, vol. viii.

of Catholic authority and unity was only recognized in the unanimity of the sacerdotal body.

The letter of Adrian to the Emperor and Empress, and the one he had written to Tarasius, were then read, but only in so far as they treated of dogmatic questions. His complaints against the title of "œcumenical" and his demands concerning the patrimony of St. Peter were passed over in silence. Nor did the legates of Rome insist. The council declared that it *approved* of the Pope's doctrine. Next were read the letters from the Patriarchal sees of the East whose doctrine agreed with that of the West. That doctrine was compared with the teaching of the Fathers of the Church, in order to verify not only the present unanimity, but the *perpetuity* of the doctrine; and the question was also examined whether the iconoclasts had on their side any true Catholic tradition. After this double preparatory examination, the council made its profession of faith, deciding that according to the perpetual doctrine of the Church, images should be venerated, reserving for God alone *the Latria* or *adoration*, properly so called.

The members of the council then adjourned to Constantinople, where the last session took place in the presence of Irene and Constantine and the entire people.

The Acts of the seventh œcumenical council, like those of the preceding ones, clearly prove that the Bishop of Rome was only first in *honor* in the Church; that his testimony had no doctrinal weight, except in so far as it might be regarded as that of the Western Church; that there was as yet no individual authority in the Church but a *collective authority*, of which the sacerdotal body was the echo and interpreter.

This doctrine is dramatically opposed to the Romish system. Let us add that the seventh œcumenical council, like the six that preceded it, was neither convoked, presided over, nor confirmed by the Pope. He concurred in it by his legates, and the West concurred in the same way, whereby it acquired its œcumenical character.

But this concurrence of the West was not at first unanimous, at least in appearance, notwithstanding the well-known concurrence of the Pope; which proves that even in the West such doctrinal authority was not then granted to the Pope, as his supporters now claim for him. Seven years after the Council of Nicea, that is, in 794, Charlemagne assembled at Frankfurt all the bishops of the kingdoms he had conquered. In this council several dogmatic questions were discussed, and particularly that concerning images. By the decisions there rendered, the council intended to reject that of the second council of Nicea, which had not been thoroughly understood by the Frankish Bishops. These Bishops reproached the Pope with his concurrence in that decision, and Adrian in a manner apologized for it.

He recognized, it is true, the orthodoxy of the doctrine professed by the council, but alleged that other motives would have impelled him to reject that council had he not feared lest his opposition might be construed into an adherence to the heresy condemned. "We have accepted the council,"[253] wrote Adrian, "because its decision agrees with the doctrine of St. Gregory; fearing lest if we did not receive it, the Greeks might return to their error and we be responsible for the loss of so many souls. Nevertheless, we have not yet made any answer to the Emperor on the subject of the council. While exhorting them to reestablish images, we have warned them to restore to the Roman Church her jurisdiction over certain bishoprics and archbishoprics, and the patrimonies of which we were bereft at the time when images were abolished. But we have received no answer, which shows that they are converted upon one point, but not upon the other two. Therefore, *if you think fit*, when we shall thank the Emperor for the reestablishment of images we will also press him further upon the subject of the restitution of the patrimonies and the jurisdiction, and, if he refuse, we will pronounce him a heretic."

The attacks of the Frankish Bishops against Adrian, although unjust, prove abundantly that they did not recognize in the Papacy the authority it claims today. The *False Decretals* had not yet been able completely to prevail over the ancient usages. Adrian replied to these attacks with a modesty that is easy of explanation, when we reflect how much he needed the Franks and their King Charlemagne

---

[253] Resp. ad. lib. Carolin. in Labbe's Collection, vol. viii.

V. Roman Bishop Authority of the 6th, 7th, and 8th Centuries 233

to establish the basis of the new Papacy. Far from mentioning that alleged authority which he so proudly strove to impose upon the East, he was willing, in respect to the Franks, to play the part of prisoner at the bar. He made advances to them to the extent of proposing to pronounce the Emperor of Constantinople a *heretic* for a mere question of temporal possessions, or of a disputed jurisdiction. But we find in Adrian, under this humble show of submission, a prodigious shrewdness in creating occasions for increasing his power. If the Franks had asked him to declare the Emperor of Constantinople a heretic, they would thereby have recognized in him a sovereign and universal jurisdiction and laid thus a precedent which would not have been neglected by the Papacy.

Adrian I died in 796 and was succeeded by Leo III, who pursued the same policy as his predecessor. Immediately after his election, he sent to Charlemagne the standard of the city of Rome and the key of *the confession* of St Peter. In return the Frankish King sent him costly presents by an ambassador, who was to come to an understanding with him upon all that concerned "the glory of the Church, and the *strengthening of the Papal dignity*, and of the Roman patriciate given to the Frankish King.[254]

Leo had some intercourse with the East upon the occasion of the divorce of the Emperor Constantine. Two holy monks, Plato and Theodore Studites, declared themselves with special energy against the adulterous conduct of the Emperor. Theodore applied to several bishops for aid against the persecutions which their opposition to the Emperor had drawn upon them. The letters of Theodore Studites[255] are replete with fulsome praises of those to whom he writes. The Romish theologians have chosen to notice only the compliments addressed to the Bishop of Rome. With a little more honesty they might as easily have noted those, often still more emphatic, that are to be found in his other letters; and they must then have concluded that no dogmatic force could be attached to language lavished without distinction of sees, according to circumstances, and with the evident purpose of flattering those to

---

254 Alcuin. Ep. 84.
255 Theod., Stud. Ep. 15.

whom the letters were addressed in order to render them favorable to the cause which Theodore advocated. The Romanists have not been willing to notice so obvious a fact. They have quoted the fulsome praises of Theodore as dogmatic testimony in favor of Papal authority, and have not chosen to see that if they have such a dogmatic value in the case of the Bishop of Rome, they must also have it no less in behalf of the Bishop of Jerusalem, for example, whom he calls "*first of the five Patriarchs*," or others, whom he addresses with as much extravagance. On these terms we should have in the Church several Popes enjoying, each of them, supreme and universal authority. This conclusion would not suit the Romish theologians; but it follows necessarily if the letters of Theodore Studites have the dogmatic value that Rome would give them to her own advantage. Moreover, if Theodore Studites occasionally gave pompous praise to the Bishop of Rome, he could also speak of him with very little respect, as we may see in his letter to Basil, Abbot of St. Sabas of Rome.[256]

At the commencement of his pontificate, Leo III had to endure a violent opposition on the part of the relatives of his predecessor, Adrian. They heaped atrocious accusations upon him.

Charlemagne, having come to Rome (800) as a patrician of that city, assembled a council to judge the Pope. But Leo was sure beforehand that he would prevail. He had received Charlemagne in triumph, and the powerful king was not ungrateful for the attentions of the pontiff.[257] The members of the council accordingly declared with one voice: "We dare not judge the Apostolic see, which is the *head* of all the churches; *such is the ancient custom!*" Men were not over nice in those days in matters of erudition. By the ancient usage the Bishop of Rome was to be judged like any other bishop; but the doctrines of the *False Decretals* had no doubt begun to spread.

---

256 Theod. Stud., Ep. 28.

257 Sismondi alleges that this mock trial and the subsequent capital punishment of Leo's accusers were prearranged, together with the coronation mentioned in the text, during Leo's visit to Charlemagne a short time previous at Paderborn. Sismondi, *Fall of the Roman Empire*, ch. xvii.—[EDITOR.]

V. Roman Bishop Authority of the 6th, 7th, and 8th Centuries 235

Ingelramn of Metz, who had used them in his lawsuit at Rome, was the chaplain of Charlemagne, and one of his first councilors.

According to this *new* code of a *new Papacy*, the Apostolic see, which could judge all, could be judged of none. Rome neglected no chance to establish this fundamental principle of her power, of which the inevitable consequence is Papal infallibility and even impeccability.

These consequences were not developed at once, but the principle was now skillfully insinuated upon one favorable occasion. Leo III justified himself upon oath. Some days later, on Christmas day, A.D. 800, Charlemagne having gone to St. Peter's, the Pope placed upon his head a rich crown and the people exclaimed, "Long life and victory to the august Charles, crowned by the hand of God great and pacific Emperor of the Romans!" These acclamations were thrice enthusiastically repeated; after which the Pope knelt before the new Emperor and anointed him and his son Pepin with the holy oil.

Thus was the *Roman* empire of the West reestablished. Rome, who had always looked with jealousy upon the removal of the seat of government to Constantinople, was in transports of joy; the Papacy, pandering to her secret lusts, was now invested with power such as she had never before possessed. The idea of Adrian was achieved by his successor. The modern Papacy, a mixed institution half political and half religious, was established; a new era was beginning for the Church of Jesus Christ—an era of intrigues and struggles, despotism and revolutions, innovations and scandals.

Pope Nicholas I of Rome

VI

THAT THE PAPACY, BY HER NOVEL AND AMBITIOUS PRETENTIONS, WAS THE CAUSE OF THE SCHISM BETWEEN THE EASTERN AND WESTERN CHURCHES.

WE have shown, first, that the Bishops of Rome did not enjoy universal authority during the first eight centuries of the Church. Second, that they were not then considered either as the centre of unity or as the source of jurisdiction. Third, that they were not supposed to be invested of *divine right* with any prerogatives whatever as successors of St. Peter.

If, after the ninth century, they put forward in respect of these three points pretensions contrary to the established and universal doctrine of the first eight centuries; if they undertook to subject the whole Church to their sovereign authority; if they assumed to be the necessary centre of unity and the source of jurisdiction; we must conclude that they have sought to usurp a power to which they had no right.

If these usurpations provoked energetic resistance on the part of the Eastern Church; if the Bishops of Rome made the recognition of their usurped power a condition precedent to reunion; it must follow that the Papacy is the first and direct cause of the division. The facts we shall allege will prove this to be so.

After the coronation of Charlemagne, there was an interval of peace between the two churches. Leo the Armenian renewed the heresy of the Iconoclasts and persecuted the Catholics. Many took refuge in Rome, and Pascal I (817) built a church for them in which they held services in Greek. This Pope even sent letters and legates to Constantinople to advocate the cause of the faith, which the majority of the bishops, with the Patriarch Nicephorus at their head, courageously defended. Leo the Armenian, hoping nothing from Rome, sought support in the Church of France. The Bishops of that church assembled at Paris and adopted several decisions similar to those of the Council of Frankfurt, of which we have spoken. Several of them were sent to Rome to give good advice to the Pope, then Eugenius II.

This was the beginning of that traditional opposition of the Church of France to the Papacy, in conformity with catholic doctrine, which has been called *Gallicanism*.

The Bishops of the Council of Paris, like those of Frankfurt, had no precise notion of the question discussed in the East; but we only desire to prove by them that they believed they had the right to contest the œcumenical character of the seventh general council, even after the Pope had concurred in it, and that they ascribed no dogmatic authority in the Church to the Bishop of Rome.

Several somewhat obscure Popes now succeeded each other until 858, when Nicholas I took the see of Rome. The Eastern Church, persecuted by iconoclastic emperors, defended the holy traditions of the Church with invincible courage. She enjoyed some tranquillity at last under the reign of Michael (842), after a persecution that had continued almost without interruption for a hundred and twenty years. Methodius, one of the most courageous defenders of orthodoxy, became Bishop of Constantinople and was succeeded (847) by Ignatius, son of the Emperor Michael Rhangabe, predecessor of Leo the Armenian. This Michael had been shut up in a monastery with his three sons, who had been made eunuchs in order to incapacitate them for reigning. Ignatius passed through all the lower degrees of the clergy and was a priest when chosen for the Patriarchal see. The Emperor Michael was a licentious man, who left his uncle Bardas to govern the empire. Ignatius drew upon himself the hatred of the Emperor by refusing to make nuns of the Empress dowager Theodora and her two daughters. He made a powerful enemy of Bardas, to whom he publicly refused communion, because of the scandal of his private life. Moreover, from the day of his consecration he had also incurred the enmity of Gregory, Bishop of Syracuse, by humiliating him and refusing to permit him to take part in that solemnity on the ground that he was accused of diverse misdemeanours; which was indeed true, but he had not been judged.

Ignatius subsequently judged and condemned him; but Rome, to which Gregory appealed, refused at first to confirm the sentence, notwithstanding the solicitations of Ignatius, and only consented when war was openly declared against Photius and his adherents.

We willingly admit that Ignatius had none but good intentions and conscientious motives in all that he did; but it is also just to acknowledge that he imitated neither the prudence of a Tarasius, nor the sublime self-denial of a Chrysostom. Naturally enough, the recollection of the imperial power, of which his father had been deprived by violence, did not dispose him to humor those who held that high position which he looked upon as the birthright of his family. The imperial court accused him of taking sides with an adventurer who fancied he had claims on the imperial crown, and he was exiled.

Many of the bishops before him had been equally exposed to the caprice of the court. Among his predecessors, and even in the see of Rome, Ignatius might have found examples of men who preferred to renounce a dignity they could no longer exercise with profit to the Church, rather than to excite by useless opposition disturbances which always injure it. He did not see fit to imitate these examples, and refused to renounce his dignity in spite of the entreaties of several bishops.

The court could not yield. It convoked the clergy, who chose Photius for their Patriarch.

Photius was nephew of the Patriarch Tarasius, and belonged to the imperial family.

His portrait is thus drawn by Fleury:[258]

"The genius of Photius was even above his birth. He had a great mind carefully cultivated. His wealth enabled him readily to

---

258 Fleury, Eccl. Hist., Lib. L. § 3, ann. 858.

find books of all descriptions; and his desire of glory led him to pass whole nights in reading. He thus became the most learned man not only of his own but of preceding ages. He was versed in grammar, poetry, rhetoric, philosophy, medicine, and all the secular sciences; but he had not neglected ecclesiastical lore, and when he came to office, he made himself thoroughly acquainted with it."

In a work latterly composed by the court of Rome, they have been obliged to say of Photius:[259] "His vast erudition, his insinuating temper, at once supple and firm, and his capacity in political affairs, even his sweet expression of face, his noble and attractive manners, made him conspicuous among his contemporaries."

But we ought first to have traced the character of Photius after those writers who are not suspected of partiality to him. Truth also demands that we should state what documents have served as the basis of all that has since been written in the Roman Church upon the important events in which he took part.

We will first mention the letters of Metrophanes, metropolitan of Smyrna; of Stylien, Bishop of Neo-Cæsarea; and of the monk Theognostus. These three men are known as personal enemies of Photius. Anastasius the Librarian was so contemptible a man that no importance can be attached to his testimony. The following is an abstract of the sentence rendered against him at Rome itself in 868: "The whole Church of God knows what Anastasius did in the times of the Popes our predecessors, and what Leo and Benedict ordered in respect to him, that the one deposed, excommunicated, and anathematized him; the other having stripped him of his priestly vestments, admitted him to lay communion. Subsequently, *Pope Nicholas reinstated him on condition of his remaining faithful to the Roman Church.* But after having pillaged our Patriarchal palace and carried off the Acts of the Councils in which he had been condemned, he has sent men out over the walls of this city to sow discord between the princes and the Church, and caused one Adalgrim, who had taken refuge in the Church, to lose his eyes and tongue. Finally, as many among you have, like myself, heard a priest, named Adon, a relative

---

[259] *The Eastern Church*, a book published under the name of M. Pitzipios, Part I, chap. 4, edition of the Roman "Propaganda."

VI. The Papacy Caused the Schism Between East and West

of his, say, he has forgotten our benefits to the extent of sending a man to Eleutherus to induce him to commit the murders you know of.[260] Therefore we order, in conformity with the judgments of Popes Leo and Benedict, that he be deprived of all ecclesiastical communion, until such time as he shall be acquitted by a council of the things whereof he is accused; and whoever communicates with him, or even speaks to him, incurs the same excommunication. If he remove himself however little from Rome, or if he discharge any ecclesiastical function, he shall suffer perpetual anathema, both he and his accomplices."

Anastasius doubtless obtained a pardon from Adrian as he had obtained it from Pope Nicholas. Rome had need of him in her contentions with the East, for he spoke Greek very well, which was then a rare accomplishment in the West. Accordingly, in the following year (869) we find Anastasius at Constantinople, engaged in the council against Photius. He translated its decrees from Greek into Latin, and added a preface in which he describes, in his own style, the acts attributed to Photius. Could such a man be regarded as a credible witness against the Patriarch of Constantinople, as a wise discriminator of facts, or as an honest narrator? May we not believe that he wished to show himself *faithful to the Roman Church* according to the condition of his first pardon granted by Nicholas?

"It is not known precisely at what time this author died. It is certain that he was still living under the pontificate of John VIII, who was elected in 872 and died in 882."[261]

There has indeed been an attempt to make the world believe in a second Anastasius, the Librarian at Rome at the same time,

---

260 Eleutherus, son of Bishop Arsenus, having debauched a daughter of Pope Adrian II, carried her off and married her though she was betrothed to another. This Pope obtained from the Emperor Louis commissioners to judge him according to the Roman law. Then Eleutherus became furious and killed Stephanie, the wife of the Pope, and his daughter, who had become his own wife. It was rumoured that Anastasius had put up his brother Eleutherus to commit these murders. At the commencement of his reign, about 868, Adrian had made Anastasius librarian of the Roman Church (V. Annales Bertin).

261 Feller, Dict. Biog. voc. Anastasius.

so as not to load the historian of the Popes with accusations which deprive him of all credibility. But no proof can be brought to sustain this assertion, which must consequently be regarded as devoid of all foundation. It is certain that Anastasius the Librarian flourished precisely at the time we have mentioned, and that no other Anastasius the Librarian is known beside the one implicated in the atrocious crimes mentioned in his sentence; who was repeatedly condemned there at Rome itself; and who only obtained pardon upon conditions which lay him open to suspicion, when he speaks of the enemies of the Roman Church.

The testimony of Nicetas David, the Paphlagonian, author of the *Life of Ignatius*, is relied on against Photius. We may even say that this writer is the great authority against him. Still, impartiality compels us to observe that Nicetas carried party spirit so far against Photius as to adopt the famous addition (Filioque) made to the creed, though not yet officially recognized as legitimate even in the West. The whole of his recital, and that of Michael Syncellus, proves that these two writers must be ranked among the personal enemies of Photius.

Now, when a historical personage is to be judged, should we defer to the opinion of his enemies? The question answers itself.

A clear and invincible argument against these authors may be drawn from their own writings, as compared with other historians such as George, Cedrenus, Zonaras, and Constantine Porphyrogenitus. The former attribute to Photius, on account of their hatred of him, the persecutions of which Ignatius was the object, while they are ascribed to Bardas by the latter, who are impartial.

How shall we decide between these conflicting accounts of the historians? We will believe neither. Photius, and the Popes with whom he quarreled, wrote letters in which their own thoughts are set forth. These letters exist; they are the most credible documents. We will hear the litigants themselves defend their own cause. This is the best mode of arriving at the truth.

VI. The Papacy Caused the Schism Between East and West

Photius received the episcopal ordination on Christmas day, 858. The following year he wrote to Nicholas I, then Bishop of Rome:

"To the most holy, sacred, and reverend fellow-minister, Nicholas, Pope of the old Rome: Photius, Bishop of Constantinople, the new Rome:

"When I consider the grandeur of the priesthood; when I think of the distance between its perfection and the baseness of man; when I measure the weakness of my powers, and recall the ideas I have had all my life of the sublimity of such a dignity—thoughts which inspired me with wonder, with stupefaction when I saw the men of our times, not to mention those of ancient times, accepting the dreadful yoke of the pontificate, and, though men of flesh and blood, undertaking, at their great peril, to fulfill the ministry of the pure-spirited cherubim; when my mind dwells upon such thoughts, and I find myself in that position in which I have trembled to see others, I cannot express the pain and the grief I experience. In childhood I took a resolution that age has only strengthened, to keep myself aloof from business and noise, and to enjoy the peaceful delights of private life; still (I should confess it to your Holiness, since in writing to you I owe you the truth) I have been obliged to accept dignities from the imperial court, and thus break my resolutions. Yet have I never been so bold as to aspire to the dignity of the priesthood. It seemed to me too venerable and formidable; above all, when I recalled the example of St. Peter, head of the Apostles, who, after having given to our Lord and our true God, Jesus Christ, so many evidences of his faith, and showed how ardently he loved him, regarded the honor of being raised by his Master to the priesthood as the crowning glory of all his good works. I also recall the example of that servant who had received one talent, and who, having hid it because his master was a hard man, that he might not lose it, was obliged to give an account of it and was condemned to the fire and to Hades for having permitted it to lie idle.

"But why should I thus write to you, and, renew my pain and aggravate my grief, and make you the confidant of my sorrow?

The remembrance of painful things embitters their evil without bringing any solace. That which has happened is like a tragedy, which took place, no doubt, in order that by your prayers we might be enabled to govern well that flock which has been committed to us, I know not how; that the cloud of difficulties hanging over us might be dispelled; that the heavy atmosphere which surrounds us might be cleared. Even as a pilot is joyful when he sees his well-directed bark driven by a favorable wind, so a church is the joy of a pastor, who sees it increase in piety and virtue, dispelling the anxieties that encompass him like clouds, and the fears inspired by his own weakness.

"A short time since, *when he who had the episcopal office before us abandoned this honor*, I found myself attacked on all sides, under what direction I do not know, by the clergy and the assembly of bishops and metropolitans, and particularly by the Emperor, who is full of love for Christ, good, just, humane, and (why shall I not say it?) more just than those who reigned before him. Only against me has he been inhuman, violent, and terrible. Acting in concert with the assembly of which I have spoken, he has given me no respite, actuated, he says, to this insistence by the unanimous wish and desire of the clergy, who would allow me no excuse; and asserting that in view of such a vote he could not, however he might desire it, permit my resistance. The assembly of the clergy was large, and my entreaties could not be heard by many of them; those who heard them took no heed of them; they had but one intention, one determined resolve—that of imposing the episcopate upon me in spite of myself.".....

We will pause here one moment. The enemies of Photius have maintained that in thus expressing himself he gave evidence of his hypocrisy; that instead of refusing the episcopacy, he had desired it. They also accuse him of falsehood in asserting that his predecessor had abandoned his dignity.

Are these two assertions true? We can better know a man by his familiar correspondence than by the gratuitous assertions of his enemies. This is certainly a principle that no one will contest. Now the familiar letters of Photius to his relative, the "Cæsar "

VI. The Papacy Caused the Schism Between East and West

Bardas, clearly prove that he left no means untried to escape from the dignity that it was sought to impose upon him. The honors which he enjoyed at court were already a burden to him, because they forced him from studies which were his only passion; he knew, that once raised to the patriarchal chair, he would be compelled to give up that peaceful life in which he enjoyed the truest delights of learning; and therefore he entreated Bardas to give another the chair.[262] What motive could he have had to write this intimately to a man who knew his tastes and was his friend?

Now did Photius seek to deceive the Pope by writing to him that Ignatius had abandoned his see? It is certain that, right or wrong, Ignatius had been condemned as a conspirator, and as such banished by the Emperor. If, under these circumstances, he had, as Anastasius the Librarian asserts, laid his church under a species of interdict, such conduct would have been criminal and opposed to that of the greatest and most saintly bishops. We have already seen Pope Martin condemned, persecuted, and banished like Ignatius, yet acknowledging the legitimacy of Eugene, elected by the Roman Church as his successor without his ever having given his resignation. St. Chrysostom, unjustly exiled, wrote in this noble language: "The Church did not begin with me, nor will it end with me. The Apostles and the Prophets have suffered far greater persecutions."

As a conclusion, he exhorted the bishops to obey whoever should be put in his place, and only begged them not to sign his condemnation if they did not believe him guilty.

Photius must have considered this custom and looked upon his predecessor as having fallen from his dignity, seeing that all the clergy except five votes[263] had elected him to succeed Ignatius. But he could not write to the Pope that Ignatius had been deposed, since he had not been canonically condemned.

He was therefore neither a hypocrite nor a liar in writing to the Pope, as we have seen. He thus continues:

---

262 Photi., Epist. ad Bard.
263 Those historians who are enemies to Photius acknowledge this.

"The opportunity for entreaty being taken from me, I burst into tears. The sorrow, which seemed like a cloud within me and filled me with anxiety and darkness, broke at once into a torrent of tears which overflowed from my eyes. To see our words unavailing to obtain safety impels us naturally to prayers and tears; we hope for some aid from them even though we can no longer expect it. Those who thus did violence to my feelings left me no peace until they had obtained what they desired, although against my will. Thus here I am, exposed to storms and judgments that only God knows of, who knows all things. But enough of this, as the phrase is.

"Now as communion of faith is the best of all, and as it is preeminently the source of true love, in order to contract with your Holiness a pure and indissoluble bond we have resolved to briefly engrave, as upon marble, our faith, which is yours also. By that means we shall more promptly obtain the aid of your fervent prayers, and give you the best evidence of our affection."

Photius then makes his profession of faith with an exactitude and depth worthy of the greatest theologian. He there refers the fundamental truths of Christianity to the mysteries of the Trinity, the Incarnation, and Redemption. He accepts the seven œcumenical councils, and sets forth in few words, but with remarkable accuracy, the doctrine there propounded.

He adds:

"Such is the profession of my faith, touching the things that belong to it and flow from it. In this faith is my hope. It is not mine alone, but is shared by all those who wish to live piously, who have in them the love of God, who have resolved to maintain the pure and exact Christian doctrine. In recording thus our profession of faith in writing, and in making known to your very sacred Holiness that which concerns us, we have as it were engraved upon marble what we have expressed to you in words; as we have told you, we need your prayers, that God may be good and propitious to us in all we undertake; that He may grant us grace to tear up every root of scandal, every stone of stumbling from the ecclesiastical order; that we may carefully pasture all those committed to us; that the multitude of our sins may not retard the progress of our flock in virtue, and thereby make our faults more numerous; that I may at all times do and say to the faithful what is proper; that on their side they may be always obedient and docile in what concerns their salvation; that by the "grace and goodness of Christ, who is the chief of all, they may grow continually in Him, to whom be Glory and the kingdom with the Father and Holy Spirit, the consubstantial Trinity and principle of life, now and evermore, world without end. Amen."

This letter savours of the taste of the age in its affected style. But it is no less a beautiful monument of orthodoxy, and, in all respects, worthy of a great writer and a great bishop.

The enemies of Photius have said that another letter, claimed to be his first letter to the Pope, was a work of hypocrisy in which he sought to win him over to his side by unworthy means, and chiefly by affecting great zeal against the iconoclasts. They have never been able to quote a line of this supposed letter. Those who invented it seem not to have remembered that the bishops could not hold the least intercourse before the usual letters of intercommunion. On this occasion, as on many others, hatred has made the forgers blind.

The *first letter* of Photius to the Pope is the one we have just translated.

It was brought to Rome with a letter from the Emperor. Nicholas I took this occasion to do an act of supreme authority in the Church. This Pope is one of those who most contributed to unfold the work of Adrian I. The Jesuit Maimbourg,[264] meaning to praise him, asserts that, "during his pontificate of nine years, he raised the papal power to a height it had never before reached, especially in respect to emperors, kings, princes, and patriarchs, whom he treated more roughly than any of his predecessors, whenever he thought himself wronged in the prerogatives of his pontifical power." This is undoubtedly true, but Father Maimbourg did not appreciate either the historical importance of what he established, nor the fatal consequences of this development of papal power. Nor did he see that this vaunted development was nothing short of a radical

---

264 Maimb., *History of the Greek Schism*.

change, and that, in, the ninth century, the Papacy was no longer the Roman patriarchate of the first eight centuries.

Nicholas did not know what had taken place at Constantinople at the time of the deposition of Ignatius and the election of Photius. He only knew that Photius was a layman at the time of his election. It is true, many canons of the West forbade hasty ordinations; but these canons did not obtain in the East, and although usage there was in favor of progressive ordinations, the history of the Church proves, by numerous examples, that these canons and this usage were occasionally passed over in favor of men of distinguished merit and under circumstances of peculiar gravity. We need only to recall the names of Ambrose of Milan, Nectarius, Tarasius, and Nicephorus of Constantinople to prove that the ordination of Photius was not without the most venerable precedent. But Nicholas desired to appear in the character of supreme arbiter. Instead of modestly putting off intercommunion with the new Patriarch until he should be more fully informed, he answered the letters of Photius and of the Emperor in this style:

"The Creator of all things has established the PRINCEDOM of the divine power which the Creator of all things has granted to his chosen Apostles. He has firmly established it on the firm faith of the Prince of the Apostles, that is to say Peter, to whom he preeminently granted the first see. For to him was said by the voice of the Lord, 'Thou art Peter, and upon this rock I will build my church, and the gates of hell shall not prevail against it.' Peter, thus called because of the solidity of the rock, which is Christ, continues to strengthen by his prayers the unshaken edifice of the universal Church, so that he hastens to reform, according to the rule of true faith, the folly of those who fall into error, and sustains those who consolidate it lest the gates of hell, that is to say, the suggestion of wicked spirits and the attacks of heretics, should succeed in breaking the unity of the Church."[265]

Nicholas then pretends to be convinced that when Michael sent to Rome, it was to fulfill the rule established by the Fathers; that

---

265 Nocol., Ep. 2d and 3d in Labbe's Collection of the Councils, vol. viii. Nat. Alexand., Eccl. Hist. Dissert. iv. in sæcul. ix.

VI. The Papacy Caused the Schism Between East and West

"without the consent of the Roman see and the Roman pontiff, nothing should be decided in controversies."

This principle was admitted in this sense, that no question of faith could be passed upon without the concurrence of the Western churches, which was commonly transmitted through the chief see of those countries; but not in this sense, that the consent of the individual See of Rome or of its bishop was absolutely necessary. Nicholas thus relied upon an error, and improperly treated it as admitted by the Emperor of the East. Upon this latter point, at least, he knew what the truth was. He next attacks the election of Photius, relying on the canons of the Council of Sardica, and the *Decretals* of the Popes Celestine, Leo, and Gelasius, whom he calls *doctors of the catholic faith*. He might have considered that the faith was not in question, but only a mere matter of discipline, and that the East had not, and was entitled not to have, upon this point, the same discipline as the West. Adrian I had forbidden in future to raise a layman to the episcopate. Nicholas relies on this as a precedent. But he does not consider whether Adrian had any better right than himself to make this prohibition. "IT IS OUR WILL," he adds, "that Ignatius should appear before our envoys, that he may declare why he has abandoned his people without regarding the rules of our predecessors Leo and Benedict... All the proceedings will then be transmitted to our superior authority, that we may judge by Apostolic authority what is to be done, in order that your church, which is now so shaken, may be firm and peaceful for the future."

Following a practice which was already established in the Roman Church, Nicholas did not permit his duties as supreme pontiff to divert his mind from the material interests of his see; accordingly, he writes to the Emperor: "Give back to us the patrimony of Calabria and that of Sicily and all the property of our church, whereof it held possession, and which it was accustomed to manage by its own attorneys; for it is unreasonable that an ecclesiastical possession, destined for the light and the service of the Church of God, should be taken from us by an earthly power."

Behold now the temporalities already invested with religious consecration!

"It is our will," adds Nicholas [these words flow naturally from his pen upon all occasions—AUTHOR], "that consecration be given by our see to the Archbishop of Syracuse, that the tradition established by the Apostles may not be violated in our time." This motive is truly strange, to say no more of it. Sicily was made subject to the Roman Patriarchate in the fourth century. After the fall of the empire, that region had remained within the dominions of the Emperor of Constantinople. Now, according to the rule admitted time out of mind in the Church, the ecclesiastical divisions should follow every change in the civil divisions. By that rule, Syracuse properly depended upon Constantinople, and not Rome. Nicholas WILLED *it otherwise*, but the law willed it thus, and the Apostles to whom he appealed had certainly never made the see of Syracuse subject to that of Rome. The letter to Photius is but an abridgment of that to the Emperor, with this difference, that Nicholas avoids the use of the ambitious expressions we have quoted. He addressed Photius as a simple layman, without giving him any episcopal title, though he knew him to have been lawfully consecrated. This affectation was big with this idea: that no bishop could bear the character of his order, except by the consent of the Roman Pontiff.

The earlier popes had never used such language either to the emperors or to their brethren the bishops. In cases where they were obliged to interfere for the defence of faith or of discipline, they did not assume the character of sovereign umpires and claimed no supreme authority; they appealed to tradition, to the canons; they did nothing without a council, and did not mix things temporal with things spiritual. We have noticed the first steps of the Papacy in its new ways and its attempts to abolish the ancient canon law.

Nicholas I thought himself prepared to treat these new pretensions as ancient and incontestable prerogatives. He thus deserves a place between Adrian I, the true founder of the modern Papacy, and Gregory VII, who raised it to its highest. But the *False Decretals* were unknown in the East. Nicholas I, instead of invoking the general principles of the œcumenical councils, quoted the *Decretals* of his predecessor, as if it were possible for those Bishops of Rome to establish universal laws. Photius, in his second letter,

VI. The Papacy Caused the Schism Between East and West 251

reminded him of the true principles with as much accuracy as moderation.

The legates of Nicholas having arrived at Constantinople, a council was assembled in that city in which three hundred and eighteen bishops took part, and which the legates attended. Ignatius appeared before that assembly, and was solemnly deposed. Everyone admits this. But the enemies of Photius represent these three hundred and eighteen bishops, who held their sessions publicly and before large crowds, as so many traitors sold to the crown. We find it difficult to believe that so many bishops can have prostituted their consciences unchecked, to a man, by any remorse, and that the people did not protest against such infamy. It is difficult to believe in this connivance of three hundred and eighteen bishops, surrounded by a crowd of clergy and people. It seems to us more probable that, in spite of his virtues, Ignatius had been raised to the Patriarchate less by election than by a powerful influence, and because of his noble blood, whereof he was indeed reproached, and that he was implicated, involuntarily, no doubt, in certain political intrigues. We see no reason to doubt the purity of his intentions; but may he not have been the tool of ambitious men? Was it not owing to their baneful influence that he did not imitate the magnanimity and the truly bishop-like self-sacrifice of a Chrysostom?

Ignatius was a second time deposed by the Council of Constantinople in 861. He appealed to the Pope; but his petition was signed by only six metropolitans and fifteen bishops.

The legates returned to Rome. Shortly after their arrival, an imperial ambassador brought the transactions of the council and a letter from Photius, thus conceived:

"To the very holy among all and most sacred brother and co-minister, Nicholas, Pope of ancient Rome. —Photius, Bishop of Constantinople, the new Rome.

"Nothing is more honorable and precious than charity; this is the general opinion confirmed by Holy Scriptures. By her that which is separated becomes united; contentions are ended; that which is already united and closely tied becomes united more closely still; she closes all doors to seditions and intestine quarrels; for 'charity thinketh no evil, suffereth long, hopeth all things, endureth all things, and,' according to the blessed Paul, 'never faileth.' She reconcileth guilty servants with their masters, insisting, in mitigation of the fault, upon their similar natures; she teaches servants to bear meekly the anger of their masters, and consoles them for the inequality of their state by the example of those who suffered the like with them. She softens the anger of parents against their children, and against their murmurs; she makes parental love a powerful weapon, which comes to their aid and prevents in families those strifes from which nature shrinks. She easily checks dissensions between friends, and persuades them to kindly and friendly intercourse. As for those who have the same thoughts concerning God and divine things, although distance separate them, and they never behold each other, she unites them and identifies them in thought, and makes true friends of them, and if perchance one of them should too inconsiderately raise accusations against the other, she cures the evil, sets all things to right, and rivets the bond of union."

This picture of the benefits of charity was intended for Nicholas, who had not practiced it toward Photius, but had shown an excessive eagerness to rebuke him. The Patriarch of Constantinople continues:

"It is this charity that has made me bear without difficulty the reproaches that your paternal Holiness has hurled at me like darts; that has forbidden me to consider your words as the results of anger or of a soul greedy of insults and enmities; that on the contrary has made me regard them as the proof of an affection which cannot dissimulate, and of a scrupulous zeal for ecclesiastical discipline, a zeal that would have everything perfect. For if charity will not permit us even to consider evil as wrong, how shall she permit us to call anything wrong? Such is the nature of true charity, that she will even regard as an intended benefit that which causes us pain. But since there is no reason why truth should not be spoken between brothers or fathers and sons (for what is there more friendly than truth?), let me speak and write to you with perfect freedom, not from a desire to contradict you, but with intent to defend myself.

VI. The Papacy Caused the Schism Between East and West

"Perfect as you are, you should have considered at the outset that it was quite against our will that we were placed under this yoke, and therefore have had pity upon us instead of rebuking us; you should not have despised us, but have had compassion on our grief. Indeed, we owe pity and kindness and not insult and contempt to those who have suffered violence. But we have suffered violence—how great, God alone, who knows the most secret things, can know; we have been detained against our wishes; we have been watched narrowly, surrounded with spies like a culprit; we have received votes against our will, we have been created a bishop in spite of our tears, our complaints, our affliction, our despair. Everyone knows it; for these things were not done in secret, and the exceeding violence to which I have been subjected was so public as to be known of all. What—should not those who have endured such violence be pitied and consoled as much as possible, rather than be attacked, evil-entreated, and laden with insults? I have lost a sweet and tranquil life; I have lost my glory (since there be who love earthly glory); I have lost my precious leisure, my intercourse so pure and delightful with my friends, that intercourse whence grief, double-dealing, and recrimination were excluded. No one hated me then; and... I accused, I hated no one, neither at home nor abroad. I had nothing against those who had the least intercourse with me, and nothing *á fortiori* against my friends. I have never caused such pain to any one as that I should reap an outrage from it, save in those dangers to which I have been exposed for the cause of religion.[266] Nor has any one so seriously offended me as to drive me to insult him. All were good to me. As for my conduct, I must be silent on that point; but everyone proclaims what that has been. My friends loved me better than their parents; as for my parents, they loved me more than the other members of the family, and knew it was I who loved them best."

The enemies of Photius themselves are forced to admit that his life was that of a man devoted to study; that as first secretary of state he possessed the greatest honors to which he could have aspired.

---

266 Photius here alludes to the resistance he had made to the iconoclastic emperors and their partisans.

How shall such admissions be reconciled with that immoderate lust after the episcopate which they attribute to him? We are nearer the truth in accepting his letters as the actual expression of his sentiments. He resisted as best he could his promotion, and it was only the will of the Emperor and that of Bardas that forced him to accept a see which no one could fill better than himself.

Photius, having drawn a comparison as true as it is eloquent between his former scholar's life and the new life that had been imposed upon him, thus continues:

"But why repeat what I have already written? If I was believed, then I was wronged in not being pitied; if I was not believed, I was no less wronged in that my words were not believed when I spoke the truth. Upon either side, then, I am unfortunate. I am reproached where I expect consolation and encouragement; grief is thus added to grief. I hear said to me, 'Men ought not to have wronged you.' Then say so to those who have wronged me, 'They ought not to have done you violence.' The maxim is excellent; but who deserves your reproaches if not those who did me violence? Who should be pitied if not those to whom violence has been done? If anyone left in peace those who did violence in order to attack those who suffered it, I might have hoped from your justice that you would condemn him.

The canons of the Church, it is said, have been violated because you are raised from the rank of a layman to the highest office of the ministry. But who has violated them? He who has done violence, or he who has been compelled by force and against his will? But you should have resisted! How far? I did resist even more than necessary. If I had not feared to excite still greater storms, I would have resisted even unto death. But what are these canons that are said to have been violated? Canons never to this day received by the Church of Constantinople. Canons can only be transgressed when they ought to be observed; but when they have not been handed down to us there can be no sin in not observing them. I have said enough—even more than was expedient—for I wish neither to defend nor justify myself. How should I wish to defend myself, when the only thing I desire is to be delivered from the tempest, and to be relieved of the burden that bears me down? It is to this degree that I have coveted this see, and only to this degree do I desire to retain it. But if the episcopal chair is a burden to you today, it was not thus at the commencement. I took it against my will, and against my will do I remain in it. The proof is that violence was done to me from the first; that from the first I desired as I do this day to leave it. But though some polite things had to be written to me, it was impossible to write to me with kindness and to praise me. We have received all that has been said to us with joy, and with thanks to God who governs the Church. It has been said to me, 'You have been taken from the laity; that is not a laudable act; therefore are we undecided and have deferred our consent until after the return of our apocrisiaries.[267] It had been better to say, 'We will not consent at all; we do not approve; we do not accept, and never will.' The man who offered himself for this see, who has bought the episcopate, who never received an honest vote, is a bad man in all respects. Leave the episcopate and the office of pastor. One who should have written me thus would have written agreeably, however falsely. But was it necessary that one who had suffered so much on entering the episcopate should suffer again in leaving it? That he who had been pushed violently into that office should be pushed from it with still greater violence? One who has such sentiments, such thoughts, must care very little to repel calumny intended to deprive him of the episcopal chair. But enough upon this subject."

In the remainder of his letter, Photius explains at great length that one Church should not condemn the usages of another, provided

---

267 The Abbé Jager, in his *History of Photius*, Book III, page 64, ed. 1854, has taken this analysis of Nicholas's letter as an assertion of Photius. He therefore adds, in a note, "*A new falsehood!*" Upon the same page he had just before written, "*An impudent falsehood! This is a new lie!*" to characterize the affirmations of Photius, saying that he remained in the bishopric against his will, and that his only ambition was to quit it. These notes are unworthy of a writer who respects himself. Moreover, before reproaching Photius for a third lie, that writer should have taken a little trouble to understand his language; he then would not have taken for a personal assertion of Photius the analysis of the Pope's letter, who had indeed said he would postpone his consent until the return of his envoys.

they are not contrary either to the faith or to the canons of the general councils. He justifies his ordination by this rule, and by the example of his holy predecessors Nectarius, Tarasitis, Nicepliortis; and also that of St. Ambrose, St. Gregory, father of the theologian, and Thalassius of Cæsarea. He shows to Nicholas that in the last council, held in presence of his legates, several disciplinary rules suggested by him were adopted because they appeared useful. He praises the Pope for his love of the maintenance of the canons, and congratulates him for it the more that, *having the primacy*, his example was the more powerful. He takes occasion from this to inform him, in conclusion, that a large number of criminals escape to Rome, under pretext of making a pilgrimage, to hide there their crimes under a false appearance of piety. He begs him, therefore, to observe upon this point the canons which prescribe to each bishop that he shall receive to communion only those who can show letters of recommendation from his own bishop.

In all ages, Rome has been thus reproached for serving as a refuge for hypocritical criminals. The Church of France wrote frequently to the Popes in the same strain as Photius did upon this occasion.

This letter of the Patriarch could not be palatable to Nicholas, for under cover of polished and elegant phrases it carried very just lessons. Photius does not use one harsh word. He does not even adopt his honorary title of œcumenical Patriarch; he recognizes *the primacy* of the see of Rome; but he does not flatter the ambition of the new Papacy, he does not bow before it, and his gentleness does not exclude firmness. Such an adversary was more dangerous to Nicholas than a violent and ambitious man. Instead of disputing with him the rights he claimed over certain churches of the Patriarchate of Constantinople, he says to him: "We would have yielded them to you if it had depended upon us; but as it is a question of countries and boundaries, it concerns the state. For my part, I should like not only to render to others what belongs to them, but even to yield a part of the ancient dependencies of this see. I should be greatly obliged to anyone who would relieve me of a portion of my burden."

VI. The Papacy Caused the Schism Between East and West

No better reply than this could have been made to a Pope who only thought of extending his power by every means. But Nicholas did not profit by this lesson, which was as just as it was moderate. He would believe neither his legates nor the acts of the council which were presented to him. He even declared to the ambassador Leo, who had been sent to him, that he had not sent his legates to depose Ignatius or to concur in the promotion of Photius; that he had not consented, and never would consent to either.

Nicholas pretended thus to judge of the legitimacy of bishops, forgetting that the canons only gave him the choice to enter into communion with the one or the other. It was well understood that before entering into relations with Photius, he must have positive information as to the legitimacy of his election; but, according to the laws of the Church, that legitimacy did not depend upon the Papal will, but upon the judgement pronounced upon Ignatius and the regularity of the election of Photius. A council of three hundred and eighteen bishops had publicly approved that election and the deposition of Ignatius. The legates had witnessed the proceedings; they gave evidence to what they had seen and heard; it was certainly enough, it should seem, to allow Nicholas to grant his communion to one whose learning and honorable character made him well worthy of the episcopate. But in taking sides with Ignatius, Nicholas was doing an act of sovereign authority. This prospect flattered his tendencies too much to permit him to eschew it. He therefore assembled the clergy of Rome to solemnly disown his legates. He subsequently wrote to the Emperor, to Photius, and to the whole Eastern Church letters which are monuments of his pride. We must give them, that the doctrine they contain may be compared with that of the first eight centuries, and that a conviction may thus be arrived at: that the Papacy had abandoned the latter in order to substitute for it an autocratic system which the Eastern Church could not accept.[268] At the beginning of his letter to the Emperor Michael, he takes it for granted that this prince has addressed himself "to the holy, Catholic, and Apostolic Roman Church, chief [head] of all the churches, which follows in all its acts

---

268 Nichol., Epist. 5 and 6.

the pure authority of the Holy Fathers," for the purpose of being informed what he should think in ecclesiastical matters.

Nicholas neglected no occasion of repeating these high-sounding phrases, which disprove themselves, for the Fathers were completely ignorant of them. Coming to the cause of Ignatius, he complains "that contrary to *his orders* a sentence had been pronounced against Ignatius; not only had they omitted to do what he had prescribed, but had done just the opposite. Therefore, he adds, since you sustain Photius and reject Ignatius, without the judgment of *our Apostolat*, we would have you to know that we do not receive Photius, nor condemn the patriarch Ignatius."

This is certainly talking like a master. He then is at pains to find differences of detail between the promotion of Nectarius and Ambrose, and that of Photius. But these differences, even supposing they were such as he makes them, were not of a nature to override a positive enactment had it been considered absolute and susceptible of no exceptions.

His letter *to the very wise man Photius* commences in this solemn manner:

"After our Lord and Redeemer Jesus Christ, who was very God before all ages, had condescended to be born of the Virgin for our redemption, and to appear as very man in the world, he committed to the blessed Peter, prince of the Apostles, the power to bind and loose in heaven and upon earth, and the right to open the gates of the kingdom of heaven; he condescended to establish his holy Church upon the solidity of that Apostle's faith, according to this faithful saying, 'Verily, I say unto thee, thou art Peter, and upon this rock I will build my Church, and the gates of hell shall not prevail against it: and I will give unto thee the keys of the kingdom of heaven: and whatsoever thou shalt bind on earth shall be bound in heaven, and whatsoever thou shalt loose on earth shall be loosed in heaven.'"

Such is the great argument on which the modern Papacy has always relied. It openly rejects the catholic and traditional interpretation of these divine words; it makes of rights granted to all the Apostles in common an exclusive and personal right in

VI. The Papacy Caused the Schism Between East and West

favor of Saint Peter; it takes its stand, contrary to all ecclesiastical law, and in virtue of a gratuitous sacrilege, as sole inheritor of chimerical prerogatives, and pretends upon these lying and fragile bases to establish the fabric of its universal autocracy. Such was the claim that Nicholas opposed to Photius; and it is now said that this Patriarch, who was perfectly acquainted with ecclesiastical antiquity, ought to have submitted to such authority! His duty was to protest as he did; and would to God that all the Bishops of the Catholic Church had imitated his courage, as firm as it was pure and moderate!

This is Nicholas's commentary upon the words of the Gospel he had quoted: "According to this promise, by the cement of the holy Apostolic institution, the foundations of the edifice, composed of precious stones, began to arise; and, thanks to Divine clemency, and by the zeal of the builders, and the solicitude of the Apostolic authority, to arise to the summit, to endure forever, having nothing to fear from the violence of the winds. The blessed Peter, prince of the Apostles, and doorkeeper of the celestial kingdom, merited *the primacy* in that edifice, as all who are orthodox know, and as we have just declared." No one, in fact, among those who are orthodox denies the primacy of St. Peter; but did that primacy give him supreme authority? No, replies Catholic tradition. Yes, answers Nicholas, who thus continues: "After him [St. Peter] *his vicars*, serving God with sincerity, and delivered from the shadow of darkness that hinders from walking in the right way, have received in a higher sense the care of pasturing the sheep of the Lord, and have carefully accomplished this duty. Among them the mercy of God Almighty has condescended to include our littleness; but we tremble at the thought that we shall answer, *first of all, and for all*, to Jesus Christ, when He shall call each one to account for his works.

"Now, as all believers come for their doctrine to this holy Roman Church, which is the chief [head] of all the churches; as they ask of her what is the purity of the faith; as those who are worthy, and who are ransomed by the grace of God, ask of her absolution for their crimes; it is our duty, who have received the charge of her, to be attentive, to keep constant watch over the flock of the Lord, the more that there are those who are ever eager to tear it with cruel fangs... It is apparent that the holy Roman Church, through the blessed Apostle Peter, prince of the Apostles, who was thought worthy to receive from the mouth of the Lord the *primacy of the churches,* is the chief [head] of all the churches; that it is to her that all must apply to know the just course, and the order to be followed in all useful things, and in the ecclesiastical institutions, which she maintains in an inviolable and incontestable manner, according to the canonical and synodical laws of the holy Fathers. Hence it follows that whatsoever is rejected by the rectors of this see—by their full authority—should be rejected, any particular custom notwithstanding; and that whatsoever is ordered by them should be accepted firmly and without hesitation."

Thus Nicholas opposed his sovereign authority to the laws, followed from all antiquity by the Church, which Photius had rehearsed to him. He next endeavors to find differences of detail in the elections of Nectarius, Ambrose, Tarasius, and that of Photius. He succeeds no better upon this point than in his letter to the Emperor Michael, and he silently passes over the other examples mentioned by Photius.

In his letters to the Patriarchs and to the faithful of the East,[269] Nicholas sets forth like views upon his autocracy. He *commands* the Patriarchs of Alexandria, Antioch, and Jerusalem to make known to their faithful the decisions of the Apostolic see.

Ignatius, by his appeal to Nicholas from the judgement passed upon him, had too much flattered the pride of the Pope. To prove this it will be sufficient to quote the superscription of his appeal papers.

"Ignatius, oppressed by tyranny, etc., to our most holy Lord, and most blessed President, Patriarch of all sees, successor of St. Peter, Prince of the Apostles, Nicholas, œcumenical Pope, and to his most holy bishops; and to the most wise, universal, Roman Church."[270]

---

269 Nichol., Epist. 1 and 4.

270 See Libel. Ignat. in Labbe's Collection, vol. viii. Many scholars doubt the authenticity of this document. Notwithstanding his friendly relations with Rome, we can scarcely believe that Ignatius could have addressed the Pope

VI. The Papacy Caused the Schism Between East and West 261

St. Gregory the Great would have rejected such titles *as diabolical inventions*, as we have already seen by his letters to John the Faster; but the Papacy of St. Gregory the Great was no more; it had given place to a politico-ecclesiastical institution, with only power for its aim. Ignatius, so long as he flattered the ambition of Nicholas, could not but be right in his eyes. Photius, who held to the ancient doctrine, and looked upon the Bishop of Rome simply as first bishop, without granting him any personal authority, could not but be wrong.

Accordingly, without further question, Nicholas pronounced anathema against him in a council which he held at Rome at the commencement of the year 863. "*We declare him,*" he says, "deprived of all sacerdotal honor and of every clerical function by the authority of God Almighty, of the Apostles St. Peter and St. Paul, of all the saints, of the six general councils, and *by the judgment which the Holy Spirit has pronounced by us.*"[271] He ventured in the sentence to accuse Photius himself of the persecutions that Ignatius had endured. This was a calumny drawn from the denunciations of the enemies of Photius, and since repeated by all the Romish writers who have spoken of the discussion between this Patriarch and Nicholas.[272] It is apparent, moreover, from all the Pope did, that he

---

in the form above quoted.

271 Labbe's Collection of Councils, vol. vii.

272 We have not noticed all that has been related by the enemies of Photius in respect to the sufferings of Ignatius. First, because these details have nothing to do with the principal question. Second, because these recitals are evidently exaggerated. Third, because history does not hold Photius responsible for them. Did not Ignatius draw upon himself the hatred of the Emperor and Bardas by his imprudent zeal by his proceedings respecting Gregory of Syracuse, and by his sentiments hostile to the government? These are questions upon which even the recitals of his partisans could not establish his innocence. We may even say that these intemperate recitals injure him by their very exaggeration. His refusal to resign provoked the violence of the court. We do not deny it, although the details of this violence are very difficult to be admitted completely. But was Photius an accomplice in this violence? We reply no, first, because impartial historians in no manner attribute it to him, and because he himself protested, in his letters to Bardas, against the violence with which his adversaries were treated. These letters, well worthy of a great and holy bishop, may be found among his correspondence.

had predetermined to bear nothing in favor of Photius in the way of proof or argument. To him a few monks, partisans of Ignatius, who had come to Rome, were better authority than a council of three hundred and eighteen bishops, beside a large number of ecclesiastics and monks, which held its sessions in presence of an immense concourse of people. It must indeed be admitted that the conduct of Nicholas must have had an altogether different motive than the defence of Ignatius or the justice of his cause. He believed himself the *depositary of divine authority, and the organ of the Holy Spirit*.

It was in this character that he claimed all his rights. But the general councils to which he appealed to support his condemnation had ordained that a bishop should only be tried and condemned by his brethren of the same province, and they had not granted any more authority to the Bishop of Rome than to the others. As for the pretensions of Nicholas to divine authority, we know what they amount to; and his reasoning is worthy of the thesis he would prove.

The Emperor Michael, when he learned the decision of the Council of Rome, wrote to Nicholas a letter filled with threats and contumely (A.D. 864), which, of course, the enemies of Photius attribute to him, alleging that the Emperor only thought of his pleasures. This is to them a conclusive argument. Nicholas replied to the Emperor in a very long letter full of apocryphal statements, false logic, and the grossest historical mistakes. We learn from this letter that the Emperor had met the Papal pretensions with a host of facts which reduced the primacy of the Bishop of Rome to its just proportions. Nicholas discusses them superficially; his reasonings are false, and he confounds some incidental proceedings with the recognition of the absolute authority which be claimed. To give an instance of his sophistry: "Observe," he writes, "that neither the

---

Shall it be only in the case of Photius that familiar letters are incompetent evidence? Romish historians pretend that his letters to Bardas were written hypocritically. But the impartial and independent writers who confirm the evidence of those letters, were they too hypocrites? Is it credible that only the enemies of Photius had the privilege of telling the truth when speaking of him? If men were to be judged by the evidence of their enemies only, who then would ever be innocent? By this system one might easily prove that Christ himself was worthy of death.

VI. The Papacy Caused the Schism Between East and West   263

Council of Nicea, nor any other council, granted any privilege to the Roman Church, which knew that in the person of Peter *she was entitled thoroughly to the rights of all power, and that she had received the government of all the sheep of Christ.*"[273]

He rests that doctrine upon the evidence of Pope Boniface. "If," he continues, "the decrees of the Council of Nicea be carefully examined, it will certainly appear that this council granted no enlargement to the Roman Church, but rather took example from her in what it granted to the Church of Alexandria." Nicholas does not add that the council had looked upon the authority of the Roman see over the suburbican churches as resting *only on usage*, and not *on divine right*; nor that if a similar authority to that of Rome was given to the Alexandrian Church, it followed that there was nothing *divine* in that authority, since a council could not give by divine authority.

It is with like force of reasoning that Nicholas endeavors to answer all the objections of his adversary against the Papal autocracy.

He concludes with a distinction between the two domains in which the priesthood and the empire should respectively act. If Michael needed to be taught that he had no right over ecclesiastical things, should not the Papacy have understood in like manner that it had no right over temporal things?

The Eastern Church was in duty bound to protest against the attempts of Nicholas.

They were contrary to the ancient law. The Ultramontanes are obliged to admit this, though indirectly. A writer,[274] who professes to write the history of Photius, but only accepts as true the assertions of the declared enemies of this Patriarch, has been forced, by the weight of evidence, to speak as *follows*:

"Schism has thrown a clear light upon the doctrines respecting the primacy of the holy see. *Never* were its prerogatives better established than in the struggle of Pope Nicholas... against the

---

273 *"Quæ in Petro noverat eam totius jura potestatis pleniter meruisse et cunctarum Christi ovium regimen accepisse."*

274 Jager, *Hist. de Photius*, liv. iv. p. 114, edit 1854.

Photian schismatics." Is it credible that before the ninth century no occasion had presented to call forth these prerogatives, if they had in fact belonged to the Roman see? The facts we have already related sufficiently answer that question. Questions of far greater moment than the deposition of a bishop had certainly been discussed between the East and West since the origin of the Church, and these questions, instead of bringing out Papal authority in relief, had reduced it to its strict limits. But in the ninth century circumstances were changed; the Papacy had sacrificed the ancient Catholic doctrine to its own ambitious dreams, and now availed itself of every circumstance to establish a spiritual autocracy as contrary to Scripture as it was to the teachings of the Fathers and the councils.

Strong in the ancient canons, Photius looked upon the excommunications of Nicholas as null, and continued to discharge his episcopal duties with a zeal and devotion that his enemies distort with remarkable dishonesty. They will only see in him a *beast of prey*, combining the most consummate hypocrisy with cruelty carried to extravagance, and do not even take the trouble to reconcile two such characters in one and the same man, and with facts which completely contradict them.

But Nicholas could not bear this contempt of his *sovereign authority*, and he availed himself of the conversion of the Bulgarians to renew the war against Photius.[275]

---

[275] At this time (866), the Emperor caused Bardas to be put to death and placed Basil, who had served him in this matter, at the head of affairs. The correspondence of Photius shows that the Patriarch had strongly reproached Bardas for his violence against Ignatius and his followers. When Bardas was dead, Photius wrote to the Emperor, congratulating him on having escaped the intrigues of Bardas. By collating these letters, we see that Photius was not on such familiar terms with Bardas that the cruelties of the Cæsar could be attributed to the Patriarch. But this conclusion does not suit the enemies of Photius, who would make him answerable for every act of violence. They therefore assert that Photius was coward enough to accuse Bardas after his death, whom he had meanly flattered during his life and had used as the instrument of his own revenge. Enemies and fanatics may thus write history, but such a course can only excite disgust in honest consciences.

VI. The Papacy Caused the Schism Between East and West

The first seeds of Christianity had been cast among the Bulgarians about the year 845.

In 864 Photius contributed powerfully to the conversion of the King Bogoris,[276] which was followed by that of all his people. He even addressed to this king a beautiful treatise upon the duties of princes. Bogoris, at war with the Germans and their Emperor Louis, thought he might appease him by asking for some Latin priests to instruct his people. He sent ambassadors to Rome in 866, shortly after the unlawful excommunication pronounced against Photius. Nicholas could not hesitate to avail himself of so rare an opportunity to extend his power in the East. He therefore sent legates to the King of the Bulgarians with a long "opinion" on the cases submitted by the latter, without stopping to ask if the statements of fact set forth in those cases were true. He did not forget[277] in his "opinion" to exalt beyond measure the Roman see, and to disparage that of Constantinople. According to him, the see of Rome[278] is, through St. Peter, *the source of the episcopate* and the *Apostolate*; therefore, the Bulgarians must accept no bishop save from Rome. It is from Rome also that they must receive doctrine. "St. Peter,"[279] he says, "yet lives and presides upon his seat; he reveals the truth of the faith to those who seek it; for the holy Roman Church has always been without spot or wrinkle; it was her founder whose confession of faith was expressly approved."

The Pope added to his legates to Bulgaria three more legates for Constantinople, giving to the latter eight letters dated on the thirteenth of November 866; they are monuments of vainglory.[280] He threatens to have Michael's letter against the Roman prerogatives ignominiously burned unless he will disavow it. He writes to the clergy of Constantinople that he deposes all those who adhere to Photius and reestablishes the partisans of Ignatius. He complains to

---

276 See Photius, Epist. Book I, letter viii.

277 See these answers in Labbe's Collection of Councils, vol. vii.

278 Resp. lxxiii.

279 Resp. cvi.

280 Labbe's Collection, vol. viii., Epist. Nichol. ix. et seq.

Bardas, that Bardas has disappointed him in all that he had hoped from his piety; he notifies Ignatius that he has reestablished him in his see, and anathematized Photius and his adherents; he flatters Theodora, the *Empress dowager*, and congratulates himself upon having taken the part of Ignatius whom she herself supported.; he implores the Empress Eudoxia to take the part of Ignatius before the Emperor, and urges upon all the senators of Constantinople that they separate themselves from the communion of Photius and declare themselves for Ignatius.

His letter to Photius, the third of the series, deserves a special mention; he gives him simply the title of man Nicholas, etc., VIRO PHOTIO. He accuses him of having "impudently violated the venerable canons, the decisions of the Fathers, and the divine precepts." He calls him *thief—adulterer*; asserts that he has failed in his own obligations, corrupted the legates, banished those bishops who refused to enter into communion with him; adding that he might justly call him a homicide, a viper, a modern Ham, and a Jew. He falls back upon the canons of Sardica, and the Decretals of his predecessors, and concludes by threatening such an excommunication as should last him during his whole life.

So *pathetic* a letter could produce but one result, that of exciting Photius to condemn the Pope.

The legates having reached Bulgaria, all the Greek priests were driven from the country, and the confirmation which they had administered was pronounced invalid. This was to insult the Eastern Church in the grossest manner, and to trample underfoot the first principles of Christian theology. Photius could endure neither this insult added to error, nor the enterprises of Nicholas. In 867 he convoked a council at Constantinople and invited the Patriarchs and bishops of the East and also three bishops of the West, who had appealed to him against the despotism of Nicholas.[281] These were the Bishop and Exarch of Ravenna, and the Archbishops of Tréves and Cologne.[282] The legates of the three Patriarchal sees

---

281 We shall have occasion to mention his circular letter.

282 Nicholas was accustomed to depose bishops, even from the greatest sees, by his own authority and in violation of the canons, according to which they

VI. The Papacy Caused the Schism Between East and West

of the East, with a host of bishops, priests, and monks, the two Emperors, and the senate, took part in that assembly.[283]

The letters of Nicholas were there read, and by a unanimous vote he was held unworthy of the episcopate, and excommunication and anathema were pronounced against him. This decision was forwarded to Nicholas by Zacharias, Metropolitan of Chalcedon, and Theodore of Cyzicus. Anastasius the Librarian declares that but twenty-one among upward of a thousand signatures with which this document was covered were authentic. We know what this man's testimony is worth. Certain it is that the document was well known in the East, and that the Council of Constantinople, which afterward annulled it, did not consider the signatures as forged. This fact speaks louder than any one mendacious writer. The sentence of the council against Nicholas was more canonical than that pronounced by Nicholas against Photius, for it was only

---

could only be judged by their fellow-bishops in their own province. Most of them took no notice of these condemnations. The Archbishops of Tréves and of Cologne met the sentence of Nicholas by a protest, wherein, amongst other things, they say: "Without a council, without canonical inquiry, without accuser, without witnesses, without convicting us by arguments or authorities, without our consent, in the absence of the metropolitans and of our suffragan bishops, you have chosen to condemn us, of your own caprice, with tyrannical fury; but we do not accept your accursed sentence, so repugnant to it, father's or a brother's love ; we despise it as mere insulting language; *we expel you yourself from our communion*, since you commune with the excommunicate; *we are satisfied with the communion of the whole Church* and with the society of our brethren whom you despise and of whom you make yourself unworthy by your pride and arrogance. You condemn yourself when you condemn those who do not observe the apostolic precepts which you yourself first violate, *annulling as far as in you lies the divine laws and the sacred canons*, AND NOT FOLLOWING IN THE FOOTSTEPS OF THE POPES YOUR PREDECESSORS." Photius did not write to Nicholas with the rude energy of these Western bishops.

283 The acts of this council were reversed by another, which was held shortly after the purpose of reinstating Ignatius. This fact, admitted by the Western writers, has not prevented certain of their number from expressing the absurd opinion that this council never was held, and that Photius invented both the council and its acts. Mr. Jager has adopted this idea in his heavy pamphlet against Photius, Book IV, p. 146.

an excommunication and not a *deposition*; now any church has a right to separate itself from the communion of those she esteems guilty, and no longer consider them as bishops.

The same year that Nicholas was excommunicated, a revolution took place at Constantinople that was to be fatal to Photius in its results. Michael was killed by Basil, whom he had associated with himself in the empire. The murderer of Bardas and Michael necessarily distrusted Photius.[284]

Moreover, Photius refused to admit the murderer to the communion. He was, therefore, shut up in a monastery. Basil reestablished Ignatius and sent ambassadors to Rome bearing the Acts of the council that had excommunicated Nicholas. This Pope had died and had been succeeded by Adrian II; who, in 868, assembled a council at Rome to condemn Photius anew. The envoy of the Emperor, in its presence, flung to the ground the Acts of the Council of Constantinople, struck them with his sword, and trampled them under foot. After this extravagant conduct he asserted that the signature of his master upon the document was forged; that the council had only been composed of some bishops

---

284 The enemies of this Patriarch, who often contradict themselves in their statements, do not agree upon the time or the circumstances of his exile. Anastasius pretends that Basil knew nothing of the dispute between Ignatius and Photius until after the death of Michael; that he informed himself of the matter as soon as he was left sole emperor, and sent two deputies to Rome, one chosen by Ignatius and the other by Photius, to plead their several cause before the Pope: that one of the deputies, the one who represented Photius, was drowned on the voyage; that the other, upon his arrival at Rome, found Nicholas dead. Nicetas, on the contrary, tells us that the day after the death of the Emperor Michael, Basil caused Photius to be imprisoned in a monastery, in order to reinstate the legitimate Patriarch. Some Western writers have hastily accepted the account of Nicetas for the sake of denying the truth of the story that Photius incurred the hatred of Basil by refusing him the communion on account of the murder he had committed. Of course these writers say that such an act of pastoral courage was incompatible with the character of Photius. This would be quite true if the great and learned Bishop had been such an one as they paint him. But, as the character they attribute to him is diametrically opposite to his real character, as it shines forth in his authentic acts and his writings, they are only, in fact, giving one more proof of their partiality.

VI. The Papacy Caused the Schism Between East and West

who happened to be in Constantinople,[285] and that the other signatures, one thousand in number, were false. The sincerity of this fanatic may well be doubted. If the signatures were false, this ought to have been proved in the East and not in the West. Instead of verifying a fact which could be so easily ascertained, the Council of Rome decided that the acts should be burnt.

Such a proceeding naturally suggests that it seemed easier to burn the Acts than to prove their falsity.

Adrian II did not fail upon that occasion to exalt the authority of the Bishop of Rome. "The Pope," he said in his council, "judges all the bishops, but we do not read that any have judged him."[286] He mentions, indeed, the condemnation of Honorius, but he pretends that the anathema which fell on him was legitimate only because it was previously pronounced on him by the see of Rome itself. This assertion is false, as we have already seen. Instead of condemning Honorius, the see of Rome had endeavored to defend him. It did not mention him at first among those to be condemned, and it was only after the condemnation by the council that Rome also decided to pronounce anathema against him.

Before separating, the members of the Council of Rome trampled underfoot the acts which anathematized Nicholas, and then threw them into a great fire.

After this expedition, Basil's ambassadors returned to Constantinople accompanied by three legates of Pope Adrian, bearing two letters: one addressed to the Emperor, the other to Ignatius. "IT IS OUR WILL," he writes to the Emperor, "that you should assemble a numerous council, at which our legates shall preside, and in which persons shall be judged according to their faults; and that in this council shall be publicly *burnt all the copies* of the acts[287] of the false council held against the Holy See, and that

---

285 If this were true, it would follow that the rest of the signatures must have been collected outside of the council and by way of concurrence. They would then gain in weight, for the signers, in that case, must have acted with the more freedom.

286 Labbe's Collection of Councils, vol. viii.

287 The historians inimical to Photius nevertheless relate that but one copy

it be forbidden to preserve any of them under pain of anathema." Adrian then demanded the Roman priests who had gone to Constantinople to complain to Photius of Pope Nicholas. The letter to Ignatius is an instruction as to the treatment of those ecclesiastics who had declared for Photius, but were now willing to abandon his cause. Adrian added to these letters a formula to be signed by the members of the council, in which they agreed to recognize him as *Sovereign Pontiff and Universal Pope.*

The council was opened at Constantinople, in the Church of Saint Sophia, on the 5th of October, 869. There were present the three Papal legates, Ignatius, Thomas, Bishop of Tyre, self-styled representative of the Patriarch of Antioch, and the priest Elias, calling himself the representative of the Bishop of Jerusalem.

The bishops who declared against Photius were brought in. They were *twelve* in number. They were permitted to take seats, and formed the whole council at the first session. At the second, *ten* bishops who had adhered to Photius entered to crave pardon for their fault. It was readily granted, and they took their places with the others. *Eleven* priests, *nine* deacons, and *seven* sub-deacons imitated the ten bishops, and were pardoned in the same manner.

Two new bishops arrived at the third session, so that the assembly was composed of twenty-four bishops, without counting the presidents. At the fourth session two bishops, ordained by the former Patriarch, Methodius, asked leave to defend the Patriarch Photius, with whom they declared they remained in communion. The council refused to hear them. The patrician Bahaner opposed this decision in the name of the Senate of Constantinople.

The legates of the Pope upheld it on the ground that the Pope had pronounced in the last resort, and it was not lawful to examine the cause of Photius any further. But being obliged to yield, they added: "Let them enter and hear the synodical decision and judgment of Pope Nicholas. They are seeking excuses, and only wish to avoid a trial." "But," said the Senate, "if they wished to avoid it, they would not cry out, *Let us be judged*—they would retire." "Let them

---

existed, carefully hidden by Photius. They say he had invented the Acts. This copy was seized, carried to Rome, and burnt at the council held in that city.

VI. The Papacy Caused the Schism Between East and West   271

enter," said the legates, "but let them remain in the lowest places." The Senate asked that three or four more bishops of the party of Photius should be admitted. "We consent to it," said the legates, "but on condition that they shall declare that they represent all the rest, and they shall only come in to hear the letter of Nicholas."

It was evident, therefore, that Rome had only caused this council to be called in order to consecrate her assumed sovereign and universal authority.

The bishops who sided with Photius, seeing that the council would not hear them, had retired. Only the first two remained, offering to prove, if the Emperor would give safe conduct to their witnesses, that Nicholas had communed with them when Photius sent them to Rome as his deputies.

The safe-conducts were not granted.

At the fifth session, Photius was forcibly brought in. He only answered, in a few words full of dignity, that he excepted to the council and would not plead to the accusations brought against him. In his eyes thirty-three bishops, assembled by the order of the Emperor, his enemy, should not presume to reverse the sentence of the three hundred and eighteen bishops who had proclaimed him legitimate Patriarch.

In the sixth session, the adjunct Elias attempted to prove that the resignation tendered by Ignatius was null and void. This fact is important, for it confirms what Photius had written to Nicholas, that *"his predecessor had abandoned his office."* At the same time, it proves that Ignatius had understood his duty in the difficult position in which he was placed; that he had at first imitated the great bishops who have always preferred to resign an office which was snatched, however unjustly, from them, rather than to trouble their Church. Left to himself, Ignatius was too virtuous not to imitate such conduct; but, in consequence of the weakness of his character, he became the tool of a few intriguers and of the ambitious projects of the Popes, who disguised their own bad designs under his virtue.

Some bishops, partisans of Photius, were introduced at the sixth session, at which the Emperor was also present. After the speeches that were made against them and their Patriarch, the

Emperor said to them, "What do you think of it?" "We will answer you," they replied, and one of them, Anthymius, of Cæsarea in Cappadocia, added, "My lord, we know your goodness and justice; give us in writing a guarantee of safety if we speak forth freely our justification, and we shall hope to show that these accusations are but idle words." This humble language only irritated the Emperor, who would not give the asked-for assurance.

The Pope's legates, as well as the Emperor, refused to hear any justification. They considered Photius and his adherents as irrevocably condemned by Nicholas, although the sentence of that Pope was anti-canonical and arbitrary. The legates constantly repeated, in tones of anger, "That it was superfluous to hear condemned persons; that they should be expelled from the assembly, since they had not come there to confess their fault and ask pardon." The supporters of Ignatius also suffered from the bitter language of the legates when they refused to sign the famous formula brought from Rome.

Photius and Gregory of Syracuse were brought in at the seventh session. An officer of the court asked them, in the name of the legates, if they would sign; Photius replied, "If they had heard what we have already said, they would not ask this question. Let them do penance themselves for the sin they have committed." This answer exasperated the legates, who overwhelmed Photius with gross language, after their wont. The same officer then asked Photius what he had to reply. "I have no answer to calumnies," he said. The bishops who sided with Photius were again solicited, but in vain, to separate from him. The Bishop of Heracleia even replied, pointing to Photius, "Anathema upon him who anathematized that bishop!" The others displayed equal energy. They insisted on their former demand of perfect liberty to defend themselves. The Emperor interposed a demurrer, saying that the council represented the Church since the five Patriarchs were represented.[288] He would not

---

[288] The Patriarchs of Antioch and Jerusalem had only false representatives. The Patriarch of Alexandria was only represented at the ninth session. In his letter to the Emperor, he declares that he knows nothing of the discussions, and that he relies on the Emperor and his bishops and clergy. His envoy was

VI. The Papacy Caused the Schism Between East and West

see that one bishop, one monk, and a priest, assuming to represent the three Patriarchs of Alexandria, Antioch, and Jerusalem, gave no guarantee, without the presence of any other bishop of these Patriarchates, and without an opportunity of communicating with the Patriarchs themselves! The friends of Photius replied that the canons, since the Apostles, proved just the opposite; that the pretended representatives of the five Patriarchates did not constitute the Church, which, on the contrary, spoke by means of the canons followed since the Apostles.

This session terminated in anathemas against Photius and his partisans. In the following session, every paper which could implicate those of this council who had taken the part of Photius against Ignatius was burned before the whole council. Finally, the council ended with some canons and a profession of faith. The acts were signed by one hundred and two bishops. This was but few when we reflect that the Patriarchate of Constantinople alone numbered at that time more than six hundred, and that the Emperor Basil had used all his influence to collect a numerous council. An immense majority of the bishops took no part in what took place at Constantinople. Some zealous friends of Photius were the only ones who would make up their minds to appear before the assembly and protest against that which was done there, and put the Emperor in the wrong by asking him to guarantee to them full liberty for their defence.

A fact worthy of remark, and of the greatest significance, is that Ignatius, who presided side by side with the legates of Rome, kept the most profound silence during the whole council. A great number of questions were discussed before him, upon which he alone could give positive information—such as that of his resignation and the attendant circumstances, the conduct of Photius toward him, and many others. Ignatius allowed them to be discussed *pro* and *contra*, without saying one word to throw light upon the debates.

Must it not be inferred from such silence that he did not know what side to take in view of the facts as he knew they had happened,

---

afterward disavowed.

and of the plausible reasons under which the Roman legates and certain intriguers covered their lying recitals?

Whatever we may choose to infer from this silence, we think that it can only be construed in favor of Photius and of his version of all that had occurred.[289] We naturally ask why Ignatius did not deny that he had abdicated or assert that it had been extorted from him by violence, since this was the gist of the whole question. We may therefore conclude that he really resigned his see, freely and conscientiously; but that Nicholas being unwilling, as he himself said, to accept that resignation, some ambitious men, personal enemies of Photius, prevailed upon Ignatius to reconsider his determination, suggesting to him as a legitimate motive the protest of the Patriarch of Rome against it.

But while he followed the impulsion of Rome in what concerned his reinstalment in his see, Ignatius did not allow himself disposed to submit to all its requirements, as in the matter of signing the Roman formula, and in the conference, which took place after the council, concerning the Church of Bulgaria.

Several members of the council, from hatred of Photius rather than from conviction, had already signed the formula which enslaved the whole Church to the Roman see. They had submitted to this demand in order that the council, from which they expected results satisfactory to their own secret desires, should not remain an impossibility. After it was over, they sent complaints to the Emperor and to Ignatius regarding their signatures, and asked that they should not be sent to Rome. They protested, moreover, against the qualified form in which the legates had signed, reserving the

---

289 It must be observed that the Acts of this council of Constantinople, considered by Rome œcumenical, are only known to Anastasius the Librarian. The authentic acts were taken from the legates by the Sclavonians, who robbed them on their return from Constantinople. Anastasius pretended that he had an exact copy of the acts, which he translated into Latin at Rome. It is therefore to the evidence of this man that we have to refer for all that relates to this council. If the acts, such as he has given them, are so favorable to Photius, is it not reasonable to think that they would be more so if they were trustworthy?

approbation of the Pope, for thereby the Bishop of Rome reserved the right to approve or to cancel, *at his will*, what had been done.

It was too late to remedy this; but the Emperor, to ease his mind in regard to the formula, caused all the signatures that could be found in the house of the legates to be taken away during their absence. The legates protested; but in vain. Ignatius did not censure this act of the Emperor, and proved, in the conference about Bulgaria, that he was not a partisan of the doctrine of the formula.

The Bulgarians, learning that a council was sitting at Constantinople, sent deputies there to know whether their church should depend upon Rome or Constantinople.[290]

The Emperor convoked the regales of Rome and the East to answer this question in presence of Ignatius: "As we have newly received the grace of baptism, we fear lest we make a mistake; we therefore ask you, who represent the Patriarchs, to what church we should be subject."

Pope Nicholas had replied to the question, but his decision was only regarded as that of a single Patriarch. The legates of Rome maintained that his decision was supreme, and must not be departed from. The Eastern legates were not of this opinion. The Romans protested that they had received no power to examine the question raised by the Bulgarians. In spite of this special pleading, the Eastern legates judged it proper to be decided. "From whom have you conquered the provinces where you dwell?" they asked of the Bulgarians; "and what church was established there then?"

"We wrested them from the Greeks," they replied; "and the Greek clergy were established there."

"In that case," said the legates, "your church depends from the Greeks; that is, from the Patriarchate of Constantinople."

"But, for the last *three years*," said the papal legates, "Rome has sent Latin priests there." This prescription of three years did not suffice, in the eyes of the other legates, to prevail over the ancient possession and they declared that the Bulgarian church should be under the jurisdiction of the Patriarchate of Constantinople. Ignatius was of the same opinion; but the Roman legates said that

---

[290] See Vit. Pap. Hadr. et Epist. Hadr. in Labbe's Collection, vol. viii.

the holy see of Rome had not chosen them for judges. "*He, only,*" they added, "*has the right to judge the whole Church*. He despises your opinion as readily as you give it lightly." As long as the condemnation of Photius was the question, that opinion had been of far greater value in their eyes. They annulled the judgment that had been rendered, and begged Ignatius not to despise the rights of the holy see *which had restored him to his*. The Emperor was angry at the pretensions of the legates. They soon left, and were robbed on the way by the Sclavonians, who took from them the authentic acts of the council.

In consequence of the decision of the Eastern legates, the Bulgarians dismissed the bishop and priests who had been sent by Rome to them, and received a Greek bishop and priests. Learning this, Adrian wrote to the Emperor of the East, threatening with excommunication Ignatius and the bishops he had sent to Bulgaria.

There is extant only a fragment of a letter from Adrian II to Ignatius. He speaks to him as a superior to an inferior; accuses him of violating the canons as they obtained at Rome; and tells him, in threatening language, that a similar course had occasioned the fall of Photius.

Such letters make it very evident that Rome had pursued the reinstallment of Ignatius not for the sake of justice, but to find occasion to do an act of sovereignty in the East. A careful reading of these documents leaves no doubt in this respect. Ignatius, in the eyes of the Pope, was as guilty as Photius the moment he refused to submit to this sovereignty.

Adrian II died in the month of November 872, and was succeeded by John VIII. This Pope took greatly to heart this affair of Bulgaria. He wrote twice to Ignatius to demand that he should renounce all jurisdiction over that church. Because the Emperor Basil (878) had asked him for legates to labour for the pacification of the religious troubles which had been rife in the East since the reestablishment of Ignatius, the Pope availed himself of this occasion to write to that Patriarch a third letter, in which he thus expressed himself:[291] "We give you this third *canonical monition* [he should have said *anti-canonical*] by our legates and letters; thereby we

---

[291] Joann. Pap. VIII, Ep., Labbe's Collection, vol. ix.

command you to send without delay to Bulgaria active men, who shall go through the whole country, and take away all those whom they may there find who have been ordained by you or by those of your dependence, so that in one month there shall remain neither bishops nor clergy of your ordination; for we cannot consent *that they should infect with their error* this new church which we have formed. If you do not withdraw them within the time mentioned, and if you do not renounce all jurisdiction over Bulgaria, you are hereby deprived of the communion of the body and blood of the Lord until *you obey*. A delay of two months from the reception of this letter is granted to you. If you remain obstinate in your violation of discipline and your usurpation, you are hereby, by the judgment of Almighty God, and by the authority of the blessed Apostle Princes, and by the sentence of *Our Mediocrity*, deprived of and deposed from the dignity of the Patriarchate which you have received through our favor."

Thus, to usurp jurisdiction over the Church of Bulgaria, the Pope does not hesitate to strike, *ipso facto*, a Patriarch with excommunication and deposition if he does not obey *his orders!* Have we observed any similar conduct on the part of the Popes of the first eight centuries?

But the bishops of the East were neither disposed to recognize the Papal authority nor to obey his anti-canonical orders. Those who supported Ignatius were as much opposed to this as the partisans of Photius.

John VIII wrote to the Greek bishops and clergy in Bulgaria a letter still more severe than that addressed to the Patriarch Ignatius. It began thus: "To all the bishops and other Greek clergy, invaders of the diocese of Bulgaria, and excommunicate by these presents He gave them thirty days to obey his orders, and promised the bishops to give them other sees on condition of leaving those they then occupied.

This was certainly acting as absolute sovereign. John wrote to the Bulgarian King and to Count Peter, who had been envoy to Rome in the time of Pope Nicholas. The substance of these letters is that nothing should be received save from the Roman Church, inasmuch as she is the source of all true doctrine. All these missives were sent by the legates Paul and Eugene. When these envoys reached Constantinople, Ignatius was dead, and Ignatius was again Patriarch (878).[292]

After some difficulties, the legates recognized Photius as Patriarch, and even said that Pope John had sent them to Constantinople to anathematize Ignatius and reinstate Photius.

Photius and the Emperor Basil sent letters and ambassadors to the Pope.[293] John was apprised of this, and seemed disposed to pacify the Church of Constantinople and to receive favorably the letters and envoys;[294] which he really did, and sent them back with letters for the Emperor and Photius. These letters of John VIII contain the most distinct answer to all the calumnies of the enemies of Photius. "In consideration," he said to the Emperor, "of the unanimity with which all the Patriarchs, even those who had been ordained by Ignatius, had acquiesced in the election of Photius, He consented to recognize him as Patriarch."

But as Photius had not waited for the recognition of Rome to reascend his episcopal chair, and regarded as null the council assembled against him, the Pope enlarged extensively upon this consideration: that necessity frequently exempts from the observance of rules. He therefore passes over these formal difficulties more readily as the legates of his predecessor had signed the acts of the council conditionally and, saving the approbation of the Pope, he gives in detail the conditions upon which he recognizes Photius: he must assemble a council and ask pardon for having reascended

---

[292] It is not our business to relate the doings of Photius during his exile. We therefore only refer to his letter those who wish for cumulative proof of the gentleness, charity, and ability whereby he regained the good graces of the Emperor Basil. These documents more than sufficiently answer the hateful statements of his enemies, in which absurdity vies with atrocity, and which, to every impartial man, only prove the blind hatred of those who composed them.

[293] Among these letters there was one in which Ignatius, near unto death, begged the Pope to recognize Photius as lawful Patriarch. Naturally enough, the enemies of Photius maintain that this letter is a forgery, but without proof.

[294] Letters of Pope John VIII in Labbe's Collection.

VI. The Papacy Caused the Schism Between East and West

his seat without a sentence of absolution; he must renounce all jurisdiction over Bulgaria; and he must receive into his communion all the bishops ordained by Ignatius. As to those of the latter who should refuse to enter in communion with Photius, he threatens them with excommunication.

These latter bishops were very few in number. The Pope wrote to the principal ones, Metrophanes, Stylienus, and John, threatening them with excommunication; and he charged the legates, whom he entrusted with his letters, to excommunicate all those who should refuse to recognize Photius as legitimate Patriarch, forbidding all, whoever they might be, to give credit to the calumnies circulated against this Patriarch.

It is, doubtless, out of respect for these commands of the Pope that the Romish writers have vied repeating these calumnies of such as Metrophanes, Stylienus, Nicetas, and other inveterate enemies of Photius, and have refused to see anything save knavery and hypocrisy in the familiar correspondence of this great man. They have left no means untried to disguise the importance of these letters of John VIII. Cardinal Baronius, in his *Annals*, goes so far as to maintain that the *feminine* weakness displayed by John in this matter gave rise to the fable of a *female pope Joan*. Everyone knows that John VIII, far from being weak in character, was energetic even to roughness; but Romish writers stick at nothing when they wish to rid themselves of facts, or even of Popes whose acts do not neatly fit into their systematic histories.

The legates with the Pope's letters having reached Constantinople, a council was called and attended by three hundred and eighty-three bishops, with Elias, who represented the Patriarch of Jerusalem.[295]

John's letters are full of the new teachings of the Papacy. He claims that he has, by divine right, the care of all the churches, and occupies the place of St. Peter, to whom Christ said, "*Feed my sheep.*" He pretends that he has been entreated to admit Photius to the dignity of the Patriarchate, and even to ecclesiastical orders; he now admits him, although he has usurped the episcopate without the consent of the holy see, but on condition that he shall ask pardon

---

[295] Collection of Councils by Father Hardouin, vol. vi.

in full council; he gives him absolution by virtue of the power he has received from Jesus Christ through St. Peter, *to bind and loose all things without exception. He commands* Photius to resign all jurisdiction over Bulgaria, and forbids him to ordain any there. In all his letters he gives *commands* and claims to exercise an absolute sovereignty of divine origin.

Such pretensions were not recognized in the East, which held to the doctrines of the first eight centuries on the subject of the Papacy. It was clear that if such letters as these were read in the council, all hope of peace was at an end. Hence only the substance of these letters was retained; every expression that could wound, or give reason to believe that the Pope wished to be Sovereign of the Church, was weeded out. Expressions of encomium in use in the East were added. These letters, as Fleury tells us, were thus modified, "*apparently in concert with the legates, who heard them read* without complaint." The first of these legates, Cardinal Peter, having asked, "Do you receive the Pope's letter?" the council replied, "We receive all that relates to the union with Photius and the interests of the Church, but not what concerns the Emperor and his provinces." By this, the Council rejected the pretensions of the Pope to Bulgaria. From such a unanimous disposition of nearly four hundred Eastern bishops, we may judge what protests the Pope's letters would have excited if the legates had not had the prudence to modify them in concert with Photius.[296] The East had always preserved this maxim, followed by all the œcumenical councils, that ecclesiastical divisions must follow those of the empire. Bulgaria, having been anciently a Greek province, depended from the Greek Patriarch and not the Latin.

When Cardinal Peter asked that the adversaries of Photius who had been excluded might be recalled, Photius replied, "The

---

296 The Abbé Jager, in his indigestible pamphlet against Photius, claims that the Pope's letters were altered by Photius alone. Would not the legates have protested against that fraud, since they heard them read in the council in their modified shape? Instead of complaining of these letters, they publicly sought to ascertain that everyone was satisfied with them. Moreover, they carried them back to Rome with the acts of the council. The Pope did not protest, and it is in Rome itself that they were afterward found.

VI. The Papacy Caused the Schism Between East and West

Emperor has only exiled *two of* them, and that for causes not ecclesiastical; we pray him to recall them."

"How did the Patriarch Photius reascend his throne?" asked Peter.

The council replied, "By the consent of the three Patriarchs, at the request of the Emperor; or rather yielding to the violence done to him, and to the prayers of the whole Church of Constantinople."

"What?!" asked Peter, "Has there been no violence on the part of Photius? Has he not acted tyrannically?"

"On the contrary," replied the council, "all took place with gentleness and tranquillity."

"Thank God!" exclaimed the Cardinal.

Thus, nearly four hundred bishops, in presence of the Pope's envoys, and in public, confounded the rare calumniators of Photius, and yet these calumniators are accepted in the West as writers worthy of faith, even while their histories give numberless proofs of a hatred akin to madness and absurdity!

When Cardinal Peter had finished his questions, Photius spoke as follows: "I tell you, before God, that I never desired this see; the majority of those here present know this well.

The first time I took it against my will, shedding many tears, after resisting it for a long time, and in consequence of the insurmountable violence of the emperor who then reigned, but with the consent of the bishops and clergy, who had given their signatures without my knowledge. They gave me guards..."

He was interrupted by the exclamations of the council, "We know it all, either of our own knowledge or by the evidence of others who have told us."

"God permitted me to be driven away," continued Photius. "I did not seek to return.

I never excited seditions. I remained at rest, thanking God, and bending before his judgments without importuning the Emperor, without hope or desire to be reinstated. God, who works miracles, has touched the Emperor's heart,[297] not for my sake but for the

---

[297] His enemies have said that he resorted to magic to dispose Basil in his favor, and some serious historians have accepted this ridiculous accusation.

sake of his people: he has recalled me from my exile. But, so long as Ignatius of blessed memory lived, I could not bring myself to resume my place, in spite of the exhortations and entreaties that were made by many upon this subject."

The council said, "It is the truth."

"I meant," continued Photius, "to make my peace with Ignatius firm in every way.

We saw each other in the palace; we fell at each others' feet, and mutually forgave each other. When he fell ill he sent for me; I visited him several times, and gave him every consolation in my power. He recommended to me those who were most dear to him, and I have taken care of them. After his death the Emperor entreated me publicly and privately; he came himself to see me, to urge me to yield to the wishes of the bishops and clergy. I have yielded to so miraculous a change that I might not resist God."

The council said, "It is thus."

Are not such words worth more, pronounced publicly as they were, and their truth attested by four hundred bishops, than all the diatribes of passionate enemies?

In the following sessions, the legates of the Patriarchal sees of Alexandria, Antioch, and Jerusalem gave unquestionable proofs that their Patriarchs had always been in communion with Photius; that the pretended legates who were present at the council of 869, under Adrian, and who had concurred in the condemnation of Photius, were only envoys of the Saracens, as Photius himself had written in his protest against that assembly.

In consequence, that council was anathematized by the legates of Rome, by those of the other Patriarchal sees of the East, and by all the bishops present.[298]

The acts of the council of 879 are as full of dignity and as high-toned as those of the council of 869 were passionate and unworthy of true bishops. Adrian's legates were more like men possessed than like judges, if we may judge from the acts preserved by Anastasius the Librarian, while the legates of John, on the contrary, displayed

---

298 Nevertheless, the Romanists call that council of 869 the *eighth œcumenical*.

VI. The Papacy Caused the Schism Between East and West

in all things as much wisdom as moderation.[299] During their sojourn at Constantinople they repeatedly saw Metrophanes, one of the worst enemies of Photius, and one of the writers who serve as guides to the Romish writers in their accounts. They requested him to furnish proofs against Photius, but could draw from him nothing but idle words. They summoned him to the council, but he refused to appear, under the false pretext of illness. "He is not so ill," said the legates, "that he cannot talk a great deal, and yet say very little." Upon his refusal to appear, he was anathematized.

---

299 The acts of the council of 879 have been found in the original at Rome with all the authentic signatures, including those of the legates of Rome; and yet the ecclesiastical historians of the West insinuate that they may have been altered. On the other hand, the acts of the council of 869 were lost by the Roman legates and are only known through Anastasius the Librarian, who pretended to have a copy; and the Western historians will not allow a doubt as to their genuineness. Is this impartial? If the acts of the council of 879 had come from the East to the West, there might be some grounds for contesting their genuineness; but they were found at Rome, and were taken from the archives of Rome to give them to the public.

Saint Photios the Great (+893)

VII

THE PAPACY, WHICH CAUSED THE DIVISION, HAS PERPETUATED AND STRENGTHENED IT BY INNOVATIONS AND HAS MADE IT A SCHISM.

FROM the facts which we have just discussed, it appears that the Papacy in the ninth century sought dominion over the Church and the position of a sovereign pontificate, the centre of unity and the guardian of orthodoxy. Its defenders are very far from contesting this; but they claim that these pretensions were not new, and to prove this they appeal to the dogmatic testimony of the Fathers, to the facts of ecclesiastical history of the first centuries of the Church, and even to the word of God.

We announced it as our special purpose to show their assertions to be false in regard to the first eight centuries of the Church, and this we have done.

We grant that after the ninth century the Popes assumed to exercise the sovereign pontificate. We have pointed out the first occasions on which Rome came before the Eastern Church with her new pretensions, and we have ascertained that the Oriental Church refused to recognize them.

It is thus beyond all doubt that it was the Papacy which provoked the division by seeking to impose a sovereignty upon the whole Church which had been unknown during the first eight centuries of the Church.

Union being reestablished, at least in appearance, between the Papacy and Photius, the Eastern Church was nonetheless separated from Rome; for there was now a radical divergency between them. Peace would not have existed even outwardly between them if the letters of Pope John had been read to the last council as they were written. In the assembly of 869 the partisans of Ignatius and Ignatius himself declared against the Papal sovereignty almost as energetically as Photius and his friends. On her side, Rome no longer did anything without asserting her pretended sovereignty, and without setting herself up as the necessary centre of unity.

The controversies between the Papacy and Photius, like their reconciliation, would have remained as unimportant as a thousand others of the same kind in the history of the Church if a radical division had not been worked out from that time in consequence of the institution of the Papacy. In following out these relations of the East with Rome, we shall meet with many attempts to reconcile the two churches at different periods. But because Rome insisted upon a recognition of her sovereignty as a condition precedent, and because the Eastern Church always appealed to the doctrine of the first eight centuries, unity could never be reestablished. It would now only be possible on condition that the Papacy should abandon its unlawful pretensions, or the Eastern Church the primitive doctrine. Now, the Eastern Church well knows that the renunciation of that doctrine would not only be criminal in itself, but would result in subjection to an autocracy condemned by the Gospel and by Catholic doctrine; hence she cannot yield without incurring guilt and without committing suicide.

And the Papacy, on its side, knows that it annihilates itself by returning to the Catholic unity with the simple character of the ancient Roman episcopate. It will not, therefore, yield any of the prerogatives which it has grown to consider as emanating from a divine source. For this cause it not only *provoked* the division in the Church, but has perpetuated and strengthened it by the pertinacity with which it has maintained what was the direct cause of it.

To this first cause we must add the successive changes which it has introduced in orthodox doctrine and the œcumenical rules of discipline. The history of its innovations would be long. From the institution of the autocracy to the new dogma of the

VII. Papal Innovation Perpetuated & Strengthened the Schism

Immaculate Conception, how many changes! How many important modifications! We may write this sad history in a special work. At this time it will suffice to consider the most serious innovation which it has permitted itself, namely, the addition which it has made to the Creed; for that addition, together with the Papal autocracy, was the direct cause of the division which still exists between the Eastern and Western churches.

It has been sought to trace the discussion respecting the procession of the Holy Spirit to remote antiquity. We will not follow the learned upon this ground, but will simply show that it was in the eighth century that it first assumed any importance.[300]

Two Spanish Bishops, Felix d'Urgel and Elipand of Toledo, taught that Christ was the *adopted* Son of God, and not his Word, *coessential* with the Father. Their error called forth unanimous complaints in the West, particularly in France, whose kings then possessed the northern part of Spain. The defenders of orthodoxy thought they had found an excellent weapon against *adoptivism* when they decided that the Son is so thoroughly one in substance with the Father that the Holy Spirit *proceeds* from him as well as from the Father.

This formula was looked upon as the bulwark of orthodoxy, and was introduced into the Creed, to which was added, in consequence, the word *Filioque (and from the Son)* after the words *proceeding from the Father.*

That addition, made by a local church which had no pretensions to infallibility, was for this very cause irregular. It was further wrong in giving a conception of the Trinity contrary to the teaching of the Scriptures, according to which there is in God but *one principal,* which is the Father, from which proceed, from all eternity, the Word by generation, and the Spirit by procession. As the quality of *a principle* forms the distinctive character of the Father's *personality,*

---

[300] It seems certain that the addition to the Creed was made by a council of Toledo in 683, and was confirmed by another held in the same city in 653. See N. Alexander, Hist. Eccl., Dissert. xxvii. While Sæcul. iv maintains that it was admitted in the Council of Toledo in 589, it has been proved that the acts of the council were altered in this particular.

it evidently cannot be attributed to the Word without ascribing to Him that which is the distinctive attribute of another Divine Person. Thus the French and Spanish bishops, wishing to defend in the Trinity the *unity of essence* or of substance, attacked the personal distinction and confounded the attributes which are the very basis of that distinction.

Another serious error on their part was in giving a decision without first ascertaining that the words which they employed were authorized by Catholic tradition. Outside of the *perpetual* and *established* doctrine, no bishop can teach anything without danger of falling into the most serious errors.

The dogmatic truths of Christianity relating to the very essence of God—that is, of the Infinite—are necessarily *mysterious*; hence no one should presume to teach them of his own authority. Even the Church herself only *preserves them as she has received them*.

Revelation is a *deposit* confided by God to His Church, and not a philosophical synthesis which may be modified. Without doubt these Spanish and French bishops had no other end in view but in the clearest manner to expound the dogma of the Trinity; but their exposition, not having the *traditional* character, was an *error*.

The design of this work does not permit us to discuss thoroughly the question of the procession of the Holy Spirit.[301] We must limit ourselves to the history of this Roman addition.

That addition was first adopted in Spain, in the seventh century, in a committee at Toledo, and was adopted by several Western churches. In 767, Constantine Copronymus having sent some ambassadors to Pepin, King of the Franks, this prince received them in an assembly known as the Council of Gentilly. As the Greeks were accused of error respecting the worship of images, so the

---

301 We recommend to those who need to be enlightened upon this important question the treatise published by Monseigneur Macarius, Archbishop of Krakow, in his *Théologie Dogmatique Orthodoxe*. This learned theologian has discussed the question, and summed up the labours of several theologians of the Eastern Church upon the subject, in such a manner us to leave no doubt. The treatise of Monseigneur Macarius is one of the most learned theological works that we have read. See *Théologie Dogmatique Orthodoxe*, French edition, vol. 1. Paris: Cherbuliez, 10 Rue de la Monnale.

VII. Papal Innovation Perpetuated & Strengthened the Schism

ambassadors accused the Franks of error concerning the Trinity, and in having added the word *Filioque* to the creed. The details of the discussion upon this subject are not extant, but it is certain that the addition was very little spread through France before the close of the eighth century, when Elipand and Felix d'Urgel taught their error. The Council of Frioul, in 791, saw fit to oppose them by approving the doctrine of the procession from the Father and the Son, but without admitting the addition of the *Filioque*, because the Fathers who composed the creed were right in using only the evangelical expression *proceeding from the Father*.[302]

Felix of d'Urgel, after having been condemned in several councils, was banished to Lyons by Charlemagne in 799. He doubtless propagated his errors in that city, and the question of the procession of the Holy Ghost was discussed there. The learned Alcuin wrote to *the brethren at Lyons*, urging them both to avoid the errors of the Spanish Bishop and also any *interpolation* of the creed. "Beloved brethren," he says, "look well to the sects of the Spanish error; follow in the faith the steps of the holy Fathers, and remain attached to the holy Church Universal in a most holy unity. It has been written, '*Do not overstep the limits laid down by the Fathers*; insert nothing new in the creed of the Catholic faith, and in religious functions be not pleased with traditions unknown to ancient times.'"[303]

This letter was written in 804. It thus appears that at the beginning of the ninth century the addition was already condemned in France by the most learned and pious men. Alcuin also censured, as we see, the usage that was beginning to prevail of chanting the creed in the service instead of reciting it.

The interpolation in the creed had, nevertheless, some advocates, who, five years later, proposed, in a council at Aix-la-Chapelle, to solemnly authorize the *Filioque*. They met with opposition, and it was decided to refer the question to Rome. Leo III was then Pope. He compromised the matter. Without positively rejecting the doctrine of the procession from the Father *and from*

---

302 Father Labbe, Collection of Councils, vol. vii.

303 Alcuin, Epist. 69.

the Son, he censured the addition made to the creed.[304] He even saw fit to transmit to posterity his protest against any innovation by having the creed engraved upon two tablets of silver that were hung in St. Peter's Church, and under which was written the following inscription: "*I, Leo, have put up these tablets for the love and preservation of the orthodox faith.*" The deputies from the Council of Aix-la-Chapelle had needed all the resources of their logic and erudition to persuade Leo III that this doctrine of the procession of the Holy Ghost might be Catholic. Their erudition was inaccurate, and consequently the opinions they rested upon it were not true. They confounded in God the *substance* with the proper character of the *divine personality*, the *essential* procession of the Spirit with His mission in the world.[305] Leo III, although he gave a hearing to their arguments, did not show himself any more favorable to the addition, nor even to the *chanting* of the creed in the services of the Church.

Nevertheless, the Creed continued to be chanted with the addition in Spain and in all the countries subject to Charlemagne. Rome only adopted that practice at the commencement of the eleventh century (about 1015) at the request of the Emperor Henry, but she seemed to agree with the other Western churches as to the substance of the doctrine. It was thus that Photius could justly reproach the Roman Church as well as other Western churches with admitting an innovation in the faith. After having been deposed by Nicholas, and after himself condemning that Pope, he sent to

---

304 Sirmond's Concil. Angiq. Gall., vol. ii.

305 This confusion is at the bottom of all the arguments of the Western theologians to this day. In support of their error, they rely upon certain texts in which the Fathers speak only of the divine substance common to the three persons, and make no mention of the essential character of the personality in each of them. This character in the Father is that of being the sole principle of the Son by generation, and of the Spirit *by procession*. Such is the doctrine of the Church, including the Roman Church herself. Such admits that the Father is the *sole principle* in the Trinity, and that such is the character of His personality, without perceiving that she contradicts herself in making of the Son *another principle* in the Trinity by her addition of *Filioque*, since she makes the personal action of the Son the same as that of the Father in the procession of the Holy Ghost.

the Eastern Patriarchs a circular letter in which he thus expresses himself upon the question of the *Filioque:*

"Besides the gross errors we have mentioned, they have striven, by false interpretations and words which they have added, to do violence to the holy and sacred Creed, which has been confirmed by all the œcumenical councils, and possesses irresistible force. O diabolical inventions! Using new language, they affirm that the Holy Spirit does not proceed from the Father only, but from *the Son* also! Who ever heard such language, even from the mouth of the impious of past ages! Where is the Christian who could admit *two causes* in the Trinity, that is to say, the Father—cause of the Son and Holy Spirit; and the Son—*cause* of the same Spirit?

"This is to divide the first principle into a double divinity—it is to lower Christian theology to the level of Grecian mythology, and to wrong the Trinity *incomprehensible* and one in principle *(iperoúsion Ke monarhitís Triados).* But how should the Holy Spirit proceed from the Son? If the procession He holds from the Father is perfect (and it is thus, since He is very God of very God), what is this procession from the Son, and what is its object?

Certainly it is a vain and futile thing. Moreover, if the Spirit proceed from the Son as well as the Father, why is not the Son begotten by the Spirit as well as by the Father? Let them say this in order that there be no piety mixed with their impiety, that their opinions may agree with their language, and they may shrink from no undertaking. Let us consider further, that if the *property* of the Holy Spirit be known in that He proceeds from the Father, the *property* of the Son likewise consists in His being begotten by the Father. But as they in their madness assert, the Spirit *proceeds also from the Son*; hence the Spirit is distinguished from the Father by more numerous properties than the Son, since the Spirit proceeding from both is something common to the Father and to the Son. The procession of the Spirit from the Father and the Son is the property of the Spirit. If the Spirit is further removed from the Father than the Son, the Son must be nearer to the substance of the Father than the Spirit.

Such was the origin of the audacious blasphemy pronounced against the Holy Spirit by Macedonius, who followed without knowing it the system and error of those who teach it in these days.

"Moreover, if all be common between the Father and the Son, assuredly that which concerns the Holy Spirit is common also, namely, that He must be God, King, Creator, Almighty, Simple, without exterior form, Incorporeal, Invisible, and absolute All. Now if the procession of the Spirit be common to the Father and to the Son, then the Spirit must also proceed from Himself, He is His own principle—at one and the same time *cause and effect.*

Even the Greeks have not gone to such length in their fables.

"One more reflection: if it were the property of the Spirit alone to have relation to different principles, He would be the only one to have a plural principle and not a single one.

"Let me add that if, in the things where there is community between the Father and Son, the Spirit must be excluded, and if the Father be one with the Son in substance only and not in *properties*, then necessarily the Holy Spirit can have nothing in common except what concerns the substance.

"You see how little the advocates of this error are entitled to the name of Christians, and that they only take it to deceive others. The Spirit proceeding from the Son! Where hast thou learned this fact that thou assertest? In what Gospel hast thou found this word? To what council belongs such blasphemy?"

Photius appeals to Scripture and Catholic tradition against the Western system. He adds that the consequence of this system is that there are in God *four* persons or *hypostases*; for the Spirit having a *double principle*, is a Being double as to personality. He further unfolds many considerations which prove in him a profoundly philosophical mind, and to which the Western theologians have answered nothing to the purpose.[306] All the arguments in favor of

---

306 The reader will soon be of our opinion if he will read without prejudice and with an unbiased mind the treatise of Monseigneur Macarius, which we have already mentioned, and the learned work of Zœrnicave, who devoted almost his entire life to the study of the question before us in all the records of tradition. The works of such as Perrone and Jager, not to mention the rest, are very meager as compared with those we speak of. This latter author

VII. Papal Innovation Perpetuated & Strengthened the Schism

pure Catholic tradition prove conclusively that particular churches never, even with the best intentions, can meddle with impunity with the sacred deposit of Revelation.[307]

Photius brought several more accusations against the Roman Church. He knew perfectly that each particular church was entitled to its own regulations, and he had laid down this soundest of principles in opposition to Nicholas himself, who sought to impose the discipline of the Western Church upon the Eastern. But in discipline we should distinguish between *Apostolic rules*, which have a character of *universality*, and private regulations.

Now, he claimed that the Roman Church violated Apostolic rules of discipline upon three principal points. First, in imposing the fast and abstinence of Saturday. Second, in making ecclesiastical celibacy a general law. Third, in regarding as void confirmation given by priests after baptism. The Roman Bishop who had been sent to the Bulgarians had transgressed the principles of orthodoxy so far as to repeat the sacrament of confirmation to those who had received it from Greek priests. This was such a flagrant violation that even the Romanists do not defend it.

Photius, in his encyclical letter, appeals to all the Apostolic sees of the East against the innovations of the *Italians*. He concludes by entreating them to adhere publicly to the second Nicene Council, to proclaim it the seventh *œcumenical*, and to declare against the innovations of the *barbarous* nations of the West who undertake to adulterate the true doctrine.

---

claims to rest his arguments upon ontological considerations to prove that the Father is the sole principle in the Trinity, although the Son is so also with him. A very original idea indeed to resort to the science of *the human being* in order to *explain the Infinite Being!* And besides, the reflections of the Abbé Jager, and those authors upon whom he relies, have this slight defect, that they are unintelligible not only to the reader, but most probably to the writers. Ambiguous phrases never make a good argument for an innovation.

307 Among the letters of Photius (Lib. II. ep. 24), there is one to the Metropolitan of Aquilela. He replies to the texts of the Latins by saying that if ten or twenty can be found in favor of the innovation, there can be found six hundred against it; whence it follows that tradition will always remain clear on this point. He also works out the same arguments as in his encyclical letter.

Photius had some reason to consider the Western people as little civilized. Since the invasion by the tribes which had transformed the West, the ecclesiastical schools and libraries had been destroyed, and the clergy were profoundly ignorant.

Charlemagne had given a strong impulse to letters; but in spite of his efforts and those of the distinguished men who aided him, the ecclesiastical sciences were in their infancy and a certain pedantry too often took their place. Now, the character of a pedant is to be quite certain about everything. The innovators therefore thought they had done a work of high religious philosophy in adding to the Creed those words of which Photius complained. They thought they had defined the nature of the Trinity better than the Nicene Council, in attributing to the Son the *personal* quality of the Father in order to prove that he had the same substance. They defended this doctrine by some misinterpreted texts from the Fathers, of whom they possessed very few works, and thus they set up a false opinion as a *dogma*, without regard to the testimony of the Apostolic churches of the East. They consulted the Popes; but the Popes, who were themselves very ignorant, swayed on the one hand by the reasoning of men whom they thought learned, and, on the other hand, desiring to avail themselves of this opportunity to do an act of sovereign authority, yielded and sanctioned the innovation even while they resisted its introduction into the Creed.

Thus was Rome influenced by error in the interest of her assumed sovereignty. And hence Nicholas felt that the Papacy itself was attacked by the encyclical letter of Photius. At a loss for how to reply, he applied to those *scholars* who, in the Church of France, were the avowed champions of the innovation. Photius had taken no notice of the Latin innovations so long as they remained in the West, and perhaps only knew of them vaguely. But when the Roman priests spread them through Bulgaria, in defiant opposition to the doctrine of the Eastern Church, and among a people brought into the faith by the Church of Constantinople, he could be silent no longer, and he drew up against the Roman Church such a bill of attainder as shall endure forever as a protest against the abuses and errors of which she has been guilty.

VII. Papal Innovation Perpetuated & Strengthened the Schism 295

Nicholas so far humbled himself that he applied to Hinemar, a famous Archbishop of Rheims, who had resisted his autocratic pretensions. He felt he had need of this great theologian of the West to resist Photius. He had received the accusations of that Patriarch through the Prince of Bulgaria. "In reading that paper," he says,[308] "we have concluded that the writers dipped their pen in the lake of blasphemy, and that instead of ink they used the mire of error. They condemn not only our Church, but the whole Latin Church, because we fast on Saturday and teach that the Holy Ghost proceeds from the Father and the Son; for they maintain that He proceeds from the Father only." Nicholas sums up some further complaints of the Greeks. Some of them are not to be found in the circular of Photius to the Easterns. "What is still more senseless," he adds, is "before receiving our legates, they would oblige them to make a profession of faith in which these articles and those who have maintained them are anathematized, and to present canonical letters to him whom they call their *œcumenical* Patriarch." We perceive by this that the Easterns, in order to preserve the ancient faith and discipline against Roman innovations, resorted to all the means in their power.

It is impossible to share the opinion of Nicholas, who chose to regard as foolish measures of caution both perfectly legitimate and canonical, which were only wrong inasmuch as they were an obstacle to his ambitious projects.

Having exhibited his grievances against the Easterns, Nicholas commanded all the Metropolitans to assemble Provincial Councils, reply to the accusations of Photius, and send the result of their deliberations to Hincmar of Rheims, who would transmit them to him. The Bishops of France assembled. Several of them entered the lists against the Easterns, particularly Æneas of Paris. Ratramn, a monk of Corbey, composed the most learned work.

No one could have done better in the defence of a bad cause. At a time when the records of tradition were very rare in the West, it was difficult to compile from the many complete instruction. The Frankish divines therefore quoted in their favor only a few texts, of

---

308 Nichol., Epist., in Labbe's Collection, vol. viii.

which many were from apocryphal works. Photius seems to allude to these labours when he says, in his letter to the Metropolitan of Aquileia, that if one could quote ten or twenty Fathers in favor of the opinions of the Latins, one might quote six hundred in support of the belief of the Church. The historical facts adduced by Ratramn in proof of the Roman primacy are completely distorted for want of proper information; and, besides, in defending that primacy, he had no intention whatever to maintain a *sovereignty of divine right*. His reasoning and his quotations, like those of Æneas respecting the celibacy of the priesthood, did not reach that question; for the Easterns did not disapprove of celibacy in itself considered, but only as a *general law* imposed upon the clergy. In this light celibacy certainly changed the general discipline of the primitive Church, and the Easterns were right in attacking it on this ground.

Under John VIII, the question of the Procession of the Holy Ghost changed its character at Rome like that of the elevation of Photius to the Patriarchal chair. The addition of the *Filioque* made to the Nicene Creed in the West was solemnly condemned in the sixth session of the council of 879. The legates of the Pope, those of the Eastern Patriarchal sees, and all the bishops concurred in that condemnation.

The Pope, upon receiving the transactions, wrote to Photius:[309]

"We know the unfavorable accounts that you have heard concerning us and our Church; I therefore wish to explain myself to you even before you write to me on the subject. You are not ignorant that your envoy, in discussing the Creed with us, found that we preserved it as we originally received it, without adding to or taking anything from it; for we know what severe punishment he would deserve who should dare to tamper with it. To set you at ease, therefore, upon this subject, which has been a cause of scandal to the Church, we again declare to you that not only do we thus recite it, but even condemn those who, in their folly, have had the audacity to act otherwise from the beginning, as violators of the divine word and falsifiers of *the doctrine* of Christ, of the Apostles, and of the Fathers, who have transmitted the Creed to us through

---

309 Joann., viii. Epist.

the councils; we declare that their portion is that of Judas, because they have acted like him, since, if it be not the body of Christ itself which they put to death, it is, at all events, the faithful of God who are his members, whom they tear by schism, giving them up, as well as themselves, to eternal death, as also did that base Apostle.

Nevertheless, I think that your Holiness, so full of wisdom, is aware of the difficulty of making our bishops share this opinion, and of changing at once so important a practice which has taken root for so many years. We therefore believe it is best not to force anyone to abandon that addition to the Creed, but we must act with moderation and prudence, little by little, exhorting them to renounce that *blasphemy*. Thus, then, those who accuse us of sharing this opinion do not speak the truth. But those who say that there are persons left among us who dare to recite the Creed in this manner are not very far from the truth. Your Holiness should not be too much scandalized on our account, nor withdraw from the healthy part of the body of our Church, but zealously contribute by your gentleness and prudence to the conversion of such as have departed from the truth, so that with us you may deserve the promised reward. Hail in the Lord, worthily venerated and catholic brother!"

John VIII spoke particularly of the *addition*; but the expressions he used prove that he condemned the doctrine, as well, which that addition represented. The word would have been no *blasphemy* if it had expressed a truth. The Papacy was changeful, then, as to the doctrine; it hesitated under Leo III; it approved the new dogma under Nicholas I; it rejected it as blasphemous under John VIII.[310]

After having ascertained this principal Roman innovation, let us now continue our account of the Roman enterprises against the East.

---

310 Several Western writers have endeavored to disprove the authenticity of this letter of John VIII. Their arguments cannot counterbalance this fact, that this letter was published from Western manuscripts. Had the Easterns invented it, as the Romanists maintain without any proof, it would have come from the East to the West, while it really went from the West to the East. This certain fact speaks louder than all their dissertations, and answers every objection.

John VIII being dead, Marin[311] was elected Bishop of Rome. He had been one of the legates of Nicholas in Bulgaria and at the council of 869. It could not, therefore, be hoped that he would follow the course of his immediate predecessor. It is thought that it was he who carried to Constantinople the letters of John approving the council of 879, except in those things wherein the legates had exceeded their powers. This exception was a mere formality, for he had received the acts; knew perfectly what had happened; very modestly urged Photius not to take it amiss, that he had demanded a submission from him; and knew the Patriarch had not been willing to make one, for this reason, that only the guilty should beg pardon.[312] Marin could not concur with the council of 879 without condemning that of 869, of which he had been one of the presidents. He therefore refused, when he was at Constantinople, to condemn himself by condemning that council, and the Emperor Basil detained him a prisoner one month for this cause.

Raised to the Roman episcopate (882), Marin had a grudge to satisfy. He hastened to condemn Photius. But his pontificate was short, and in 884 he was succeeded by Adrian III, who also condemned the Patriarch of Constantinople. The Emperor Basil wrote very energetic letters to this Pope, but they only arrived at Rome after his death and were delivered to his successor, Stephen V (885), who had been the intimate friend and confidant of Marin, against whom the Emperor's letters were particularly directed. Stephen undertook his defence. We will quote some passages of his letter, which are well worthy of notice.[313]

"As God has given you the sovereignty of temporal things, in like manner we have received *from him*, through St. Peter, Prince of the Apostles, *the sovereignty of spiritual things*. To us is committed the care of the flock; this care is as much more excellent as the heavens are above the earth. Hear what the Lord said to Peter, *Thou art Peter*, etc. I therefore entreat your Piety to honor the name and dignity of the Prince of the Apostles by conforming to his decrees; for the

---

311 Known also as Martin II.

312 Joann., viii. Epist.

313 Steph. V, Epist. Labbe's Collection, vol. ix.

episcopate in all the churches on earth owes its origin to St. Peter, by whom we instruct all the faithful, teaching them wholesome and incorruptible doctrine."

Here is a clear enunciation of *Papal sovereignty* and Papal *infallibility of divine right.* Stephen pretends that the legates of Pope Sylvester, at the first Council of Nicea, established this principle, "That the *first bishop* could not be judged by anyone." Such an assertion was worthy of the erudition of that age. As a consequence of his doctrine of the episcopal character, Stephen claims that Photius never was anything but a layman, since he did not derive his episcopate from Rome.

"Did not the Roman Church," he adds, "write to you to hold a council at Constantinople? I ask you, to whom could it write? *To Photius, a layman?* If you had a Patriarch, our Church would often visit him by letters. But, alas! The glorious city of Constantinople *is without a pastor,* and if the affection that we bear toward you did not lead us to bear patiently the insult to our Church, we should be obliged to pronounce against the prevaricator, Photius, who has so basely spoken against us, more severe penalties than our predecessors. We do not presume, in thus speaking, to fail in the respect due to you; we speak in our own defence and that of Pope Marin, who held the same sentiments as Pope Nicholas."

Thus Nicholas had bequeathed to Marin the sentiments which the latter had bequeathed to Stephen. As for the acts of John VIII, they were completely ignored. Photius did not change as easily as the Popes, and he followed the rules of ancient law with moderation and intelligence.

It appears from the letter of Stephen V that the Papacy was no longer so very defiant toward the emperors of the East. The Roman Empire of the West had crumbled with Charlemagne. From its fragments had sprung a thousand little independent states, forever quarreling among themselves. The feudal system was organizing; the Papacy no longer saw a powerful prince at hand to protect it. Rome itself was a prey to the quarrels of several hostile parties. Meanwhile the Mussulmans continued their conquests. Checked in the East by the Emperor Basil, they were pouring in upon the West, and Rome itself was threatened. John VIII knew that Rome could obtain better aid from the Emperor of the East than from the divided princes of the West. His successors, with less cleverness, implored the same assistance without sacrificing any of their contemptible personal grudges. It was only fair that they should not succeed.

Had the Papacy been happily inspired, it might have availed itself of its influence in the West to arouse the Princes against the Mussulmans and unite them with the Emperor of the East in that great struggle. But Rome preferred to indulge her antipathies against a Church which set up the doctrine and laws of the primitive Church in opposition to her usurpations. She aroused the West as much against the Eastern Christians as against the Mussulmans, and thus introduced a radical fault in those great movements of nations known as the *Crusades*. The conception of these expeditions was grand, and for the West it led to some useful results. We do not deny it; but historical impartiality demands that it should be confessed, at the same time, that the Papacy, which set these expeditions on foot, failed to give them the character of grandeur they would have had if, instead of circumscribing them to the West, it had united in a fraternal embrace the Eastern Christians with the Crusaders.

Rome sacrificed all to her hatred of the Eastern Church.

The Emperor Basil died shortly after receiving the letter of Pope Stephen V. Leo the Philosopher, son of Basil, succeeded him upon the throne of the East. He drove Photius from the see of Constantinople, to put there his own brother Stephen. As a pretext for this usurpation, he sent two of his officers to the Church of Saint Sophia, who ascended the pulpit and publicly read off the crimes which it pleased the Emperor to impute to Photius; and the Patriarch was next accused of having been concerned in a plot, the object of which was to place one of his relatives on the throne. Not a single proof of this charge could be adduced. Then Leo had Bishop Stylien, who was a personal enemy of Photius, brought to court and the two composed an infamous letter for the Pope (886) in which they collected all the accusations of the enemies of Photius—accusations which had been declared to be *calumnies* by John VIII and by a council of four hundred bishops. This letter of Stylien is

VII. Papal Innovation Perpetuated & Strengthened the Schism

one of the Principal documents of which the Western writers have made use in their accounts of what they call the *schism of the East*.³¹⁴

Its value may be estimated at a glance. Stylien's letter only arrived at Rome after Stephen's death (891). Formosus, his successor, replied that Photius had never been anything more than a layman; that the bishops whom he had ordained were likewise nothing but laymen; that he was therefore condemned without need of any trial; that the bishops, his adherents, should be treated with mercy but only as laymen.³¹⁵ The Pope who wrote this answer was exhumed by Pope Stephen VI. His putrescent corpse was cited, judged, and condemned. John IX reversed this judgment of Stephen VI. These facts and the atrocious immoralities of the Popes of that period are covered by Romanists with a veil of complaisance. They have anathemas only for a great Patriarch who, by his virtues and ecclesiastical learning, deserves to rank with the most illustrious bishops of the Church.

There is no doubt that Photius died the same year that Formosus wrote his famous letter to Stylien against him, that is, in 891.³¹⁶

The Eastern Church holds Ignatius and Photius in equal veneration. She has declared anathemas against all that has been written against either of them. She is perfectly wise in this decision. It was her will that these two Patriarchs should be judged by themselves and by their own writings, without reference to other writings dictated by passion. Now, Ignatius wrote nothing against Photius; and the latter, in his numerous writings, never attacked Ignatius. After the restoration of Ignatius, and the reconciliation of Photius with the Emperor Basil, they saw each other, forgave each other, and it may be said that Ignatius died in the arms of Photius

---

314 The Abbé Jager innocently says, "The letter of Stylien is a historic monument upon which we have frequently drawn." *Hist. of Phot.*, book ix. p. 387, edit. 1854.

315 See Labbe's Collection of Councils, vols. viii. and ix.

316 M. Jager, who thinks himself a historian of some weight, says that Photius died in 891, adding that this was *several* years after the letter of Formosus. That letter, however, as well as the pontificate of Formosus, only dates from the year 891, as Stephen V, his predecessor, had only died in that same year.

according to what this latter Patriarch declared before four hundred bishops in the council of 879.

It is therefore dishonest to appeal to the testimony of a few enemies of Photius who were Greeks on the ground that they belonged to the Eastern Church. That Church has disowned them, and has had the wisdom to warn her faithful that calumnies inspired by blind hatred, whether they come from Greeks or Latins, are alike to be condemned.[317]

Stylien, Bishop of Neo-Cæsarea, and an enemy to Photius, remained in correspondence with the Popes after the death of that Patriarch. John IX wrote to him in the year 900,[318] to this effect: "it is *our will* that the decrees of our predecessors (concerning the Patriarchs of Constantinople) should remain inviolate"; but this Pope did not attempt to reconcile those of John VIII with those of Nicholas, both of whom were equally his predecessors. Five years after, the court of Rome had some relations with the East to sanction an act of injustice. The Emperor Leo VI, having married for the fourth time, had thereby violated the discipline of the Eastern Church, sanctioned even by civil laws. The Patriarch Nicholas besought him to have the case examined by the five Patriarchal churches. Leo feigned to consent, and wrote to Sergius III, Pope of Rome; to Michael, Pope of Alexandria;[319] to Simeon, Patriarch

---

317 The Abbé Jager sees an *astonishing contradiction* in the conduct of the Greek Church (*Hist. of Phot.*, book ix, p. 392). This is the fault of his eyes, which by the effect of a singular mirage have made him see things quite different from what they are in reality. A historian who starts with the principle of only listening to the enemies of the person whose history he is about to write, must necessarily find contradictions in those who have followed an opposite course. The question is, whether in judging a man it is expedient to refer exclusively to his enemies. There is in the work of the Abbé Jager a *contradiction* much more *astonishing* than that which he imputes to the Greek Church. It is the *Satanic character* he ascribes to Photius, side by side with that which shows forth from the letters he has quoted of this great man. Mr. Jager did not perceive that Photius, by his letters, belies all these infamous accusations that he renewed against him.

318 See Collection of Councils, by Father Labbe, vol. ix.

319 The Patriarch of Alexandria took the title of Pope as well as the Bishop of Rome, and still preserves it.

VII. Papal Innovation Perpetuated & Strengthened the Schism

of Antioch; and to Elias, Patriarch of Jerusalem. The Patriarchs sent legates. The Emperor bribed them. The faithful bishops were exiled.

Nicholas was deposed and Euthymius put in his place; and, finally, a dispensation was granted to the Emperor for his fourth marriage. Thus did Rome sustain the unjust deposition of a Patriarch who was guilty of nothing more than of maintaining the rules of church discipline. For in all things, she acted less in accordance with justice than with her own interest. If she had taken the part of Ignatius, it was because she feared the opposition of Photius to her sovereignty. If she so readily sacrificed Nicholas, it was in order to do an act of authority in the East. Power was her sole object. Pope Sergius could not indeed be fastidious upon the subject of the illicit marriage of Leo, for he was himself the lover of the infamous Marozia, and had by this adulterous connection a son who was a Pope like himself.[320] Such a Pope could not understand the delicacy of conscience of the Patriarch Nicholas. After the death of the Emperor Leo, Euthymius was driven away and Nicholas reinstated. This Patriarch was even placed at the head of the regency during the minority of the young Emperor Constantine, surnamed Porphyrogenitus. Reinstalled in his see, he wrote (A.D. 912) to Pope Anastasius III, the successor of Sergius, to complain of the conduct of his legates at Constantinople. "They seem,"[321] he wrote, "to have come from Rome for no other purpose than to declare war against us. But since they *claimed the primacy in the Church*, they ought carefully to have ascertained the whole affair, and written a report of it, instead of consenting to the condemnation of those who had incurred the displeasure of the Prince only for their detestation of incontinency. It is not, indeed, to be wondered at that two or three men should be taken by surprise; but who could have supposed that Western bishops would confirm that unjust sentence by their votes without knowledge of the cause? I learn that the pretext of *dispensation* is brought forward, as if by a

---

320 Rome was then governed by three prostitutes, Theodora and her two daughters Marozia and Theodora, who disposed of the Popedom in favor of their lovers and adulterine children.

321 Nicol., Epist. in the Collection of the Councils, vol. ix. Appendix.

dispensation debauchery could be authorized and the canons violated. Dispensation, if I am not mistaken, is intended to imitate the mercy of God; it extends its hand to the sinner and lifts him up, but it does not permit him to remain in the sin into which he has fallen."

This perfectly just doctrine was not that of Rome. At one time, under pretence of observing the canons, she would throw an entire kingdom into confusion, as under Nicholas I, in relation to the marriage of Hloter; then again she could *give dispensation* without difficulty in equally important cases. This was because her study was always to establish the principle of her absolute power over laws as well as men. Her will was her law, and the interest of her sovereignty her only rule.

The Patriarch Nicholas felt the consequences of the palace intrigues; he was banished and again reinstated. Peace was finally reestablished in 920 by an imperial decree which again recognized the discipline for which Nicholas had suffered persecution. This Patriarch wrote to Pope John X to renew friendly relations between the churches of Rome and Constantinople. But John X was more engrossed by his adulterous amours with Theodora, Marozia's sister, than by the affairs of the Church.

For a century there was scarcely any intercourse between the churches of Rome and Constantinople which did not tend to reunite them in matters of doctrine.[322] In 1024, the Patriarch Eustathius attempted to have himself recognized at Rome as the ecclesiastical chief of the East, in the same way as the Pope was chief of the West. His envoys were on the point of succeeding—thanks to their money, of which the court of Rome was very greedy; but the intrigue transpired and caused some agitation, principally in Italy. The court of Rome did not dare to go further. This fact proves, at least, that the Bishops of Rome and Constantinople were not at strife. Those of Rome were mostly unworthy of their place; their political business and the struggles which prevailed in most of the Western churches were as much as they could attend to, and they did not trouble themselves with the Eastern churches, where their

---

322 Nat. Alex. in Eccl. Hist. Dissert. IV. Sæcul. ix. et. x.

VII. Papal Innovation Perpetuated & Strengthened the Schism 305

sovereignty was always opposed. But the contest recommenced in 1053, when Leo IX was Bishop of Rome.

Having received letters of communion from Peter, the new Patriarch of Antioch, Leo affected, in his answer, to tell him that he held the third rank in the Patriarchate, thus ignoring the Patriarch of Constantinople—notwithstanding the decrees of the œcumenical councils, which had given him the second rank, the third to the Patriarch of Alexandria, and the fourth to the Patriarch of Antioch. At that time Michael Cerularius was Patriarch of Constantinople; he had written a letter to John, Bishop of Trani, against several disciplinary or liturgical practices of the Latin Church.[323] Cardinal Humbert, having read this letter at the Bishop's house, translated it into Latin and sent it to Pope Leo IX. The Pope wrote to the Patriarch of Constantinople in unmeasured terms. The Patriarch then wrote a second letter against the Latins, completing his accusations. The most serious one was that of adding the *Filioque* to the Creed. Leo IX should have calmly answered these accusations; proved that many of them were unfounded; and excused several Latin usages upon the principle that discipline may vary in different countries, provided the regulations of the Apostles and of the œcumenical councils are kept inviolate; confessed, in fine, that many of the accusations made by the Patriarch were just, and undertaken the reform of the Western Church. But Leo IX only cared for the injury that he thought was done to his pretensions as sovereign head of the Church, and he wrote to Michael Cerularius under the influence of that thought.[324]

After a long exordium upon the unity of the Church, he claims that unity to be in the Roman Church, which has received that high prerogative from God through St. Peter. That Church, having received as its foundation Jesus Christ through St. Peter, is the unshaken rock against which the gates of hell shall never prevail. There can, therefore, be no error in the Roman Church,

---

323 This letter may be found in the Annals of Baronius. See Letters of Leo IX. in the Collection of Councils. Nat. Alesand., Eccl. Hist. Synop. Sæcul. xi. c. iv.

324 Leo IX, Ep. in Labbe's Collection of Councils, vol. ix.

and it is only through pride that the Eastern Church makes those accusations. He attacks that Church on account of the heresies that have sprung up in her bosom; but he does not observe that no church can be made responsible for heresies she has condemned, whilst the Roman Church was herself accused of having taught error in lieu of sound doctrine. He ventures to recall the opposition of the ancient Bishops of Rome to the title of œcumenical, but does not remark that the Popes had usurped the thing as well as the title, although not officially introduced in all their acts; he falsely maintains that the first Council of Nicea declared that no one could judge the Bishop of Rome, and that he was the chief of all the churches. He cites an apocryphal grant of Constantine to prove the sovereign power of the Pope in a temporal as well as a spiritual point of view. He thinks also that he has subdued the *impudent vanity* of those who contested the rights of the Papacy. He resorts to those texts of Scripture which at all times have constituted the meager arsenal of the Papacy. He maintains that Constantinople owes to the Holy See the second rank that she occupies among the Patriarchal Churches. As for the Roman Church, she has an exceptional rank, and to attack her rights is to attack the Church Universal, of which she is the divine centre. Pride and jealousy alone could suggest such sacrilegious intentions.

Such is the substance of the first letter of Leo IX to the Patriarch Michael Cerularius. Politics envenomed these first discussions. The Normans were attacking the empire.

The Emperor Constantine Monomachus, too weak to resist all his enemies, resolved to ask the aid of the Germans and Italians, and to this end applied to the Pope, who had great influence over those people. In order to conciliate the Pope, he wrote to him that he ardently desired to reestablish friendly relations, so long interrupted, between the churches of Rome and Constantinople. He persuaded the Patriarch Michael to write in the same strain to Leo IX, who at once sent three legates to Constantinople with a letter for the Emperor and another for the Patriarch (1054).

He begins by felicitating the Emperor upon the pious desire he had communicated to him, but very soon comes down to the

VII. Papal Innovation Perpetuated & Strengthened the Schism

rights of the Roman see. "The Catholic Church," he says, "mother and immaculate virgin, although destined to fill the whole world with her members, has nevertheless but one head, which must be venerated by all. Whoever dishonors that head claims in vain to be one of her members." That head of the Church is Rome, whose power the great Constantine recognized by his grant. Now, as Bishop of Rome, he is the Vicar of God charged with the care of all the churches. He therefore wishes to restore its splendour to the Roman Episcopate, which for a long time has been governed by mercenaries, he says, rather than pastors. The Emperor of Constantinople can aid him in this work by restoring the estates which the Roman Church possessed in the East, and by checking the enterprises of the Patriarch Michael, whom he accuses of ambitious projects against the churches of Alexandria and Antioch.

In his letter to Michael Cerularius, Leo IX first acknowledges the receipt of the letters written to him by that Patriarch in favor of a pacification. "We shall have peace," he tells him, "if you will, in future, abstain from overstepping the boundaries set up by the Fathers." This is just what the Eastern Church said to the Papacy. Leo then finds fault with Michael for his ambition, his luxury, and his wealth. Did such blame fall with a good grace from the mouth of a Pope? He adds, "What a detestable, lamentable, sacrilegious usurpation is yours, when in speech and in writing you call yourself *universal* Patriarch." Then he mentions the opposition of St. Gregory to this title; and this brings him to the pretended rights of the Church of Rome. "The Roman Church," he says, "is not, as you allege, a *local* church; is she not the head and mother? How could she be this if she had neither members nor children? We proclaim this openly because we believe it firmly; the Roman Church is so little a local church that, in all the world, no nation which presumes to disagree with her can any longer be regarded as belonging to the Church. It is thenceforth only a conventicle of heretics—a synagogue of Satan! Therefore let him who would glory in the name of a Christian cease to curse and attack the Roman Church; for it is vain in him to pretend to honor the Father of the family if he dishonors his spouse!"

Is it surprising that the Eastern Church energetically protected against this sacrilegious doctrine?

Cardinal Humbert was chief of the legates of Leo IX, who were bearers of these letters. The Emperor received them with distinction, and Humbert opened the discussion at once. He entered upon the defence of the Latin Church and made sundry accusations against the Greek Church, showing that the Greek Church had her own peculiar discipline and her own peculiar abuses as well as the Latin Church. His writings were translated into Greek by the Emperor's order.

The Patriarch Michael refused to communicate with the legates. Without doubt he knew that it was a foregone conclusion with the Emperor to sacrifice the Greek Church to the Papacy in order to obtain some aid for his throne. The letter he had received from the Pope had enlightened him sufficiently as to what Rome meant by union. The legates proceeded to the Church of Saint Sophia at the hour when the clergy were preparing for the mass. They loudly complained of the obstinacy of the Patriarch, and placed upon the altar a sentence of excommunication against him. They went out of the church, shaking the dust from their feet and pronouncing anathemas against all those who should not communicate with the Latins. All this was done with the Emperor's consent, which explains why the Patriarch would have no intercourse with the legates. The people, convinced of the Emperor's connivance, revolted. In the moment of danger, Constantine made some concessions. The legates protested that their sentence of excommunication had not been read as it was written; that the Patriarch had the most cruel and perfidious designs against them.

However that may be, and had Michael even been guilty of such wicked designs, this manner of acting was none the more dignified or canonical. Michael has been further accused of making groundless complaints against the Latin Church. Several of these were, in fact, exaggerated; but it has not been sufficiently observed that the Patriarch, in his letter, only echoed the sentiments of all the Eastern churches. Ever since the Papacy had attempted to impose its autocracy upon them, there had been a strong reaction in all

VII. Papal Innovation Perpetuated & Strengthened the Schism

these churches. On the spur of this sentiment, everything had been sought out that could be laid at the door of the Roman Church, which by her bishops held herself out as the infallible guardian of sound doctrine. Michael Cerularius was only the interpreter of these complaints; he would never have had enough influence to impose his grievances, true or pretended, upon the whole Christian East; so that those who call him the consummator of the schism, commenced under Photius, have but superficially understood the facts. What made the strength of Photius against the Papacy was that all the churches of the East were with him, in spite of political intrigues, imperial influence, Papal violence, and the spite of relentless enemies. Therein lay the strength of Michael Cerularius also. This Patriarch possessed neither the learning, the genius, nor the virtues of Photius; but he spoke in the name of the East, and the East recognized its own sense in his protests against the innovations of Rome. The Emperor, jealous of the influence he had acquired, banished him, and was endeavoring to have him deposed by a council when he heard of his death (1058).

After the death of the Patriarch Michael, intercourse between Rome and Constantinople became even less frequent than before. We hear of one legate sent in 1071, by Pope Alexander II, but rather for a political object than from motives of religion. He thought that the Eastern Emperors might be of great help in the Crusades.

Gregory VII, who soon after ascended the Papal chair (in 1073), raised the Papacy to its greatest height by skillfully taking advantage of the divisions caused by the feudal system to extend the influence of the Church, which he summed up in the Bishop of Rome. But he did not use his influence to reconcile the West with the East; and besides, the antagonism was too great between the two churches to allow the diplomatic negotiations of the Popes with the Emperors of the East to have any useful result. The Papacy had spread throughout the West the idea that the Greeks were schismatics and dangerous enemies of the Church, while the Easterns regarded the people of the West in the light of barbarians who were Christians only in name and had tampered with the faith and the holiest institutions of the Church.

Hence the distrust of the Crusaders on the part of the Greeks, and the violence of the Crusaders against them. We are not concerned with those expeditions in this work. We will only notice this acknowledged fact, that the Crusades only strengthened the antipathy which had long existed between East and West, and that if any attempt were made to reconcile them, it was ever the emperors, acting from motives of policy and interest, that took the lead. These emperors never ceased to think of their Western possessions. They watched the contests between several of the Popes and the emperors of the West. These contests, as animated as they were protected, were caused by the Papacy, which, in virtue of its spiritual sovereignty, pretended to overrule the temporal powers. Alexis Comnenus endeavored to turn them to account. He sent (A.D. 1112) an embassy to Rome announcing that he was inclined to proceed thither to receive the imperial crown from the hands of the Pope. This step did not lead to anything more but it proves that the emperors of that period had a decided tendency to conciliate Rome from motives of mere policy. Manuel Comnenus (A.D. 1155) sought the alliance of the Pope and of Frederic, Emperor of the West, against the Normans, who had wrested Sicily from the empire of Constantinople. Upon that occasion, Pope Adrian IV sent legates to Manuel with a letter for Basil, Archbishop of Thessalonica, in which he exhorted that bishop to procure the reunion of the churches.[325] Basil answered that there was no division between the Greeks and Latins, since they held the same faith and offered the same sacrifice. "As for the causes of scandal, weak in themselves, that have separated us from each other," he adds, "your Holiness can cause them to cease, by your own extended authority and the help of the Emperor of the West."

This reply was as skillful as it was wise. The Papacy had innovated; it enjoyed a very widespread authority in the West. What was there to prevent its use of that authority to reject its own innovations or those it had tolerated? It was in the power of the Church of Rome to bring about a perfect union between the two churches. But the Papacy had no such idea of union; no union could exist in its view

---

325 Adrian iv. Ep. 7.

VII. Papal Innovation Perpetuated & Strengthened the Schism

except upon the submission of the Eastern Church to its authority. But the Eastern Church, while maintaining the ancient doctrine, was in an attitude of continual protest against this usurped authority, and was not disposed to submit to this unlawful yoke.

The emperors continued their political intrigues while the Church was in this situation. They kept on good terms with the Emperor of the West so long as he was friendly with the Papacy; but as soon as new struggles arose, they profited by them to renew their applications to the Popes respecting the imperial crown. Alexander III being at war with Frederic, Manuel Comnenus sent him (A.D. 1166) an embassy to make known to the Pope his good intentions of reuniting the Greek and Latin churches, so that Latins and Greeks should thenceforth make but one people under one chief. He asked, therefore, the crown of the whole Roman empire, promising Italy and other material advantages to the Roman Church. The Pope sent legates to Constantinople. Two years later (A.D. 1169) Manuel sent a new embassy to Alexander, offering to reunite the Greek and Latin churches if he would grant him the crown he solicited. The Pope refused, under pretext of the troubles that would follow that grant. Notwithstanding this refusal, the most friendly relations existed between the Pope and Manuel, at whose request a Cardinal sub-deacon, named John, went to Constantinople to work for the union of the churches. But Manuel's tendencies were not approved of by the Greeks, who detested the Latins not only for religious reasons, but also from resentment for the violence they had suffered from the Crusaders. And accordingly, after Manuel's death, the Latins were massacred without mercy at Constantinople (A.D. 1182). Cardinal John was one of the victims. Andronicus, who had instigated the massacre, was elected Emperor. He died shortly after, and was succeeded by Isaac Angelus, who was dethroned by his brother, Alexis Angelus. Innocent III was Bishop of Rome (A.D. 1198). Since Gregory VII, no other Pope had had so much influence in the West. Alexis Angelus hastened to follow the policy of the Comneni: he sent ambassadors, with a letter to the Pope from him, and another from the Patriarch John Camaterus, in order to prove to him that they desired to procure a union between the churches. Innocent dispatched legates to Constantinople, bearing letters in which he exalted the Roman Church beyond all measure. The Patriarch gave the legates his answer, which began thus:

"To Innocent, very holy Roman Pope, and our beloved brother in the Lord Christ, John, by the Divine Mercy, Archbishop of Constantinople, Patriarch of New Rome, love and peace from our Lord and Saviour Jesus Christ." Here is the substance of his letter:

"In reading the letter you have sent to our Humility, we have approved of the zeal of your Holiness for our mutual union in the faith. But I will not conceal from you what has greatly embarrassed me in your letter. It amazes me, in fact, that you call the Church of Rome *one* and *universal,* since it is well established that the Church is divided into particular churches, governed by pastors, under one sole, supreme pastor, Jesus Christ. And what I do not further understand is that you call the Church of Rome *the mother* of the other churches. The mother of the churches is that of Jerusalem, which surpasses them all in antiquity and dignity. I cannot, therefore, plead guilty to the accusation, which your Holiness makes against me, that I divide the single and seamless coat of Christ. When, on one side, we behold our own Church, carefully preserving the ancient doctrine of the Procession of the Holy Ghost, and, on the other, your Church fallen into error on this point, we may well ask you: which of them has rent the coat of Christ?

"I am not the less disposed, for all that, to second the kind intentions of the Emperor for good."

The Emperor also answered the Pope, who replied in two letters from which we will give some extracts. He writes to the Patriarch: "The primacy of the Roman see has been established not by man, but by God, or rather, by the Man-God; this can be proved by numberless evangelic and apostolic evidences, confirmed by canonical constitutions which attest that the most holy Roman Church was consecrated in Saint Peter, the prince of the Apostles, to be the mistress and mother of all the others." Innocent cites many texts from Scripture, interpreting them in his own way.[326] He wonders that the Patriarch is ignorant of these interpretations then

---

[326] We have already determined their true sense in the first chapter of this work.

VII. Papal Innovation Perpetuated & Strengthened the Schism

he undertakes to answer the two questions which he had put to him: "You ask me," he says, "how the Roman Church is *one* and *universal*. The universal Church is that which is composed of all the churches, according to the force of the Greek word *Catholic*. In this sense, the Roman Church is not universal, it is only a part of the Universal Church; but the first and the principal part, like the head in a body. The Roman Church is such because the fulness of power resides in her, and that only a part of that fulness overflows to the others. That *one* Church is therefore universal in this sense, that all the others are under it. According to the true sense of the word, the Roman Church only is universal, because it is the only one that has been raised above the others...

"You ask me how the Roman Church is the mother of the churches? She is so not according to time but according to dignity. The Church of Jerusalem may be regarded as the mother of the faith, because that faith came first from her bosom; the Church of Rome is the mother of the faithful, because she has been placed over them all by the privilege of her dignity." Innocent then congratulates the Patriarch upon his desire for unity, and adds that he owes *respect* and *obedience* to the Roman Church and to its bishop as to his chief; that he will receive him upon condition that he shall be subject as a *member should be to the head*, but that if he refuse *respect* and *obedience*, he will proceed against him and the Greek Church.

Innocent III liked to talk like a master. He expresses himself in the same manner in his reply to the Emperor. He declares his willingness to call a council, although the constitution of the Church is not synodal; that he will invite the Patriarch to it; *that if he will there submit to the Roman Church, and render it the obedience which he owes to it, peace shall be made with him.* He begs the Emperor to see that the Patriarch appears at the council thus disposed; and concludes this letter also with threats.

He did not carry them into execution, however; for he knew that to secure the success of the Crusade which was then organizing, he must keep on good terms with the Greek Emperor. He therefore wrote to the Crusaders who had just left Venice and were on their way to Constantinople, "Let none among you flatter himself that he may be permitted to invade or pillage the land of the Greeks, *under pretext that it is not sufficiently submissive to the Holy See*, or that the Emperor is an usurper, having wrested the empire from his brother. *What crimes he or his subjects may have committed*, it is not for you to judge; and you have not taken the Cross to avenge that injury."

The Crusaders knew perfectly well that their success would insure their absolution. They had made a treaty at Venice with the young Alexis, son of Isaac and nephew of the Emperor. This prince promised that if the Crusaders should give him back the throne his uncle had usurped, be would subject the Greek Church to the Papal sovereignty and join the Crusaders against the Mussulmans.

Upon reaching Constantinople, the Crusaders showed the young Alexis to the people, but soon perceived that they would excite no sympathy in this manner. They then determined to force him upon the city, which they took by assault. They sent news of this to the Pope by a letter in which they sought to excuse themselves for having attacked the Greeks.[327] "The cruel usurper of the empire (Alexis Angelus) had harangued the people and had persuaded them that the Latins were coming to ruin their ancient liberty and subjugate the empire to their laws and to the *authority of the Pope*. This so excited them against us and against the young Prince that they would not listen to us." They pretended to have been first attacked by the Greeks; they related what the old Emperor Isaac, together with his son Alexis, was doing for them, and took good care to add, "He further promises to *render you that obedience* which the Catholic emperors, his predecessors, have rendered to the Popes, and to do all in his power to *lead back the Greek Church to that obedience*."

One of the chiefs of the Crusaders, the Count of St. Paul, wrote, on his part, to the Duke of Louvain: "We have so much advanced the cause of the Saviour that the Eastern Church, of which Constantinople was formerly the metropolis, *being reunited to the Pope its head*, with the Emperor and all his empire, as it was *formerly, recognizes herself as the daughter of the Roman Church and will humbly obey her for the future*. The Patriarch himself is to go to Rome

---

327 See Villehardouin; see It. Godef. ad ann. 1203; Raynold. Annal.; Innocent III, Epist.

VII. Papal Innovation Perpetuated & Strengthened the Schism

to receive his pallium, and has promised the Emperor on his oath to do so. The young Alexis wrote in the same strain to the Pope. "We own," he said, "that the chief cause which has brought the pilgrims to succor us is that we have voluntarily promised, and upon oath, *that we would humbly recognize the Roman Pontiff as the Ecclesiastical head of all Christendom, and as the successor of St. Peter, and that we would use all our power to lead the Eastern Church to that recognition,* understanding well that such reunion *will be very useful to the empire* and most glorious for us. We repeat to you the same promises by these presents, and we ask your advice how to *woo back* the Eastern Church."

It was, therefore, well understood that union meant nothing but submission to the Roman see. The Crusaders and their *protegés* knew that only such promises could lead Innocent III to approve what he had at first censured. The experiment succeeded. Innocent replied to Alexis that he approved of his views as to the reunion of the Eastern Church. If he would remain faithful to his engagements, he promised him all manner of prosperity; if he should fail, he predicts that he will fall before his enemies.

Innocent then replied to the Crusaders. He feared that they had only exacted from Alexis the promise to subject the Eastern to the Roman Church in order to excuse their own fault. "We will judge by these results," he said, "whether you have acted sincerely: if the Emperor sends us letters-patent that we may preserve as authentic proof of his oath; if the Patriarch sends us a solemn deputation to recognize the primacy of the Roman Church, and to *promise obedience* to us; and if he asks of us the pallium, *without which he cannot legitimately exercise the Patriarchal functions."*

Could the Eastern Church recognize such a doctrine as being that of the first eight centuries?

The Crusaders soon quarreled with Alexis, who, when he was Emperor, at once forgot his promises. But this young prince had alienated the Greeks by ascending the throne by means of the Latins. He was dethroned, and Constantinople fell into the power of an adventurer. The Crusaders decided that this man had no right to the crown, and that the Greeks were to be treated without much consideration, *since they had withdrawn from their obedience to the Pope.*

They, therefore, took possession of the city and placed one of their number, Baldwin, Count of Flanders, on the throne. Constantinople was sacked; all its churches polluted, pillaged, and laid waste.

The Latin Empire of Constantinople began in 1204 and ended in 1261. During that period of about half a century, the hatred between the Greeks and Latins assumed fearful proportions. The Marquis of Monferrat, chief of the Crusaders, wrote to the Pope that, if Constantinople had been taken, it was principally to *do a service to the holy see and to bring the Greeks back to the obedience which was due to it*. "After our miraculous conquest," he adds, "we have done nothing except for the sake of reuniting the Eastern Church to the holy see; and we await your counsel for that result."

In his reply, Innocent censures the excesses and sacrileges of which the Crusaders had been guilty. "The Greeks," he adds, "notwithstanding the bad treatment they suffer from those who wish to force them to return to the obedience of the Roman Church, cannot make up their minds to do so because they only see crimes and works of darkness in the Latins, and they hate them like dogs... But the judgments of God," continues the Pope, "are impenetrable, and hence we would not judge lightly in this affair. It may be that the Greeks have been *justly* punished for their sins, although you acted *unjustly* in gratifying your own hatred against them; it is possible that God may *justly* reward you for having been the instruments of His own vengeance." It is evident that Innocent III was calm enough to make subtle distinctions in the presence of a city of bloodshed and rains. The rest of his letter is worthy of the foregoing: "Let us leave," he says, "these doubtful questions. This is certain, that you may keep and defend the land which is conquered for you by the decision of God; upon this condition, however, that you will restore the possessions of the churches, and *that you always remain faithful to the holy see and to us.*"

The Papal sovereignty was the great and single aim. Crimes became virtues, provided the authority of the holy see was propagated and sustained.

Not content with approving the taking of Constantinople, Innocent undertook to establish firmly the new empire. He

VII. Papal Innovation Perpetuated & Strengthened the Schism

accordingly wrote to the bishops of France a circular, of which this is the substance: "God, wishing to hallow His Church by the reunion of the schismatics, has transferred the empire of the *proud, disobedient, and superstitious* Greeks to the *humble, pious, catholic,* and *submissive* Latins. The new Emperor, Baldwin, invites all manner of people, clerical and lay, noble and villain, of all sexes and conditions, to come to his empire to *receive wealth* according to their merit and quality. The Pope, therefore, *commands* the bishops to persuade everyone to come; and he promises the Indulgence of the Crusade to those who will go to uphold the new empire."

Baldwin having begged the Pope to send him some Latin ecclesiastics to strengthen the Papal Church in the East, Innocent wrote a new circular to the bishops of France. "Send," says he, "to that country all the books you can spare, at least to have them copied, that the Church of the East may agree with that of the West in the praises of God!" Thus the venerable liturgies of the East found no grace in the eyes of the Papacy. It was a new church it wished for in the new Latin-Greek Empire.

Baldwin established a Latin clergy at Constantinople, and named the canons, whom he installed at Saint Sophia. These elected the Venetian, Thomas Morosini, for their Patriarch. Innocent found no irregularity except in his elective character; therefore, instead of confirming the election, he directly appointed Thomas to the Patriarchate. His letter deserves to be quoted: "As for the personal character of the Patriarch elect, he is sufficiently known to us and to our Brethren the Cardinals, because of the long sojourn he has made with us. We know he is of a noble race, and of proper life, prudent, circumspect, and sufficiently learned. But having examined the election, we have not found it canonical because, laymen having no right to dispose of ecclesiastical affairs, the Patriarch of Constantinople should not have been elected by the authority of any secular prince. Besides, the Venetian clergymen, who call themselves canons of Saint Sophia, could not have the right of election, not having been established in their Church either by ourselves or our legates or deputies. For this reason we have cancelled the election in full Consistory."

Then the Pope declares that, wishing to provide for that Church, the care of which is specially his, he appoints the same Thomas Patriarch in *virtue of the fulness of his power.*

Nothing can be legitimate in the Church, except by this full power; such was the claim of the Papacy.

Innocent defended the ecclesiastical possessions of which a part had been appropriated by the Crusaders. "It is not expedient," he said, "for the holy see to authorize this act. Moreover, since their treaty was made with the Venetians—*for the honor of the Roman Church, as they say in nearly every article*—we cannot confirm an act which detracts from that honor."

Innocent conferred upon Thomas Morosini, who was only a sub-deacon, the diaconate, the priesthood, and the episcopacy; then he published a bull, in which he thus expresses himself: "The prerogative of grace which the holy see has given to the Byzantine Church proves clearly *the fulness of power that this see has received from God*, since the holy see has put that Church in the rank of Patriarchal Churches. It has drawn it, as it were, from the dust; it has raised it to the point of preferring it to those of Alexandria, Antioch, and Jerusalem; it has placed it next to the Roman Church, above all others."

Innocent recognized *the fact* that the Church of Constantinople had the second rank in the Church. But he ascribed this to the Roman see, although that see had protested against the decrees of the œcumenical councils of Constantinople and Chalcedon, which had given that Church the second rank in spite of Rome. It was thus that the Papacy in the Middle Ages distorted history to find proofs in support of its pretensions.

The Greek Patriarch of Constantinople, John Camaterus, resigned and retired to Thrace. He was succeeded by Michael Autorian, who crowned Theodore Lascaris Emperor of the Greeks. They both fixed their residence at Nicea in Bithynia.

The French and Venetians quarreled about the new Latin Patriarch and the division of the ecclesiastical property. Thomas applied to the Pope, who replied in a long letter from which we will quote an extract: "Of the four beasts which are about the

VII. Papal Innovation Perpetuated & Strengthened the Schism

throne, Ezekiel put the eagle above the others, because, of the four Patriarchal Churches, represented by the four beasts, which surround the holy see *as its servants*, the Church of Constantinople has the preeminence."

Thus Rome was the throne. The imperial eagle, the type of Constantinople, was to be the first of the symbolic beasts that adored it. Such was Innocent's modest notion of his authority. He thus gives a divine origin to the preeminence of Constantinople, because it had come from the holy see—God's organ. After this preamble the Pope gives Thomas some instructions, among which we will notice the following: "You ask me how you should arrange the bishoprics in those countries where there are only Greeks, and in those where they are mixed with Latins. In the first you must consecrate Greek bishops, if you find any, who will be faithful to you and are willing to receive consecration from you. In mixed bishoprics you will ordain Latins, and give them preference over the Greeks... If you cannot bring the Greeks to the Latin ritual, you must suffer them to keep their own until the holy see otherwise orders." Such was the policy constantly followed by the Papacy in respect to the *united Greeks*; to tolerate them until they could be made to submit.

From that epoch there were in the East, by Papal authority, two Catholic churches opposed to each other. Schism was thenceforth an accomplished fact (1206). As the Bishop of Thessalonica justly wrote to Pope Adrian IV, no schism really existed before that period. There had merely been a *protest* of the Eastern Church against the Roman innovations. This protest was anterior to Michael Cerularius and even to Photius. It took a more decided character under those Patriarchs, because Rome innovated more and more and wished to impose her autocracy upon the whole Church; but in reality the schism had not taken shape. As Fleury judiciously remarks, respecting the intercourse between Manuel Comnenus and Alexander III, "It cannot be said that in his day the schism of the Greeks had yet taken shape."[328] This cursory remark of the learned historian, who cannot be suspected of partiality for the Greek Church, has an importance which everyone will understand. It necessarily follows from it that

---

328 Fleury, Eccl. Hist., liv. ixxiii. § 32.

neither Photius nor Michael Cerularius created the schism. Who then was its author? It would be impossible to point one out among the Greeks. To our minds it is the Papacy, which, after having called forth the protests of the Eastern Church, and strengthened them by its own autocratic pretensions, was really the founder of the schism.

The true author of it is Pope Innocent III. It had been commenced by the Latin Church of Jerusalem; it was consummated by that of Constantinople.

This is the testimony of authentic and impartial history. The Papacy, after having established the schism, strengthened it by establishing Latin bishoprics in cities where Greek bishoprics had existed since Apostolic times. When the Latin bishops could not reside there, Rome gave them titles in *partibus infidelium*, as if the Apostolic Church of the East had none but *infidels* among its members.

Innocent III died in 1216. His successors continued his work. But the Greek Emperors of Nicea, on the verge of being overcome by the Latin Emperors of Constantinople, bethought themselves to resume the policy of their predecessors toward the Papacy. At the entreaty of the Emperor John Vataces, the Patriarch Germanus wrote to Pope Gregory IX (1232). His letter was filled with the best sentiments.[329] He first calls upon Jesus Christ, the cornerstone which joins all nations in one and the same Church; he acknowledges the primacy of the Bishop of Rome, and declares that he has no desire to contest it; and he adds: "Let us seek, with all possible care, who have been the authors of the division. If we ourselves, then point out to us the wrong we have committed and apply the remedy; if the Latins, then we cannot believe that it is your determination to remain outside of the Lord's heritage, through ignorance or criminal obstinacy. All acknowledge that the division has sprung from different beliefs, from abolishing canons and changing the ritual that has come to us by tradition from our fathers. Now all are witness that we ask supplicatingly to be reunited in the truth, after a profound examination to be made thereof, so that we may no longer

---

329 See this letter in Labbe's collection of Councils, vol. xi.; also in the historian Matthew Parris.

VII. Papal Innovation Perpetuated & Strengthened the Schism

hear from either party the imputation of schism." After having drawn the picture of the woes which that imputation of schism had drawn upon them from the Crusaders, Germanus exclaims, "Is it this that St. Peter teaches when he recommends the pastors to govern their flocks without violence or domination? I know that each of us believes himself right, and thinks that he is not mistaken. Well then, let us appeal to Holy Scripture and the Fathers."

Germanus wrote in the same way to the Cardinals who constituted the Pope's council. "Permit us," he writes to them, "to speak the truth; division has come from the tyrannical oppression that you exercise, and from the exactions of the Roman Church, which is no mother, but a stepmother, and tramples upon the other churches just in proportion as they humiliate themselves before her. We are scandalized to see you exclusively attached to the things of this world, on all sides heaping up gold and silver, and making kingdoms pay you tribute." Germanus then demands a thorough examination of the questions that divide the Church; and to show the importance of such an examination, he calls attention to the fact that a large number of nations agree with him.

Gregory IX[330] did not follow Germanus upon the ground which this Patriarch had taken. He accuses the Greek Church of too much submission to the temporal power, whereby it had lost its liberty; but he does not say wherein the liberty of the Church lies. For every Christian that liberty consists in the right to preserve revealed doctrine and Apostolic laws in their integrity. From this point of view, has not the Eastern Church been always more free than the Western? Whether a Church sacrifice the truth to an Emperor or to a Pope-King, it is equally servile in either case. Is it not wonderful to hear the Papacy talk thus of liberty to the Eastern Church while in the very act of attempting her subjugation, and after it had enslaved the Church of the West? Gregory IX, instead of accepting the discussion proposed by Germanus, promised to send him two Dominicans and two Franciscans to explain to him his intentions and those of the Cardinals. These monks actually set out for Nicea in the following year (A.D. 1233), bearing a letter to the Patriarch

---

330 Greg. IX, Ep. in Labbe's Collection of Councils, vol. xi.

Germanus in which the Pope compared the Greek schism to that of Samaria. It will be granted that the comparison was not very exact.

In fact, Rome was neither Jerusalem, nor the universal temple, nor the guardian of the law. These titles rather belonged to the Eastern Church than to the Roman, which had altered dogmas and Apostolic laws while the other had piously preserved them. In the same letter Gregory IX claims, as head of the Church, the twofold power, spiritual and temporal; he even maintains that Jesus Christ gave that power to St. Peter when he said to him, "Put up thy sword into the sheath."[331] This interpretation of the text is worthy of the opinion it was cited to sustain. Gregory IX concludes by attacking the use of leavened bread for the Eucharist. "That bread," he said, "typifies the corruptible body of Jesus Christ, while the unleavened bread represents his risen and glorious body."

The four Western monks were received at Nicea with great honors. They conferred with the Greek clergy concerning the procession of the Holy Ghost; the report is still extant that was made in the West.[332] In this report the monks claim to have had the advantage, as may well be imagined; but by their own showing, they confounded *substance* with *personality* in the Trinity—the *essential* procession, with the temporary sending of the Holy Spirit upon the Church; they misquoted Scripture and the Fathers; they could give no reason for the addition made to the creed; and they likened that addition, irregularly made, and involving a new dogma, to the development that the *œcumenical* Council of Constantinople had given to the creed of the first *œcumenical* Council of Nicea.

As for the Eucharist, the discussion concerning it was quite insignificant. Before they retired, the monks declared to the Emperor that, if the Greeks wished to unite with the Roman Church, they must subscribe to her doctrine and submit to the Pope's authority. It appears, therefore, that they had not come to inquire what was the true doctrine, and whether or not the Papal authority was legitimate; union to them, as to the Pope, meant nothing but *submission*. The Patriarch Germanus did not understand it; so, therefore, he called

---

331 Gospel acc. to St. John 18:11.

332 Ap. Raynald. ad Ann. 1233.

a council to examine the points of difference existing between the Greeks and Latins.[333] That assembly was held at Nymphæum. According to the account of the Nuncios themselves, their only triumph was in asking the Greeks why they no longer submitted to the Pope, after having formerly recognized his authority. If we may believe them, the Greeks were very much embarrassed by this question, and kept silence. Such a remark is sufficient to show with how little honesty their account was composed. Certainly the most ignorant of the Greeks knew that the Papal authority had never been recognized in the East. After long discussions upon the procession of the Holy Spirit, and upon unleavened bread, the Emperor summoned the Nuncios and said to them, "To arrive at peace, each side must make concessions; abandon your addition to the creed, and we will approve of your unleavened bread." The Nuncios refused. "How then shall we conclude peace?" asked the Emperor. "Thus," replied the Nuncios: "You shall believe and teach that the Eucharist can be consecrated only in unleavened bread; you shall burn all the books in which a different doctrine is taught; you shall believe and teach that the Holy Ghost proceeds from the Son as well as from the Father, and shall burn all the books that teach the contrary. The Pope and the Roman Church will not abate one iota of their belief; the only concession that can be made to you is not to oblige you to chant the creed with the Latin addition. Such was the substance of the reply of the Nuncios. The Emperor was much annoyed at it, and at the last session of the council the two parties separated, mutually anathematizing each other. No other result could have been anticipated.

About thirty years after this Council (A.D. 1269), Michael Palæologus reentered Constantinople and destroyed the Latin empire, which had only lasted fifty-seven years. The Papacy now saw vanish its most cherished hopes. Urban IV, the reigning Pope, wrote to Louis IX, King of France, urging him to take up the defence of the Latin Emperor, "expelled by the schismatic Greeks, to the shame of the West." He endeavored to arouse the whole of Europe and caused a Crusade to be preached against Palæologus.

---

333 Raynald. ad Ann. 1233; Wading. Annal. Min. ad Ann. 1233.

The Emperor sought to move the Pope by embassies and presents, and promises to work efficiently for the union of the churches. This policy, first adopted by the Comneni, and now resumed by Palæologus, resulted in two solemn assemblies—the second Council of Lyons and that of Florence, in which it was sought to fix upon a basis of union. All endeavors to do this proved futile, because the Papacy had no notion of having its supreme and universal authority, nor its doctrines, called in question. Clement IV formally declared this in a proposal for union which he sent to Michael Palæologus by four Franciscans.[334] According to the same Pope, Michael was guilty of the division existing between the churches, because if he chose to use his power, he could force all the Greek clergy to subscribe to the demands of the Pope. To use that power—i.e., to force the Greek clergy—was the only way to secure his empire against the enterprises of the Latins. Thus, according to Clement IV, interest, brute force, and threats were the true means of obtaining unity. Michael Palæologus was particularly in danger of an invasion on the part of Charles, King of Sicily. Remembering that Clement IV had written to him that the only mode of protecting himself against the Latins was to unite the churches, he wrote to Gregory X to express to him his own good intentions in this respect.

It is not our purpose to give a detailed account of the relations between Gregory and Michael. We need only say that the latter acted solely from political motives; that he abused his imperial power to persuade some of the bishops to favor his projects; that he persecuted those who resisted him; that some bishops, who were traitors from interested motives, made all the concessions that the Pope demanded; that their course was disavowed by the rest, notwithstanding the dreadful persecutions that this disavowal drew upon them; in fine, that reunion, instead of being established by those intrigues and acts of violence, only became more difficult than ever.

Such is, in substance, the history of what took place at the second Council of Lyons (1274) in regard to the reunion of the churches,

---

[334] Raynald, Annal. Eccl.; Labbe's Collection of Councils, vol. ix.; Wading., Annal. min.; Pachymeros, *Hist. Orient.* book v.

VII. Papal Innovation Perpetuated & Strengthened the Schism   325

and of what took place in the Greek Church after the Council. It is all political, and has no religious character. Gregory X declared peace at Lyons upon the basis laid down by Clement IV. But this union was only made with Michael Palæologus and a few men without principles. The Church of the East had no share in it. Rome herself was so persuaded of this that Martin IV excommunicated Michael Palæologus for having tricked the Pope under pretext of reunion (1281). Andronicus, who succeeded Michael (1283), renounced a policy in which there was so little truth.

But it was resumed by John Palæologus for the Council of Florence.

In the interval between these two assemblies of Lyons and Florence, several parleys took place between the Popes and the Emperors, but they resulted in nothing because the Eastern Church, instead of drawing nearer to the Church of Rome, was increasing the distance between them in proportion as the Papacy became more proud and exacting.

Still, John Palæologus succeeded, by using all his authority, in persuading a few bishops to attend the Council of Florence.

There were two distinct periods in that assembly: that of the doctrinal expositions, and that of the concessions.

By the doctrinal exposition it was made apparent that the Eastern Church differed from the Roman upon many fundamental points, and that she maintained her doctrine against Papal innovations, because that doctrine had been bequeathed to her by the Apostles and the ancient Fathers.

The concessions were inconsistent with the doctrinal exposition. Why? Because the Pope and the Emperor of the East used all the resources of their despotic power to overcome the resistance of the Greeks; because the Pope, in spite of his formal engagements, left to perish with hunger those Greeks who did not yield to his demands, while at the same time the Emperor of the East rendered their return to their country an impossibility; and, because the Papacy was able to gain over some ambitious men whose treachery it rewarded with a cardinal's hat and other honors. But the Papacy did not succeed, for all that, in obtaining from the Council of Florence any distinct recognition of its pretended sovereignty. For that assembly, even while it proclaimed that sovereignty of *divine right*, inserted in its decree one clause which annulled it and declared it a sacrilegious usurpation.

In fact, that sovereignty can only be a usurpation if we seek to determine its character by a reference to the œcumenical councils.

Thus was iniquity false to herself in that famous assembly, which was nothing more than a conspiracy against sound doctrine, which, under the name of a union, promulgated only a mendacious compromise, broken before it was concluded; the abettors of which were anathematized by the Eastern Church; of which the Church of the West, represented in a great majority by the Council of Basle, condemned the principal author, Pope Eugene, as a *heretic, a schismatic, and a rebel against the church.*

Since the sad drama of Florence, the Papacy has not attempted to subjugate the Eastern Church. It has preferred to endeavor to disorganize her, little by little, in order gradually to attain to her enslavement. Its policy has been to pay an outward respect to the Eastern ritual and doctrine; to profit by every circumstance, particularly by all conflicts between nationalities; to insinuate itself and lend its authority as a support and a safeguard to national rights; to be contented, at first, with a vague and indeterminate recognition of that authority, and then, by all manner of hypocrisy and deceit, to strengthen that authority in order to turn it afterward against the doctrines and ritual for which at first it feigned respect. This explains the contradictory bulls issued by the Popes on the subject of the *united* of all churches. The *united* Greeks of the East and of Russia, the *united* Armenians, the *united* Bulgarians, the *united* Maronites, etc., etc.

If, as we hope, we should ever publish a special work on the points of difference between the Eastern and Roman Churches, we shall exhibit in its details, and with proper references to authorities, the *policy* of the Papacy. We shall detect that policy at work in the assemblies of Lyons and of Florence; in all the relations between the Popes and the Emperors of Constantinople, since the establishment of the Latin kingdoms of the East; and in the contradictory bulls that have emanated from Rome from that time to our own.

Our object in the present work has been only to prove:

First: That the Papacy, from and after the ninth century, attempted to impose upon the universal church, in the name of God, a yoke unknown to the first eight centuries.

Second: That this ambition called forth a legitimate opposition on the part of the Eastern Church.

Third: That the Papacy was the first cause of the division.

Fourth: That the Papacy strengthened and perpetuated this division by its innovations, and especially by maintaining as a dogma the unlawful sovereignty that it had assumed.

Fifth: That by establishing a *Papal Church* in the very bosom of the Catholic Church of the East, it made a true schism of that division by setting up one altar against another altar, and an illegitimate episcopacy against an *Apostolic* episcopacy.

We have proved all these points by unanswerable facts. It is therefore with justice that we turn back upon the Papacy itself that accusation of *schism* of which it is so lavish toward those who refuse to recognize its autocracy, and who stand up in the name of GOD and Catholic tradition against its usurpations and sacrilegious enterprises.

We say now to every honest man: On the one side you have heard Scripture interpreted according to the Catholic tradition; you have heard the Œcumenical Councils and the Fathers of the Church; you have heard the Bishops of Rome of the first eight centuries.

On the other side you have heard the Popes subsequent to the eighth century. Can you say that the doctrines of the one and of the other are identical? Are you not compelled to acknowledge that there are concerning the Papacy two contradictory doctrines: the divine doctrine, preserved during eight centuries even in the bosom of the Roman Church—a doctrine which condemns every idea of autocracy or sovereignty in the Church of Jesus Christ; and the Papal doctrine, which makes of that autocracy an essential and fundamental dogma of the Church, a dogma without which the Church cannot exist?

Which is the doctrine that every Christian must prefer? That of GOD, or that of the Pope? That of the Church, or that of the Court of Rome?

You must choose between the two. Are you in favor of the divine doctrine, preserved by the Church? Then you are a Catholic Christian. Are you in favor of the doctrine of the Papacy? Then you are a *Papist*, but you are not a *Catholic*. This name only belongs to those who, in their faith, follow *Catholic tradition*. That tradition contradicts the Papal system; hence you cannot be a Catholic and accept this system. It is high time to cease playing upon words and to speak distinctly; be a *Papist* if you will, but do not then call yourself a *Catholic*.

Would you be a *Catholic*? Be no longer a *Papist*. There is no possible compromise; for *Catholic* and *Papist* are words which mutually deny each other.

VII. Papal Innovation Perpetuated & Strengthened the Schism

Saint Peter's Basilica at the Vatican, Old Rome.

INDEX

A

Acacius, his contest with Rome, 171-175.
Adrian I, the first Pope, 223-230.
—— The False Decretals, published during the reign of, 225, *et seq.*, *note*.
Adrian II claims to be Autocrat of the Church, 268-276.
Agapitus at Constantinople, 178.
Alcuin opposes the addition *Filioque*, 289.
Ambrose of Milan, his doctrine unfavorable to the Papal authority, 152-155.
Appeals to Rome, nature of, 78.
Athanasius of Alexandria, affair of, unfavorable to Papal authority, 110-115.
Augustine of Hippo, his doctrine opposed to Papal authority, 38, 155-160.
Aurelian, Emperor, decision of, alleged in proof of Papal authority, 81.
Authority, Papal, condemned by the Word of GOD, 33-49.
Avitus of Vienne, his doctrine opposed to Papal authority, 75, 92.

B

Baptism of heretics, discussion upon the, 66.
Basil of Cæsarea, his doctrine opposed to the Papacy, 152.
—— of Thessalonica, letter of, to the Pope upon the means of ending the division between the churches, 310.
Bulgarians converted by Photius, 265.
—— Ignatius endeavors to preserve his jurisdiction over the, 275, et seq.
—— Why they applied to Rome, 265.
—— Answer of Pope Nicholas to the, 265, et seq.

C

Chief, Christ the, of the Church, 33, *et seq.* (See Head.)
Chrysostom, affair of John, unfavorable to the Papacy, 120-126.
—— Doctrine of John, opposed to the Papacy, 139-148.
Clement of Rome, letter of, 52-54.
Council of Antioch, Canon of, explaining a text of St. Irenæus, 65.
—— of Constantinople deposes Ignatius and recognizes Photius, 251.
—— falsely called by the Romans the eighth œcumenical, 270, et seq.
—— acts of, not authentic, 274, *note*.
—— opposed to the so-called eighth œcumenical, 279, et seq.
—— Acts of, authentic, 283, *note*.
—— of Jerusalem, 41.
Council of Nicea, (first œcumenical,) contrary to papal authority, 85-88.

Index

—— of Constantinople, (second œcumenical,) contrary to Papal authority, 88.
—— of Ephesus, (third œcumenical,) contrary to Papal authority, 93.
—— of Chalcedon, (fourth œcumenical,) contrary to Papal authority, 88-93.
—— œcumenical, (fifth,) opposed to Papal authority, 181-182.
—————— (sixth,) opposed to Papal authority, 215-219.
—————— (seventh,) opposed to Papal authority, 224, 230-232.
—— of Sardica, opposed to Papal authority, 112-115.
—— *in Trullo*, opposed to Papal authority, 219.
Councils, the œcumenical, were neither convoked nor presided over, nor confirmed by the Bishops of Rome, 93, 108-109, 182, 214, *et seq.*, 230-232.
Crusades, the, ill-planned by the Papacy, 300.
Cyprian, controversy of, upon the baptism of heretics, 66-67.
—— doctrine of, contrary to Papal authority, 64, 72-76, 84, 131, *et seq.*
Cyril of Alexandria, doctrine of, contrary to the Papacy, 150-152.
—— Church of Africa, opposed to the Papal sovereignty, 157.

D

Decretals, (see False Decretals.)
Dionysius of Alexandria, his doctrine concerning the Roman primacy, 67, 71.
—— his alleged appeal to Rome, 79.
Dispensation, what is a, according to the Church of Constantinople and according to the court of Rome, 303-304.
Division, character of the, between the Eastern and Western Churches, 29, *et seq.*
Donatists, the affair of the, unfavorable to Papal authority, 115-120.

E

Easter, discussion concerning, 54-59.
Empire, (Latin,) foundation of, at Constantinople, 314-316.
—— Fall of, 323.
Epiphanius, his doctrine contrary to the Papacy, 137.
Eusebius of Cæsarea, testimony of, against Papal authority, 129.
—— upon the first œcumenical councils, 94.
—— upon the discussion concerning the baptism of heretics, 66.
—— upon the discussion concerning Easter, 58.
—— upon the Letter of St. Clement of Rome, 52-53.
—— upon the affair of Dionysius of Alexandria, 79.
—— upon the affair of Origen, 78-79.
Eustathius, the Patriarch, his overtures to the court of Rome, 304.
Excommunications, nature of the, of the Bishops of Rome In the first centuries, 72.

F

False Decretals, the basis of the Papacy, 225, *et seq.*, *note*.
Fathers, doctrine of the, contrary to Papal authority, 39, note, 40, note, 127-129, 164, (See their names.)
Filioque, addition of, to the Creed, 242, *et seq.*
Firmilian, his doctrine concerning the Roman primacy, 68-70.
Florence, Council of, and the false union proclaimed there, 325-326.
Frankish Bishops of the eighth century opposed to the Papal sovereignty, 232, 238, 267.

G

Gelasius of Rome, erroneous doctrine of, 175-176.
Germanus, letter of the Patriarch, to Pope Gregory IX, 320-321.
—— to the Cardinals, 321.
—— assembles the Council of Nymphæum, 323.
Greeks, (united,) policy of Rome in respect to the, 318, 319, 325.
Gregory IX, his singular accusations against the Eastern Church, and his doctrine concerning Papal prerogatives, 320-322.
Gregory X and Michael Palæologus, 324.
Gregory Nazianzen, text of, upon the Church of Constantinople, 65.
—— doctrine of, contrary to the Papacy, 148.
Gregory of Nyssa, doctrine of, contrary to the Papacy, 149.
Gregory of Syracuse and Ignatius of Constantinople, 239.
Gregory the Great, Bishop of Rome, opposed to Papal authority, 182-206.

H

Head, or *caput*, meaning of the word, 115.
—— change in its meaning, and its official origin, 207-208.
Hilary of Poitiers, doctrine of, unfavorable to the Papacy, 135-136.
Hippolytus of Ostia, doctrine of, unfavorable to Papal authority, 73, note.
Honorius, Bishop of Rome, his heresy, 208.
—— condemned after his death by the sixth œcumenical Council and by the Bishop of Rome himself, 218.

I

Iconoclasts, matter of the, a proof against Papal authority, 112.
Ignatius of Constantinople deposed, 245, 277, 278.
—— his appeal to Rome, 250, 260.
—— doubtful authenticity of his appeal papers, 260, *note*.
—— reinstated by the Council of Constantinople, called by Romanists the

Index

eighth œcumenical, 270, *et seq.*
—— his silence during that council, 273.
—— threatened by Adrian II, 276.
————— John VIII, 276, 277.
—— reconciled to Photius, 281-282.
Innocent III., Letters of Pope, to the Patriarchs and Eastern Emperors, and his doctrine on the pretended rights of the Roman see, 315-317.
—— excuses the crimes of the Crusaders because of their devotion to the see of Rome, 316.
—— endeavors to establish firmly the Latin Empire of Constantinople, 316.
—— the real author of the schism between the two Churches, 316-317.
—— doctrine of, concerning the prerogatives of the see of Constantinople, 317.
Irenæus admonishes Pope Victor, 57.
—— Text of, touching the primacy of the Roman Church, 57-65.

J

Jager, (Abbé,) draws his information regarding Photius from Stylien, 301, *note*.
—— calling himself the historian of Photius is guilty of an absurdity for the sake of insulting Photius, 255, *note*.
Jager, (Abbé,) indirectly acknowledges the changes which took place during the ninth century in the authority of the Bishop of Rome, 263-264.
—— errors of this pretended historian, 255, *note*, 267, *note*, 268, *note*, 278, *note*, 280, *note*, 292-293, *note*, 301, *note*, 302, *note*.
Jerome, doctrine of, opposed to Papal authority, 164-168.
John Camaterus, Patriarch, Letter of to Innocent III, 311.
John the Faster, Bishop of Constantinople, his title of œcumenical, 182-207.
John, (St.,) text of, relative to St. Peter, 44.
John VIII, threatens Ignatius with deposition, 276-278.
—— claims the right to depose the Greek Bishops and clergy of Bulgaria, 278.
—— his legates recognize Photius as legitimate Patriarch, 278.
—— Letters of, modified, 279-280, *et seq.*
—— letter of, against the addition *Filioque*, 297.

L

Lambs and sheep, 44-46.
Latin Empire, foundation of, at Constantinople, 316.
—— Fall of, 316.
Leo VI, Emperor, violates church discipline, 302.
—— is condemned by the Patriarch of Constantinople, 302-303.
—— absolved by the Court of Rome, 302-303.
Leo I, Bishop of Rome, doctrine of, opposed to Papal authority, 89-92, 138-139.

Leo III, opposed to the addition *Filioque*, 289-290.
Leo IX, Pope, his relations with Constantinople, and his doctrine concerning her rights, 157-160.
Luke, (St.,) Texts of, relating to St. Peter, 42-44.
Lyons, Second Council of, and the pretended reunion of the Churches, 324.

M

Macarius, Monseigneur, his treatise upon the Procession of the Holy Spirit, 288, *notes*, 292, *notes*.
Maimbourg, (Father,) a Jesuit, indirectly admits the change that took place during the ninth century in the authority of the Bishops of Rome, 247.
Matthew, (St.,) Text of, "Thou art Peter," etc., 36-42.
Michael Cerularius, his protest against the Roman innovations, 157-159.
—— excommunicated by the legates of Leo IX, 308.
—— general character of his protest, 308-309.
Monothelites, matter of the, a proof against the Papal authority, 208-219.
Morosini, (Thomas,) first Latin Patriarch of Constantinople, 317-318.

N

Negotiations between Rome and Constantinople, why they were useless, 308-311.
Nicholas, Patriarch, his relations with the court of Rome, 302-304.
Nicholas I, Pope of Rome, 238.
—— strengthens the new Institution of the Papacy, 247.
—— new doctrine contained in his letters, 248, *et seq.*, 259, *et seq.*, 262, *et seq.*, 266 *et seq.*
—— declares against the council that deposed Ignatus, and recognized Photius, 269.
—— autocratic pretensions of, 256, *et seq.*
Nicholas I deposes Photius, 261.
—— is anathematized by the Council of Constantinople, 267, et seq.
—— his reply to the Bulgarians, 265.
—— applies to the Western Bishops to reply to the protest of Photius, 295.
Novatians, matter of the, unfavorable to Papal authority, 82-83.
Nymphæum, Council of, discussions between the Greeks and the Latins respecting the addition *Filioque*, 323.

O

Object of this work, 29, *et seq*, 327.
Œcumenical, title of, 182-207.
Optatus of Melevia his doctrine opposed to Papal authority, 161-162.

Index

Origen, his pretended appeal to Rome, 78.
—— his doctrine opposed to the Papacy, 151.

P

Palæologus, (Michael,) his policy toward Rome, 324.
—— (John,) his policy, 325.
Papacy, origin of the, 224.
—— first pretensions to the, condemned, 56, 69-71.
—— opinions against the: (see Fathers.)
        Ambrose of Milan, 154-155.
        Augustine, (St.,) 155-160.
        Avitus of Vienne, 75.
        Basil of Cæsarea, 152.
        Chrysostom, (St. John,) 139-148.
        Council of Nicea, 85-88.
        —— Constantinople, 88.
        —— Ephesus, 93.
        —— Chalcedon, 86-93.
        —— Fifth Œcumenical, 181-182.
        —— Sixth " 216-219.
        —— Seventh " 224, 230-231.
        —— Sardica, 112-115.
        —— in Trullo, 219-220.
        Cyprian, (St.,) 63, 72-76, 83-84, 130, *et seq.*
        Cyril of Alexandria, 150-152.
        Dionysius of Alexandria 67-71.
        Epiphanius, 137.
        Eusebius, 129.
        Firmilian, 68-71.
        Gregory Nazianzen, 148-149.
        Gregory of Nyssa, 148-150.
        Gregory the Great, 182-206.
        Hilary of Poitiers, 135-136.
        Hippolytus of Ostia, 73, note.
        Jerome, 164-166.
        Optatus, 161.
        Origen, 151.
        Tarasius, Bishop of Constantinople, 223.
        Tertullian, 63, 73, 75-77, 130.
        Theodore Studites, 233-234.
Papal authority contrary to God's Word, 33-49.
Paul of Samosata, affair of, 80.
Paul, (St.,) doctrine of concerning the Church, 33, 41.

Peter, (St.,) doctrine of concerning the Church, 36.
Photius, his election and character, 240, 241, *et seq.*, 254.
—— slandered by Stylien, according to the Emperor's order, 300-301.
—— Biographers of, 240-242.
—— first letter of, to Pope Nicholas, 243, *et seq.*
—— second letter of, 251.
—— Injustice of the accusations brought against, 261-262, *note*.
—— exiled by the Emperor Basil, 268.
—— arbitrarily condemned, 270, *et seq.*
—— reinstated by a legitimate council, 278.
—— apology of, 281, *et seq.*
—— reconciled with Ignatius, 282.
—— protest of, against the Roman Innovations, 291, *et seq.*
—— again arbitrarily deposed by the Pope, 298, *et seq.*
—— exiled a second time, 300.
—— death of, 301.
Policy of the Eastern Emperors toward the court of Rome, 309-311, 319.
Polycrates, answer of, to Victor, 56.
Primacy of Peter according to Scripture, 46-49.

R

Rock, Jesus Christ the, of the Church, 36, *et seq.*
Rome and Constantinople, antagonism between, 169-180, 222, 285.
Rome, first attempts of the Bishops of, to increase their authority, 172-177, 210, 212, 222, 229, 235.
—— its rupture with the Empire of the East, 222.
—— radical change in the doctrine of, In the ninth century, concerning the authority of its bishop, 237.
—— Council of, against Photius, 268.
—— innovations of, 285-288.
—— variations of, relative to the addition *Filioque*, 296.
—— false policy of, 300.

S

Sardica, Council of, opposed to the Papal sovereignty, 112, 113.
Sheep and lambs, 44-45.
Summary of this work, and consequences which flow from it, 327.
Stylien, an enemy and calumniator of Photius, 300, 302.

Index 337

T

Tarasius, Bishop of Constantinople, opposed to Papal authority, 223-224.
Tertullian, doctrine of, opposed to Papal authority, 76, 130, 134-135, 136.
Theodore Studites, opposed to Papal authority, 233-234.
Three Chapters, matter of the, a proof against Papal authority, 178-181.

U

Union, conditions of, according to the envoys of Gregory IX to the Council of Nymphæum, 323.
Union, the political, decreed at the second Council of Lyons, 324.
―― second, decreed at Florence, 324.
Urban IV, (Pope,) causes a Crusade to be preached against the Greeks, 323.

V

Victor, Bishop of Rome, admonished by Polycrates of Ephesus, 56-57.
―― by Irenæous of Lyons, 57-58.
Vigilius, Bishop of Rome, falls into error and submits to the sixth œcumenical council, 179-181.

W

West, the Popes contribute to the establishment of a new Roman empire in the, 222.

UNCUT MOUNTAIN PRESS TITLES

Books by Archpriest Peter Heers

Fr. Peter Heers, *The Ecclesiological Renovation of Vatican II: An Orthodox Examination of Rome's Ecumenical Theology Regarding Baptism and the Church*, 2015

Fr. Peter Heers, *The Missionary Origins of Modern Ecumenism: Milestones Leading up to 1920*, 2007

The Works of our Father Among the Saints, Nikodemos the Hagiorite

Vol. 1: *Exomologetarion: A Manual of Confession*
Vol. 2: *Concerning Frequent Communion of the Immaculate Mysteries of Christ*
Vol. 3: *Confession of Faith*

Other Available Titles

Elder Cleopa of Romania, *The Truth of our Faith*
Elder Cleopa of Romania, *The Truth of our Faith, Vol. II*
Fr. John Romanides, *Patristic Theology: The University Lectures of Fr. John Romanides*
Demetrios Aslanidis and Monk Damascene Grigoriatis, *Apostle to Zaire: The Life and Legacy of Blessed Father Cosmas of Grigoriou*
Protopresbyter Anastasios Gotsopoulos, *On Common Prayer with the Heterodox According to the Canons of the Church*
Robert Spencer, *The Church and the Pope*
G. M. Davis, *Antichrist: The Fulfillment of Globalization*
Athonite Fathers of the 20th Century, Vol. I
St. Gregory Palamas, *Apodictic Treatises on the Procession of the Holy Spirit*
St. Hilarion (Troitsky), *On the Dogma of the Church: An Historical Overview of the Sources of Ecclesiology*
Fr. Alexander Webster and Fr. Peter Heers, Editors, *Let No One Fear Death*
Subdeacon Nektarios Harrison, *Metropolitan Philaret of New York*
Elder George of Grigoriou, *Catholicism in the Light of Orthodoxy*
Archimandrite Ephraim Triandaphillopoulos, *Noetic Prayer as the Basis of Mission and the Struggle Against Heresy*
Dr. Nicholas Baldimtsis, *Life and Witness of St. Iakovos of Evia*
On the Reception of the Heterodox into the Orthodox Church: The Patristic Consensus and Criteria
Patrick (Craig) Truglia, *The Rise and Fall of the Papacy*
St. Raphael of Brooklyn, *In Defense of St. Cyprian*
The Divine Service of the Eighth Œcumenical Council
The Orthodox Patristic Witness Concerning Catholicism
Hieromartyr Seraphim (Svezdinsky), *Homilies on the Divine Liturgy*

Select Forthcoming Titles

Cell of the Resurrection, Mount Athos, *The Mystery of Christ: An Athonite Catechism*
Acts of the Eighth Œcumenical Council
Fr. Theodore Zisis, *Kollyvadica*
St. Raphael of Brooklyn, *On the Steadfastness of the Orthodox Church*
George (Pachymeres), *Errors of the Latins*
Fr. George Metallinos, *I Confess One Baptism*, 2nd Edition
St. Maximus the Confessor, *Opuscula: Theological and Polemical Works*
Fr. Peter Heers, *Going Deeper in the Spiritual Life*
Fr. Peter Heers, *On the Body of Christ and Baptism*
Athonite Fathers of the 20th Century, Vol. II

This Edition of

THE PAPACY
ITS HISTORIC ORIGINS AND PRIMITIVE RELATIONS WITH THE EASTERN CHURCHES

written by Abbe Vladimir Guettée typeset in Baskerville printed in this two thousand and twenty fourth year of our Lord's Holy Incarnation is one of the many fine titles available from Uncut Mountain Press, translators and publishers of Orthodox Christian theological and spiritual literature. Find the book you are looking for at

uncutmountainpress.com

**GLORY BE TO GOD
FOR ALL THINGS**

AMEN.

www.ingramcontent.com/pod-product-compliance
Lightning Source LLC
Chambersburg PA
CBHW060550080526
44585CB00013B/506